FINDING GOD
IN ALL THINGS

FINDING GOD IN ALL THINGS

ESSAYS IN HONOR OF MICHAEL J. BUCKLEY, S.J.

Edited by Michael J. Himes
and Stephen J. Pope

A Crossroad Herder Book
The Crossroad Publishing Company
New York

1996

The Crossroad Publishing Company
370 Lexington Avenue, New York, NY 10017

Printed in the United States of America

Library of Congress Cataloging-in-Publication Data

Finding God in all things : essays in honor of Michael J. Buckley
   S.J. / edited by Michael J. Himes and Stephen J. Pope.
     p. cm.
   Includes bibliographical references.
   ISBN 0-8245-1629-X (pbk.)
    1. Theology. 2. Atheism. 3. Religion and science. 4. Catholic
universities and colleges. I. Buckley, Michael J. II. Himes,
Michael J. III. Pope, Stephen J., 1955-
BR50.F48 1996
230'.2–dc20
                                   96-31325
                                      CIP

Contents

Part II
RELIGION AND SCIENCE

Part III
THEOLOGY AND SPIRITUALITY

Acknowledgments

The editors received a great deal of assistance in completing this book from a number of graduate students. Cara Anthony, Anna Bonta, Joseph Curran, Mary Lee Freeman, Mark Graham, Edward Hogan, Brian Hughes, Thomas and Lisa Kelly, Richard Miller, Michael Moreland and Deborah Wallace assisted in editing and revising the contributors' manuscripts. Many of them are students of Michael Buckley in the Department of Theology at Boston College, and their immediate willingness to be of service to our project bespoke deep gratitude for the work and wisdom of their mentor. This project would not have been completed without their dedication and generosity, attributes which flow from their own devotion to "finding God in all things."

Introduction

In *At the Origins of Modern Atheism*, Michael Buckley wrote,

> The question about the existence of God is so profoundly and pervasively human that it inescapably involves a circle in which all of the human disciplines figure and condition one another. There is a depth at which human beings confront the great issues of life that lies beneath the formal separation of the sciences and of the sciences from the humanities.[1]

This conviction lies at the heart of his distinguished career on the faculties of Gonzaga University, the Jesuit School of Theology at Berkeley, the Gregorian University, the University of Notre Dame, and Boston College, where he is now professor of systematic theology and director of the Jesuit Institute. He has taught and written in the history and philosophy of science, systematic and ascetical theology, the history of atheism, the nature of higher education, and methodology for cross-disciplinary study. He has influenced students and colleagues in the faculties in which he taught and far beyond in his work as executive director of the Committees on Doctrine and Pastoral Practices of the National Conference of Catholic Bishops (1986–89) and as an officer and later president of the Catholic Theological Society of America (1989–92). In gratitude for his career and his continuing contributions to the field of theology especially, we have invited a number of Father Buckley's friends, colleagues, and former students to join in this collection of essays honoring him on the occasion of his sixty-fifth birthday.

The essays deal with four areas which have been central to Father Buckley's research and writing. They are the relationship between belief and unbelief, the connection between religion and science, the interpenetration of theology and spirituality, and the nature and value of higher education within a Catholic context.

Peter Hünermann begins the first section, "Atheism and Belief," by reflecting on the meaning of the most fundamental of theological questions, "Does God exist?" Although in the context of modernity and what some now call "postmodernity" the question is posed in a very different way from that in which Thomas Aquinas asked it in the *Summa Theologiae* I, q. 2, a. 3, he demonstrates that Thomas's way of answering the question remains illuminating for those who ask it now. David Burrell then explores Thomas's "metaphysics-cum-semantics" and seeks to show that his way of unfolding language about and, more importantly, in praise of God reveals the depths of all human language. Louis

Dupré moves the discussion from the thirteenth to the eighteenth century in order to test the validity of Michael Buckley's thesis on the dialectical origin of modern atheism. In doing so he defends the claim that the project of modernity remains vital and important, although unfinished. Nicholas Lash urges that the contemporary "crisis in our thinking about God" cannot be countered by a doctrine of God which unbalances the tension between the three articles of the creed. He suggests that we seek a becoming modesty in our claims to speak about God, a modesty based on an appreciation of creaturely contingency which can be learned and purified in the shared life of the church. The faith of the Christian community rests on its relationship to Christ, and Roger Haight addresses the impact of contemporary "Jesus research" on christology and the church's faith in Christ. Finally, following Michael Buckley's insistence that one of the root factors in the emergence of modern atheism was theologians' bracketing of religious experience as theological resource, Elizabeth Johnson examines the contemplation of the natural world as revelatory of the Spirit. The experience of the sacramentality of creation, she suggests, may be an important theological resource in the ongoing dialogue with modern atheism.

The second group of essays, "Religion and Science," begins with Charles Hefling's thoughtful review of the problems inherent in the conversation between theology and natural science. He makes an important contribution to this collection by cautioning against too easy attempts to sort out these problems and reminds us that there are many sciences, many theologies, and many philosophies. Evolutionary thought within contemporary science and its significance for theology are common themes in the next three essays. John H. Wright seeks to explore the relationship of spirit and matter as it is uncovered in human consciousness. In a new and highly sophisticated way of asking the perennial question of the one and the many, Ernan McMullin looks at two different understandings of evolution and asks whether the contingency of evolution makes the notion of cosmic purpose impossible. And William R. Stoeger writes on how the triune God both transcends and subsumes time in an evolving universe. Concluding this second section, Albert R. Jonsen turns our attention to the practical roles of religion and science in formulating the basic lines of the discipline of bioethics, specifically dealing with the role of moral ambiguity in contemporary medical-moral decision-making.

The loss of the sense of transcendence is a hallmark of the modern Western world. In his insightful article which opens the third section on "Theology and Spirituality," Paul Crowley discusses the resources within Christian theology for the recovery of transcendence, especially in the human confrontation with suffering. Employing Karl Rahner's notion of "Christian pessimism," Vaclav Havel's description of the fate of those who lack a sense of transcendence, and Michael Buckley's theological analysis of unbelief, he explores the relevance of the symbol of the cross to our time. In the next essay, Brian Daley turns to Gregory of Nyssa, who is often described as the father of the tradition of mystical theology, and asks how accurate that description is. He carefully lays out the dynamics of mystical union in Gregory's writings, showing how they foreshadow later developments in Christian mysticism. Lawrence Cunningham introduces another patristic writer and another major strand of Christian spirituality. He examines John Cassian, one of the principal figures in the development of monasticism, especially in regard to a theme which is most often associated with Ignatian spirituality, discernment. The theme of Ignatian spirituality is continued in the subsequent essay by William B. Spohn. He compares Ignatius's discernment, the habit of "finding God in all things," with the analysis of religious affections by Jonathan Edwards, the most influential theologian within the Calvinist tradition and one of the shapers of American religious thought. To close part 3, Thomas Rausch notes Michael Buckley's significant interest in the theology and spirituality of the priesthood. In his article he takes up a pressing current issue in the Catholic Church: the connection between the community and the Eucharist and how that connection affects our understanding of the role of the priest.

There has been much discussion in recent years of the nature and role of the Catholic university and whether and how the Catholic character of universities in the United States can be fostered, a discussion in which Father Buckley is an important participant. This provides the theme of the fourth group of essays, in which four distinguished Catholic educators address issues concerned with Catholicism and the university. David Hollenbach begins by centering the Catholic university's role in the long tradition of Christian humanism — but with an important difference. He calls for a humanism which takes account not only of the heights to which we can rise but also of the depths to which we can descend. The centrality of the cross in Christian life and thought must shape a humanism which can address the suffering of the twentieth century; key to the Catholic identity of the university must be a commitment to justice for the oppressed. Next William B. Neenan and Frederick Lawrence enter into direct conversation with Michael Buckley's writings on the qualities which make a university authentically Catholic. The first uses Boston College, the Jesuit university of whose faculty Father Buckley is a member, as a test case for what works and what needs improvement in Catholic universities. Lawrence's essay points to the politicization of universities in American life — including Catholic universities — and calls for the recovery of the university as a center of conversation. Lastly, Lisa Sowle Cahill enters the discussion by approaching the Catholic university from the ethical field. She stresses the importance of the Catholic university as a center of rigorous and open intellectual inquiry for both the church's teaching office and its pastoral ministry.

As epilogue to the collection, Leo O'Donovan offers his reflections on Michael Buckley's life as a priest, a member of the Society of Jesus, a theologian, and a teacher. The editors join with him and all the contributors to the volume in expressing their personal and professional gratitude to their colleague, mentor, and friend on his sixty-fifth birthday.

MICHAEL J. HIMES
STEPHEN J. POPE

Note

1. Michael J. Buckley, S.J., *At the Origins of Modern Atheism* (New Haven: Yale University Press, 1987), 360f.

Part I

ATHEISM
– AND –
BELIEF

1

Does God Exist?

Reflections on the Fundamental Question of Theology

– PETER HÜNERMANN –

At the outset of his tract on God, Thomas Aquinas places the discussion of the question *An Deus sit?* — "Whether God exists?" The question is treated in three articles. That God exists is not for human beings a self-evident truth, *per se nota*. Rather, it must be demonstrated that God exists. Thomas sets out this demonstration by means of five arguments. As one examines these concise and important lines of demonstration it becomes apparent that for contemporary theology the question "Does God exist?" is raised in an entirely new context. This new context of thought is clearly seen in the question which must be answered as a preliminary step: "Is the question of the existence of God a meaningful question?" There are a number of theologians in recent decades who have regarded the question of God's existence as meaningless. In his *Systematic Theology*, Paul Tillich stated: "Thus the question of the existence of God can be neither asked nor answered.... It is as atheistic to affirm the existence of God as to deny it."[1] For Tillich, as for many other theologians, the point is that "to exist" always means "to exist in space and time." Based on such considerations some authors in the 1960s and '70s spoke of the compatibility of atheism and Christianity, indeed, of an atheistic faith in God.

So the question must be clarified: Is the affirmation "God is" a meaningful statement? To clarify the issue more precisely it is necessary to refine the use of the word "is" in the affirmation.[2]

I

A review of the different ways in which the word "is" may be used clearly shows two types of use. In the first, the word "is" serves as the copula; for example, "London is the capital of Great Britain." Through the copula the predicate is connected to the subject. It expresses a partial or total identity of the subject and the predicate. In the second, we have

the absolute or verificatory use of the word "is." Again some examples
will make this clear: "Troy is no more." In this sentence no particular content is attributed to the expression "Troy." Instead, the predicate
says of "Troy" that it no longer exists. Frege and Russell have maintained that "is" used in this absolute sense refers to the concept. The
example just given demonstrates the opposite: this "is" refers to Troy
itself.[3]

There is an interesting similar example: "There are other women in
Achaia." Here too the verb "is" is used not in the copulative sense but in
the sense of existence. This example is interesting because Russell seems
to say that there are no actual plural subjects but only concepts. But
there are not only plural subjects in such sentences. There are also all-
encompassing statements of this kind: "There is no one who can escape
death."

Closely connected to this absolute sense of the word "is" is the so-
called verificatory sense. This has to do with the affirmation of the
truth-claim of a particular statement or with expressing confirmation
and assent to it. For example: "That is true!" or "May it be as you
say!" While propositions with "is" as a copula refer to the subject and
unpack its semantic content, in propositions using "is" in its absolute or
verificatory sense a subject or state of affairs is affirmed as such. At the
same time, in such an affirmation the one advancing the proposition, the
speaker, is revealed as an asserter, an affirmer. In this affirmative use of
speech the speaker acts as asserter and gives assent; he expects others to
agree with his claim.

From these few examples one conclusion immediately follows: none
of the typical propositions cited using "is" in its absolute sense is trivial
or foolish. All these statements are meaningful, and it makes a difference whether this "is" is affirmed or negated. We can understand the
difference between something being the case and not being the case. This
use cannot be reduced to the copulative function. And so when Tillich
claims that one who affirms or denies the existence of God is as much
an atheist as a theist, he is confining himself to a notion of the use of the
word "is" which is obviously impoverished.

A second conclusion follows from these examples: the *semantic*
meaning of the word "is" — and this is evident in its use as a copula
and in its absolute and verificatory use — is clearly indefinite. "To be"
is said in multiple ways. By contrast, "to be" in its absolute and verificatory use has a definite *pragmatic* meaning: the verb lets us declare a
reality to be the case, to exist, to be real. At the same time the pragmatic
meaning of "to be" is defined by whatever the subject of the statement
happens to be.

From this it follows immediately that when I say that God exists and
affirm this as a Christian, I am not objectifying God in a simple, con-

crete, spatial or temporal way. Rather the statement means that God, to whom the propositions of the Christian faith refer, is not imaginary but is real even apart from the thought and belief of the one making the affirmation. This is an essential presupposition of faith.

A third conclusion is implicit in this: any such affirmation of the existence of God includes a free relationship between the subject speaking and the reality whose being (in the sense of existence) is affirmed. In the verificatory affirmation or (which means the same thing) in the absolute use of this little word "is" there is already posited (from a transcendental point of view) the truth-relation and so the subsistent subject of the act of speaking.[4]

II

The considerations set forth here demonstrate not only that raising the question of the existence of God can be meaningful. They also show the meaning and significance of the proofs for God. To anticipate the conclusion of this second line of thought now presented as a thesis, proofs for God can only exercise an auxiliary and essentially negative function as regards the affirmation that God exists. First, let us ask how people act and respond when they raise the question, "Does something or other exist in fact?" In the overwhelming majority of cases, we find that we put faith in someone who attests to the existence of some particular thing. Based on the person's witness and the credibility of the thing in question, we agree with his or her judgment and so affirm the existence of the thing. When a third person inquires about the basis of our affirmation, we reply as a matter of course, "This other person told us so."

We refrain from agreeing with another person's testimony only when there are reasonable and plausible grounds which tell against the reality of the matter in question. In that case, the person with whom we do not agree will say to us, "Convince yourself. See for yourself." This is an entirely proper response. Since the affirmation of existence involves a pragmatic kind of speech in which at one and the same time the self-subsistence and actuality of the thing in question and the affirming subject are constituted together in a free act, their linking together is fundamentally free. The "yes" to anything can always spring only from freedom. It can arise in absolutely no other way whatsoever. This means that there is no possibility of forcing or coercing someone into this "yes" to the existence of anything. We can only convince ourselves.

Such a "yes" obviously presumes that there are no rational and plausible objections or that they can be dealt with. And when such objections are removed, then everything leads us to conclude that the thing in question is a reality. In that event, there is incumbent on a person's conscience the obligation to agree with the facts to which the other person has testified. In his *Grammar of Assent* Newman has explicated the role of conscience in the genesis of assent. Assent has to do with a free and therefore responsible moral act. The verificatory use of "is" is a speech-act which denotes assent. The basis for positing this responsible moral act, namely, that any objections have been dealt with, that "everything speaks for it," so that one is obligated to posit the act, moves us to a different plain than that on which theories, logical consequences, in short, semantic explications are located.

Basically, there are two possible ways to resolve contradictions and objections to the judgment of existence.

The first way of becoming convinced is when the things, persons, or matters in question are of such sort that one can encounter them in some form in space and time. But when one tries to duplicate the experience of the person who first testified to their existence, one inevitably finds that they are not at the same point in time, perhaps not at the same point in space. One no longer finds them at the same location. Changes have occurred — and necessarily so. Thus one can never precisely duplicate another's experience. A "perfect reproduction" and "one-hundred-percent control" are impossible. Thus if on the basis of one's own encounter with a thing or a person, one agrees with a witness's judgment about their existence, then despite the fact that there continue to be irreconcilable discrepancies and differences between the two encounters, the force of particular objections is weakened and the weightiness of the other person's judgment is shown. This also holds true in the study of the natural sciences. Because of their specialized methods, they minimize their experiential differences, even though they cannot fully and finally overcome them.

There is a second and much more common way of becoming convinced of something's existence. It has to do with cases when an immediate encounter is not possible. There are situations in which one can be "put on the track" of things, matters in question, or persons only through other things, matters, and persons. In such cases, what sorts of problems and objections can arise? First of all, there may be questions stemming from the doubtful reliability of the witness. Secondly, there may be objections founded on reasons of general character. There is no possible way to construct an argument of chiefly singular character to prove the nonexistence of something. This means, however, that objections of general character must be answered by a style of argument which resolves the force of the opposed general reasons. Such arguments do not yield a proof of existence in the strict sense. Rather, these arguments converge on the things whose existence is under debate in such a way that the general assumptions which militate against them are refuted and sufficient grounds are given to render the judgment of their existence plausible, unassailable, perhaps even obligatory. These sufficient grounds should be seen as stepping-stones, as it were, making assent possible in that they pave the way to the matter in question. But they do not compel assent in the theoretical sense.

Let us apply these considerations to the proofs for God. Thomas formulates his question *An Deus sit?* and its answer through the proofs for God within a cultural context which presumes that at least some people believe in God. They affirm God's existence. Thus, at the conclusion of each of the proofs for God, Thomas says that what has been demonstrated in the argument is what everyone calls God.

To this statement of belief in God one can obviously oppose a quite different way of thinking. But as has been noted, objections and counter-assumptions — apart from questions about the personal unreliability of the witness — always arise from a general counterview of the world. What are the counterassumptions which especially come into play here? If God is understood to be the creator and disposer of the world and of history, then the counterassumptions which would tell against the reality of God must be the self-subsistence, independence, autonomy, and self-sufficiency of the world, the human person, and history. These are the assumptions which view as unfounded and silly the radically opposed position grounded in faith, namely, that everything is to be thought of as dependent on God.

Thomas deals precisely with these counterassumptions in his five proofs for God. Let us exemplify this from his first proof.[5] In his first argument Thomas begins by observing that everything in the world is moved. Here, as is usually the case with Thomas, movement is to be understood in the widest sense as change, as becoming and passing away, as waxing and waning. This observation of a basic quality of reality as we always and everywhere experience it is formulated in a general abstract principle: movement is nothing other than reducing something from potency or possibility to act or reality. Movement has to do with not-yet-being, being-possible, becoming-real. The passage from possibility, potency or virtuality to actuality requires something in being, something which possesses its own actuality and can cause or mediate or effect this passage. Nothing can in the same way and at the same time be both possible and actual. Thus Thomas finally formulates the general principle: "Everything which is moved must be moved by another." We would misunderstand this statement of Thomas were we to fail to notice that, under his terms of movement, act, and potency, he is describing the experience of reality as we actually find it. Reality is characterized by becoming and passing away, by movement in the ontological sense. Thus, by the same token, it is understood as in relationship. The reality we experience is, first of all, reality as finite, brought into being, caused, effected. We meet no reality which is absolute and self-subsistent.

At this point in the course of his thought Thomas seemingly makes an unexpected leap. He states: "Here, however, we must not go on to infinity, for then there would be no first mover and consequently nothing else which moves.... Thus it is necessary to arrive at a first mover which is not moved by anything else." How are we to understand the course of argument which Thomas pursues here? Obviously he abandons the kind of thinking which he has employed to this point. For such a way of thinking would indeed stretch off endlessly into absolute infinity. Now Thomas firmly fixes his attention on this finite, incomplete, waxing and waning reality and deals with it as a whole. And because he is dealing with the whole of finite reality, he also deals with the concrete being of the human person who is part of this reality and who recognizes himself as one being in this fluctuating and transient reality. But to the view of such a person, this finite reality which comes into being and passes from being, this endlessly restless finitude appears as a contradiction. It turns out to be unintelligible, totally unthinkable. Why is anything moved if everything is totally dependent on another finite, i.e., conditioned, instrument or cause or event? Indeed, why is there any movement and not absolute immobility? But a solution to this contradictory situation — if we are to maintain the rationality of thought and the rationality of the world — requires a radically different way of thinking. In order to maintain this limited and finite movement of all reality we must affirm an unmoved mover, an unconditioned actuality. Typically Thomas says that it is necessary "to arrive" at a first mover.

First and foremost, what Thomas has demonstrated is a negative conclusion. The world with all its persons and things cannot be understood on its own. The world, the human person and history would then be contradictory. Thus a very powerful obstacle to accepting the reality of God is removed. Through the course of his argument Thomas shows that this objection brought against God's existence, i.e., that the world is intelligible on its own, does not stand up to scrutiny. Such an understanding of reality, if seriously thought through, leads to a dead-end. It yields humanity no meaningful orientation and no direction for life or thought. Reality, history, the individual existence of the person — all finally become unintelligible. Thus has Thomas led those who advance objections to the assent to God's actuality to the point of a conversion: humanity and the world demand to be understood from a perspective quite opposed to theirs. Only in this way can their partial and dependent reality be shown to be thinkable and rational rather than contradictory. Thomas calls this other which is the first mover an *aliquod*. One might also call it the X which is defined by its function of resolving this contradictory predicament. Precisely in this situation of contradiction the function of this X is discerned. It is to be the source of that movement, that reduction to absolute actuality, the *movens non motum*, the unmoved mover. Thus it is seen to be an X which meets the requirements of the general principles and lines of thought employed in the arguments replying to the objections.

Thomas himself recognized the peculiar quality of this carefully hedged result of his argument for God. He concludes this first "proof for God" with the statement: *Et hoc omnes intelligunt Deum,* "And this all understand as God." He sometimes concludes the other proofs with the phrase, "All call this God." Thus one can correctly say that Thomas's argument converges on God. It leads up to the decisive point of a conversion of thought and develops from the logic of its line of thought a hypothesis, namely, that of the first mover, in which believers recognize God without making God absolutely identical with this conception.

What has Thomas accomplished with this proof as regards the person who up to now has refused to give his assent to faith? He has undermined this person's counterassumptions and brought his thinking to a point where the evidence for God can seem plausible to him. For he must at least agree with this: there is something outside the world in its constant becoming which I must presume as an unmoved mover if this changing world is not to be unthinkable.

The structure of Thomas's other arguments is very similar. He regularly starts with the most basic traits of reality, those characteristics which he sees everywhere, and analyzes them. The result of this investigation is always the same: there are certain fundamental and constant qualities to reality; these exist in various relationships and contexts; but the whole does not cohere, it does not finally make sense or provide any ultimate direction for human beings. Only when a person considers the Whence of reality — as we have already described with regard to the quality of movement in reality — and articulates this Whence in light of both the basic quality which was the starting point and the contradiction to which the analysis of reality has led, do we find a rational relation.

As a result of these various negative arguments we reach a point X with predicates which are drawn from our experience of reality but which, in the words of Anselm, are to be thought in such a way that nothing greater can be thought: the unmoved mover or *actus purus,* being itself, etc. These terms are simply juxtaposed. They are neither referable to one another nor deducible from one another.

These terms come from the transcendental determinations of the existent, that is, those fundamental qualities of reality which are found in everything that is. When they are each thought of at their maximum beyond all limited things, they attain that conceptual level to which the so-called proofs for God lead as result. The transcendentals can only be discovered, never deduced from one another or from something else.

Thus reality — according to Thomas — is essentially and inescapably plural but not organizable by itself. There is no encompassing but purely natural ordering-principle of any kind whatever. And likewise there are a plurality of intelligible presuppositions needed to resolve the contradictions of reality.

We should note here a parallel to recent developments in the philosophical analysis of the present. For Lyotard modernity, i.e., the modern world and its basic understanding of reality, is marked by three central governing ideas.[6] He characterizes these central ideas as meta-narratives. The first is the emancipation of humanity in the Enlightenment, the second the teleology of spirit in idealism, and the third the hermeneutic of meaning in historicism. He finds the distinguishing mark of the present in the fact that these unifying themes "have fallen into decay, not only as regards their explicit content but even in the whole style of thought. Totality as such has become obsolete and we end up with a dissolution of the parts."[7] Thomas's intellectual analysis deals with this plurality of reality.

If the *demonstratio Dei* which Thomas offers effectively removes counterassumptions and leads our thinking directly to the point of conversion and the emergence of an X with unconditioned predicates so that as a result an assent to God — a God to whose existence other human beings give testimony — becomes plausible, then the question unavoidably arises: How does God enter into our thought? How can we talk about God to whose existence assent is freely given by human beings, when by intellectual argument all that appears is an X, an Absolute which is to be qualified as unmoved mover, *actus purus,* being itself, etc.? Freedom demands that its "yes" be spoken not blindly and irresponsibly. The removal of contrary assumptions is important. It is a *conditio sine qua non.* The point of conversion and the hypothesis of the mysterious X are undoubtedly steps in the right direction. But how does God arise for human beings?

III

The elements of an answer are found in Thomas. He does not raise the question itself with the same explicitness as we have raised it.

a. The first answer to the question goes as follows: God has always revealed Godself to humanity; God is intimately implied in our thinking, of course, *in aliquo communi,* in a general fashion, and *sub quadam confusione,* in a certain undifferentiated and confused way.[8] Thomas makes this more precise: "In so far, namely, as God is the beatitude and the salvation of the human person." Happiness is that toward which the human person's whole being is ordered. And it is precisely in this, according to Thomas, that God encounters the person, even though with a certain obscurity. Thomas strongly emphasizes this: "This does not mean that we know absolutely that God exists, just as to know the person approaching does not mean that we know Peter, even though Peter is the person approaching. For many believe the perfect good for human beings, which is happiness, to be wealth, but others to be pleasure, and still others something else."[9]

Two points should be noted in this terse passage: first, happiness is that perfection which makes the human person happy in every respect and that means at every moment in the course of his existence. Here we are precisely not dealing with a particular aspect of the person's existence, *one* quality of his reality, as one or other has been picked out and specially thematized in the proofs for God. Here the human being is set before us as a whole and in his totality.

Second, it is presupposed that the human being does not possess his happiness in himself but that it is given to him. He is ordered to it, it is granted to him, imparted to him. This basic structure is also seen in the fact that a human being can falsely locate his happiness in something which cannot make him happy in all ways and cannot make him happy as a whole.

Thus the human being is described as one who essentially is related externally to his goal in such a way that, in his whole being and with all his unique abilities, he cannot help being other than the source of his own happiness. In this fact of his being, Thomas perceives the method and means by which God is intimately present to human beings and by which they already — albeit in an undefined way — always know God and are related to God.

b. A second, more significant answer is found in Thomas in connection with his discussion of the name "God."

With reference to the language of faith, Thomas maintains that the absolutely ineffable and sublime divine mystery is designated by the name "God." The origin of this name, however, is God's action toward and governance of humanity and the world. "Of course, all who speak of God intend to name the God who exercises universal providence over all things."[10] "For this name is used in order to refer to that which exists above all things, which is the principle of all things and which is distinct from all things. For those who name God intend to refer precisely to this."[11]

Thomas says of this sovereignty of God from which the name "God" is derived, this *operatio propria Dei*,[12] that we "experience it constantly" — *experimur continue*.[13]

If one were to inquire how Thomas understands this "constant experience," the answer would have to be that it is not some one experience or the experience of some one thing *in* the world. Since the *operatio* of which Thomas speaks is the universally grounding, preserving, and directing *operatio*, it must refer to an experience of the world and ourselves and all our thinking and acting as a whole. At most, individual experiences could be included in this to the extent that they are references to or signs of this whole.

In his reflections on language Ludwig Wittgenstein has noticed this kind of experience.[14] Among Wittgenstein's numerous notes on religious language is found this statement: "You cannot hear God speak with another unless you are the one addressed — this is a grammatical observation."[15] Here Wittgenstein is emphasizing two things: in this speaking the human being becomes a fully individual addressee; it is a speech which one cannot simply listen to but which only the person in his irreducible and unalterable selfhood can hear. It is a speaking which employs no words external to the person but is rather a speaking in which the human person is radically and totally fulfilled as hearer. The explanation, "This is a grammatical observation," means that Wittgenstein is dealing here with the general rules by which all speech of any kind is governed. By grammar Wittgenstein means the rules governing the linguistic act which makes speaking and hearing possible. The human being must be perfected as a hearer if he wants to hear God speak. This dictum is clarified by other statements of Wittgenstein: "God does not reveal himself *in* the world."[16] Another statement illustrates the same thought: "Giving us a new sense — I would call that revelation."[17] If the human being is realized as the one addressed — standing before God who addresses him — then it also follows that God does not reveal God-self in the world but rather that God develops in the world a new sense, that God gives a new sense to humanity and to the world.

When one considers these and similar statements of Wittgenstein, one gets closer to what Thomas means by the "experience" of divine providence over all things. It is the way of encountering the world and one's own existence as posited by God which is disclosed in the act of naming God. For Thomas, God is a name in which the most profound disclosure of the world and existence is laid open — through the mediation of conversion. Here conversion does not mean merely a physical phenomenon but rather that transformation of existence, and so of the understanding of existence, by which the human being no longer lives for himself, through his own will-to-live, for his own purposes, but accepts the world, others, and himself as given by God.[18] Religious language describes conversion[19] as the religious experience of the world.[20] This conversion is not a human accomplishment. Instead, what is humanly accomplished is experienced by the converted as gift and blessing; conversion is the manifestation of God and a pledge given by God. Obviously this conversion exercises its mediation through religious language, through its witness to God, and through human interactions which are marked by this kind of conversion. In undergoing conversion one also experiences the world in a new way. Augustine has described this experience of the world in his metaphor of the great cry of all things proclaiming to human beings, "We did not make ourselves!"[21] This conversion is, of course, a lifelong process in which the human person increasingly forms his identity by invoking God.

In conversion and the act of naming God, i.e., invoking God as God, there is a concomitant transformation of the results of the "proofs for God." These arguments led to formulations such as the unmoved mover, *actus purus,* being itself, etc. We have seen that in these formulations expressing the requirements for the possibility of orienting the human being in his thinking about reality, the transcendentals, i.e., the universal qualities of reality, are in each case the starting point. In each case the result of the argument was the semantic expression of the various transcendental qualities of reality understood under the form of *id quo maius cogitari nequit.*

Now, in conjunction with the naming and invocation of God as God, the facts which we have just described gain a new meaning. When all reality is understood to be a gift given by God, these facts which have been inferred gain a transformed context of meaning. The transcendental qualities of reality in their manifold, various, and divergent forms point to their divine origin. God must possess the various perfections found in the world which are manifested in these transcendental qualities, but in a way surpassing the finite and also in such a way that these qualities, in themselves multiple, are in God one and the same. Thus the transcendental qualities, understood in the form of *id quo maius cogitari nequit,* attain the status of the name "God," as those attributes which truly belong to God and are proper to God, without pretending that they express God as he is in Godself. In this connection, Thomas speaks in his tract on the names of God of those designations of God which are proper to God but which cannot capture in words the *natura Dei.*[22] Thus these names of God which result from thought form the inner structure of the name "God," protect this name "God" from misunderstandings and too narrow interpretations and safeguard its all-encompassing breadth.

So, as a result of our study, we conclude that the arguments which Thomas presents in the five ways first become proofs for God through our conversion, because only in conversion and in the naming and invocation of God do we discover that the conclusions to which the arguments lead are identical with God himself. Only as a result of conversion is that statement possible with which Thomas concludes his proofs: *hoc omnes nominant Deum.*[23]

(English translation by Michael J. Himes)

Notes

1. P. Tillich, *Systematische Theologie* (Stuttgart: Evangelisches Verlagswerk, 1956), 1:274f.; English trans.: *Systematic Theology* (Chicago: University of Chicago Press, 1951), 1:237.

2. In what follows I am drawing on the work of C. H. Kahn, in W. M. Verhar, ed., *The Verb Be and Its Synonyms: Philosophical and Grammatical Studies* (Dortrich: Reidel, 1973), and on E. Tugendhat, "Die Seinsfrage und ihre sprachliche Grundlage," *Philosophische Rundschau* 24 (1977): 161–76.

3. See·G. Frege, *Die Grundlagen der Arithmetik* (Darmstadt: Wissenschaftliche Buchgesellschaft, 1961), and B. Russell, "Logic and Knowledge," *Essays 1902–1950*, ed. R. C. March (London: George Allen and Unwin, 1971), 175–281.

4. See H. Krings, *Transzendentale Logik* (Munich: Kosel-Verlag, 1964), 318: "Through its affirmation a being is revealed and manifested as what it is.... In the affirmation not only is the transcendental act realized in its form, but in it as well is posited the truth which is the transcendental revelation of what the being itself is. At the same time as the transcendental I is realized through the transcendence implicit in the affirmation, so too the being itself is realized."

5. For the following, see *Summa Theologiae* I, q. 2, a. 3.

6. J. F. Lyotard, *La condition postmoderne: Rapport sur le savoir* (Paris: Editions de Minuit, 1979).

7. Wolfgang Welsch, *Unsere postmoderne Moderne*, 3d ed. (Weinheim: VCH, 1991), 32.

8. *Summa Theologiae* I, q. 2, a. 1, ad 1.

9. Ibid.

10. Ibid., I, q. 13, a. 8.

11. Ibid., I, q. 13, a. 8, ad 2.

12. See ibid., I, q. 13, a. 9, ad 3.

13. Ibid.

14. For the following, see R. Wimmer, "Anselms 'Proslogion' als performativ-illokutionärer und als kognitiv-propositionaler Text und die zweifache Aufgabe der Theologie," in F. Ricken, ed., *Klassische Gottesbeweise in der Sicht der gegenwärtigen Logik und Wissenschaftstheorie* (Stuttgart, Berlin, Cologne: W. Kohlhammer, 1991), 174–200.

15. Ludwig Wittgenstein, *Schriften*, 2d ed. (Frankfurt am Main: Suhrkamp, 1980), 5:429.

16. See Ludwig Wittgenstein, *Schriften*, 2d ed. (Frankfurt am Main: Suhrkamp, 1963), *Tractatus Logico-Philosophicus*, 6:432; [English trans.: *Tractatus Logico-Philosophicus*, trans. D. F. Pears and B. F. McGuiness, International Library of Philosophy and Scientific Method, 2d impression corrected (London: Routledge and Kegan Paul, 1963), 149.]

17. Ludwig Wittgenstein, *Schriften* (Frankfurt am Main: Suhrkamp, 1964), 2:172.

18. On this conversion and on "experience" as the rediscovery of the holy, see B. Casper, K. Hemmerle, and P. Hünermann, *Besinnung auf das Heilige* (Freiburg, Basel, Vienna: Herder, 1966); also, P. Hünermann, *Der Durchbruch geschichtlichen Denkens im 19. Jahrhundert: Johann Gustav Droysen, Wilhelm Dilthey, Graf Paul York von Wartenburg. Ihr Weg und ihre Weisung für die Theologie* (Freiburg, Basel, Vienna: Herder, 1970), 403–17; and P. Hünermann,

Jesus Christus — Gottes Wort in der Zeit: Ein systematische Christologie (Münster: Aschendorff, 1994), 34–51.

19. In this context Richard Schaeffler has published important studies; see his *Kleine Sprachlehre des Gebets* (Einsiedeln, Trier: Johannes Verlag, 1988), and *Das Gebet und das Argument: Zwei Weisen des Sprechens von Gott: Eine Einführung in die Theorie der religiösen Sprache* (Düsseldorf: Patmos, 1989).

20. See Gerhard Krüger, *Religiöse und profane Welterfahrung* (Frankfurt am Main: Klostermann, 1973).

21. Augustine, *Confessiones* 11, 4, 6.

22. See *Summa Theologiae* I, q. 13, a. 2 and a. 3.

23. In the context of the reflections presented here we could not discuss how conversion takes place on different "depth-dimensions" and as a result makes possible distinctive experiences of the divine. The author has outlined these differences both in *Durchbruch des geschichtlichen Denkens* and in *Jesus Christus — Gottes Wort in der Zeit;* see note 18.

2

Beyond Idolatry

On *"Naming"* the One — God

– DAVID B. BURRELL, C.S.C. –

If naming things is a demand endemic to the human species, a practice which the earlier Genesis account links with the very origins of humankind (2:19) and which Aristotle exploits in constructing a science of *whatever is*, commensurate with that species of animal which "by nature desires to know" (*Meta.* 1.1), then praising God becomes second nature to those naming animals who are brought to recognize themselves as creatures of a free Creator. It is characteristic of Thomas Aquinas to link these two imperatives of human nature, so that the praise such creatures render to their Creator will befit their nature as naming animals, and so be as articulate as possible.[1] Yet his correlative insistence on the uniqueness of that Creator, whose free act of creating signalled a complete absence of need for fulfillment, would seem to remove such a One from the theater of human discourse. How can we articulately praise the One whom we know "in knowing that we do not know what God is" (DN 7.4 [731])?[2] St. Thomas insists, however: not only can we praise such a One articulately, but elucidating that very activity will display how it is we can use language at all. The "metaphysical semantics" of discourse *in divinis* offers a clue to our complex "ordinary" activities of naming. Creation, as the connection which secures "the distinction," affords the key.[3]

Naming cannot simply be assimilated to describing. We may even resent school chums calling us by a name which marked certain distinctive features.[4] Naming seems to respond to a call to a yet deeper familiarity than "talking about" someone. What we call *names* of God seems to partake of something of both, however, since terms like "just" have a quasi-descriptive dimension as well. Yet if we reflect on the "call" which the use of a term like "justice" evokes, we see that it lies in part with the self-transcendence built into the term (which we shall be examining), yet also with the *appeal* which it holds out to us. So God's "names" at once relate (1) us to God, (2) God to us, and (3) us to ourselves. How? Their semantic structure (3) recalls us to ourselves, as in Socrates' realizing that he could be named the wisest person in Hellas only because he realized that he was not wise; their givenness in the Scriptures (2) introduces God to us, and their aspiration-character (1) orients us to God. We shall see how this multiple structure works itself out in the metaphysical semantics of Aquinas, culminating in his treatment of the proper way to use "attributes" to name and hence to praise the one God.

It is safe to say that the very dilemma which so discouraged Maimonides from hoping that one might succeed in "naming" God encouraged Aquinas in his inquiry. That is, the ontological *simpleness* of divinity, yielding the One in whom "essence and existence are perfectly identical" (GP 1.57), means that "composition is inconceivable" in God, so that we cannot even "mean to say that an attribute of *unity* is added to His essence" (1.57) when we insist that God is one. What Maimonides clearly sees Aquinas will explain. The very "composition" of a declarative sentence, in which adjectives are predicated of a subject, as in "God is just," has the infelicity of presupposing that the subject of which one is speaking is itself composed. Such is the force of the Aristotelian working axiom that the structure of assertive discourse mirrors the structure of its subject. Yet for Aquinas, what one who understands this fact is able to do, when speaking of God, is to recognize that "we use concrete nouns for God...to indicate [God's] subsistence and completeness," and "abstract nouns to indicate [God's] simplicity" (ST I, q. 13, a. 1, ad 3, ad 2). The key is the recognition that our language may be inadequate to the subject at hand, plus our capacity to factor that recognition into our use of statements involving predications about God.

In his treatment of this topic in the *de Potentia*, Aquinas suggests that such a capacity is grounded in the fact of creation brought to consciousness: *as* God understands many creatures in one act of understanding, *so* our intellect, ascending from the multiplicity of creatures to God, understands that there are many notions relating imperfectly to one God (see q. 7, a. 6, ad 5). The very possibility of an ascent of the mind to something so simple and unitary as God, then, presupposes the fact of a creating emanation from that One. Those features of this world which we recognize to be perfections may be used to ascend to an imperfect understanding of their source because we know the world to be patterned according to divine wisdom. The crucial note of "imperfect understanding" stems from the previous article, which signals the metaphysical gap between source and effect: "perfections of created things may be said to be similar to God [*assimilantur*] after the manner of [God's] unitary and simple essence" (7.5).[5] So terms signifying perfections can be said to "signify what God is, yet imperfectly and deficiently," since though they derive from God as their source, their manner of being in God is totally other than their manner of being in creatures. Only difference-in-similarity can distinguish authentic use from "projection," and while the operative notion of *creation* signals this difference, it can also be detected in the way in which one employs "divine names" — either conscious of one's imperfect grasp or not.

Aquinas offers a comparison to help understand the relation-cum-disrelation: "*As* created things are little by little assimilated to God [*assimilantur*], however imperfectly, by means of these perfections, *so* our intellect is informed by the similitudes [*speciebus*] of these perfections" (q. 7, a. 5). As I read this comparison, he is reminding us that our intellect, as a unitary power of understanding, is informed by various perfections *as we apprehend them* (*speciebus*), yet that same intellect is also able to recognize how, as perfections, they may lead one to their unitary source in God. What distinguishes perfections from other predicates is the way in which their ordinary use requires operative space between our mode of apprehending them and their import beyond any conditions accompanying their accustomed use. Hence Aquinas's celebrated use of the hitherto grammatical distinction between *modus significandi* and *res significata*: our manner of understanding and what the term signifies. And given all that we have said so far about God's manner of being, it is not surprising to hear him say that while our manner of understanding shapes our use of such expressions, it is *what* the terms signify, the *res significata*, which is "properly said of God, indeed *before* they are said of creatures" (q. 7, a. 5, ad 8).

It is this stipulation — that a privileged set of terms may be used properly of Creator and of creatures, and that any one of these terms is said primarily of God rather than of creatures — which sets the parameters for Aquinas's resolution of the metaphysical and semantic dilemmas (which Maimonides identified) in the human project of "naming" God. The first part of the stipulation incorporates his particular way of assimilating Aristotle on "analogous" terms, and the second part recalls the perspective of pseudo-Dionysius regarding the human mind's capacity to ascend to that One whence all-that-is emanates. And both parts of the stipulation require us to move beyond the formation of concepts (or formulae) to the activity of judgment, which Aquinas associates with the act of "combining" predicate with subject to *assert* that something is the case. A normal act of asserting amounts to a claim that what one has formulated is indeed the case; while the act of judgment involved with the use of analogous terms announces that a use is appropriate in a domain where we may not be able to formulate the conditions of its application, yet we have reason to believe that it is applicable there.[6]

This requires some explication. The privileged set of terms includes the transcendentals as well as evaluative terms more generally. Aristotle had already reminded us that "being" is said in many ways, and that the same is true of "one," "true," and "good." What it means for a statement to be one statement will differ from what it is for a letter to be one letter, or a syllable to be one syllable. As a result, there will be no formula (definition) for such terms which does not itself contain a similarly analogous term. Yet Aristotle also insisted that the diverse ways of using "being" were systematically related to one principal use, namely, assertions about individual existing things. So we may surmise, more generally, that other analogous terms will share the semantic structure of "being": while able to function properly in diverse contexts, they will nevertheless be related to a primary, "at home" use. Here is where Aquinas exploits the initially grammatical distinction between *modus significandi* and *res significata*. He justifies his novel use of it by reference to the originating *fact* of creation, contending that the terms we use to praise God, say in reciting the psalms, may indeed "express something of what God is" (ST I, q. 13, a. 2), provided that *we* understand how such terms have a dual domicile. They are (as *res significata*) "used properly of God, and in fact more appropriately than they are used of creatures, for these perfections belong primarily to God" (q. 13, a. 3); yet by their *mode of signification,* "they are predicated of [God] in the category of substance [i.e., intending to express something of what God is], but fail to represent adequately what [God] is, [for] since we know [God] from creatures we can only speak of [God] as they represent [God]" (q. 13, a. 2). What saves the language-user from semantic schizophrenia, however, is the explicit reminder of creation:

> Any creature, in so far as it possesses any perfection, represents God and is like to him, for he, being simply and universally perfect, has pre-existing in himself the perfections of all his creatures. (q. 13, a. 2; see also q. 4, a. 2)

If it is the capacity of the human mind to make judgments which explain the working of analogous terms as we use them — and we use them in many circumstances other than these rarefied ones; it is the background *truth* of creation which assures our capacity to use them here, that is, to use properly of God expressions whose "reach" we can assert but not otherwise know. In other words, the fact that we are able to distinguish, in a privileged class of terms, *what*-they-signify from our *manner*-of-signifying (which their normal use embodies) does not imply that we are thereby in a position to know what we mean when we use them of God. That is, we can assert them to be true of God, understanding (as we have seen) that "attributes" are not *attributed to* God after the fashion in which the ordinary declarative sentence "God is just" presumes them to be. We also understand that we are not using them to assess God, since although "God is known from the perfections which flow from [God] and are to be found in creatures, [they nevertheless] exist in [God] in a transcendent way, [whereas] we understand such perfections...as we find them in creatures, and as we understand them so we use words to speak of them" (ST I, q. 13, a. 3). Understanding, that is, how it is that we understand them, and understanding them as well to be true of God as their source, we understand that we do not understand their *manner* of being so in God. It is in that precise sense that we do not know what we mean when we assert them to be true of God, yet we know that we are asserting something true of God: that God is the source of justice. That is why we are not using "just" to assess God in asserting God to be just, even though we are relying on the "differential" character it possesses as an assessment term to so employ it.

Yet rather than leave us without moorings — as those who demand some "univocal core of meaning" for analogous terms keep complaining — this demand that we "ascend" to the point where we can acknowledge that the expressions which we use are "more appropriately" said of God than of creatures is what assures us that we are using these terms properly when we use them according to our own proper manner of understanding and signifying. (Aquinas does not make this last point explicitly; I am offering it as a gloss on the pregnant remarks of Mark Jordan at the end of his careful exegesis of Aquinas's treatment of the "divine names" in the *de Potentia*[7]). We will be able to see this more clearly if we reflect on the class of evaluative terms, which forms an illustrative subset of analogous expressions. Such expressions have an inertial tendency to a conventional or ethnocentric use. A "just political arrangement," for example, will spontaneously be understood within certain parameters by, say, a Marxist or by a classical liberal. (I am not speaking here of self-conscious political theorists, who may have sufficient sophistication to recognize their contextual bearings, but rather of those of us who might fit the categories but not have reflected on the fact.) We need something of the deliberate historical placement elaborated, say, by Alasdair MacIntyre in his recent *Whose Justice? Which Rationality?*,[8] to grasp how the assessment-term "just" will acquire a different set of "truth-conditions" as it operates in one sociopolitical framework after another. Nor is this feature of assessment-terms like "just" threatening to one who comes to understand it across such contexts, since that same person can recognize *what* it is to which these different cultures and thinkers were aspiring in aspiring to their particular set of just arrangements. We will not be able to formulate this *res significata* outside a particular context, except in the most formal of terms, one or more of which is bound to be analogous itself, yet we will be able to identify the aspiration and hence the particular embodiment.

In other words, it is this very capacity for transcontextual recognition which allows us to use the assessment-term "just" properly in any particular context: that is, neither ideologically nor ethnocentrically. It is this capacity which Aquinas linked with our capacity for judgment of truth/falsity, and when it is used with terms expressing divinity, such an enhancing of our capacity for judgment so exercises our use of assessment-terms that we ought to be warned off misusing them in a conventional sense. Much like Jesus' mocking of the Pharisees' conventional use of "sinner" in Luke 15, pointing toward the transcendent reference point of the One who is Creator of all provides one with a vantage from which other uses of the term are acknowledged to be appropriately context-bound. And our attempt to speak of the One can supply such "purchase" even when we cannot be said properly to know *how* the terms we use to signify God do in fact signify God. Just as knowing-by-faith may grant a certain perspective even when it cannot cast any direct light on the divine-human relationship (as "light" faith is usually "darkness"), so one's recognition that "just" and "justice" said of God make reference to the divine as the source of justice can free us from pretending to a context-free (or "absolute") use of the term in human affairs. Again, knowing *that* such terms express something of what God is as the source of the perfection at issue does not supply us with a transcendent *use* of the expression ("God is just"/"God is justice"), yet the very effort to enhance our power of judgment to the point where we can make such a complementary assertion truthfully (see ST I, q. 13, a. 2) should alert us to the contextual character of our uses of "just."

Here is where the genius of Aquinas's treatment shows itself. By placing his discussion of "divine names" in the wake of his acutely metaphysical probe into what-God-is [not], as he does in the *Summa Theologiae,* or even embedding it within the relevant treatment of divine simplicity, as he does in *de Potentia,* St. Thomas accepts the stark challenge of Rabbi Moses: how might our discourse about or praise of the one God be able to assert anything of a God so uniquely other — or "otherly unique"? The challenge is a formidable one, and Aquinas accepts it on Maimonides' own terms: God is indeed the One in whom essence and existence are perfectly identical (GP 1.57, ST I, q. 3, a. 4). Moreover, that ontological formulation of divine *simpleness* has both metaphysical and religious import. As he organizes his treatment of what-God-is-[not] in the *Summa Theologiae,* it simulates Aristotle's methodological demands for any scientific inquiry: that one first establish the nature of the item in question (presuming, of course, that it exists), in order to be able to demonstrate therefrom its essential properties. Yet "since God is altogether outside the order of creatures" (ST I, q. 13, a. 7), and so cannot be captured in the genus/difference framework so as to yield a *quiddity* (or *mahiyya* [Ibn-Sina]), what-God-is (for Ibn-Sina, God's *dhat*) will have to be established in a *sui generis* manner which nevertheless yields a comparable result.[9]

Aquinas's strategy turns on a conception of God "as the beginning and end of all things and of reasoning creatures especially" (ST I, q. 2, Pro.), and after offering some plausible reasons which would lead reasonable people to acknowledge the presence of such a One (I, q. 2), he proceeds to locate that one metaphysically by showing that it cannot be: composed (I, q. 3), indifferent or inert (I, q. 5), limited (I, q. 7), subject to generation or corruption (and hence temporal) (I, q. 9), or multiple or even one of a kind (I, q. 11). The upshot is a God who can be seen to be supremely One in the fullest rabbinic sense of that expression: because its essence (*dhat*) is to-exist, it is not one of those things which derive from it, all of which are "composed" of *what*-they-are and the fact *that* they are (I, q. 3). Moreover, as the one who simply *is*, God is eminently desirable to intentional beings, so neither indifferent nor inert, since existence is naturally desirable (I, q. 5). Furthermore, such a one could neither be "limited" to a place *in* an ontological scheme (I, q. 7) nor subject to motion or change (I, q. 9), and finally, since no "other" could logically share in such a uniquely determining ontological description, God must be supremely One: neither sharing the stage with another nor happening to be the only one of its kind (I, q. 11). For the ontological placement, by way of simpleness, goodness, limitlessness, and unchangeableness is designed to deliver the divine analogue of Aristotle's *kind*: the divinity so presented is none other than God, whose most proper name is "the One who is" (I, q. 13, a. 11).

There is little doubt that the congruence of this highly metaphysical treatment with the Vulgate translation of God's response to Moses' demand to know the divine name (Exod. 3:14) confirmed Aquinas's novel appropriation of Avicenna's distinction of *existence* from *essence,* and the use to which he put it to articulate God's uniqueness: that with God alone is the nature simply to-be. Yet the mutual illumination between religious and philosophical perspectives need not turn on a translation, nor is it limited to that coincidence. Aquinas even distinguishes the Vulgate translation "qui est" from the "Tetragrammaton [itself] which is used to signify the incommunicable and, if we could say such a thing, individual substance of God" (ST I, q. 13, a. 11, ad 1). This shows a characteristic semantic sophistication: that a term may be used in a fashion not directly connected with its lexical meaning. Yet he also exploits that meaning when he argues that "[the One] who is" indeed most appropriately functions as the name of God. For this expression secures "the distinction" of Creator from creation: "no [created] form or nature *is* its nature or quiddity; so it is that the name proper to God is "[the One] who is, as is clear from Exodus 3:14, because it names, as it were, God's proper form" (deP 2.1). Aquinas says "as it were" because it is actually the semantic peculiarity of "[the One] who is" which makes it "most appropriate for [naming] God, since it does not determine a certain form to God, but signifies indeterminate *to-be* "(deP 7.5). This leads him to make the general observation: "since we cannot comprehend divine things, it is more fitting that we signify them by common nouns which signify something indefinitely..., whence it follows that this name '[the One] who is,' which signifies, according to John Damascene, an infinite sea of substance, is most fittingly said of God, as is clear from Exodus 3:14" (deP 10.1 ad 9). A more pointed argument for "[the One] who is" as God's proper name is given in his commentary on *The Divine Names* of pseudo-Dionysius, where he adopts the Neoplatonic valuation of *to-be* (*esse*) over *life* and *wisdom*. By way of clarification, he notes that "to-be itself is compared to life and other such [perfections] as the thing participated to those participating in it, for life itself is a kind of being (*ens*); hence to-be (*esse*) is prior and simpler than life and other such [perfections], and so is to be compared to them as their act" (DN 5.1[635]). Aquinas's adaptation of this text reminds us forcibly how *existing* is never a mere given for him, but the freely bestowed created participation in God's own life which is itself the source of all subsequent perfections which creatures enjoy.

In the *Summa Theologiae*, Aquinas actually weaves a more evocatively religious perspective into his otherwise severely formal elaboration of the divine nature (what-God-is[not]), matching each "formal feature" with a complementary assertion more resonant with a posture of praise. Structurally, the treatment of questions 3–11 displays a zipper-like pattern, with the (left) logical side completed in each instance by its religious analogue, culminating in a oneness where philosophers, rabbis, and mystics often merge:

Simpleness (I, q. 3)	Perfection (I, q. 4)
Goodness in general (I, q. 5)	Goodness of God (I, q. 6)
Limitlessness (I, q. 7)	God's existence in things (I, q. 8)
Unchangeableness (I, q. 9)	God's eternity (I, q. 10)
Oneness of God (I, q. 11)[10]	

And if we remind ourselves that the role of the "five ways" of ST I, q. 2 is to convince fair-minded inquirers of his day that of their various explanatory schemes each displays an incompleteness which requires something of another order to complete it, then the entire scheme of questions 2–11 may be seen to be grounded in a Creator who is "in act and in no way in potency" (I, q. 3, a. 1).

The meaning of that expression will be allowed to develop, in unfolding the oneness of God through a simpleness articulated as the One whose essence is to-exist, and thence to remarking the further coincidence of divine attributes (or "properties," in Aristotle's sense of that term) with the "names" or descriptors of God offered in the Scriptures. When we return to this point, the more metaphysical elaboration of the divine nature shifts to the background to exercise a more regulative function, just as kind-talk does in our ordinary discourse — we normally know *what* we are talking about! Yet in the case of divinity, one's metaphysical commitments will have to be more intrusive, more explicitly regulative, experience shows, since the background we normally presume is that of our world: of creation, then, and not of its Creator. This underscores the importance of a clear-headed metaphysics-cumsemantics when treating the issues involved in humans' discourse about and praise of their God. This is a conviction which I share with Mark Jordan and David Braine, who has eloquently stated and elaborated the case for metaphysics *in* theology in his recent study: *The Reality of Time and the Existence of God*.[11] It is this conviction which links each of us so explicitly with Thomas Aquinas and explains why Jordan insists, at the close of his article on divine names, that:

> the doctrine of the divine names is the surest philosophical approach to the nature of God. Any other treatment, unless it is placed after the doctrine of the names, is bound to fall into dialectical idolatry as result of mistaking the logic of the terms which name divine attributes. (183)

One can verify this contention nearly wherever one looks; I can only hope that this essay has contributed to persuading some inquirers of its truth.

Notes

1. The final argument which Aquinas gives in support of these names expressing something of what God is reminds us of the "intention of those who speak of God" — an intention usually suffused with praise (ST I.13.2).

2. References to Aquinas's works will be by abbreviation: DN=*In Librum de Divinis Nominibus Expositio;* deP=*Questiones Disputatae de Potentia;* ST=*Summa Theologiae.* Moses Maimonides' *Guide for the Perplexed* (=GP) will normally be cited in the Freidlander translation (New York: Dover, 1956) rather than the more recent and usually preferred Pines translation (Chicago: University of Chicago Press, 1963), since Freidlander's philosophical terminology is more standard.

3. For closer development of this point, see my *Knowing the Unknowable God* (Notre Dame, Ind.: University of Notre Dame Press, 1986), and Robert Sokolowski's study to which mine is singularly indebted: *The God of Faith and Reason* (Notre Dame, Ind.: University of Notre Dame Press, 1982).

4. I am indebted to al-Ghazali for this observation regarding naming from descriptive features; see *Al-Ghazâlî on the Ninety-Nine Beautiful Names of God*, trans. David Burrell and Nazih Daher (Cambridge: Islamic Texts Society, 1992), 179.

5. For "imperfectly signify" see Herbert McCabe's appendix in his translation of questions 12–13 of *Summa Theologiae: Knowing and Naming God* (London: Eyre and Spottiswoode, 1964), 104–5.

6. See Gregory P. Rocca, O.P., "Aquinas on God-Talk: Hovering over the Abyss," *Theological Studies* 54 (1993): 641–61.

7. Mark Jordan, "The Names of God and the Being of Names," in Alfred J. Freddoso, ed., *The Existence and Nature of God* (Notre Dame, Ind.: University of Notre Dame Press, 1983), 161–90, esp. 182–83.

8. Alasdair MacIntyre, *Whose Justice? Which Rationality?* (Notre Dame, Ind.: University of Notre Dame Press, 1988).

9. See *Knowing the Unknowable God*, 39–41.

10. This is developed further in chapter 2 of my *Aquinas: God and Action* (Notre Dame, Ind.: University of Notre Dame Press, 1979).

11. David Braine, *The Reality of Time and the Existence of God* (Oxford: Oxford University Press, 1988).

3

The Dialectic of Faith and Atheism in the Eighteenth Century

– LOUIS DUPRÉ–

Atheism has from the beginning been a steady companion of religious belief. Michael Buckley implicitly refers to atheistic precedents in more religious ages when adding the qualifier "modern" to the title of his insightful *At the Origins of Modern Atheism*. Modern atheism differs from the earlier ones, however, by its absolute character. Eighteenth-century unbelief rules out *any* kind of traditional religious interpretation of reality. This absolute character of modern atheism makes the final chapter of Buckley's study, "The Dialectical Origins of Atheism," intriguing. How can a position that excludes any dialogue with its opposite still relate to an "other?" That question inspired the following pages and its answer confirms the legitimacy of Buckley's thesis.

I

Modern atheism is dialectical because modern thought created a thoroughly ambiguous condition with respect to religious faith. It allowed the atheistic conclusion as well as the religious one. But one conclusion implicitly continued to refer to the other. The same thinkers who estranged the modern mind from its religious beliefs forced it to reconsider them.

The mechanistic philosophies of Descartes and Newton had opened the road to materialism but, as Malebranche and Clark prove, they also justified the spiritual interpretations their originators had given to their own thought. Michael Buckley has carefully traced the continuing impact of the "mother" philosophy on its atheist heirs. Following his lead I propose to pursue the lateral relations atheists entertained with their religious cousins. The existence of such relations ought not to surprise us. Atheism can preserve its identity only by the grace of the belief it negates. Contemporary secular humanism has severed the link with religion altogether. For that reason it refuses to characterize its position as

38

"atheistic." Nietzsche may well have been the last dialectical atheist: he remains fully engaged with the religious principles he denies. The battle ended at the beginning of this century. Lenin's and Sartre's vigorous anti-theism must be considered a rearguard action. But in the eighteenth century the two positions were intimately related. Behind each believer stood an atheist, and behind each atheist a believer. One reacted to the other's claims.

Eighteenth-century atheism merely brought to a head profound conflicts that had long affected Christian theology and that had played a major part in dividing the Christian churches during the Reformation. In the wake of the religious wars a search for common principles was undertaken. The outcome of it transformed theism in a way its champions themselves had not realized. To be sure, the quest for a common basis reaches far back in the history of monotheist thought. Serious philosophical reflection on religious unity had begun in the cultural encounter of the three monotheist faiths in the Middle Ages. The ninth-century Baghdad thinker al-Kindi had already proclaimed the rational, and therefore universal, nature of all revealed faith. His rational universalism — as that of the many who followed him — had been essentially religious. Al-Farabi (d. 980) and Ibn-Sina (Avicenna), who held similar ideas, were deeply spiritual men. In Christianity the idea of a religious universality based on reason had been, at least in part, accepted by Aquinas. Renaissance thinkers such as Ficino, Pico, and Bodin fully embraced it mostly on the common basis of the Neoplatonic idea of the soul's natural longing for its divine origin.

The search for philosophical unity undertaken after the Reformation was different. It bore the scars of the theological meltdown of the fourteenth and fifteenth centuries. Nominalist theology had thoroughly eroded the notion of *form* on which much of earlier philosophical structures had rested. Christians had used this Greek notion for construing their own synthesis of nature and grace. The primeval form was God's own Word, exemplar of all earthly forms, and the realm of nature, reflecting this divine origin, was through divine grace called to return to it. There had been tensions — the iconoclastic episode in Byzantine history is one we best remember. But not until Scotus did the contrast between the universal Greek form of unblemished perfection and the exemplary form incarnated in a human individual subject to suffering and death turn into a conflict.[1] The fundamental opposition between Christian individualism and Greek universalism rendered the postulate of an a priori harmony between nature and the divine model on which the synthesis of nature and grace had been based a dubious assumption. After the nominalist crisis the entire relation between created reality and its divine origin had become uncertain. A less ambitious, less theological basis for religious concord had to be found. The new philosophies of the seventeenth century provided a modest substitute: through efficient causality all creatures depended on the same Creator.

Pascal exaggerated when he called this causality as conceived by Descartes no more than the divine hand flip that started the world's mechanism. Descartes never restricted the divine creative impulse to a single event after which God withdrew. On the contrary, he insisted that creation is a never-ending process without which the cosmos would immediately return to nothingness. Moreover, the mind depended as much on divine assistance for its operation as the material universe. Not only does God guarantee its truth; God constitutes the essential condition without which no knowledge of the finite could exist at all. Each finite perception presupposes a horizon of divine infinity. My continued existence and acting, even as the continued order of nature, depends at each moment on God. No direct link ties Descartes to eighteenth-century materialism.

Nevertheless Christian thought proved to be unprepared for the mechanistic world picture. Though continuously preserved by God, the system of motion is endowed with a relative autonomy that enables it to rule itself. In the earlier conception divine causality had not only secured a steady inflow of power: it had also directed this power. According to Newton, no new divine intervention was needed for motion to start. The state of rest is no more "natural" than that of motion. Unnecessary hypotheses of divine interventions beyond creation and preservation would destroy the coherence needed in a scientific system. Again, as amply appears in the "General Scholium," Newton's own view was thoroughly religious. Yet it was the mechanism of Newton's system, not his religious vision, that supplied the scientific basis for the deist and later the atheist theories.

The eighteenth century pitted universal reason against particular revelation. The two had previously remained united by principles such as *fides quaerens intellectum* or *intellectus quaerens fidem*. Faith calls for the insight of reason, but any understanding of the divine requires the light of revelation. Deism was to disrupt that balance in favor of unaided reason. To be fair to the deist position we must recognize that two Christian principles supported it: (1) faith must be a *rationabile obsequium*, able to withstand the test of reason; (2) God wants the salvation of all persons. Moreover, the earlier advocates of a religious universalism based their position on the idea of an aboriginal divine revelation to the entire human race. The content of this revelation had generally been lost in idolatry, yet had left some vestiges in all religions. The theory of a primeval revelation had existed since the Renaissance. But the origins of modern deism may be traced to a small group of learned and deeply pious Anglican divines, mostly graduates of Emmanuel College at Cambridge, who attempted to give the idea of a universal religion a basis in human nature. In the Christian Platonic tradition, initiated by Ficino and Pico, they stated that the soul naturally longs for God and that this longing has been fulfilled by a universal revelation. The Cambridge Platonists, especially Ralph Cudworth, enriched the idea of a universal revelation by empirical descriptions of the direct experience of God's presence in the soul and of the traces of an underlying monotheism in polytheist religions. They attempted to substantiate their theory on the bases of Egyptian religion as interpreted through Plutarch, Iamblichus, and of Greek and Roman philosophy. Their concept of a "natural" religion was in fact a Neo-Pythagorean and Neoplatonic monotheism.

Their claim, however, was far more comprehensive. In all ancient religions, they stated, one supreme God rules over all others. This henotheism prepared the human race for the fullness of a monotheist revelation. According to Cudworth, the ancient monotheist revelation had become corrupted into a base polytheism through the fault of the poets, "the grand depravers and adulterators of pagan theology."[2] They had unduly personified what, at least among the Greeks, had been metaphorical entities. Philosophers, however, had persistently recognized a single God. The masses possessed only the hidden truth of polytheism.

What Cudworth interpreted as the genuine, though hidden truth of popular religion, later deists considered an untruth useful for maintaining moral standards among the masses. The universality of the Cambridge theory, then, rested on an original revelation the truth of which was revived in the Christian revelation. Their theory had been a response to a religious question that had arisen *within* the Christian community: How can the entire human race partake of a truth essential to salvation conveyed in a historically circumscribed faith? Their universalism rested on Christian faith; that of the deists on reason allegedly opposed to the particularity of revelation.

Could the deist theory itself claim any genuinely *religious* support? Interestingly, some deists appeal to the same argument the Cambridge Platonists had invoked: the presence in polytheist religions of a single high God from whom all power derives and who sanctions the moral world order. Voltaire in the first of the four so-called *Homilies Delivered in London in 1765* insists that the Egyptians "recognized a supreme God despite all their superstitions." He then extends his argument to the Indians and the Chinese and concludes: "Thus you see that all civilized peoples — Indians, Chinese, Egyptians, Persians, Chaldaeans, Phoenicians recognized a supreme God."[3] Some students of comparative religion have since then come to consider the existence of a "meagerly personified" god who received little or no worship a rather common feature of archaic religions. This supreme god shows some similarity with the deist godhead.[4] What distinguishes the deist interpretation of this primitive monotheism from the Christian is that, according to the latter, the knowledge of one God originates not in reason but in a primordial revelation.

II

The slide to a rationalist deism occurred almost imperceptibly. According to Herbert of Cherbury, the idea of one supreme Being, avenger of good and evil, to be worshiped by a moral life, had been implanted into the human mind independently of all revelation. But most often John Locke's *The Reasonableness of Christianity* (1695) is singled out as the founder of religious rationalism. His philosophical theology developed in the *Essay on Human Understanding* as well as his *Letter on Toleration* undeniably influenced later deist theories. But Locke's work itself is neither deist nor rationalist in the ordinary sense of that term. For Locke revelation is an indispensable complement to reason, not only for those who lack the leisure or the mental capacity to follow complex philosophical arguments. It is needed for enriching the thin religious content of philosophical theology, as well as for teaching religious doctrines and practices (e.g., concerning resurrection and afterlife) necessary for salvation. On the other hand, reason prepares the mind for accepting revelation and always remains the critical norm of what truly belongs to revelation. No position contrary to reason can be revealed by God. Locke considered Scripture essential and infallible, but the church interpretations of it subject to the critique of reason. While preparing *The Reasonableness of Christianity as Delivered in the Scriptures* (1695) he wrote to an acquaintance: "This winter I have been carefully considering in what the Christian faith consists. I have drunk for myself from the Holy Scriptures, but I have held aloof from the opinions of sects and systems."[5] The outcome was, for its time, a remarkable work of exegesis of the four gospels intended to prove that Jesus was indeed the Messiah announced by the Hebrew prophets.

At the very beginning of his work Locke rejected the thesis that Christianity is no more than "a natural religion," that is, that it contains nothing *above* reason. That theory was emerging at the time, as the title of John Toland's *Christianity Not Mysterious, Or a Treatise Shewing, That There Is nothing in the Gospel Contrary to Reason, nor Above it* (1596) indicates. For Locke, faith, being an assent "not thus made out by the deductions of reason but upon the credit of the proposer, as coming from God," goes by its very nature beyond reason.[6] Nonetheless *The Reasonableness of Christianity* was immediately accused of atheism and Socinianism by John Edwards, a Calvinist divine.[7] Locke answered only the second charge, pointing out that his position, contrary to Socinius's, was entirely based on Scripture and not on independent reason. Further controversy followed and Locke in *A Second Vindication of the Reasonableness of Christianity* explicitly and, I think, sincerely declared that he wrote his treatise for the benefit of "those who thought that there was no need of revelation at all" or of those who considered the articles for salvation incompatible with their way of reasoning — the two objections "which were with most assurance made by Deists against Christianity but against Christianity misunderstood."[8] In a (Second) Reply to the Bishop of Worcester concerning the resurrection of the dead he had already written: "the reason of believing any article of the Christian faith...to me and upon my grounds, is its being a part of divine revelation" (*Works* IV, 303). In light of those declarations it appears astonishing that Locke's treatise became a rallying text for early deists. While for him revelation, though inaccessible to independent reason, remains conformed to reason, for his alleged followers, revelation never exceeds reason.

The miracles of the gospel presented, of course, a special case. Could one regard them as surpassing the natural course of events without running contrary to the laws of reason? In *The Reasonableness* Locke had not entered into this problem. But two radical deists, Anthony Collins and Thomas Woolston, perceived the difficulty and disposed of it on the basis of Locke's own scriptural argument. Collins attacked the validity of Locke's fundamental argument: that Jesus had fulfilled the biblical prophecies. That so-called "fulfillment" was so vague that any religious teacher could claim to have done so. Woolston completed this critique by denying the credibility of the miracles that were supposed to support the fulfillment.[9] Once the bond that had linked scriptural revelation to reason was broken, the theory of rational religion entered into conflict with revelation.

Nevertheless, for all their hostility to scriptural authority deists continued to rely heavily on the theological legacy of the gospel. Their "rational" monotheism remains in essence biblical, endowing God with the traditional attributes of justice, goodness, omnipotence. Their moral code also continued to borrow from the gospel. This was even the case after deism developed into atheism. Moreover, deists display an amazing loyalty to their attenuated idea of God. Voltaire, who had assaulted the Christian and biblical faith with unprecedented vehemence (most acerbic in the anonymous *An Important Study by Lord Bolingbroke* [1767]), wrote equally scathing attacks upon atheism in his *Questions on the Encyclopédie,* in the dialogue *The Sage and the Atheist,* and in the *Philosophical Dictionary.* Deists felt as passionately concerned about the survival of rational religion as they felt hostile to the terrors of "superstition." Their position, however antagonistic to Christian theology, maintained a secret but ambivalent relation with it. They continued in fact a rationalization process that had already started in thirteenth-century theology.

Albert and Aquinas had still succeeded in developing a remarkably harmonious synthesis of revelation with Aristotelian philosophy. Later theologians, however, tended to rationalize the language of revelation without regard for its symbolic nature. Erasmus and the early Reformation temporarily restored the existential, dynamic quality of God-talk. But soon rationalism reinvaded theology: the language of Lutheran Orthodoxy and of the Reformed Church was hardly less univocal than that of late scholasticism. Nowhere does this appear more obvious than in the seventeenth-century conflict between freedom and the traditional Christian idea of election. All solutions, the Calvinist and Jansenist ones as well as the Molinist, resulted in heavily anthropomorphic, univocal representations of God's will. Pascal's mordant wit pilloried the Molinist position in the *Lettres provinciales*. Voltaire ridiculed the Jansenist one in the adventures of the *ingénu* Huron. Eventually the entire structure of rational theology came under attack by the "philosophes" — only to make place for the rationalism of the deists.

Deist rationalism despised the pseudo-rationality of theology. It claimed to rely *exclusively* on reason. But what was really at stake was an inversion from theocentrism to a radical anthropocentrism expressed in the absolute sovereignty of reason, that rendered any discourse about God impossible and inevitably led to atheism. Already seventeenth-century philosophy had shifted the function of the immanent and the transcendent factors that had traditionally determined meaning and value. Rather than reflecting a divinely established order, meaning and value now were considered to originate in the mind itself. For Descartes, the father of modern philosophy, God had still played an indispensable, if not primary part, in the attainment of truth. Even for Kant, the *idea* of God continued to fulfill a vital function: it secured the ultimate unity of knowledge, the reliability of the moral universe, and the very possibility of scientific investigation. But the traditional relation between autonomous reason and revelation was undermined once the idea of God came to be viewed as being itself a product of autonomous reason.

I mentioned that deists continued to pattern this idea on a Christian model and to draw much of their moral value system from the gospel. But these dependencies remained unacknowledged, if not openly rejected. Thus unresolved tensions appeared on all sides. On the one hand the deists claimed that God sanctions the moral law. On the other hand they defined the nature and norms of conduct in exclusively human terms. This inconsistency appears already in Locke (in other regards not a deist), who added a divine sanction to his moral utilitarianism. That God merely sanctions what humans effectively accomplish by their own wits and on their own behalf appears even more clearly in Voltaire, who blandly defines virtue as "what is useful to society."[10]

III

The transition to atheism became inevitable once deists became aware of the inconsistency of a position that both asserted an exclusively human source of meaning and value and yet persisted in proclaiming the same source dependent on a transcendent principle. As La Mettrie acutely perceived, the deist concern was not with the existence of God as such but with the alleged need for a transcendent theoretical and moral support for an autonomously human position. Such a support, he argued, was no longer needed in a consistently mechanistic worldview:

> I do not mean to call in question the existence of a Supreme Being. On the contrary it seems to me that the greatest degree of probability is in favor of this belief. But since the existence of this being goes no further than that of any other toward proving the need of worship, it is a theoretic truth with very little practical value.... Let us not lose ourselves in the infinite, for we are not made to have the least idea thereof, and are absolutely unable to get back to the origin of things. Besides it does not matter for our peace of mind, whether matter be eternal or have been created, whether there be or be not a God.[11]

The agnostic La Mettrie's claim with regard to the "usefulness" of God in a mechanistic philosophy holds equally true for deism, as deists gradually came to realize. Deism had been an intermediate position that succeeded only in maintaining itself on the basis of a practical need. How could moral norms be preserved, especially among the uneducated, without some divine sanction? As the answer to this question became ever more uncertain under the attacks of agnostics and atheists, deism lost much of its raison d'être and developed into atheism. The pragmatism underlying both positions vividly illustrates the inverted relation between immanence and divine transcendence.

The atheist conclusion implicit in the deist premises appears obvious in Hume's *Natural History of Religion* (1757). The very title indicates how far modern thought had moved away from asserting the indispensability of a transcendent principle of meaning: that principle itself is now presented as having a "natural" (i.e., purely immanent) origin in the human mind. Early deists had sidestepped the question of the historical origins of religion. They had repudiated the Renaissance notion of a primeval revelation but had provided nothing to replace it. Most of them assumed the existence of some universal religious instinct. But how did that account for the "superstitious" character of religion? To Hume the assumption of a primary religious instinct appeared unwarranted. Historical evidence indicated religion to be derived from emotions such

as fear that were not religious themselves. That religion had no supernatural origin was, in the Christian culture, an unprecedented assertion.
Yet no less significant was Hume's denial that religion originated as a
reaction to a nonreligious emotion. It implied that a variety of reactions
to that primary emotion were possible, including nonreligious ones.

> Some nations have been discovered, who entertained no sentiments of reli-
> gion, if travellers and historians may be credited; and no two nations, and
> scarce any two men, have ever agreed precisely in the same sentiments.
> It would appear, therefore, that this preconception springs not from an
> original instinct or primary impression of nature, such as gives rise to self-
> love, affection between the sexes, love of progeny, gratitude, resentment;
> since every instinct of this kind has been found absolutely universal in all
> nations and ages and has always a precise determinate object, which it
> inflexibly pursues.[12]

The full implication of Hume's account of the origin of religion appeared shortly afterward when Baron d'Holbach based his aggressively
atheist theory on it: "The first theology of man was grounded on fear
modelled by ignorance."[13] For d'Holbach, however, ignorance was in itself already sufficient to inspire religion. To be sure, Hume left a door
open to the rational justification of religion: some philosophical arguments might still prove the existence of God, independently of human
emotions.

Hume himself pretended strongly (though with dubious sincerity)
that this was indeed the case: "The whole frame of Nature bespeaks an
intelligent author; and no rational inquirer can, after serious reflection,
suspend his belief a moment with regard to the primary principles of
genuine Theism and Religion." Skeptical readers doubted that after the
exhaustive, "natural" interpretation of *Natural History,* such an argument was likely to be forthcoming. They were right. In his posthumously
published *Dialogues concerning Natural Religion* Hume not only closed
the door to any support of traditional religion; he made sure to plug
all loopholes through which a deist argument might escape. Indeed,
Hume's assertion that a genetic interpretation left the logical validity
of the idea of God intact must have seemed to himself "a lame ex-
cuse if there ever was one," as Freud called such a possibility after his
own genetic explanation of religion.[14] Even the popular assumption of
an original monotheism which several deists implicitly held (independently of any primitive revelation) proved untenable. "It is a matter of
fact incontestable, that about 1700 years ago all mankind were poly-
theists" — with the exception of a few philosophers and one or two
nations, "and that not entirely pure" (Section 1). Primitives do not raise
such abstruse theoretical questions as whether there might be one cause
behind the multiple phenomena to be feared. Even after monotheism has

become solidly established the uneducated continue to return to "mediating powers," indestructible survivals of a primitive polytheism. Nor did monotheism emerge as a conclusion of reason, but rather by a *natural* development of polytheist religion. Gradually religious worshipers attributed more and more powers to one god. Originally that one god was no more than the top of the polytheist hierarchy. That this concentrated product of fear and superstition coincided "with the principles of reason and true philosophy" (!) (Section 6) Hume ascribes to chance.

Even the pragmatic argument that had shored the deist thesis, namely, that only religion provides an adequate basis for morality, has lost its power for Hume. No link joins virtuous conduct to religious belief. How could superstition ever induce moral behavior? Has religious fanaticism not been responsible for the most heinous crimes? Hence, Hume piously concludes, "it is justly regarded as unsafe to draw any certain inference in favor of man's morals from the fervor or strictness of his religious exercises" (Section 10). In refuting the pragmatic argument, the bulwark of deism, Hume moves beyond La Mettrie's indifference: for him religion is a negative moral value.[15] Once the focus of religion was transferred from God as "valuable in Himself" (as Scheler was to express it later) to a God who is valuable only for us, the discovery that no particular human value depended on his existence soon followed. The transition from a deist pragmatism to atheism occurred quite naturally. A passage in *Dialogues concerning Natural Religion* sets the stage. When Cleanthes, extending La Mettrie's metaphor to the entire cosmos, argues that the world seems like a huge machine, Philo aptly replies that a machine is a typical *projection* of the human mind, and hence inappropriate for proving the existence of a transcendent Creator.

Does atheism still preserve a dialectical relation to faith? Was its development out of deism more than a straightforward movement toward an unqualifiedly secularist worldview? The coarse materialism of d'Holbach and La Mettrie appears to leave little room for any but an unqualifiedly negative relation to religion proper. But that materialism is an atypical, extreme expression of a more comprehensive shift in the relation between immanence and transcendence. That shift itself remains intrinsically dialectical. Even in its atheist expressions it continues to maintain a more than negative relation to transcendence. As Feuerbach was to point out later, the attribution to nature of qualities once reserved to God still bears a religious significance. That significance had appeared more obvious in early modern thinkers. Bruno and Spinoza were called atheists by their contemporaries, but both retained a notion of transcendence *within* nature that distinguishes their thought from d'Holbach's plain naturalism. A surplus of meaning beyond the merely factual continues to indicate that, for them, the appearance of things alone does not suffice to justify them, but requires a transcendent foundation.

Their thought marked in this respect a return to later Greek, particularly Stoic and Neoplatonic, philosophy, which also had located the transcendent *within* rather than above the cosmos. Christian thinkers had, from the fourth century on, adopted much of the Neoplatonic vision but, faithful to the biblical idea of God, they had originally interpreted the Neoplatonic One as a God who stands entirely *above* creation. For Plotinus and his followers, however, the One dwells within the real of which it constitutes the very core. The Neoplatonic conception did not support the dialogical relation between God and the soul, typical of biblical faith. Still the development of Christian mysticism shows that the idea of the indwelling God was not altogether incompatible with that faith. How else do we explain the ease with which Augustine, Ruusbroec, John of the Cross, and so many other spiritual Christians through the centuries moved back and forth between dialogue and introversion?

Nevertheless a substantial difference separates these ancient and the Christian modes of thinking about the relation between transcendence and immanence from the ones of deism and atheism. The difference, already noticeable in Bruno, consists in the modern turn toward the subject, which transforms transcendence from an a priori condition of thought and value into an object of the mind among others. The slide toward atheism this transformation effected was slow and gradual, accomplished with many hesitations, and, until the age of deism, rarely followed through to the end. Descartes himself, often held responsible for the anthropocentric turn, continued to view the presence of God in the Augustinian tradition as the necessary condition for the mind's meaning-giving activity. The "philosophes" of the eighteenth century were more consistent, and no one more so than Denis Diderot. His spiritual development brought him from traditional Christian theism to deism, to pantheism, and finally to materialist atheism. In a chapter on "The Atheistic Transformation of Denis Diderot" Michael Buckley has traced that development with much wit and insight. In the final part of this essay I shall attempt to show the continued presence of the dialectic in Diderot's thought as well as the inevitability of his slide into atheism.

Diderot's first writing on religion, the *Pensées philosophiques* of 1746, proves to be particularly revealing for this purpose. Written in the aphoristic mode of Pascal's *Pensées,* to which it is meant to reply, the text speaks in many voices — theist, deist, skeptic, atheist. The discord of conflicting opinions results in a uniquely dialectical composition. A deist voice stresses the presence of God as He dwells in the cosmos and the human heart: "We do not sufficiently emphasize [God's] presence. People have banished the Deity from their midst and relegated God to a sanctuary. The walls of a temple limit our view of Him."[16] Yet in another entry a different (skeptic?) voice points out how much the subjective quality of our perception, what Diderot calls *le tempérament,* defines the nature of the experience. The God whom one person experiences as object of love is for another an object of fear. "Does piety follow the law of the wretched temperament? Alas, how can we deny it!" (no. 11, 277). The young Diderot already shows a mature awareness of the subjective predicament as it was affecting the modern concept of transcendence.

Not all restrictions imposed on our knowledge of God are due to the subjective nature of religious feelings. Reason itself surrounds the idea of God with boundaries of its own. Any truth claim must be assessed exclusively on the basis of reason, the deist posits. "C'est à la raison qu'il faut s'en tenir" (no. 52, 301). Yet the restriction of reason, as the mechanist philosopher conceives it, allows no statement about the transcendent ever to attain the certainty that geometry and physics possess (no. 59, 304). Indeed, reason so conceived excludes the very notion of a supernatural revelation as well as the possibility of any miraculous "signs" of revelation. Exasperated by Pascal's notion of an authority beyond reason, the skeptic exclaims: "Find me the reasons. Why harass me with miracles when all you need to defeat me is a syllogism?" (no. 50, 300). Truth is to be found exclusively in the human mind and wherever the mind falls short in attaining it, it must remain satisfied with the quest for it. "One must require from me that I seek the truth, not that I find her" (no. 29, 288). (Lessing was to rephrase this even more poignantly: the quest for truth is preferable to the given truth.)

Does the contemplation of nature convey any rational evidence to support the existence of a transcendent reality? That is what Diderot investigated in his next discussions, the *Letter on the Blind* (1749) and the *Thoughts on the Interpretation of Nature* (1753). The *Letter* contains a pseudo-historical account of the death of the Cambridge professor of mathematics, the blind Nicholas Saunderson. A minister called to his bedside attempts to awaken the patient's faith by evoking the marvelous order in the universe. Saunderson admits the order, but questions whether it conveys any insight about its origin. Could "the hatching matter" out of which the universe evolved not have produced its order and coherence? Only those forms might have survived that fitted in with the rest and were able to perpetuate themselves. Even now the earth continues to produce "monstrous forms" and, by a self-regulating mechanism, to abort the ones incompatible with the already existing order.[17] Diderot dearly paid for placing these irreverent questions in Saunderson's pious mouth. But, undeterred by censorship, he proceeded to answer them himself in yet another aphoristic writing, *Thoughts on the Interpretation of Nature.*

What had been skeptical questions now received a pantheist reply. This time the biologist Maupertuis served as mouthpiece of Diderot's opinions. Why, he wondered, do we fear to attribute to the material universe as a whole perceptive qualities, such as we observe in all animals? If we overcome this irrational fear, we may find nature itself capable of introducing the modifications we ascribe to the Creator. Nothing prevents the sum of all molecules to be to some extent "endowed with the powers of thought and feeling."[18]

> If faith did not teach us that animals sprang from the hands of their Creator just as we know them... might the philosopher not suspect, having given himself up entirely to his own conjectures, that the particular elements needed to constitute animal life had existed from all eternity, scattered and mixed with the whole mass of matter; that these elements happening to come together, had combined because it was possible for them to do so.[19]

The purpose of Diderot's rudimentary hypothesis of a spontaneous evolution of the species was more theological than scientific, namely, to show that a creative transcendence might well reside *within* the universe — like a divine world soul — rather than above it. Though Diderot ascribes the immanent power to "hatching matter," he has not yet fully embraced d'Holbach's self-explanatory materialism. Transcendence is not absent from his theory, but has become thoroughly immanent in the cosmos itself. A dialectical relation with a theist creationism is preserved, even though his believing contemporaries considered the outcome plain atheism. Of course, Diderot's contemporaries were not wrong in detecting a direct link between the early skepticism and the later atheism. Once the process of increasing immanentization of the transcendent became part of the modern project, it would eventually reach the point where no surplus of meaning justified any further talk of transcendence. In following this line of reasoning to the very end Diderot was more consistent than others before and after him.

The question, then, inevitably occurs: Was there an alternative? Is theism still compatible with the modern mindset? How I would conceive the beginning of an answer to that momentous question I have sketched in the conclusion of *Passage to Modernity*. The modern idea of unlimited creativity as envisioned by the early humanists soon derailed when this creativity became detached from the transcendent and cosmic components with which it had been integrated in a single ontological synthesis. Before the eighteenth century this rarely resulted in the radical forms of deism and atheism, because few thinkers followed the basic premises of modern thought through to their final conclusion. They were able to abstain from doing so because of the theological consequences; both the conception of these premises *and* their application had still been uncertain. Eighteenth-century rationalism hardened what had remained fluid and canonized what had still been open options in the early modern period. I do not believe that eighteenth-century rationalism allowed any theist alternative. The solution, if there be any, lies not in adjusting rationalist thought but in totally overcoming it. Attempts to do so have, of course, long been on the way. Must they aim at a complete *reversal* of modernity, as some postmodernists claim? I think not. Instead, we ought to return to, and elaborate, the fundamental principle of modernity as it was first enunciated half a millennium ago: human creativity must and can be developed in full integration with the transcendent and cosmic components of the ontotheological synthesis. Contrary to current anti-modernist theses I consider the program of modernity not obsolete or in principle wrongheaded, but unfinished.

Notes

1. On this complicated story the reader may consult my *Passage to Modernity* (New Haven: Yale University Press, 1993), chap. 1.

2. Ralph Cudworth, *The True Intellectual System of the Universe* (Andover: Gould and Newman, 1837), 473.

3. *Voltaire on Religion: Selected Writings,* trans. and introduced by Kenneth W. Appelgate (New York: Frederick Ungar, 1974), 51–52.

4. Gerardus Van der Leeuw, *Religion in Essence and Manifestation* (New York: Harper and Row [1938] 1963), chap. 18. The theory of a universal aboriginal revelation was revived with some scientific claims by Andrew Lang and P. W. Schmidt. Today it has largely been abandoned.

5. John Locke, "Letter to Limborch" as quoted in Harald Hoffding, *A History of Modern Philosophy* (New York: Dover, 1955), 1:388.

6. John Locke, Essay IV, 18, 2.

7. John Edwards, *Some Thoughts concerning the Several Causes and Occasions of Atheism, especially in the Present Age, with some Brief Reflections on Socinianism and on a Late Book entitled: "The Reasonableness of Christianity as delivered in the Scriptures."*

8. *The Works of John Locke,* 10 vols. (London, 1823), 7:188.

9. Thomas Woolston, *Discourses on the Miracles of Our Saviour* (1727–29). On the development of Lockean thought into deism, see Peter Gay, *The Enlightenment: An Interpretation* (New York: Random House, 1968), 374–80.

10. Voltaire, *Eléments de philosophie de Newton* (1738) in *Oeuvres* (Paris 1785), 38:63.

11. Julien Offray de La Mettrie, *L'homme machine: Man a Machine* (La Salle, Ill.: Open Court, [1912] 1993), 50–51 (French ed.), 122 (English ed.).

12. David Hume, *The Natural History of Religion,* Introduction. Since so many editions of this work exist I simply refer to the number of the short sections.

13. Baron d'Holbach, *The System of Nature,* trans. H. D. Robinson (New York: Burt Franklin, [1868] 1979), 170.

14. Sigmund Freud, *The Future of an Illusion,* trans. James Strachey, in *The Complete Psychological Works,* vol. 21 (London: Hogarth Press, 1961), 32.

15. Frank Manuel, *The Eighteenth Century Confronts the Gods* (New York Atheneum, 1967), 168–83.

16. *Pensées philosophiques,* no. 26 in Denis Diderot, *Oeuvres complètes,* vol. 1 (Paris: Le club français du livre, 1969), 286.

17. *Lettre sur les aveugles* in *Oeuvres complètes,* 2:197–99.

18. *Pensées sur l'interprétation de la nature* (no. 50), in *Oeuvres complètes,* 2:758. In a letter to Charles Pineau Duclos dated September 10, 1765, Diderot stated quite openly: "Sensibility is a universal property of matter, an inert property in inorganic or senseless bodies...a property rendered active in the same bodies by their assimilation into an animal substance, one that is living" (quoted in Michael Buckley, *At the Origins of Modern Atheism* [New Haven: Yale University Press, 1987], 232).

19. *Pensées sur l'interprétation de la nature* (no. 58), 769. Translation taken from *Diderot's Selected Writings,* ed. Lester G. Crocker (New York: Macmillan, 1966), 86.

4

Among Strangers and Friends

Thinking of God in Our Current Confusion

– NICHOLAS LASH –

The departure lounge in any busy airport is a restless space in which a continuously shifting crowd of strangers mingles, somewhat nervously, against a background of piped music and occasional obscure commands. An uninformed observer might be puzzled by the mix of apparently quite aimless, random movement and coordinated group activity: shopping, drinking, the announcement of delays; exchange of tickets, tidying of litter, meeting friends, inspecting luggage, gathering up lost children. Except, however, on rare occasions of comprehensive crisis (a bomb threat, for example) there seems to be no single center of activity, giving purpose and direction to the whole. Much of what happens in the lounge is admittedly affected, often indirectly, by what goes on in the control tower. But the officials in that high and distant building, misjudging both their power and their grasp of what is going on, may overestimate the limited, though not unimportant, sense in which their work situates them at the "center" of the airport's life.

"The problem with atheism is that it is not a problem. It is a situation, an atmosphere, a confused history."[1] Allegory has its dangers, but to consider contemporary Catholic Christianity as a kind of airport lounge may at least remind us how particular are the standpoints, of experience and expectation, from which each of us engages the confusion that is our common plight.

If there is, today, a crisis in our thinking about God, the variety of standpoints from which this crisis is experienced and hence described is irreducibly diverse. This diversity does not, itself, constitute the crisis. However, if badly handled and misunderstood, it undoubtedly contributes to its deepening.

To illustrate this, we might set out from the self-evident observation that a crisis in our thinking about God is a crisis about truth. Some people interpret this in epistemic terms, as referring to a crisis of credibility: the culmination of three hundred years' erosion, by the acids of secular modernity, of reasoned belief in God's existence. Others, however, construe it in ethical terms: it is trust in God's reliability and lovingkindness, his unswerving faithfulness, rather than belief in his reality, which is now under the more fundamental threat.

The warrants for both interpretations can, of course, be found in certain features of the account of truth and of God's truthfulness which Christianity inherited and developed from Judaism. Which account comes most readily to mind depends, in part at least, upon the different patterns of experience which differently shape faith's quest for understanding. Thus, in contexts dominated by the preoccupations of "Enlightened" secularity, questions concerning the existence of a sovereign Creator of the world still stand at center stage. Elsewhere, however, experience of injustice, slavery, and oppression sets questions about the trustworthiness of God, the reliability of the Redeemer's love, at the forefront of concern.

Thus, on the basis of experiential differences, now this, now that aspect of the mystery gets presented as the norm or center of the whole. It is as if the history of Christianity were a struggle for supremacy between the three articles of its Creed; a struggle tempting the participants to polemicize into opposition mutually indispensable distinctions lying at the very heart of Christian (which is to say trinitarian) apprehension of the mystery of God.

Thus, for example, in a recent essay on Christianity after Communism, Jozef Tischner distinguished two "currents" in Catholicism after Vatican II, which he labelled "catechetical" and "evangelical." The former grounds its account of human value in the doctrine of creation, the latter in the doctrine of redemption. So far, it might seem, so good. But Tischner then begins to turn the polemical screw. Where attitudes to the crucifixion are concerned, the catechetical current "is a breeding-ground for Manichaeism," whereas the other "places grace in the foreground." Catholics of the former kind "are intent on making a show of their convictions," whereas the latter deepen belief in "the discovery of the heroic dimension of the gospel." Thus it is, he concludes, that "we are in an age in which one set of Christians" (most of whom, apparently, inhabit "the liberal countries of Western Europe") is engaged in a determined struggle for the loosening of church discipline, while the others (most of whom, one suspects by now, are found in Poland) "accept persecution and years of imprisonment for faithfulness to the church and her discipline."[2]

The lesson that I would draw from this is as follows. I entirely accept Father Tischner's contention that intra-ecclesial differences run deep, run, indeed, as he contends, to the heart and center of the gospel. As I understand the Creed, however, each of its three articles says something about the *whole* of Christian faith. There are three articles because there are, in God, three persons. If, however, our recognition of the unity of God, and of God's world, is not to be compromised, such understanding as we gain from the standpoint provided by any one of the three articles will require correction from the standpoint of the other two. Thus it is that the very *form* of our confession of faith provides a pattern of restraint upon the range of its misuse.[3] (Hence, after a brief section on the question of God's being, I have grouped the issues I shall comment on under headings evoking each of the articles in turn.)

It follows that while different "currents" of Catholic thought and action will, indeed, be patterned more closely now to this, now that, article of the Creed, each will require and should expect corrective pressure from other currents, patterned to the other articles. There is thus laid upon all schools and currents in the church the endless labor of attempting accurately to understand and, in some measure, sympathize with, those whose different experience differently shapes their action and their understanding.

Triumphalisms of every kind, what I earlier described as the "struggle for supremacy" between particular perceptions of the whole, are, or should be, as alien to the ethos of Catholicism as is liberal relativism. Viewed doctrinally, both are failures to live, and think, and argue within the strenuous requirements of the Creed.

One final comment before concluding these preliminary remarks. It is often suggested that the difficulty experienced these days by so many people in knowing quite what it would be appropriate or sensible to say or think of God is itself evidence of the weakness of belief which characterizes contemporary European culture: of the extent to which God has become a stranger in our house. Yet finding speech concerning God unproblematic would surely be unreliable evidence of faith. It would seem better to say, with Karl Rahner: "We are just discovering today that one cannot picture God to oneself in an image that has been carved out of the wood of the world...this experience is not the genesis of atheism, but the discovery that the world is not God." Or, as my Cambridge predecessor put it: "The futility of so much confident speech concerning the ultimate...is something that only the thrust of a recognizable family of metaphorical expressions can convey."[4] He had in mind expressions such as "hiddenness" and "invisibility," for God's invisibility is not diminished by his appearance in the world, nor his hiddenness cancelled by the utterance in time and place of his eternal Word.

A Question of Being

The story of the rise and fall of modern deism (or theism, for the two terms were, originally, identical in sense) is the story of a twofold dissociation. It is, first, a tale of the dissociation (between Bacon's day and

Diderot's) of memory from argument, of narrative from reason. With the fusion, in the seventeenth century, of the late scholastic passion for univocity and the Renaissance rediscovery of Stoicism's "nature" (homogeneous in all its parts, an *ens commune* construct of one kind of stuff and of one set of forces) there was born a new ideal for the working of the mind: "a science that has an unequivocal language with which it speaks and uniform objects of which it speaks." No time nor patience now for narrative, or poetry, or paradox. Theologians and scientists alike developed a single-minded passion for pure prose.[5]

Secondly, it is a story of the dissociation of things measured from the measuring observer, of objects from subjects, things from thoughts. This twofold dissociation entails, in its turn, a cleavage in the concept of philosophy. On the one hand, philosophy is now transformed into natural philosophy which, in turn, becomes mechanics. On the other, philosophy transmutes into epistemology and consideration of the content of the conscious mind.

On the side of the object, God, the maker of the system of the world and its ultimate explanatory principle, can be quietly disposed of once it is acknowledged that the system needs no such explanation. On the side of the subject, God becomes a useful fiction, symbolic of whatever each one dreams of as the fulfillment of his or her restless striving: money, sex, peace, security, self-importance, power (and atheism, on this side, is little more than the insistence that these things be called by their proper names).

Notwithstanding the best efforts of d'Holbach or Feuerbach or Freud, however, people have not ceased to "believe in God." But belief has never been so dangerously ambivalent. Each U.S. dollar bill still bears the message "In God we trust," but it is difficult to imagine the publication, in any century before our own, of a book entitled: *The God I Want*.[6] And yet we should not, perhaps, exaggerate the novelty of our predicament. Edward Gibbon's eighteenth-century description of the world of ancient Rome has an uncomfortably contemporary ring: "The various modes of worship...were all considered by the people, as equally true; by the philosophers, as equally false; by the magistrates, as equally useful."[7]

Under the impact of this century's appalling suffering, dazzling achievement, and deepening confusion, the paradigms of "modernity" have slowly lost their grip. If, nevertheless, we find our thinking about God (and human beings and the world) to be in crisis, this is because we do not yet know whether "postmodern" culture will heal the dualisms and dissociations through the incorporation of modernity into some more nuanced and more comprehensive story, or whether, one-sidedly rejecting the one-sidedness of the age now ending, we shall slide into fresh sectarian conflict, irrationalism, and despair.

Thus, where the Christian doctrine of God is concerned, one of the most striking features of mainstream twentieth-century theology has been the setting aside of modern "theisms" and the recovery of comprehensively trinitarian consideration of the mystery of God. And yet, this recovery, although now several decades old, is still not mediated, either philosophically into other discourses and disciplines, or pastorally into the general conversations of the culture.

To see this, we need do no more than notice that most of our contemporaries still find it "obvious" that atheism is not only possible, but widespread and that, both intellectually and ethically, it has much to commend it. This view might be plausible if being an atheist were a matter of not believing that there exists "a person without a body" who is "eternal, free, able to do anything, knows everything" and is "the proper object of human worship and obedience, the creator and sustainer of the universe."[8] If, however, by "God" we mean the mystery, announced in Christ, breathing all things out of nothing into peace, then all things have to do with God in every move and fragment of their being, whether they notice this and suppose it to be so or not. Atheism, if it means deciding not to have anything to do with God, is thus self-contradictory and, if successful, self-destructive.

Playfully, Jean-Luc Marion has asked: "With respect to Being, does God have to behave like Hamlet?"[9] All human beings have their hearts set somewhere, if only on themselves, and the object of our worship is where our hearts are set. But if Christianity is (like Judaism and Islam) best regarded as a kind of school in which we wean each other from the worship of created things into adoration of the mystery of God alone; if, in other words, the first question to be asked concerning God, and our relationships with God, is not "to be or not to be?" but what is it that we worship, that we take as God; then this has not yet been communicated widely outside the confines of specialist theology.

A Question of Contingency

There is still no better summary description of the subject-matter of "that theology which pertains to holy teaching" than that it treats of God and of "all things," *omnia*, in their relationship to God as their beginning and their end, their origin and destiny.[10] But to accept this view of things, and to accept all things as made by God, *ex nihilo*, is to accept contingency: to acknowledge the absolute dependence of all worlds on God. And this we find it difficult to do, for we are frightened of the dark and nervous of dependence. Such fears are by no means unfounded and, lacking the resources to dispel them, we oscillate between Promethean ambition and nihilist despair.

Among the more surprising runaway bestsellers in recent years, in

Britain, has been an essay by one of the leading theoretical physicists of our time: Stephen Hawking's *Brief History of Time*. According to Hawking, a complete explanation of the world, which would include an explanation of why the universe exists, "would be the ultimate triumph of human reason — for then we would know the mind of God." An earlier reference to quantum theory's abolition of the necessity for appeal "to God *or some new law* to set the boundary conditions for space-time" makes clear that Hawking's God is only an explanation of the world.[11] The "triumph" which he seeks, the knowledge of God's mind, is thereby tinged with pathos, for why should we suppose an explanation to bring peace?

Some scientists, sensing this, give more dangerous expression to their rejection of contingency, dreaming of descendants with "the advantage of containing no organic material at all," free from "the biological ball and chain," and thus, at last, capable of becoming "lords of the universe."[12] We should not underestimate the influence on our culture of the fear of death, the contempt for the flesh, the terror of contingency, which drives these dreams.

It is, of course, integral to such fantasies to suppose that human beings are not, in the last resort, *animals* at all. Instead of creatures fashioned of flesh, determinate in time and place and circumstance, we suppose ourselves small godlets dropped on earth, "angels fallen into flesh,"[13] mind-things of (potentially) unlimited and unrivaled power. The last two centuries have seen this power unleashed to the irreversible destruction of the fragile wealth and beauty of the world.

Feminists have rightly emphasized the element of *machismo* in this disastrous posturing of "modern man." It is with much less justice, however, that ecological movements tend to lay the blame on Jewish and Christian doctrines of creation. The "dominion" over other living things which men and women are required to exercise is husbandry, not despotism (see Gen. 1:28). It is the modern world, not ancient Israel, which takes absolute power, unconstrained by circumstance or duty, as paradigm of kingship.

Ask most people what God makes when he creates the world, and they will list the kinds of things which the natural sciences describe: whirling gases, deep seas and rock formations, galaxies and stars. "Life" may be mentioned, but probably in some rather vague and general way. Almost certainly missing from the list will be such items as rituals and relationships, languages and symbols systems, trade and agriculture. It is as if God did not make the things that human beings do; as if God's self-gift, creative graciousness, were less immediately constitutive of promises and symphonies than of plutonium and silt. Or is it that we think that God made matter, whereas we, like God, are made of "mind"?

The healing of the deep-laid dissociative dualisms which plague our modern imagination cannot but be a slow, laborious, and costly process. The place to start, it seems to me, is with the recognition that the doctrine of creation out of nothing is not, in itself, good news. It is realism, not cowardice, which makes us frightened of the dark. And it is prudence which makes us suspicious of dependency, for slavery is as familiar a feature of the world as friendship.

The only school in which to learn acceptance of contingency would be one in which we learned, not merely that God makes the world *ex nihilo,* but that the "nothing" out of which he makes it is the non-necessity, the *gratuité,* of love, and in which, moreover, we also learned that *what* he makes, in love, is harmony and friendship, homecoming and peace. In the Christian scheme of things, these things are discovered, not from the first article of the Creed, the confession of our createdness, considered on its own, but from that first article considered in relation to the second (which speaks of sonship) and the third (which tells us of the Spirit's gift). It is, in other words, only within the pattern provided by the Creed in its entirety that we discover, not only that God makes the world, but that God makes the world parentally, and that the world God makes parentally is the temple of his peace.

This is the kind of school the church exists to be: a place within the wider culture in which this reading of contingency, of all things' createdness *ex nihilo,* could be, not merely stated, but — in all our common life and labor — even now displayed. Only through such sacramental instantiation of its truth can the doctrine of God's creation of the world become, again, good news.

A Question of Meaning

That reason's truths are necessary and those of history merely accidental, as Lessing and his contemporaries supposed, is not, itself, a necessary truth, but merely how things seem to people who (as I put it earlier) have dissociated memory from argument, narrative from explanation. Our problem, these days, is rather different. What worries us is not that reason's truths alone seem really true, but rather that, having unmasked "Reason" as but another idol, another construct of our restless vanity, we mistrust claims to final, comprehensive explanation. Assertions by those who exercise authority that X is absolutely true, or Y a rule without exceptions, are heard less as "good news" than as *diktat.* Nevertheless, the correlative crumbling of truth into subjectivism, into what "makes sense for me," is a madness that gives comfort only to the rich and powerful. Thus it is that, speaking and scribbling endless quantities of words, we seem to have forgotten what it would be like to hear some single word, one *logos,* bearing the burden of the meaning of the world, and to hear this word uttered not to our condemnation or oppression but to all things' deliverance, as gospel, joy.

After Auschwitz and Kolyma, all claims that everything does, in the end, make sense, are suspect. Nor is it, by any means, only God that now seems difficult to understand. Human beings are hardly more intelligible. A certain careless atheism supposes that it is "religious" truth that has been called in question. But in what "secular" story would all our killing fields find mention as but unfortunate episodes in an otherwise quite satisfactory tale? In those dark forests, it is the sense not simply of religion but of everything (Aquinas's *omnia* again) that risks unraveling.

It is, perhaps, the very notion of truth "claimed," "asserted," that we should set question marks against. "Claims" are what *I* stake over against *you,* and the gesture of "assertion," which, in ancient Rome, both set slaves free and bound them into servitude, now connotes my power rather than your liberty. The heart of the matter seems to be that, if there is sense or meaning in the world, it goes before our finding and waits more upon our trust than on our ingenuity. Truth, in the last analysis, is not our achievement, let alone our plaything or our property, but a gift received, a presence recognized.

This was the thesis of a remarkable essay by George Steiner, in which he argued that "any coherent understanding of what language is and how language performs...is, in the final analysis, underwritten by the assumption of God's presence." Many of his readers must have found this statement quite bizarre. He went on to argue that the only way back to recognition of that presence would be through the practice and acknowledgement of what he called "the core of trust within logic itself, where 'logic' is a *Logos*-derivative and construct." There would be "no history as we know it, no religion, metaphysics, politics or aesthetics as we have lived them, without an initial act of trust, of confiding," so fundamental as to be constitutive of the relation between word and world.[14] The crisis of our time arises from the fracturing of that relation.

"In the beginning was the Word." But how might that Word now be heard? How might the world, in all its savagery and darkness, its bewildering and uncontrollable diversity, be given sense as utterance of that constituting Word? The temptation, for the Christian, is to take shortcuts toward the answer. Theology, as the Anglican Bishop of Monmouth reminds us, is "perennially liable to be seduced by the prospect of bypassing the question of how it *learns* its own language." Theologies east and west, Catholic and Protestant, conservative and liberal, all tend in one way or another to operate "with a model of truth as something ultimately separable *in our minds* from the dialectical process of its historical reflection and appropriation." Under the influence of this model, we grow impatient with "debate, conflict, ambivalence, polysemy, paradox. And this is at heart an impatience with learning, and with learning about our learning."[15]

In the previous section I described the Christian life as schooling in contingency. From the standpoint of the present meditation on the meaning of the world, its constitution by the *Logos,* we could call the church a school of contemplation, a place where people learned to learn, educated each other in attentiveness.

Before the mystery of God, teachableness or docility is contemplation, receptivity: that generous attentiveness of which Mary's "Fiat" is the paradigm. Such contemplation, such attentiveness, is patient (and patience connotes suffering); it is "appropriation of the vulnerability of the self in the midst of the language and transactions of the world."[16] It is the very form of God's self-utterance in Gethsemane.

There are, it seems to me, three areas in particular in which this theme of the necessity of learning how to learn, of Christian faith as patience and docility, is, at present, of particular importance. The first of these I mentioned earlier, when I suggested that the duty of attempting accurately and generously to understand and represent the words and deeds of those from whom we differ has its roots in the doctrine of God's Trinity. The appropriate character of Christian disagreement is a strictly theological topic, and by no means merely a question of church order or Christian ethics. As such, it is, at present, dangerously neglected.

The other two areas I have in mind would be, on the one hand, the relations between what we loosely call "church" and "world" and, on the other, the relations between Christianity and other religious traditions. The simple point that still needs insisting on is this: the recognition that there is always something to be *learned* — whether from geneticists and sociologists, historians and literary critics, psychologists and philosophers, or from not only Judaism, Islam, Buddhism, and Hinduism, but also from folk religion and even New Age cults — is not a suspect concession to "liberalism," but a necessary implication of the doctrine that the Word which is, in Jesus Christ, incarnate, is the selfsame Word in the one utterance of which God makes all worlds. It is worth remembering that Aquinas's answer to the question as to whether the diversity of things is due to God was: Yes, because no single creature could give God adequate expression. Not even, by implication, God's own humanity, particular flesh (see Luke 4:18; Isa. 61:1).

To confess that all things (*omnia*) have, in God's self-utterance, their existence, origin, and destiny, is to confess that, in the end, all things make sense. And the sense they make is shown in him whose story — from conception through Calvary to the Father's side — is summarized in the second article of the Creed. That article, however, considered on its own, does not lack ambivalence, for it ends in judgment. This utterance of God, this meaning of the world, this judgment, is good news only if it is forgiveness and not condemnation. And this we learn, not from the second article considered on its own, but only in that gift of life, outpouring of the Spirit, acknowledged in the third.

This, then, is the kind of school the church exists to be: a place within the wider culture in which contemplativity, attentiveness, openness to truth, all truth, might — even in present darkness, conflict, and confusion — be learned in patient labor waiting on the ending of God's utterance, God's Word of peace.

A Question of Life

In personal relations, distance is a metaphor for lack of interest or affection. We say of people, for example, that they are very "close" to each other, or that they have grown "far apart." The God of modern theism seems very far away: is this an indication of our lack of interest in God, or of God's unconcern for us? Both answers have been given. According to the former, the Western world is "secularized," a place of weak and waning faith, less interested in, or influenced by, religious issues than were previous periods in European history.

Bookshops (at least in Britain) suggest a different story. They may stock few, if any, titles of serious theology or biblical criticism, but they display shelf upon shelf piled high with spirituality, the occult, New Age, Sufism, reincarnation, mysticism, black magic, Tantrism, astrology, and Tarot. If this is "secularity," its atmosphere is restless, irrational, and superstitious; driven by a poignant and unstructured yearning for something less impersonal and remote ("distance" again!) than the lifeless systems of which academic experts, from quantum physics through to economics, seem to speak.

If our societies are, as is often said, materialist, then this is a materialism obsessed with spirit. And everyone agrees, it seems, that spirit is a good thing. But what does it connote? With what do we contrast it? Spirit is not-matter, not-body, or (in certain New Age and charismatic circles) not-reason. When church leaders are exhorted, or exhort others, to concentrate on "spiritual" affairs, the implication seems to be that these are matters loftier than, and different from, such down-to-earth concerns as preaching good news to the poor and liberating the oppressed.[17]

It is, moreover, not unknown for even educated Christians to suppose that the distinction drawn, in Romans 8, between flesh and spirit is *more or less* the same as that which we might draw between the body and the mind. So firm the grip in which our imagination is held by the dualisms of modernity that we hardly notice the extent to which, at the heart of Scripture's talk of God as Spirit (and of the world as the effect of, and as affected by, the Spirit that is God) the contrast drawn is between not-life, or lesser life, or life gone wrong, and *life:* true life, real life, God's life and all creation's life in God. Spirit is life outpoured, beyond imagination and control, like wind, the breath of God.

According to the Nicene Creed, the mystery we confess as God is Holy Spirit, life-giving Lord. God gives all life, is intimate to every movement, animates all action, fuels freedom, breaks down barriers, breathes dead bones dancing. This line of thought, generating a sense of all things (*"omnia"* again) as a kind of organism pulsating to the heartbeat of life-giving Spirit, has some affinity with the gathering recognition — from our economics and our politics to so-called "chaos theory" in mathematics — that the whole system of the world forms one single, vulnerable, complex web of life.

Of course such thoughts are dangerous: all worthwhile thoughts are. Christianity is not pantheist. We do not worship "nature" or the world. Life, all life, the life we share, the life that we are called upon to cherish and enhance, true life, eternal life, is *given,* has a whence, a referent. God gives, and what God gives is nothing less than God. But God's God-given life is ever in the movement of the giver's hand, is ever being-given. Christian speech concerning the givenness of God, whom we call grace and life, is speech unceasingly referring the given to the giving. "Gift," as used of God, attempts to name a relationship of origin.[18]

In other words, where the grammar of Christian discourse is concerned, pantheism is a mistake of the same kind as agnosticism and fundamentalism. It freezes one "moment" in the movement of our life in God, mistaking what it finds there for a description of divinity. There is nothing that God simply "is": not silence, speech, or life. But, in the silence that is God, God speaks, and what God speaks is life, in God.

Pantheism distorts the sense of God, but does so neither more nor less than the contraction of the territory to which discourse concerning God refers from all things, *omnia,* to some small margin of our private lives, the supposedly safe Sunday-space we think of as "religion."

I have mentioned our deepening recognition of the interdependence of the constituents of the world. But interdependence is not, in itself, good news. The McDonald's sign in every city may be a symptom, not of human solidarity, the dawn of the communion of saints, but rather of the abolition of particularity, diversity, and freedom beneath the wheels of juggernauts beyond accountability and control. We have still good reason to be frightened by voices such as that of Teilhard de Chardin, proclaiming in 1936: "Fascism opens its arms to the future. Its ambition is to embrace vast wholes in its empire. And in the vigorous organization of which it dreams, it is more anxious than any other system to allow for the preservation of the élite (which means the personal and the Spirit)."[19]

To discover the conditions in which the announcement of interdependence would be good news, we must go back to the beginning. If God is life, enlivening Spirit, and if all life, vitality, joy, freedom, are therefore signs and tokens of God's presence, then the right name for God's absence from the world is death. Not mere mortality (for this is, after all, a function of contingency) but deadliness, extinction, the remorseless weight and burden of the world construed as fate.

Individuals still feel guilt. But, notwithstanding our fondness for blaming other nations, other social classes, other groups and "currents" in society, for our common plight, it is as fate, necessity, rather than as guilt, that we experience the shared and public burden of the world. The gray pervasiveness of our despair (of which disillusion with political process is but one indication) perhaps arises from the recognition that necessity is not, by definition, transmutable into freedom. Whereas, if we were guilty, we might at least cry out for forgiveness.

There is no theory or hypothesis that could transform the world. Despair, however, overlooks a *fact*. The fact is that forgiveness occurs. Friendship and reconciliation may be fragile, but they are facts, and so are peace, and joy, and gentleness.

There is a useful notion in philosophy: that of the "performative utterance." Such utterances do not describe, propose, prepare the ground for action; they enact what they announce. Promises are performative. So is God's Word. God speaks: a world exists, a garden flourishes. God speaks: light shines in darkness, prisoners are freed, the dead are raised to life. The outpoured Spirit is what God, speaking, does.

What, on a Christian reading of the world, we learn from the fragile fact of friendship, then, is that we have been forgiven. It is in contrition, in friendship's bonds renewed, that guilt is retrospectively acknowledged. There are, in my opinion, few more succinct summaries of the gospel than this: We have been made capable of friendship. The "we" is unrestricted, it refers to everybody, past and present, near and far and, by analogy, to every feature of that web of life of which we form a part. We "have been" made: the passive voice protects the primacy of grace, the givenness of things. Made "capable of" friendship, rather than "made friends," for it is as *duty* that we hear the Word's announcement of the way all things are made and made to be.

There are no short cuts to friendship. How could there be, when even God's announcement of the fact, God's self-performing utterance of love, exacts his agony and crucifixion? The "sponge full of vinegar" given to the dying Christ is an allusion to Psalm 69, which contains the plea: "Let not the flood sweep over me, or the deep swallow me up" (Mark 15:36; Ps. 69:15 [see 69:21]). It is as if God's utterance, which makes the world, is itself threatened by the chaos that it sets in place as "nothing."

A prayer in the Gelasian Sacramentary says of the Holy Spirit that he is himself the forgiveness of all our sins: "ipse est omnium remissio peccatorum."[20] If, in the third article of the Creed, the mystery of God is confessed as given life, communion, friendship, it is in the second article that we acknowledge the price love's utterance, as forgiveness, pays.

This, then, is the kind of school the church exists to be: a place within the wider culture in which forgiveness is found, in which the godliness of life is celebrated, and in which a foretaste of all things' final friendship even now occurs.

Home or Away?

If God is a stranger in our house, then it is quite certain that our house is not our home, for we are made to be at home with God. That we are not yet at home is not, in itself, occasion for surprise. For we are travellers, pilgrim people (hence the image from which this article set out was that of an airline terminal). We are not yet at home. Nevertheless, according to the gospel, God has already, even now, made himself at home with us, "pitched his tent" among our dwellings (see John 1:14). Before we take false comfort from the fact that we are still away from home, therefore, we need more carefully to formulate the paradox of our predicament.

If the subject-matter of that theology which pertains to holy teaching is, indeed, the mystery of God and of all things, *omnia,* in their relationship to God, then a crisis in our thinking about God will be a crisis in our thinking about not merely God but everything.

Christian thinking is *fides quaerens intellectum.* Failure to attain that glimmer of understanding of the mystery of God which has, even now, been made accessible to us is, *eo ipso,* misunderstanding of the world of which we form a part. If there is, indeed, a crisis in our thinking about God, then this will show itself, will find expression, in crisis and confusion in our thinking about science and politics, ethics and economics, birth and death and poetry and peace.

And if this crisis has, at present, a distinctive shape, a particular configuration, this distinctiveness consists in the extent to which people — even devout, well-educated Christian people; even priests and bishops (not to mention theologians!) — fail to realize this. If, however, we continue to act, and think, and study, as if relationship with God was mediated by something less than everything, by "religion" for example, or by the church alone, if (to turn it round the other way) we continue to behave as if God was one of the particular objects, things, or topics, with which we have to do, then we Christians, who have been called to clarify the darkness, will merely contribute to its deepening.

To recapitulate. Under the heading of "A Question of Being," I suggested that it is an implication of the trinitarian character of Christian faith that there is no overarching single head, no ultimately privileged

descriptive category (neither "being," nor "truth," nor "love") in terms
of which the mystery of God is best considered. In the following sections, I tried to indicate why the church is to be thought of as a kind
of school, within the wider culture, in which the practice and theory
of contingency, and sense, and common life, might be learned, and purified, and deepened. This is, perhaps, another way of saying that the
church exists to be a place in which the fact and possibility of friendship
among those who had been strangers, of homecoming after exile, might
be discovered and displayed.

Notes

1. Michael J. Buckley, *At the Origins of Modern Atheism* (New Haven: Yale
University Press, 1987), 13. Few scholars in the English-speaking world have
done more than Michael Buckley to clarify that "confused history." In gratitude
for his redoubtable achievement, and in celebration of our friendship, it gives me
great pleasure to offer these reflections, an earlier version of which served as one
of the preparatory papers for the second Congress of the European Society for
Catholic Theology (see the second issue for 1994 of the Society's house journal,
E.T., 195–208), which took place in Freising in Germany in August 1995, and in
which Mike Buckley took part. The papers reflected the theme of the Congress,
which was: "God — A Stranger in our House?."

2. See Jozef Tischner, "Christianity in the Post-Communist Vacuum," *Religion, State and Society* 20 (1992): 334–35.

3. See Nicholas Lash, *Believing Three Ways in One God: A Reading of the
Apostles' Creed* (Notre Dame, Ind.: University of Notre Dame Press, 1992).

4. Karl Rahner, "Science as a 'Confession'?," *Theological Investigations*
3, trans. Karl-H. and Boniface Kruger (London, 1967), 391, 390 (essay first
published in *Wort und Wahrheit* 9 [1954]: 809–19); Donald M. MacKinnon,
"Metaphor in Theology," *Themes in Theology: The Threefold Cord* (Edinburgh,
1987), 69 (first published in the *Scottish Journal of Religious Studies,* 1984).

5. Amos Funkenstein, *Theology and the Scientific Imagination from the
Middle Ages to the Seventeenth Century* (Princeton, N.J.: Princeton University
Press, 1986), 41; see 72.

6. C. Rycroft et al., *The God I Want* (Indianapolis: Bobbs-Merrill, 1967).

7. Edward Gibbon, *The History of the Decline and Fall of the Roman Empire,* 6 vols. (London, 1853), vol. 1, chap. 2, 36; quoted (from a different
edition) by Michael J. Buckley, "Experience and Culture: A Point of Departure
for American Atheism," *Theological Studies* 50 (1989): 458.

8. This definition of what those who believe in God understand themselves
to believe has been offered by a most distinguished and devoutly Christian philo-
sophical theologian: see Richard Swinburne, *The Coherence of Theism* (Oxford:
Clarendon Press, 1979), 1. For some discussion, see my *Easter in Ordinary:
Reflections on Human Experience and the Knowledge of God* (Charlottesville:
University Press of Virginia, 1988), 98ff.

9. Jean-Luc Marion, "Preface to the English Edition," *God without Being:
Hors-texte* (Chicago: University of Chicago Press, 1991), xx; English trans. of
Dieu sans l'être: Hors-texte (Paris, 1982).

10. See Thomas Aquinas, *Summa Theologiae* Ia, q. 1, a. 1, ad 2; q. 1, a. 7. c.

11. Stephen W. Hawking, *A Brief History of Time* (London: Bantam, 1988), 175, 136; emphasis added.

12. For an excellent discussion of this material, see Mary Midgley's 1990 Gifford Lectures, *Science as Salvation: A Modern Myth and Its Meaning* (London: Routledge, 1992); for the quoted phrases, see 152, 153, 159.

13. Fergus Kerr, *Theology after Wittgenstein* (Oxford: Basil Blackwell, 1986), 168, where he discusses the antiquity and power of the Origenist myth.

14. George Steiner, *Real Presences: Is There Anything in What We Say?* (London: Faber, 1989), 3, 89. In the 1990 Aquinas Lecture, in Cambridge, I tried to draw out some of the rich theological implications of Steiner's essay: see Nicholas Lash, "Friday, Saturday, Sunday," *New Blackfriars* 71 (March 1990): 109–19.

15. Rowan Williams, "Trinity and Revelation," *Modern Theology* 2, no. 3 (1986): 197–98, second emphasis added.

16. Rowan Williams, "Theological Integrity," *New Blackfriars* 72 (1991): 148.

17. See *Summa Theologiae* Ia, q. 47, a. 1.

18. See Aquinas, *Summa Theologiae* Ia, qq. 37, 38, for some brief discussion of which, see my chapter on "Donation" in *Believing Three Ways in One God*.

19. Pierre Teilhard de Chardin, "The Salvation of Mankind," *Science and Christ* (New York: Harper and Row, 1968), 140–41; English trans. of *Science et Christ* (Paris: Éditions de Seuil, 1965).

20. *Liber Sacramentorum Romanae Aeclesiae Ordinis Anni Circuli* (*Sacramentarium Gelasianum*), ed. L. C. Mohlberg (Rome: Herder, 1968), lxxx, no. 639.

5

Jesus Research and Faith in Jesus Christ

– ROGER HAIGHT, S.J. –

I begin with an incident. I teach an introductory course on the church, and one of the early considerations of the course deals with the relationship between Jesus and the origins of the church. Historical study of the New Testament has raised the question of whether and in what sense Jesus founded a church similar to what actually arose by the beginning of the second century. In the course of a discussion of this material a woman made a statement to this effect: I wonder if others found this material paradoxical. On the one hand the Catholic doctrine affirms that Jesus is God. On the other hand we are asking whether Jesus intended a church or knew one would arise.

This incident which occurred within the boundaries of the faith community is a version of the perennial tension between the historian and the believer which became acute during the nineteenth century but has remained a generative topic of discussion. What is the relation between the knowledge gained by the "objective" historian through critical research into Jesus of Nazareth and the faith of the believer, including the public belief structure that gives expression to that existential commitment? The tension between these two kinds or differentiated formalities of conscious engagement with Jesus of Nazareth is so basic that it must be seen as part of the elemental structure of Christian faith itself.

A vigorous interaction between historical science and christological belief has been going on for the last two centuries. This history has generated a variety of different methods of construing and appropriating this active relationship, and we shall consider two of them in the course of this essay. The issue is particularly pressing at present for a number of reasons: one is the enormous output of and interest in the historical reconstruction of first-century Christianity generally and, more particularly, the person of Jesus himself. Another is the fact that this material has become available to a broad audience that transcends theologians. Still another is the potential confusion that is generated by the results of this historical research, as is indicated by the opening story.

There is at least a tension and at times a conflict between two ways of thinking about Jesus of Nazareth, or between two distinct languages about Jesus, the doctrinal and the historical. Doctrinal language interprets Jesus of Nazareth on the basis of an encounter of faith, or the experience of salvation that Jesus mediates for the Christian. The doctrinal language of faith portrays Jesus in transcendent terms as being intimately related to God and, finally, divine. Historical language is also interpretive; but it is this-worldly and portrays Jesus in terms of his life in this world. Today an enormous output of historical Jesus research very frequently presents Jesus in a way that seems at odds with doctrine. A particularly striking example is provided by John Hick: What does it mean to say, on the one hand, doctrinally, that Jesus is an incarnation of God and, on the other, with historians, that Jesus was unaware of his divinity?[1]

The question that I wish to address can be focused by the following question: How does historical study of Jesus of Nazareth, that is, Jesus research, influence faith in Jesus Christ, including theological understanding of Jesus Christ? How does Jesus research come to bear upon and influence doctrinal construal of Jesus? From that point of view I will try to define a connection between the two languages.[2]

This straightforward question would not yield an equally clear answer across the discipline of christology. Christology is pluralistic in both method and content. However, the thesis, method, and framework for my discussion of the topic are all contained in the following proposition: a way of understanding and measuring the influence of Jesus research on christology lies in the category of the imagination. I propose that by looking at imagination as playing a key role in understanding one will also find in it a common ground, in some instances a battleground, in and through which these two languages are interacting. However, I do not conceive the goal of these reflections as breaking new ground. The new ground is being broken by the steady interaction between these two languages and the constructive efforts of describing the positive role of the imagination in knowing. More modestly I intend simply to use the category of imagination to describe what is going on in this interchange between historians and theologians in such a way that it can be seen as not destructive but constructive and salutary.

I will be able to do this in a five-part development. I begin by presenting the framework of the discussion, including an account of the imagination. I shall then consider possible imaginative construals that attend some of the classical christological doctrines. How do people imagine Jesus in the light of christological doctrine? In the third section I will consider the premises and the content of Jesus research and how they are reshaping the imaginative portraits of Jesus. Then, fourth, I will compare two theologians who deal with this issue and measure them in terms of the thesis proposed here. And as a conclusion I will draw out the impact of Jesus research on christology in a few theses that show some of its positive consequences.

The Framework for this Discussion

Let me begin by describing briefly the framework of this discussion. Our pluralistic theological situation makes it necessary to lay out some of the presuppositions and premises of any particular discussion. In this case, the main premises can be reduced to two: the conception of imagination being enlisted in these considerations and the christological framework that underlies my discussion. In both instances I will be operating loosely within the context of a Thomistic Aristotelian tradition.

Imagination

The imagination is the subject of an enormous literature in a wide variety of disciplines announcing innumerable theories of its nature and function. My goal has nothing to do with establishing a theory of the imagination but in simply laying down a number of axioms that may be confirmed by common experience. In Thomas's faculty psychology, the imagination is a fairly discrete inner power of the human spirit that, as it were, warehouses or stores up the concrete sensible images that are received through the external senses.[3] In what follows I consider the imagination not as a discrete power of the human spirit, but as one of many functions or activities of the human mind that is mixed up with and implicated in other cognitive processes. And rather than describe an integral picture of imaginative activity, I will limit myself to three propositions that will be useful for this discussion.

The first of these is that all human knowledge enters the mind through the mediation of sense data and the imagination. This view reflects the empiricism of Aristotle. According to Thomas, in terms of objective content the human mind is born like a clean slate upon which nothing is written.[4] It stands in relation to the whole of reality as a pure potency ready to be filled with content. This content comes to it through the five senses, which mediate external reality to the human spirit. The sensible images from the material world are cleared in the mind by what Thomas calls internal senses, two of which are imagination and memory. These provide the immediate resources for intellectual or conceptual knowledge. It is finally the active, spiritual intellect itself that discerns within these concrete and particular images immaterial and universally relevant ideas. Thomas calls this process abstraction, a drawing out of universal truth or meaning from a material, sensible datum.[5]

Second, this foundational empiricism yields the proposition that "the intellect knows nothing but what it receives from the senses."[6] And this can be expanded to include the imagination: all human knowledge is drawn from the material world through the senses and the concrete images that are formed and stored up by the imagination. Thus it follows that there are no concepts, or words, or more generally languages that do not also bear with them an imaginative residue. Abstraction of a universally relevant idea from a particular imaginative datum does not mean leaving our contact with physical, sensible reality behind. Rather it means discovering and grasping universally intelligible meaning within the concrete and specific. I am suggesting that even our most abstract ideas and propositions always carry along, or imply, or create some concrete imaginative construal.

Third, imagination in Aquinas has a passive and an active dimension. It is passive in the sense that it receives and stores images of the external world. It is active in the sense that it divides and combines received images and constructs new ones. For example, from the received image of gold and the image of a mountain the imagination can construct the picture of a golden mountain.[7] On this basis one can speak of a twofold function of the imagination: it is both conservative and creative. The passive storing of images to which all knowledge is bound keeps our speculative reasoning in touch with reality; it prevents imagination from becoming fancy or fantasy. The active dimension of imagination is the principle of creative discovery and invention in poetry, in art, and in the breakthroughs of science.

Christological Framework

The christological framework within which I am operating here builds on a philosophy of religion which shares deep resonances with the Aristotelian empiricism of Aquinas. On the one hand, this empiricism rules out an immediate contact with God. All our knowledge of God is mediated through the world, through some finite, historical medium; there is no universal nonmediated religion. On the other hand, all our knowledge is tied to a particular time and place in history in such a way that even universally relevant knowledge is conditioned by unique, specific, and individual images. This rules out a religion based on reason or a natural theology. All religion is historically mediated. The central medium that defines Christianity is the event and person of Jesus of Nazareth. Christianity is the religion in which faith in God was and is mediated by the external historical medium, Jesus of Nazareth.[8]

Given this fundamental understanding of the historical ground of Christianity, christology developed out of the specific experience of the disciples of Jesus, more specifically the experience of salvation from God being mediated or made present and available to them through Jesus. My purpose here is not to go into detail in describing this experience nor how it developed within the realization that Jesus was raised by God. It is sufficient to say that the New Testament bears witness to various

interpretations of how Jesus is savior and how he is to be understood
relative to us and relative to God. Moreover, this interpretation continued as Christianity spread into the Greek and Roman worlds and their
intellectual cultures. The classical christological doctrines of Nicaea and
Chalcedon are public interpretations referring back to Jesus of Nazareth
that also respond to specific historical problems that were raised in those
particular historical contexts. Beneath them, as the ground and rationale
for their intelligibility, is the same ground that underlies the New Testament witness, namely, the experience of Jesus as the mediator of God's
salvation.

Let me sum up this first part of this discussion, which lays the ground-
work for what follows. I am working within the framework of a theory
of knowledge and of religion that takes our contact with the sensible
world as the starting point and basis of all knowing, including religious knowing. This means that the imagination will have an important
role in the way we construe things, even the personal, spiritual, eternal, and transcendent reality of God. All knowing in this world involves
the imagination. This anthropology and epistemology lead to the view
that Jesus is the concrete historical foundation of Christian faith and
that the history of christology is the history of interpreting Jesus of
Nazareth. In the next two parts I will consider the imaginative understandings that accompany the classical doctrinal interpretations of Jesus
and the imaginative understandings that are being proffered by Jesus
research.

Classical Christological Doctrines and the Imagination

I now want to briefly outline the imaginative construal of Jesus of Nazareth that is implied in the classical christological doctrines of Nicaea
and Chalcedon. I can be brief here because my goal is not to prove anything, but to point to what I think is common experience. The premise
of this description is that all language and concepts have an imaginative residue. I shall not analyze the genesis of the classical doctrines,
which would be necessary if one wished to uncover their historically
generated theological meaning. I am less interested in their technical
meaning, and more interested in the imaginative understanding they
generate.

The doctrine of Council of Nicaea in 325 affirms that what is incarnated in Jesus, namely, God's Word or Son, is not less in stature than
God the Father; it is rather of the very same stuff as God. Jesus, then,
is truly and properly divine. So great was the stress on Jesus' divinity,
however, that Jesus' humanity seemed to get lost in some conceptions
of him. This resulted in controversies that led the Council of Chalcedon in the middle of the fifth century to declare that Jesus Christ is

truly divine and truly human, of the same nature as God and of the same nature as human beings. Jesus Christ is one proper individual, but this individuality unites within itself a distinct human and divine nature.

In one sense one could say that this formula righted the imbalance left in the wake of Nicaea, for Jesus was now declared to be consubstantial with human beings. But from another perspective Jesus' divinity still held the upper hand. For the theology surrounding the formula allowed certain forms of speech that are paradoxical. Because the one person Jesus Christ had two integral natures, one could affirm of him that which pertained to either one of the natures. One could say, for example, that Jesus suffered, because he did so in his human nature. One could also say that Jesus in his earthly life was God. One could affirm of Jesus' knowledge and consciousness what was proper to God. Thus, although one could read the classical doctrine as simply a confession of faith that Jesus is simultaneously and integrally divine and human without any explanation, still the theology of the time allowed one to say undialectically that Jesus was God. The portrayal of Jesus left by the council was that Jesus was a divine individual who also bore an integral human nature.

If this is an accurate description of these classical doctrines, what is the imaginative portrayal of Jesus that they communicate? The overwhelmingly most significant image the doctrines portray is that Jesus is God. It is not that we have a direct image of God; rather, we know God through this-worldly images by denying all limits in the positive qualities that are predicated of God.[9] And these characteristics can now be predicated of Jesus. Jesus is really infinite being, all-knowing, all-powerful. In himself he is substantively, or hypostatically, God.

Originally it was Jesus who supplied Christians with their images of God. But when the classical doctrines are the starting point of one's christology, one is introduced to Jesus by way of the doctrine. The affirmation "Jesus is God" is accompanied by some imaginative construal that controls one's reading of the gospel accounts of Jesus. It is not surprising that Jesus worked miracles, although one might recognize the astonishment of those who experienced them for the first time. It is not surprising that Jesus cured from a distance, or walked on water, or calmed the storm, or raised people to life, for he was himself the agent of creation. The doctrinal imagination, once it is internalized, forms a kind of master pattern that reinforces itself by a literal construal of the miracle traditions in the gospels. One may at this point recall the anecdote that began this discussion. It was a doctrinal imagination that caused the surprise that Jesus, being divine, could have been ignorant of the movement that would grow up after his death and evolve into a church.

Jesus Research and the Imagination

We pass now to Jesus research and ask about the bearing of the imagination upon the quest for the historical Jesus. I have divided this discussion into three simple points: first, the role of imagination in historical reconstruction; second, the content of Jesus research; and third, the effect of Jesus research on the imagination of those who read it.

How does imagination enter into the process of reconstructing the past? R. G. Collingwood, historian and philosopher of history, responded to this question in the first half of this century. History, he said, is not written on the basis of collecting and collating authoritative witnesses. Rather the historian assumes a certain autonomous responsibility for reconstructing the past by selecting, adding to, and amending the sources.[10] First of all, negatively, by the principle of analogy, historians reject what appears to be impossible according to commonly accepted laws of nature.[11] And, positively, historians exercise autonomy by constructing an integral, in some measure unified, and plausible picture of a specific part of history and a coherent narrative. This is done by what Collingwood calls an a priori or necessary imagination that interpolates into the evidence. This imagination is not freewheeling fancy but a priori, that is, bound to the evidence by necessity. For example, if the sources say Caesar was in Rome, and later in Gaul, one must interpolate the journey even when the sources do not mention it. If a ship appears on the horizon at one point and some time later at a different point on the horizon, we are "obliged to imagine it as having occupied intermediate positions when we were not looking."[12] We necessarily imagine "the under side of this table, the inside of an unopened egg, the back of the moon."[13] When the historian considers Jesus as a human being, the humanity of Jesus presents another example of an instance that requires all sorts of necessary, imagined data about him.

Generalizing on Collingwood's analysis one will have to say that the imagination that controls interpretation is *both passive and active*. On the one hand, if it were not objective and passive, keeping close to the evidence received, imagination would turn into fancy, and in that measure stray from the truth. But, on the other hand, if it were not subjective, active, and creative, one could not assemble a coherent and continuous account of this truth. Therefore both the passive and active dimensions of imagination that were noticed by Thomas have an essential role in historical reconstruction.

This plainly appears in the contents of Jesus research today where there are, among others, two distinguishable but overlapping kinds of research. The one focuses on the overall portrait of Jesus and relies more on an active imagination; the other focuses more on Jesus' teachings and actions and remains more closely dependent upon the sources. Regarding the first, however, there is no single portrait of Jesus that is beyond dispute. There is a great diversity in the pictures of Jesus that emerge from the relatively limited sources the historian has to work on. Much of the diversity comes in trying to decide the genre of Jesus, that is, the basic historical role he assumed or projected, the type of character he appeared to be. Most admit that because Jesus was a Jew he should be understood in the terms of some position or role known in the Jewish world of his time. For example, the Galilean Jesus was probably or surely not a priest, or an Essene, or a Zealot, or a scribe, or a lawyer.

Positively there are at least three major generalized portraits of Jesus that are currently being exploited in Jesus research: Jesus was a prophet, or a holy man, or a philosopher-poet. A strong case has been made by many that Jesus appeared as a prophet, or the eschatological prophet, and presented his teaching in an apocalyptic way.[14] Others depict Jesus as a healer, an exorcist, and a wonder-worker who proffered forgiveness of sins.[15] Still others see Jesus as a wandering, Cynic-like, philosophical figure who taught a countercultural message and dramatized it by a simple life of poverty.[16] As the judgment about the genre of a text gives a first interpretation of the data contained in it, these large interpretations of Jesus shape the content and meaning of his message in different ways. It is probable that all of these types contribute something true about Jesus and one should not judge between them too quickly.[17]

There is more consensus when the imagination stays closer to the evidence about the basic message of Jesus: that he preached the kingdom of God, that he went around teaching, healing, and doing good, that he associated with the poor and the outcasts of society, that he criticized structures and practices that were dehumanizing, that he told parables and performed symbolic actions that dramatized the kingdom of God, that these dramatizations reversed everyday patterns of thought, and that his ethics of the kingdom of God were radical. However one depicts Jesus, one should take into account that he was publicly executed as a criminal. Jesus was a public figure who rubbed authority the wrong way.[18]

Finally, what is the impact of these imaginative historical reconstructions of Jesus on the imaginations of those who read and study them? The answer to this question is simple and blunt: one cannot but be impressed by the humanity of Jesus. Negatively, the historian as historian and not as theologian can present to us nothing more than Jesus as a human being. The divinity of Jesus is a datum of faith and not empirical event. Moreover, on the supposition of Jesus' humanity, the imagination can and must interpolate all sorts of data that are not explicitly supplied by the texts but which are necessarily implied by them, namely, the implications of being a human being. In doctrinal terms, these are the characteristics that attend upon Jesus' being "consubstantial with us as to humanity, like unto us in all things but sin (see Heb. 4:15)."[19] In sum, historical research presents us with a Jesus who overwhelms our imaginations as being thoroughly human. What then is the impact of this upon christology?

Two Current Views on Jesus Research and Christian Faith

As a help in responding to this question of the impact and significance of Jesus research relative to Christian faith I want to compare two current views on the matter and relate each to this understanding of the role of imagination in the encounter with Jesus Christ. The two theologians are Schubert Ogden and Jon Sobrino.

Schubert Ogden

Schubert Ogden approaches the relationship of Jesus research to Christian faith in Jesus Christ by first establishing that the question that is addressed to Jesus in christology is an existential and religious question. It is not an objective question aiming at knowledge about Jesus as he was in himself; it is a question about God, about ultimate self-identity and destiny, and about Jesus as the medium of the answer to these two deep issues.[20] Given the nature of the christological question, he then asks about the subject matter of christology, the object or referent of the term "Jesus" when Jesus is accepted in faith as the Christ. Is this Jesus the object of Jesus research, "the actual Jesus of the past insofar as he is knowable to us today by way of empirical-historical inquiry using the writings of the New Testament as sources?"[21]

Ogden's response to the question revolves around two distinctions. The first is between what he calls the "empirical-historical Jesus" and the "existential-historical Jesus." The empirical-historical Jesus is "the actual Jesus of the past insofar as he is knowable to us today by way of empirical-historical inquiry using the writings of the New Testament as sources."[22] By contrast the existential-historical Jesus is Jesus insofar as one is existentially moved by an encounter with him. This is Jesus engaging human subjectivity existentially by mediating a response to the religious question. The distinction is similar to H. Richard Niebuhr's distinction between external and internal history as illustrated by Lincoln's reference to the birth of a nation at the beginning of his Gettysburg Address. The United States was founded on the historical events that included the Declaration of Independence, the Revolution, and the writing of the Constitution. But when Lincoln recalled the bringing forth of a nation in his Gettysburg Address, he was not recalling merely empirical events; he was appealing to the impact and meaning of those events on the patriots in his audience, to the shared ideals of liberty and justice contained in those events which have shaped the American personality. Analogously, the existential-historical Jesus is Jesus insofar as he has been encountered religiously by people and has shaped their lives. It is a participatory knowledge of encounter that defines the formality of how Jesus is grasped.[23]

Secondly, Ogden distinguishes between a "Christ kerygma," which is the developed message of the meaning of Jesus Christ as found in Paul and John, and the "Jesus kerygma," which is the earliest witness of faith to Jesus and is "accessible through critical analysis of the synoptic gospels."[24]

On the basis of these distinctions, Ogden can state his basic thesis as follows: "I contend that the Jesus to whom the earliest witnesses point as 'the real locus of revelation' is the existential-historical Jesus, and therefore neither the empirical-historical Jesus nor their own witness of faith, save insofar as it is solely through their witness that this event of revelation is now accessible and continues to take place."[25]

The implications of these distinctions and Ogden's position are several. The distinction between the existential-historical Jesus of faith and the empirical-historical Jesus means that "what can or cannot be inferred concerning the empirical-historical Jesus has no bearing whatever on the point of christology."[26] The subject of christological assertion is not Jesus in himself, but Jesus' meaning for us as a medium of God. But this is supplied by the Jesus kerygma, which is the earliest existential-historical witness to Jesus. On the one hand, there may be empirical data about Jesus that can be retrieved by historical research, but this has no bearing upon the claim that Jesus is the Christ. On the other hand, christological formulations too have to be controlled and normed by a historical study of Scripture. But this historical quest for the norm of christology is not a quest for an empirical-historical Jesus but for the Jesus kerygma or earliest witness to Jesus as the Christ. In this way Ogden embraces the new quest for the historical Jesus, but he makes it clear what this quest reaches is not an empirical-historical Jesus but the existential-historical Jesus of the Jesus kerygma.

Jon Sobrino

In *Jesus the Liberator* Jon Sobrino defines the historical Jesus in such a way that it corresponds to what Ogden calls the existential-historical Jesus. The gospels presuppose and were written out of faith in Jesus as the Christ. But this faith needed to hold on to its historical referent: "it was not enough to confess Christ; it was necessary to refer back to Jesus, and to the reality of Jesus."[27] Two things then must be held together. Ogden calls these two existential faith and Jesus; Sobrino calls the two theology and Jesus. Sobrino describes the gospels as history and theology simultaneously. They are not factual information but theology;

but they are theology that is historicized. No history of Jesus without theology; and no theology of Jesus without writing a history of him.[28]

Sobrino offers an analytic account of how the historical Jesus functions in his christology. He first contrasts what liberationists are up to with other European theologians and then sums up his position in four points. First, by the historical Jesus Sobrino means "the history of Jesus," the words, actions, attitudes, and spirit that make up his history.[29] And the core of what is important in this history of Jesus is Jesus' "practice with spirit." By practice he means "the whole range of activities Jesus used to act on social reality and transform it in the specific direction of the Kingdom of God. The 'historical' is thus primarily what sets history in motion, and this practice of Jesus, which in his day set history in motion, is what has come down to our time as a history set in motion to be continued."[30] To practice Sobrino adds the phrase "with spirit," designating the attitudes and intentions with which Jesus did what he did: his spirit of mercy, his concern for others, his partiality for those who suffer. This "practice with spirit" is the formality or aspect of the historical Jesus material that Sobrino makes central.

Then, secondly, within this practice with spirit one can discern the person of Jesus: his practice provides a framework for organizing the various elements of his ministry. The way to understand Jesus the person is through a consideration of the various aspects of his practice. And, thirdly, the link between the historical Jesus and faith in him as the Christ is also mediated through practice. That is, the practice of discipleship, of following Jesus, is a prior condition for faith's appreciation of him as the Christ. "It is, in the last resort, a matter of affinity and connaturality, beginning with what is most real in Jesus."[31] To get to faith in Jesus as the Christ, one needs a prior experience or prior affinity, and this comes through discipleship, a participation in the practice of Jesus. "In the case of faith in Christ, the prior objective phenomenon necessary is the phenomenon of the historical Jesus and the prior subjective experience is being his disciple."[32]

Finally, Sobrino describes liberation christology as gospel christology. He has a good appreciation of the critical limits of Jesus research. But his interest lies more in using Jesus material within the context of faith and presenting Jesus as the Christ narratively. This means telling how Jesus is the Christ in story form, in a history that opens up to following him: to discipleship, practice, and ethics.

Role of the Imagination

In the views of both Ogden and Sobrino there is room for a role of the imagination in appreciating Jesus, although this is given significantly greater play in Sobrino's narrative christology. But in both cases it is, as it were, *faith's* imaginative portrayal of Jesus in the past that is the object of our appreciation of Jesus today. Both Ogden and Sobrino affirm that the basis of christology, insofar as it is christology, is not an objective, empirical historical account of Jesus of Nazareth. Such will never generate what Christian faith recognizes in Jesus; faith transcends what the discipline of history can determine. What is preserved for us in the New Testament as the norm of christology is Jesus perceived as the Christ, a mixture of empirical datum and faith's appreciation, a duality of history and theology, or kerygmatic Jesus. This distinction between the transcendent and gratuitous character of faith's appreciation of Jesus and the empirical details about Jesus which appeal to the imagination grants faith a degree of autonomy and protects it from being jerked around by the latest historical hypothesis.

But no matter how much one presses this side of the distinction, and it is crucial that one do so, it does not break an intrinsic bond between Jesus in his "empirical" historical actuality and the faith's appreciation of Jesus. One must distinguish between subjectivity and objectivity, but one cannot sunder their continuity completely. The distinction between an existential-historical Jesus and an empirical-historical Jesus is a formal distinction in the way the knower knows the object; the material object, Jesus, is common to both. The existential-historical Jesus is still Jesus; internal history is an appreciation of external history; theology cannot be separated from history. Therefore the results of empirical historical research on Jesus enter into, even though they do not by themselves control, christological construal. The way this occurs is through the imagination.

The role of empirical history can be explained in terms of the role of the imagination in faith's construal of Jesus. All subject-object encounter entails the imagination. Christian faith is encounter with God mediated through Jesus of Nazareth, so that the Christian conception of God is not confirmed by Jesus, but is mediated by Jesus. One cannot step out of a historical mediation of God to compare what one encounters through it with a direct or unmediated concept of God. Negatively, therefore, one cannot say that Christian faith would remain the same if Jesus of Nazareth never existed. Nor could one continue to maintain the faith assertions mediated through Jesus if in fact Jesus were the opposite of all that the Jesus kerygma attributed to him. On the contrary the dynamic of Christian faith, even though its object is God mediated through Jesus, assumes a continuity between what is asserted of Jesus and the empirical historical reality of Jesus. This is shown in the natural curiosity to know more about Jesus upon which Jesus research feeds. The role of the imagination in knowing correlates with this intrinsic bond between understanding and concrete historical mediation. Knowing is never separated from concrete images of the object known. But this means that the implicit imaginative portrayal of Jesus that accompanies all Christian faith will either remain naive and unreflective, as in a dogmatic imagination that is exclusively nurtured by doctrine, or will itself be the object of critical reflection. It is precisely the task of theology as critical reflection on the witness of faith to develop a critical understanding of faith.[33] But this necessarily includes a critical image of Jesus. And it is achieved by the discipline of history. In sum, the role of history is to establish within faith a critically reflective image of existential-historical Jesus.

The Impact of Jesus Research on Christology

Let me conclude this discussion by outlining the impact of Jesus research upon christology generally. The pieces are in place and need only be drawn together. I will do this by presenting four propositions, which I shall also briefly explain.

First, there will be a tension between the historical reconstruction of Jesus and the transcendent and doctrinal aspects of christology. Where a doctrinal christology has generated a docetic and monophysitic imagination, this tension will amount to a clash of opposition. Docetic and monophysitic christologies do not include a reckoning of Jesus as absolutely a human being like all other human beings; Jesus is imagined as simply God on earth in human clothing. This imaginative view of Jesus Christ will be directly challenged by Jesus research. This is a significant observation if Karl Rahner was correct in asserting that a majority of Christians are implicitly monophysitic. But even in a balanced or orthodox christology there must be a tension between the humanity and divinity of Jesus.

Second, historical research that tries to reconstruct the figure of Jesus forms a starting point and suggests a structure for relating the humanity and divinity of Jesus. This research makes it clear that Jesus of Nazareth is the subject matter of christology, even though he is only the subject matter of christology when and insofar as he mediates a response to the existential religious question. Epistemologically the existential response to Jesus or to God through Jesus leads back to Jesus. Knowledge of transcendence begins with the world, history, and sense data. For the Christian, that data is Jesus, and God is not known apart from Jesus. And the divinity of Jesus, too, is not known apart from Jesus, but must be imagined as *within* or as a dimension of the integral human being Jesus of Nazareth. Another way of putting this is that the human being Jesus cannot be left behind in the affirmation of Jesus' divinity. Jesus of Nazareth is a sacrament or symbol or concrete medium making God present to history. An imaginative historical construal of Jesus cannot be neglected or even played down in a critical christology. Rather doctrinal christology should assume into itself an imaginative historical portrayal of Jesus' human career.[34]

Third, Jesus research functions as a negative norm in the fashioning of an integral christology. By a negative norm I mean that one cannot affirm of Jesus what is positively excluded by a consensus of history. For example, a necessary imaginative judgment recognizes that as a finite human being Jesus was limited by his historical particularity; he had limited insight, judgment, and knowledge. This is confirmed by the historical evidence. Thus any christology that depicts Jesus as essentially constituted with God-like knowledge is false by the criterion of history. Or again, it is the consensus of Jesus research that the idea of the kingdom of God was central to Jesus' preaching and action; it formed a center of gravity for his public ministry. A christology that fails to give any attention to this dimension of Jesus is less than adequate. Here one sees the conservative role of the passive dimension of the imagination. The passive imagination stores the historical images of Jesus, and doctrine about Jesus is bound to stay close to the imaginative memory of him.

Fourth, Jesus research provides a positive guide for christological interpretation. Here the active dimension and the creative role of imagination come into play. Jesus as he is imagined to be in his historical life provides a guide for Christian understanding of God and of human existence. This is what it means to say that Jesus reveals God. His teaching and his person open up the imagination for its encounter with and construal of God. Jesus also mediates to the Christian imagination a way of understanding human existence. Since Jesus was a figure of the past, this requires imaginative and creative interpretation today, not rote or literal imitation. But it is Jesus of Nazareth who is the subject matter of this hermeneutics.[35]

In sum, in these four ways Jesus research is having a dramatic influence on christology today. This historical research is not something to be feared, but to be welcomed as enriching our knowledge of Jesus and our impulse to discipleship.

Notes

1. John Hick, *The Metaphor of God Incarnate: Christology in a Pluralistic Age* (Louisville: Westminster/John Knox Press, 1994), 30.

2. It may be useful simply to note the questions that are not being directly addressed here. I am not asking whether or how one can get to faith from history. Nor am I asking what faith adds to history or how religious questioning engenders a distinctive religious interpretation of historical data. Rather I am presupposing faith as a given and asking about the way it is influenced by historical research. In this way I hope to reveal something about the structure of faith and thereby also shed some light on these other questions even though they will not be formally entertained.

3. Thomas Aquinas, *Summa Theologiae* (hereafter ST) I, q. 78, a. 4. For

a brief account of Aquinas's theory of the imagination, see Ray L. Hart, *Unfinished Man and the Imagination: Towards an Ontology and a Rhetoric of Revelation* (New York: Herder and Herder, 1968), 318–34. Also Jacques Maritain reviews Thomistic psychology and epistemology with an eye to imaginative artistic creativity in *Creative Intuition in Art and Poetry* (New York: Pantheon Books, 1953), 95–145.

4. ST I, q. 79, a. 2.

5. ST I, q. 79, a. 4.

6. ST I, q. 78, a. 4, obj. 4; English translation: *Summa Theologica: Complete English Edition in Five Volumes,* trans. by the Fathers of the English Dominican Province (Westminster, Md.: Christian Classics, 1961).

7. ST I, q. 78, a. 4.

8. For an account of the necessity of historical mediation for all our knowledge of God see John E. Smith, "The Disclosure of God and Positive Religion," in *Experience and God* (New York: Oxford University Press, 1968), 68–98.

9. Aquinas, ST I, q. 13, a. 2.

10. R. G. Collingwood, *The Idea of History* (New York: Oxford University Press, 1956), 235. John McIntyre, *Faith, Theology and Imagination* (Edinburgh: The Handsel Press, 1987), 109–15 provides a synopsis and commentary on Collingwood.

11. Collingwood, *The Idea of History,* 239–40.

12. Ibid., 241.

13. Ibid., 242.

14. A good representative of this position today is Edward P. Sanders, *Jesus and Judaism* (Philadelphia: Fortress, 1985).

15. Geza Vermes, *Jesus the Jew* (Glasgow: Fontana/Collins, 1973) is a thorough study of Jesus from this perspective.

16. Burton L. Mack, *The Lost Gospel: The Book of Q and Christian Origins* (San Francisco: Harper, 1993) develops this genre of Jesus on the basis of Q, the gospel sayings source common to Matthew and Luke.

17. See for example Marcus J. Borg, *Jesus: A New Vision: Spirit, Culture, and the Life of Discipleship* (New York: HarperCollins, 1987); idem., *Meeting Jesus Again for the First Time: The Historical Jesus and the Heart of Contemporary Faith* (New York: HarperCollins, 1994).

18. Edward Schillebeeckx, *Jesus: An Experiment in Christology,* trans. John Bowden (New York: Seabury, 1979), is a fine retrieval of the message and posture of Jesus. Jesus is represented as the eschatological prophet. Also Gerd Theissen, *The Shadow of the Galilean: The Quest of the Historical Jesus in Narrative Form* (London: SCM, 1987), provides a balanced imaginative portrayal of Jesus in the form of a story.

19. Council of Chalcedon, *Enchiridion Symbolorum,* ed. H. Denzinger and A. Schönmetzer (Freiburg im Breisgau: Herder, 1963), n. 301, 108.

20. Schubert M. Ogden, *The Point of Christology* (Dallas: Southern Methodist University Press, 1992 [orig. 1982]), 20–40.

21. Ibid., 44.

22. Ibid.

23. It is important to note, however, that the distinction between the empirical-historical Jesus and the existential-historical Jesus is not an "adequate" distinction; Jesus as a historical figure is common to both terms of the distinction.

24. Ogden, *The Point of Christology,* 51.

25. Ibid., 59–60.

26. Ibid., 60.

27. Jon Sobrino, *Jesus the Liberator* (Maryknoll, N.Y.: Orbis Books, 1993), 59.

28. "Presenting the history of Jesus, however theologized, is the best way of giving truth and substance to believers' faith and encouragement to their lives. And this is, in my view, the permanent value of the specific way of going back to Jesus that the Gospels offer" (Jon Sobrino, *Jesus the Liberator* [Maryknoll, N.Y.: Orbis Books, 1993], 60).

29. Ibid., 50–51.

30. Ibid., 51.

31. Ibid., 54.

32. Ibid., 55.

33. See Schubert M. Ogden, "Toward Doing Theology," *Journal of Religion* 75 (1995): 1–14.

34. This cannot be escaped on the basis of the pluralism of the reconstructions of Jesus, because in fact all christologies imply some conception of the character of Jesus. A critical christology will recognize this implicit necessity and lay out its implied image of Jesus in dialogue with historians.

35. At this point one must raise the question of *how* a critical imaginative portrayal of the existential-historical Jesus comes to bear on Christian experience, spirituality, and moral life. William C. Spohn addresses this question in "Jesus and Ethics," *Proceedings of the Catholic Theological Society of America,* 49 (1994): 40–57. He examines the epistemology of Jesus as a concrete universal and shows that "Jesus functions normatively in Christian ethics through the paradigmatic imagination and moral discernment, which are distinctive ways of exercising moral authority" (46). He analyzes how the Christian imagination entertains significant paradigmatic reactions of Jesus, scenarios of how he acted, and narratives that made up his life. In so doing the Christian is influenced and formed in a variety of ways: in his or her ability to perceive moral issues, in the habits of reacting in parallel situations, and more generally in developing a certain character individually or communally. All of this is based on the perception of patterns in concrete life that are analogous to the patterns displayed concretely in Jesus and imaginatively entertained. Something parallel to this analysis of Spohn's could be developed in response to the knowledge of God mediated by Jesus.

6

Heaven and Earth
Are Filled with Your Glory

Atheism and Ecological Spirituality

– ELIZABETH A. JOHNSON, C.S.J.–

The great insight that emerges at the end of Michael Buckley's *At the Origins of Modern Atheism* discloses the critical self-alienation that developed within Christian theology as it attempted to respond to the attacks of Enlightenment thinkers on belief in God.[1] Instead of appealing to its own primary material, namely, christology with its center in the person and teaching of Jesus the Christ and religious experience with its focus on personal witness and event empowered by the Spirit, theology abandoned its distinctive turf in favor of philosophy with its inferential method of reasoning toward the existence of God. In this way theology did indeed find common ground on which to dialogue with atheism, but at the price of its own unique evidence: "It is not without some sense of wonder that one records that the theologians bracketed religion in order to defend religion."[2] If this were done only as a first step, the results might not have been so impoverished. But it remained the continuing and total option of most major thinkers, with natural theology, or philosophical reasoning from the world to God done from the privileged position of the spectator, never intersecting with mystical theology, or critical description and analysis of participatory religious experience, a meeting that would have fertilized and extended the theological reach of the former.

The challenging implication for contemporary Western theology being done in a cultural context where atheism is now a given is clear: do not repeat this major mistake. In an illuminating essay on atheism and contemplation, Michael Buckley himself gives an example of how particular religious experience can be put into critical dialogue with atheism, facing off the two around the issue of projection.[3] Some popular and theological images of God do indeed bear the mark of being devised by way of extension from believers' psyches, as atheism charges. But the ancient path of contemplation, which is becoming one of the great religious movements of our times, draws persons into the purifying darkness of an apophatic moment that breaks all divine images open. As a result of this existentially difficult and religiously profound not-knowing, persons are moved experientially into the vision of the incomprehensible mystery of God.[4] Reflecting on this experience, mystical theology uses a panoply of intellectual tools to highlight how the descent into darkness, dryness, the desert foils projection through the ineffable experience of receiving what is conceptually beyond human grasp or objectification, the mystery of God who is love. The transforming power of contemplation convinces believing persons that God is beyond form and beyond control, certainly not like they may have originally imagined. Rather than being a projection, the focus of religious awareness becomes incomprehensible holy mystery "known" in and through the breakdown of projections, itself an event of disclosure.

The legitimacy and necessity of the appeal to religious experience, and contemplation as one such experience: I have sketched these key ideas from Michael Buckley's corpus because they provide the present essay with its justification and method. In gratitude and celebration on the occasion of this fine theologian's sixty-fifth birthday, I would like to focus on one particular type of contemplation growing rapidly in contemporary religious experience, namely, the gaze upon the beauty, intricacy, and dynamism of the natural world as revelatory of divine Spirit, and explore its potential for dialogue with atheism.

The cultural context of this religious experience is contemporary consciousness of the earth, an understanding shaped by the dialectic of new knowledge about the world discovered and popularized by contemporary science in tension with realization of how human predation is currently spoiling nature. On the one hand, perception of the vast age, size, and complexity of the universe, awareness of the cosmic processes that have created and continue to create it, appreciation of the infinitesimal reality of matter at the atomic and quantum levels, realization of the marvelous complexity of biological evolution up to and including the human species, and understanding of the interconnectedness of all life — all of this knowledge gives rise to the sense that the world is a wonder. On the other hand, cognizance of the rapid depletion of life-supporting planetary systems and habitats and of the concomitant killing off of other species through human practices of pollution, unbridled reproduction, and consumptive use of land and sea engenders a contrast experience whereby the treasure of nature is known to be under mortal threat. Wonder at the world in the face of wasting the world: for many religious persons today this experience provides a new entry to an ancient form of contemplation along with a fresh ethical consequence, namely, acts of prophetic witness and repair of the world.[5]

This development in the history of spirituality joins the dialogue with atheism insofar as it draws its originating knowledge from a scientific community many of whose leading contributors and popularizers publicly reject religious interpretations of the cosmos. Prominent scientists such as Stephen Hawking, Carl Sagan, Edmund O. Wilson, and Stephen Jay Gould, along with many others, have raised critical consciousness about the wonder and wasting of the world even as they profess skeptical agnosticism about religious ideas and, in truth, consider such ideas to be essentially illusory and supportive of false consciousness.[6] While such is not the position of all scientists, a small but significant number of whom are newly engaging philosophers and theologians in dialogue,[7] the scientific culture as a whole does spawn indifference and even hostility to religious ideas to the degree that it lifts the legitimate, practical atheism of scientific method to the ontological level of interpretation of the world as a whole. In the face of this thought pattern, no amount of inference from natural phenomena to divine mystery as origin, sustaining ground, and goal of the world can succeed.

But might the specifically theological appeal to religious experience of the natural world and the consequent moral passion to protect it not allow believing persons to render a more credible account of the hope that is in them? The fact that the world is simply there, in splendor and fragility, gives rise to wonder, leading to a religious sense of the living, loving, creative Matrix who grounds it, quickens it, and attracts it toward the future. In such experience the cosmos as a whole and in a special way the earth with its community of life, now under threat, is seen as a sacred place disclosive of the presence of divine mystery. The life-giving Spirit of God, *Dominus et vivificantis,* encircles, pervades, and energizes the world, gifting it with its own intrinsic, self-organizing powers that have led to magnificence beyond our imagination, including our own human race, now responsible for the ongoing fruitfulness of the world. For such a religious vision, the biblical bush still burns and we take off our shoes.

It appears to me that this ecological religious vision of the world among many good Christian people is generating a new "natural theology," one quite different from the Enlightenment type based on philosophical inference. For one thing, nature and history, the impersonal and personal worlds, can no longer be strictly separated once one realizes that nature is the result of a historical process still going on and that humanity is kin to all other creatures in the community of life, emerging from and being continuously sustained by the world itself. For another, the theological procedure is not deduction from the known to the unknown but critical reflection on the presence and absence of holy mystery being experienced positively in and through the beauty of the world and negatively by contrast with its destruction and in the summons to resist its destruction.

In the spirit of Buckley's insight about the value of religious experience in crafting a theological response to atheism, this essay will explore (all too briefly) what might well be called ecological contemplation in both its mystical and prophetic aspects, testing whether these specific Christian experiences may contribute to theology's dialogue with atheism.

Mystical Insight

> The world is charged with the grandeur of God.
> It will flame out, like shining from shook foil.
> It gathers to a greatness, like the ooze of oil,
> Crushed...[8]

More than a century after Gerard Manley Hopkins penned these ecstatic words, his poetic intuition grows ever stronger in believing persons who encounter the dazzling variety and profound interconnectedness of the world, its denizens, and its systems. At times, some are swept up in an oceanic feeling of oneness with the universe as a whole. Others awaken to the delight of particular forms of matter, each one of which has its own intricate, spirit-filled reality. Writing of her goldfish, for example, Annie Dillard displays an eloquent if poignant detail:

> This Ellery cost me twenty-five cents. He is a deep red-orange, darker than most goldfish. He steers short distances mainly with his slender red lateral fins; they seem to provide impetus for going backward, up, or down. It took me a few days to discover his ventral fins; they are completely transparent and all but invisible — dream fins. He also has a short anal fin, and a tail that is deeply notched and perfectly transparent at the two tapered tips. He can extend his mouth, so it looks like a length of pipe; he can shift the angle of his eyes in his head so he can look before and behind himself, instead of simply out to his side. His belly, what there is of it, is white ventrally, and a patch of this white extends up his sides — the variegated Ellery. When he opens his gill slits he shows a thin crescent of silver where the flap overlapped, as though all his brightness were sunburn.
>
> For this creature, as I said, I paid twenty-five cents. I had never bought an animal before. It was very simple; I went to a store in Roanoke called "Wet Pets"; I handed the man a quarter, and he handed me a knotted plastic bag bouncing with water in which a green plant floated and the goldfish swam. This fish, two bits' worth, has a coiled gut, a spine radiating fine bones, and a brain. Just before I sprinkle his food flakes into his bowl, I rap three times on the bowl's edge; now he is conditioned, and swims to the surface when I rap. And, he has a heart.[9]

As Sallie McFague comments on this passage, the juxtaposition of twenty-five cents with the elaborateness, cleverness, and sheer glory of

this tiny bit of matter named Ellery is frankly unnerving.[10] For the intricacy of this little creature calls forth wonder, and suddenly its worth
is sensed to be priceless.

Such experiences with the extraordinary quality of even the mundane world are to the fore in our ecological times. Since, as Michael
Buckley has observed, "God has emerged again and again in the history of wisdom as the direction toward which wonder progresses,"[11]
wondrous experience of the natural, bodily world including ourselves
leads contemplative persons to sense the grandeur of God drawing near
and passing by in and through the magnificence of creation. They know,
not just with their minds but with a certain kind of experiential feeling,
that the utterly transcendent holy God is utterly immanent in the world,
present and active in its creatures and dynamic processes. How to ex-
plicate this? The biblical concept of glory and the Thomistic category
of participation offer theology intellectual tools with which to bring
religious experience to language.

Consulting the Scriptures: Glory

In the Hebrew Scriptures a plethora of metaphors is used to refer to
divine presence and engagement throughout the world. These metaphors include the spirit of God, the angel of the Lord, the word of
God, the wisdom of God, and the glory of God, among others. Theologically speaking, these figures are not intermediaries between God
and the world. Rabbinic interpreters consistently warn against this
idea, as if God were so distant that some kind of go-between were
needed. Rather, these are biblical circumlocutions that signify the one,
transcendent God's nearness to the world in such a way that divine transcendence is not compromised. Since glory is the metaphor least likely
to be personalized, although even it like the others receives a christological interpretation in early Christian reflection ("He is the brightness
of God's glory" — Heb. 1:3), it has the potential to articulate divine
relation to the world in a way that is somewhat congruous with the
apophatic character of much contemporary belief. This is a wager that
needs exploring.

In ordinary speech "glory" is a word that signifies splendor, magnificence, brilliance, luster, rich ornamentation, power, and worth. It
connotes something beautiful and desirable. The Hebrew word for glory,
kabod, derived from the verb meaning "to weigh heavily," weaves these
connotations round with a sense of heaviness or deep importance, so
that glory signifies a certain weighty radiance.[12] When used in reference
to the mystery of God, the kabod YHWH is a light-filled metaphor
meaning the weighty radiance of divine presence in the world, the
heavy, plump, fat brightness of God's immanence drawing near and
passing by to enlighten, warm, and set things right. The more the

infinite transcendence of God was stressed in Israel's experience, the more *kabod YHWH* became a technical term in the biblical books for divine presence within the world and its happenings. Though God dwells beyond the heavens and can be compared with nothing created, the approach of divine glory signifies the self-disclosure of God's being, the publicly engaged, unhidden character of the incomprehensible Holy One.

In the wisdom of Scripture, however, the glory of God is never directly perceived. Rather, it is revealed in and through the world and its events. Chief among these revelatory bearers is the natural world with its power and beauty: "The heavens are telling the glory of God," exults the psalmist (19:1). Typically in the Bible the approach of divine glory is depicted by a cloud or the land's fruitfulness or fire or a thunderstorm with its crashing noise, flashing lights, and rushing waters. Indeed all of the natural world is *capax Dei,* capable of revealing the unseen, hidden Creator. As Isaiah's mystical vision of the One who is "holy, holy holy" perceives, heaven and earth are full of God's glory (6:3).

In the biblical vision, glory is thus a category of divine immanence perceived through the world's participation in divine beauty. The world shares in the weighty radiance of God: the starry heavens sing of it, other natural creatures reveal it in flashes of speed, methods of feeding, and all their intricate, mysterious workings (Job 38–41). Human beings, too, reflect divine splendor, and when they realize this in moments of insight they "give glory" to God. This response entails upwelling sentiments of praise and thanks, as well as efforts to correspond to divine glory through their own loving deeds of righteousness.

But divine glory (divine presence and action) is not confined to the beauty and magnificence of the world. Sin, sorrow, and injustice mar the world's well-being. Therefore, the *kabod YHWH,* never directly perceived, is also manifest in and through historical events of peace-making and liberation. The Exodus narrative makes great play with this symbol, using it to bespeak the God who frees the Israelites from slavery and accompanies them in the glory of cloud, smoke, and fire through the desert, to Mount Sinai, and thence into their own covenanted history.

In this connection, and to an extraordinary degree, the glory of God is a biblical theme of religious hope. Uttering words of comfort to people suffering the distress of Babylonian exile, Isaiah proclaims that "the glory of the Lord *will be* revealed" (Isa. 40:5), namely, when they are delivered. Then they will see a resplendent manifestation of divine power in a historical moment of liberation and homecoming, sign of that even greater future day when evil will be overcome and the whole world will be filled with the *kabod YHWH.* Yearning for salvation, for victory in the struggle with evil, for deliverance for the poor and cessation of violence against the needy is expressed in the hope that God's glory will dwell in the land (Ps. 85:9), or will fill the earth (Ps. 72:19), or will shine throughout heaven and earth (Ezek. 43).

Biblically, then, the glory of God does not point to God as a bigger and better Solomon sitting on a throne in isolated splendor. Rather, it signifies divine beauty flashing out in the world and in particular bent over brokenness and anguish, moving to heal, redeem, and liberate. It is a synonym for God's elusive presence and action in the midst of historical trouble. As such, it is a category of relationship and help.

It is interesting to me how resonant the biblical term "glory" is with *ruah, sophia,* and *shekinah,* those great grammatically feminine metaphors of God's indwelling power and concern. Hopkins himself associates the glory of God with *ruah,* the spirit of God, ending his poem about God's grandeur with a hopeful, maternal metaphor: "the Holy Ghost over the bent world broods with warm breast and with ah! bright wings."[13] The book of Wisdom consistently connects God's glory with *sophia,* saying of wisdom that "She is a pure radiance of the glory of the Almighty" (7:25); "She is the brightness that streams from everlasting light" (7:26); and "She is more splendid than the sun, and outshines every constellation of the stars; compared with the light of day she is found to excel, for day gives place to night, but against wisdom evil does not prevail" (7:29–30). In the writings of early rabbinic Judaism glory and the *shekinah* are used as equivalents, the *shekinah* being God's compassionate spirit who accompanies the people, suffering the tragedies of history with them and occasioning hope. Here the typical expression of the *kabod shekinah YHWH,* the glory of God's indwelling spirit, signifies no mere feminine dimension of God but the radiance of God as She-Who-Dwells-Within, divine Spirit in compassionate engagement with the conflictual world as source of vitality in the struggle.[14]

The correlations, the mutual amplifications, at times even the identity, between the glory of God and the divine metaphors of *ruah, sophia,* and *shekinah* indicate that we are dealing with the active presence of great beauty that can fittingly be imaged in female metaphors, itself a critical move against the historical dominance of patriarchal metaphors that have come to reify divine being and thus block mystical experience. In the film *Steel Magnolias,* which deals with the life struggles of a group of women in the American South, there is a memorable scene where in the midst of beautifying preparations for a wedding, an older woman says delightedly, "What distinguishes us from the animals is our ability to accessorize." You have to hear these words uttered in an inimitable southern drawl to appreciate their impact! The ability to accessorize might well describe what the glory of God has wrought in the world, so filled with the marvels of even a twenty-five cent goldfish as well as fragmentary shapes of freedom and justice happening amid destruction and despair. She has adorned the world with beauty and her own gracious radiance shines out, even in the darkness.

The New Testament taps deeply into these meanings of glory, now translated by the Greek word *doxa*. It proclaims that the weighty radiance of divine presence is in the world in a new way through the very human flesh of Jesus the Christ, whose ministry makes strikingly manifest how divine glory operates: the blind see, the lame walk, the dead are raised up, the poor have the gospel preached to them (Matt. 11:5). It is especially in the light of Easter, as the crucified one is raised to glory by the power of the Spirit, that divine *doxa* pervades the world. Glory rests on the whole community of believers, women as well as men, who are thereby being transformed amid weakness and sin into the image of Christ (2 Cor. 3:18). The natural world, too, is involved in this drama of salvation, groaning in the present age but with the hope that it "will obtain the freedom of the glory of the children of God" (Rom. 8:21). The orientation toward promise is strong throughout these writings: "Christ in you, the hope of glory" (Col. 1:27). Once again, glory is a category of participation in God's redeeming beauty that draws near to share the brokenness of the world in order to heal and set free.

To sum up the biblical data: the glory of God is a luminous metaphor for the elusive nearness of the transcendent God glimpsed in and through the wondrous processes of nature, the history of freedom, and communities where justice and peace prevail. Using the term "glory of God" signifies that the incomprehensible holy mystery of God indwells the natural and human world as source, sustaining power, and goal of the universe, enlivening and loving it into liberating communion.

Consulting Aquinas: Participation

The meaning carried in the biblical notion of the glory of God is cast in a more ontological framework by medieval scholasticism, but the two are uncannily consistent with each other. At the heart of Aquinas's vision of God's creative relation to the world is the evocative idea of participation. Through the act of creation God, whose essence is the very livingness of being itself, gives a share in that being to what is other than Godself:

> Whatever is of a certain kind through its essence is the proper cause of what is of such a kind by participation. Thus, fire is the cause of all things that are afire. Now, God alone is actual being through divine essence itself, while other beings are actual beings through participation.[15]

As to ignite is the proper effect of fire, so too is giving a share in being the proper effect of the Mystery of Being. Hence, all that exists participates in its own way in divine being through the very gift of creaturely existence. It is not as if God and creatures stood as uncreated and created instantiations of "being" which is held in common by both. Rather, the mystery of God is Being itself who freely shares being while creatures participate. Nor is the gift of being given only once in the instant when a creature begins to exist, but continuously in a ceaseless act of divine creation. To cite another of Aquinas's fiery analogies, every creature stands in relation to God as the air does to the light of the sun. As the sun is light-giving by its very nature whereas the air is bright and illuminated only so long as it is lit by the sun, so also God alone simply exists (divine essence is *esse*) while every creature enjoys existence insofar as it participates in being (creaturely essence receives the gift of being).[16]

The category of participation affects theological understanding of both God and the world. Continuously creating and sustaining, God is in all things not as part of their essence but as the innermost source of their being, power, and action. There is, in other words, a constitutive presence of God at the heart of things. Conversely, in its own created being and doing, the world continuously participates in the livingness of the One who simply is. Every excellence it exhibits is a participation in that same quality unimaginably present in the unknowable mystery of God. Take the key example of goodness. Since "it befits divine goodness that other things should be partakers therein,"[17] every created good is a good by participation in the One who is good by essence. It follows that "in the whole sphere of creation there is no good that is not a good participatively."[18] In possessing their own specific goodness, creatures share in divine goodness. This is the intelligible basis for speech about the transcendent mystery of God, for in knowing the excellence of the world we may speak analogically about the One in whose being it shares.

One of the strengths of Aquinas's vision is the autonomy he grants to created existence through its participation in divine being. He is so convinced of the transcendent mystery of God (*esse ipsum subsistens*) and so clear about the *sui generis* relation of God to the world that he sees no threat to divinity in allowing creatures the fullest measure of agency according to their nature. In fact, it is a measure of the creative power of God to raise up creatures who participate in divine being to such a degree that they are also creative and sustaining in their own right. A view to the contrary would diminish not only creatures but also their Creator: "to detract from the perfection of creatures is to detract from the perfection of divine power."[19] This is a genuinely noncompetitive view of God and the world. According to its dynamism, nearness to God and genuine creaturely autonomy grow in direct rather than inverse proportion. That is, God is not glorified by the diminishment of the creature but by the creature's flourishing. The nature of created participation in divine being is such that it grants creatures their own integrity without reserve, while in turn they become symbols in and through which divine mystery may be asymptotically glimpsed.[20]

Result: Earth a Sacrament

Contemplative appreciation of the glory of God flaming out in the natural world, undergirded by the theological notion of created participation in uncreated being, gives rise to the realization that the world itself is a revelation and a sacrament: revelation, because the invisible grandeur of God can be glimpsed and known experientially in the splendor of the universe, its balance, complexity, creativity, diversity, fruitfulness; and sacrament, because the mystery of divine, self-giving presence is really mediated through the richness of the heavens and the earth. Participating in the glory of God, our whole planet is a beautiful showing forth of divine goodness and generosity. By being simply and thoroughly its magnificent self, it bodies forth the glory of God that empowers it, being as it were an icon. And, in keeping with the biblical theme of glory, this carries with it a note of promise. Pervaded and encircled by the glory of God, nature's beauty, intricacy, wildness, richness, order, and novelty are a sacrament of hidden glory not yet fully revealed.[21]

In the light of mystical insight resulting from contemplative religious experience, the many-faceted ecological crisis suffered by the living planet Earth becomes a matter of intense religious concern. For human beings are rapidly fouling and even destroying the primary sacrament of God's glory, one with its own intrinsic value before God. The critical praxis of justice for the earth, flowing from contemplative attentiveness, becomes in turn an engaged, practical form of religious experience in its own right.

Prophetic Stance

If it be the case that, as John of the Cross writes, "contemplation is nothing else than a secret and peaceful and loving inflow of God, which, if not hampered, inflames the soul in the spirit of love,"[22] then the soul so enkindled responds to divine love by trusting correspondence to divine affections for the world. This dynamic, so basic to Jewish and Christian faith, finds its characteristically contemporary interpretation in the dictum of political and liberation theologies that God is not only to be contemplated but also to be practiced. If the heart of divine mystery is turned in compassion toward the world, then devotion to this God draws persons into the shape of divine communion with all others. "Be merciful, just as your Father is merciful" (Luke 6:36): to deny one's connection with the suffering need of others is to detach oneself from divine communion.[23]

The praxis of mercy toward the poor as constitutive of the Christian life is rooted in this realization. So too is committed work on behalf of peace, human rights, economic justice, and the transformation of

social structures. For those who engage in this work out of deep contemplative experience, it is far from mere activism or simple good deeds.
Rather, solidarity with those who suffer, being there in commitment to
their flourishing, is the locus of encounter with the living God. Through
what is basically a prophetic stance, one shares in the passion of God
for the world.

In the midst of the present ecological crisis, the vision of the natural world as a sacrament of the glory of God motivates contemplative
persons to extend this justice model to embrace the whole earth. If the
creative glory of God pervades the whole world which is a sacrament
of divine fecundity and beauty, then ecological abuse that weakens or
destroys the earth's flourishing is contrary to God's intent. The human
selfishness, greed, irresponsibility, and ignorance that are newly impov-
erishing nature need to be challenged both concretely and systemically.
The preferential option for the poor must now include vulnerable, voice-
less, nonhuman species and the ravaged natural world itself, all of which
are kin to humankind. In the memorable words of Brian Patrick,

> Who is our neighbor: the Samaritan? the outcast? the enemy? Yes, yes,
> of course. But it is also the whale, the dolphin, and the rain forest. Our
> neighbor is the entire community of life, the entire universe. We must love
> it all as our self.[24]

Loving these neighbors as their very selves, committed religious persons
develop moral principles, political structures, and lifestyles that promote
their thriving and halt their exploitation. For the prophetic passion flowing from contemplative insight, action on behalf of justice for the earth
participates in the compassionate care of God who wills the well-being
of the whole interdependent community of life and opposes whatever
mars or destroys divine glory in the world. Human beings become, quite
literally, partners and co-redeemers with "the Love that moves the sun
and the other stars."[25] In carrying forth this project, naming and then
transforming ecological abuse form two interrelated religious acts.

Naming the Abuse

In order to right a wrong, it must first be brought into the open
and faced squarely as an evil. Prophetic consciousness infused with
the glory of God in the world therefore urges upon the religious and
civic communities the realization that the earth, its life-giving systems,
and the diversity of creatures it has brought forth are currently undergoing massive assault from human beings on an unprecedented scale.
Ever-expanding consumer demands that fuel endlessly swelling growth
economies are plundering the planet. These human pressures, coupled
with exploding human populations, are destroying the health of planetary ecosystems. Pollution of waters, air, and soil; build-up of toxic

and nuclear wastes, destruction of vast stretches of habitat — these are symptomatic of deep abuse. Living species that took millions of years to evolve and that form the life context of humanity's own emergence are disappearing without a trace; we will never see their like again. Much has already been irretrievably lost, and if human beings do not change their ways, the days are fast coming when, in Catherine Keller's eloquent phrase, the planet will be uninhabitable except by the very rich, the very armed, and the insect (and in the end, maybe just the insect).[26]

Human beings are woven into the planetary fabric of life; there is no human community without the earth, soil, air, water, and other living species. We evolved amid this radiance of abundant life and are interdependent with it for our own flourishing. So wasting the world has dire consequences for the well-being of present and future human generations as well and is, in fact, a practice of intergenerational irresponsibility. Degradation of the earth is also interwoven with social injustices among human beings, for it is poor people, people of color, and colonialized nations that bear the brunt of exploitation of land, resources, and their own labor for the benefit of the wealthy, industrialized nations. In fact, structures of social domination are chief among the ways that exploitation of the earth is accomplished.[27] But degrading the planetary ecosystems also has significance beyond the human troubles that result. For the world itself is a marvel, the result of millions of years of creative process still underway. Damaging or even destroying it nips its future promise in the bud and begins to wipe out one of the magnificent bright spots of the universe.

We have a duty to know this; turning our face the other way does not make us innocent. As with any wrongdoing, to remain silent in the face of evil is to be an accessory to the fact. By contrast, naming the evil as an injustice that ruptures divine communion is an act of spiritual practice. In this spirit, prophetic wisdom brings the sins of biocide, ecocide, and geocide to light.

Part of the difficulty in facing this, however, is a certain religious worldview prevalent in Christianity for many centuries according to which the world is merely a backdrop for the drama of human salvation; human beings are individual sinners to whom grace comes as the call to set their minds on the things above, not below; and the gracious mystery of God is utterly transcendent and unrelated to the earth. Supporting this worldview is a thought pattern of hierarchical dualism inherited from ancient Greek philosophy and intensified in Cartesian philosophy according to which matter and spirit are profoundly divided with the latter assigned a higher value. This basic assumption works its way out in key contrasts: soul over body, reason over emotions, what is active over what is passive, autonomy over interdependence, what is conscious and personal over what is inert and natural, and therefore history over nature, the whole system being at root a program of alienated mind pitted against its own matter.

The vantage point of feminist analysis of sexism makes clear that in each of these pairs, the category related to spirit (the transcendent, heavenly principle) is identified with masculine reality while matter (the lowly, earthly principle) is considered feminine. Within the system of hierarchical dualism, the linkage between women and the earth is symbolic as well as practical, both considered inferior, even dangerous, and subjected to men's control. Women whose bodies give physical existence to humanity thus become the oldest symbol of the connection between social domination and the domination of nature. The oft-used phrase "the rape of the earth" and other such linguistic metaphors reveal the extent to which the symbolic identification of women and nature issues in actual effects, the exploitation of nature being logically coherent with violent sexual attack upon women.[28]

In this alienated dualism of body and soul, it is virtually unthinkable to assign the earth a serious religious value. By concentrating on the salvation of the immortal soul and denigrating the bodiliness of human nature, patriarchal theology also disregards the larger matrix of physical life, the whole world in which human selves are embedded. Consequently, one may ignore the world, trivialize it, flee it, use it, subdue it, rape it, at best one may even responsibly steward it, but to embrace and cherish it as a precious creation is not envisioned as a way of holiness. Removing sacred value from the earth, seeing it almost as the index of the anti-divine, is a Christian factor contributing to the present assault on the earth, its life-systems, and its diversity of creatures. By contrast, imbued with the contemplative realization of the earth as a sacrament of divine glory, contemporary prophetic consciousness names what has gone awry and seeks a new paradigm that reconfigures the mystery of God, all humans, and the earth in deep interconnection.

Transforming the Abuse

Saving the earth requires hard choices and courageous deeds in the political, social, economic, and cultural arenas. To reflect upon and promote such critical praxis, theology has need of thought patterns that disrupt human dominance and promote the whole community of life. I would like to suggest that one such configuration consists of the basic categories of memory, narrative, and solidarity. As originally developed in the practical foundational theology of Johannes Baptist Metz, these categories function in an emancipatory way in the service of suffering and defeated human beings.[29] It seems to me that they have the capacity to serve the same way with regard to the exploited earth and its creatures.

Memory is a category that serves to rescue lost or threatened identity. Witness the fact that every dominating power tries to wipe out defeated peoples' traditions, while political protest and resistance is fed by the subversive power of remembered sufferings and freedoms. Memory is not understood here as mere nostalgia. Rather, it is an incalculable visitation from the past that energizes persons. By evoking the sufferings and victories of those who went before, it galvanizes hope that new possibilities can be realized. There is danger in such remembrance for it interrupts the omnipotence of a given situation, breaking the stranglehold of what is currently held to be plausible. The future is opened up in a new way by the surplus of meaning carried in the act of remembering.

Memory is most often communicated by narrative, which preserves the uniqueness of experiences of suffering and victory, preventing them from being reduced to any theory. In the widest sense life itself has the character of a story, and concrete reality is expressed better through narrative than through abstract thought. In oppressive situations, telling certain tales of courage and witness, violence and defeat, has disclosive and transformative power. Robert McAfee Brown has described the method of survivor and witness Elie Wiesel:

> You want to know about the kingdom of night? There is no way to describe the kingdom of night. But let me tell you a story.... You want a description of the indescribable? There is no way to describe the indescribable. But let me tell you a story.... [30]

Within the political experience of unjust suffering, narrated memory is a subversive language with practical effects. Telling dangerous stories does not bring intelligibility to the suffering, as if this could ever make sense. But evocative telling of tales of tragedy and triumph births hope and resistance in the midst of darkness.

The memory of suffering and freedom retold through narrative creates, strengthens, and then expresses solidarity. In Christian political theology this category does not refer to a common feeling with those in our immediate class or neighborhood, or even optimistic sympathy for the less fortunate. Rather, it connotes a partnership of desires and interests with those in need, with those most in need, perhaps causing us loss. In a vital community one enters into common reflection and action against the degradation which so defaces others, and does this with the sense that these others are part of oneself. The universality of this category, furthermore, is shown in the fact that it does not include only the living; rather, solidarity involves an alliance with the dead, especially with those who have been overcome and defeated in history. The narrative memory of the dead creates a solidarity backward through time, which emphasizes the common character of the destiny of all creatures. It is thus a category of help, support, and togetherness, by means of which the dead can be affirmed as having a future, the living who are oppressed and acutely threatened can be raised up toward becoming genuinely free, and a more promising future can be created for those yet to be born. This historical solidarity between the living and the dead in view of the future breaks the grip of dominating forces and empowers transformative praxis toward a fulfilling future for *all,* guaranteed only when the value of the most despised is assured.

Memory, narrative, solidarity: the dynamic of their interaction in the context of a threatened earth can release new energies for protection and deliverance. Think of the power for transformation if, encountering the glory of God in the sacrament of the earth, Christian people with their pastors and theologians *remembered* the earth with its life-systems and diversity of plants and animals, many going extinct; told the story of its amazing, ancient, creative complexity and ongoing destruction; and did so in solidarity with all earth's creatures, including species long or recently dead. Think of the practical effect of including the living earth and its creatures in every liturgical prayer that is offered for others, every lesson about loving one's neighbor, every ethical discernment about justice and peace. Narrative memory of the earth in solidarity with all the earth's creatures, living and dead, calls present destructive political, economic, and social systems into question and turns people toward innovative praxis in the personal and social order, empowering a prophetic edge to the contemplation of God's glory.

Conclusion

Decrying early modern theology's self-estrangement that permitted atheism to make significant headway, Michael Buckley concludes that the pattern will inevitably recur if the cognitive claims of religious reason are split off from experience:

> If an antimony is posed between nature or human nature and god, the glory of one in conflict with the glory of the other, this alienation will eventually be resolved in favor of the natural and the human. Any implicit, unspoken enmity between god and creation will issue in atheism....The origin of atheism in the intellectual culture of the West lies thus with the self-alienation of religion itself.[31]

In the light of this insight, this essay has explored aspects of one increasingly widespread religious phenomenon, ecological spirituality, to ascertain whether its theological interpretation may contribute to the dialogue with atheism.

Several conclusions result. Unlike Heidegger before the God of theism (the precise theological construct rejected by atheism), one can certainly dance before the living God whose glory shines through the resplendent tapestries of cosmic processes and life on earth. Moreover a powerful sense of the transcendence and immanence of God, the two increasing in direct rather than indirect proportion, arises from this religious encounter with divine glory in the world, thus reinforcing the deep wisdom of the Jewish and Christian traditions that calls for moral responsibility for what is so beloved of God. Here there is no inferential proof that would refute atheistic argument against the existence of God, but rather witness that the Creator Spirit abides with the world and galvanizes human beings to its care and defense. One might even argue that religion can foster the moral inspiration to act ethically in our dealings with nature better than can a worldview in which the universe has no ultimate point.[32] This argument would not be conclusive, however. In the end, contemplative experience that heaven and earth are filled with God's glory and the praxis of ecological justice which overflows as an intrinsic element of this prayer stand with their own integrity, pointing to the power of faith in a world ever so in need.

Notes

1. Michael Buckley, *At the Origins of Modern Atheism* (New Haven: Yale University Press, 1987).

2. Ibid., 345.

3. Michael Buckley, "Atheism and Contemplation," *Theological Studies* 40 (1979): 680–99.

4. Theology is forever in debt to Karl Rahner for placing this realization at the center of contemporary Western theology; see his "The Concept of Mystery in Catholic Theology," *Theological Investigations* 4 (New York: Seabury, 1974), 36–73.

5. Brian Swimme and Thomas Berry, *The Universe Story: From the Primordial Flaring Forth to the Ecozoic Era* (San Francisco: HarperCollins, 1992), is a choice example of this earth consciousness with its religious and ethical implications.

6. Representative examples of their work include Stephen Hawking, *A Brief History of Time: From the Big Bang to Black Holes* (New York: Bantam Books, 1988); Carl Sagan, *Cosmos* (New York: Ballantine Books, 1980); Edmund O. Wilson, *The Diversity of Life* (New York: Norton, 1992); Stephen Jay Gould, *Wonderful Life: The Burgess Shale and the Nature of History* (New York: Norton, 1989).

7. One opening bell for dialogue was sounded by Robert Jastrow, *God and the Astronomers* (New York: Norton, 1978); an excellent synthesis of scientific and religious viewpoints is Arthur Peacocke, *Theology for a Scientific Age: Being and Becoming — Natural, Divine, Human* (Minneapolis: Fortress, 1993); see the series of books resulting from dialogue co-sponsored by the Vatican Observatory and the Center for Theology and the Natural Sciences, Graduate Theological Union, Berkeley: Robert Russell, et al., eds., *Physics, Philosophy, and Theology* (1988), and *Quantum Cosmology and the Laws of Nature* (1993), distributed by University of Notre Dame Press.

8. Gerard Manley Hopkins, "God's Grandeur," *A Hopkins Reader*, ed. John Pick (Garden City, N.Y.: Doubleday, 1966), 47.

9. Annie Dillard, *Pilgrim at Tinker Creek: A Mystical Excursion into the Natural World* (New York: Bantam Books, 1975), 126.

10. Sallie McFague, *The Body of God: An Ecological Theology* (Minneapolis: Fortress, 1993), 210.

11. Buckley, *At the Origins of Modern Atheism*, 360.

12. For what follows, see Gerhard Kittel, ed., *Theological Dictionary of the New Testament* (Grand Rapids: Eerdmans, 1964), 2:232–51.

13. Hopkins, "God's Grandeur," 48.

14. For more detailed discussion, see Elizabeth Johnson, *She Who Is: The Mystery of God in Feminist Theological Discourse* (New York: Crossroad, 1992), 82–93.

15. Thomas Aquinas, *Summa Contra Gentiles* III, 66:7; hereafter SCG. Edition used is translated by Vernon Bourke (Garden City, N.Y.: Doubleday, 1956).

16. *Summa Theologiae* I, q. 104, a. 1; hereafter cited as ST. Edition used is translated by the English Dominicans (New York: Benziger, 1956).

17. ST I, q. 19, a. 2.

18. ST I, q. 103, a. 2.

19. SCG III, 69:15.

20. For further explanation of this view see Piet Schoonenberg, "God or Man: A False Dilemma," in his *The Christ* (New York: Seabury, 1971), 13–49.

21. For diverse approaches to the theme of the earth as revelation and sacrament, see Sallie McFague, *The Body of God* as well as her *Models of God: Theology for an Ecological, Nuclear Age* (Philadelphia: Fortress, 1987); Jürgen Moltmann, *God in Creation: A New Theology of Creation and the Spirit of God* (San Francisco: Harper and Row, 1985); John Haught, *The Cosmic Adventure* (New York: Paulist, 1984); essays in Charles Birch, et al., eds., *Liberating Life: Contemporary Approaches to Ecological Theology* (Maryknoll, N.Y.: Orbis Books, 1990); Michael J. Himes and Kenneth R. Himes, "Creation and an Environmental Ethic," in their *Fullness of Faith: The Public Significance of Theology* (New York: Paulist, 1991), 104–24; and Denis Edwards, *Jesus the Wisdom of God: An Ecological Theology* (Maryknoll, N.Y.: Orbis Books, 1995).

22. *Dark Night of the Soul* 1, chap. 10, no. 6, quoted by Buckley, "Atheism and Contemplation," 695.

23. The classic statement of this position remains Abraham Heschel, *The Prophets* (New York: Harper & Row, 1962); an eloquent restatement is offered by Jon Sobrino, *The Principle of Mercy* (Maryknoll, N.Y.: Orbis Books, 1994). See Charlene Spretnak, *States of Grace* (San Francisco: HarperCollins, 1991), for discussion of the wisdom of the Semitic social justice tradition in relation to the wisdom of other religious traditions.

24. Cited in Michael Down, *Earthspirit: A Handbook for Nurturing an Ecological Christianity* (Mystic, Conn.: Twenty-Third, 1991), 40; for foundations of an environmental ethic, see James A. Nash, *Loving Nature: Ecological Integrity and Christian Responsibility* (Nashville: Abingdon, 1991).

25. Dante, *The Divine Comedy: Paradise,* trans. Dorothy Sayers and Barbara Reynolds (Harmondsworth, England: Penguin Books, 1962), canto 33, line 145.

26. Catherine Keller, "Talk about the Weather: The Greening of Eschatology," in Carol Adams, ed., *Ecofeminism and the Sacred* (New York: Continuum,

1993), 36; see also her "Women against Wasting the World: Notes on Eschatology and Ecology," in Irene Diamond and Gloria Feman Orenstein, eds., *Reweaving the World: The Emergence of Ecofeminism* (San Francisco: Sierra Club Books, 1990).

27. See Drew Christiansen, "Ecology, Justice, and Development," *Theological Studies* 51 (1990): 64–81, for review of the moral discussion.

28. Pioneering analysis has been done by Rosemary Radford Ruether in her works *New Woman, New Earth* (San Francisco: Harper and Row, 1975); *Sexism and God-Talk: Toward a Feminist Theology* (Boston: Beacon, 1983); and *Gaia and God: An Ecofeminist Theology of Earth Healing* (San Francisco: HarperCollins, 1992). For a synthesis, see Elizabeth Johnson, *Women, Earth and Creator Spirit* (New York: Paulist, 1993).

29. Johannes Baptist Metz, *Faith in History and Society* (New York: Seabury, 1980).

30. Robert McAfee Brown, *Elie Wiesel: Messenger to All Humanity* (Notre Dame, Ind.: University of Notre Dame Press, 1983), 6–7.

31. Buckley, *At the Origins of Modern Atheism*, 363.

32. Argument well made by John Haught, *The Promise of Nature: Ecology and Cosmic Purpose* (New York: Paulist, 1993).

Part II

RELIGION
– AND –
SCIENCE

7

On the Difficulties of Dialogue between Natural Science and Christian Theology

– CHARLES HEFLING –

Perhaps the most gratifying extracurricular activity I have taken part in as a university professor is a faculty seminar that for some years has regularly brought together colleagues from different departments for cross-disciplinary discussion. Our stated topic has been "God and the world of the sciences," and the disciplines represented have been biology, chemistry, geology, philosophy, physics, and theology. All of us have, I think, learned a great deal in the seminar, in large measure because of Michael Buckley, who is not only its institutional sponsor but also an active and articulate participant. But one thing we have certainly learned is that conversation of the kind we have been engaged in is difficult. Even to formulate clearly such questions as might best specify and orient our discussion has proved to be no simple task.

Probably the same would be true in some measure of any attempt at crossing disciplinary boundaries. Academic culture today demands of scholars a degree of specialization that works against their giving serious attention to other fields of inquiry than their own. But between theology or religious studies on the one hand, and the natural sciences on the other, conversation is especially problematic. I propose in this essay to suggest some of the reasons why.

I

Genuine attempts on the part of scientists and theologians to understand one another's thinking are less rare than they used to be, though still infrequent enough. John Polkinghorne, who has himself written extensively on issues involving both science and theology, observes that when an expert in one of these disciplines does try to engage the other in conversation, it is more often a scientist attempting a dialogue with theology than the other way around. There are exceptions of course. Thomas Torrance for one, and Michael Buckley for another, have approached the relations between religious belief and scientific inquiry from the theological side. But for the most part theologians seem inclined to keep themselves to themselves, at least where science is concerned.

What explains this shyness? Loss of nerve, for one thing. "Extinguished theologians," T. H. Huxley opined, "lie about the cradle of every science as the strangled snakes beside that of Hercules." Triumphalist rhetoric though his statement is, it does not entirely miss the mark. When the "warfare of science with theology" was being waged, most of the casualties were, in fact, suffered on the theological side. If theologians today decline to enter the fray at all, they are at least avoiding strangulation. But there are other reasons, less unworthy, as well. It can be argued that theology should have no dealings with science, not because it is dangerous, but because there is no theologically relevant reason to take account of science in the first place. Two strong trends in contemporary theological thought make such an argument. Though otherwise they have not much in common, they agree in conceiving the theological task as one that precludes from the outset any interaction with science. One of these might be characterized as a linguistic-biblical-narrative trend; the other, as an existential-pastoral-spirituality trend.

By a linguistic-biblical-narrative trend, I mean an approach to theological discourse which insists that whatever Christianity has to say it says on grounds which are unique to itself and to which it has an exclusive claim and an exclusive access. Christians, in brief, speak a language of their own. As the discipline which reflects upon and regulates that language, theology is thus an in-house activity. It belongs to a discrete community, which is itself constituted as the community it is by the fact of speaking in this specific way. Other forms of discourse, those of physics or biology, say, are similarly contained within definite communities, so that however interesting or important they may be in other connections they are no concern of Christians *qua* Christian. Science is "spoken" in the laboratory: theology is "spoken" in the church.

An extreme exemplification of this trend can be found in the peculiarly North American phenomenon of fundamentalism, insofar as it takes its methodological stand on an exclusivistic reading of the *sola scriptura* principle. But the same trend can take forms that are anything but simplistic; witness the nuanced grandeur of Karl Barth's *Church Dogmatics*. From Barth, with a strong infusion of Ludwig Wittgenstein's views on language, descends the increasingly influential program for theology proposed by George Lindbeck in *The Nature of Doctrine*,[1] which is explicit in its exclusion of scientific knowledge as beyond the theological pale. Nor is it a purely Protestant move to confine theology to what is thought to be uniquely Christian territory. By insisting that Christian ethics should be elaborated solely on the basis of Jesus' love-command, instead of the more traditionally Catholic basis of natural law, or that a truly Christian doctrine of God should begin and end with the Trinity, to the exclusion of what used to be called natural theology, theologians of whatever stripe are insisting that theological discourse is *sui generis*.

Much the same is true, *mutatis mutandis*, of what I have called a existential-pastoral-spirituality trend in contemporary theology. Here it is not revealed truth, however, that provides the specifically Christian basis for theological thought, but the truth of lived experience. Conversion, prayer, and liturgical participation, especially in the paschal mystery, give theology all it needs by way of motivation and subject-matter. The emphasis thus falls not on language but on the *Lebenswelt*, not on texts but on devotion, not on God as disclosed or mediated but on God as personally and immediately present. Theology itself, for those who follow this second trend, is to be pursued less as an intellectually rigorous theoretical discipline than as one that issues in concrete *praxis*. Mystagogy, not pedagogy, is central.

Because of its often tacit assumption that the character of religion is not primarily cognitive, theology that follows the existential-pastoral-spirituality trend need not concern itself about potential conflict with the truth-claims of cognitive disciplines, the natural sciences included. As with the first trend, there are both Protestant and Catholic forms, and the two trends can overlap or merge. The special experience of liturgical worship, for example, and the special language associated with it, can combine to become the matrix of a theological program essentially unrelated to scientific knowledge.

My characterization of these two trends is not meant to be an exhaustive map of theological options, and I would stress that they are trends and not ideal types. The one point I am making is that there exist at present strong reasons (beyond mere self-preservation) for theologians to limit their conversation to their own guild, without even trying to talk with scientists about science. For those who take a linguistic-biblical-narrative position, conversation is ruled out because only Christians have the appropriate grammar and vocabulary; for those who take an existential-pastoral-spirituality position, it is ruled out because only Christians know what to talk about. On the one hand conversation is impossible in principle, on the other irrelevant in practice. Consequently both positions promote, if not an intellectual isolation of the Christian community, then at least a kind of sectarianism where the sociology of knowledge is concerned. Neither trend, to put it differently, has much affinity with theology as Thomas Aquinas thought of it — "science of God *and of all things* in their relations to God."

Now, the trends I have sketched are not the only options available to the Christian theologian at present, but they do make themselves felt, and where one or the other of them predominates, any theologian who does think that attempting to communicate with scientists is important will be open to criticism from within his or her own discipline. Have theologians any reason to stick their necks out by making the attempt? One possible reason lies in the fact that there are scientists who have no qualms about pronouncing on theological matters. When the Big Bang is called "the moment of creation"; or when no less prestigious a physicist than Stephen Hawking says that the unified field theory for which he and his colleagues are searching will be "the ultimate triumph of human reason — for then we should know the mind of God";[2] or when the equally eminent sociobiologist E. O. Wilson proposes that religious narratives play a role in human evolution and offers the "evolutionary epic" as a functionally superior alternative for human adaptation and natural selection in the future[3] — when statements like these are made, it would seem that theologians ought to have something to say in response. For even if it is objected (as it rightly could be) that in issuing these pronouncements the scientists who issue them are not talking science but scientism, "science out of bounds," it remains that they *are* scientists and that what they say therefore carries considerable weight in our culture. So, for instance, if creation in the properly theological sense does not name an event at all, the Big Bang or any other, somebody needs to explain the difference.

Explaining the difference, and answering such challenges as Hawking's or Wilson's, would be an exercise in the branch of theology traditionally known as apologetics. And such a defense would be a conversation of sorts. It would be largely negative, however, and largely ad hoc. Moreover the fact that some scientists still want to keep up the old warfare with theology is not perhaps the most promising point of departure for genuine communication. A more positive reason for theologians to open a dialogue with science lies in a definition of their craft that does not entail the "sectarianism" toward which both the trends discussed above seem to be headed.

One such definition would be that theology is *fides quaerens intellectum*, faith in quest of understanding. That venerable phrase has been interpreted in more ways than one, but there are grounds for thinking it means, not establishing faith, but throwing light on what is already established; not proving or demonstrating the truth of religious beliefs, that is, but understanding what religious people believe. It is one thing to be quite certain that two and two are four, and something else to understand, through the theory of numbers and mathematical operations, why that is so. The same thing applies to religious beliefs: it is one thing to hold them as truths, and another to give an intelligent account of what they mean.

Now *if* what theology is for is, among other things, the understanding of what religious people accept in faith as true, *and if*, to refer again to Thomas's definition of theology, the scope of the understanding that theology seeks extends to "*all* things in their relations to God," then the theological quest for understanding will almost by definition be open to what is known about "all things" by those who specialize in knowing about them — by, among others, scientists. This approach is not a strict logical alternative to either of the trends with which I began. To conceive theology as *fides quaerens intellectum* is to posit in some sense a cognitive element in religious faith; but it is not to deny the non-cognitive aspects on which the existential-pastoral-spirituality approach concentrates. Nor does conceiving the subject-matter of theology as all-inclusive deny that Christianity is committed to such "revealed" tenets, specific to itself, as would be insisted upon by the linguistic-biblical-narrative approach. In contrast with the isolationism of those two options, however, this one implies that theologians will *want* to hear what scientists have learned about those subdivisions of "all things" that fall under their respective sciences. There is a kind of obligation to enter into conversation with science, not in order to refute scientism (unless perhaps incidentally) but in order to throw light on the relations in which the things scientists study stand to God.

II

Everything I have said so far is highly general. I have pointed out that a disinclination, on the part of theologians, to engage the natural sciences in conversation can find respectable justification in either or both of two contemporary trends that eliminate such a conversation, more or less a priori. By way of corrective I have suggested, also on a priori grounds, that conversation between theology and science might be relevant if the scope of theological inquiry embraces, in principle, everything that exists, and if the goal of the inquiry is to grasp the intelligibility of what faith accepts. But it is one thing to urge that such an interaction could be relevant, and something else to show how it might take place. That a quest for theological understanding should lead to the laboratory is possible in the abstract. Is it possible concretely? The best way to show that it is would be to produce a good example. Are there any good examples, then?

There are. I have already mentioned John Polkinghorne's remark that a disproportionate number of those engaged in dialogue at the "interface" of science and theology are scientists. Polkinghorne himself is one of them. A theoretical elementary-particle physicist by training, a professor of mathematical physics, and a member of the Royal Society of London, Polkinghorne has more recently taken holy orders in the Church of England and become president of Queens' College, Cambridge. Those of his recent publications which are not about quantum

physics are on theology and science, and these I propose to examine here, beginning with one of the most recent, his contribution to
a symposium held in Dunedin, New Zealand, in 1993. Six major papers were delivered, culminating (in the published proceedings) with
Polkinghorne's essay "Theological Notions of Creation and Divine
Causality."[4] This paper is in many ways an epitome of the position he
had developed in previous writings, to which it not surprisingly makes
frequent reference.[5] Thus it offers a good introduction to his way of
conducting a dialogue, even though the conversation partners are both
Polkinghorne himself, in different capacities.

The two Christian beliefs to which Polkinghorne has given most attention — he has written a book on each — are creation and providence,
and these are the ones he concentrates on in the Dunedin paper. His aim
is to promote an understanding of these beliefs, by asking how each of
them stands in relation to contemporary science, specifically physics. His
first methodological precept in this regard is that "the insights of science
are to be taken absolutely seriously and...the way we think theologically about creation and providence must be consonant with what we
know about the history and process of the physical world."[6] Thus Polkinghorne has found himself agreeing with Jürgen Moltmann, as against
one branch of the existential-pastoral-spirituality trend, that "no theological doctrine of creation must be allowed to reduce the understanding
of belief in creation to the existential self-understanding of the person. If God is not the Creator of the world, he cannot be my Creator
either."[7] Yet, at the same time, he faults Moltmann's big book on creation for discussing space without mentioning General Relativity, and
for its merely occasional, and even then cursory, references to scientific
insight elsewhere.[8]

As for his own efforts at understanding creation, Polkinghorne clears
the way by showing that the consonance of this doctrine with physics has nothing to do with the Big Bang, one way or another. The
choice between big-bang and steady-state cosmologies is theologically
neutral, because creation in the Christian sense refers not to temporal
beginning — that is deism, not Christianity — but to ontological origin.[9] What is, however, relevant is the effectiveness throughout physics
of mathematical reasoning. The physical world is intelligible; its intelligibility is "part of scientific founding faith." But the form of the
laws that constitute its intelligibility is always mathematical, and moreover developments in mathematical thinking have at times run ahead of
the discovery of physical laws that can only be expressed in terms of
the developed mathematics. These facts raise a question. Why should
mathematics be the key to the scientific strategy of understanding?
Polkinghorne considers that the question is all but unavoidable. The explanatory power of mathematics, itself the work of human minds, lies in

its correspondence with the physical world, and simply to dismiss this correspondence as a brute fact will not do. If it is a fact, it is an intelligible fact; yet in this case science itself cannot provide the intelligibility for which the *why*-question calls. Here, "in the account of its own domain of knowledge, science fails to slake that thirst for an understanding through and through which is the natural desire of the scientist. Its laws are not sufficiently self-explanatory to be treated as self-contained; they raise questions which point beyond their own power to answer."[10] If the universe is a creation, however — if it has as its origin an intelligence that bears some resemblance to the human intelligence that is capable of discovering and formulating, say, quantum field theory — then the mathematical intelligibility of those physical laws which obtain throughout the universe is itself intelligible.

Anyone who is familiar with old-fashioned "rational theology" will recognize Polkinghorne's logic here. It echoes the reasoning used in "cosmological" arguments for the existence of God. All such arguments, however naive or sophisticated, confront a demand for complete explanation, "that thirst for understanding through and through" which Polkinghorne speaks of, with the world's inability to explain itself completely. The gap between the demand, the "thirst," and its satisfaction drives the quest for understanding beyond what science, as science, can explain. Yet Polkinghorne's is not an updating of rational theology in its standard form. There are two significant differences.

1. The first difference, not an unimportant one, is that whereas theistic arguments *a contingentia mundi* traditionally begin with some particular feature of the world, commonly motion, and argue that only if there exists a God is that feature intelligible, Polkinghorne goes a step further by arguing that it is not the intelligibility of any particular feature but *intelligibility itself* which is incomplete, an unexplained brute fact, apart from God. Not any particular answer, but the fact that answers can be reached at all, stands in need of explanation. In other words, the way in which science answers questions about the world raises a "meta-question" about the character of the answers science arrives at, a question that science itself cannot answer.[11]

2. This is not to say that Polkinghorne is offering a sort of meta-proof of God's existence. That is the second difference. There is no logical entailment or apodictic demonstration, he insists, in his move from a mathematically structured universe to the doctrine of creation. The most he will claim is that there is a "deep and satisfying consonance" or a "marvelous congruence."[12] The doctrine of creation does add a level of intelligibility to the physicist's account of the universe, and conversely physics illuminates belief in a Creator, but in itself the doctrine is grounded not in syllogistic reasoning but in religious experience.[13]

That the intelligible universe exists because there exists an intelligent Creator is not, of course, the whole of what Christianity has to say about God. Even if creation is understood as continuous ontological dependence rather than as a single event in the past, the doctrine of God's providence adds that the Creator also interacts with what is created. Providence, for Polkinghorne, is an essential component of Christian theism, and his treatment of this further doctrine is in some ways more interesting and original than what he says about creation. Nevertheless creation will be my focus here, partly because it is conceptually prior to providence but also because it leads directly to questions of the sort which, I want to argue, have to be faced if any responsible conversation between theology and science is to go forward.

Questions of just this sort were, in fact, raised at the Dunedin conference by one of the responses to Polkinghorne's paper, given by Jack Dodd, president of the Royal Society of New Zealand. Dodd is a physicist, like Polkinghorne, but not a believer. "Atheist" he considers too absolute a name for his position on the question of God, and he prefers "agnostic" or "skeptical atheist." His unbelief notwithstanding, Dodd acknowledges that the idea of God as Creator comes closest to being, for him, convincing. What, then, does he make of the "unreasonable effectiveness" of mathematical laws?

On this score Dodd holds two closely related views. The first involves denying that there *are* any physical laws in the strong sense of the word. There are only hypotheses, imaginatively constructed. These may in time be promoted to the status of theories; eventually they may even come to be called, by courtesy as it were, "laws." Repeated experimental testing can show that some particular theoretical construction is reliable, but that does not make it true. *"There is no such thing as scientific truth,"* according to Dodd, if scientists are being properly honest and properly skeptical.[14] From this it follows, secondly, that the "metaquestion" which Polkinghorne thinks mathematical intelligibility raises simply does not arise for Dodd.

It is important to specify the difference between Dodd and Polkinghorne. In his paper Polkinghorne had alluded to quantum field theory as bringing together in a single intelligible whole the seemingly paradoxical facts that quantum entities such as light sometimes behave the way waves behave and sometimes the way particles do.[15] The properties of particles and those of waves are incompatible, but the fact that both can be observed experimentally in the case of certain kinds of radiation has, since 1927, been explained in a single, consistent way that has its proper expression in mathematical terms. For Polkinghorne this explanation (to which we shall return below) is a prime instance of the "unreasonable effectiveness" of mathematics. Not for Dodd. He denies that either the wave-description of quantum entities or the particle-description is really a description at all, if by description is meant an account that corresponds to what these entities actually are. They are only models. Accordingly their being incompatible presents no urgent problem; nor does the fact that quantum field theory resolves their incompatibility mean that it gives any better account than theirs of what really is so. Mathematics, in Dodd's judgment, is not a key to the nature of radiation or fundamental particles; it is only "the language which scientists have constructed as appropriate for describing the properties that we observe."[16]

Dodd's response goes on to more properly theological matters, but the most basic question is already decided as soon as he has taken the stand I have just outlined. Polkinghorne's claim that a chastened form of natural theology answers a question which science raises, but which science does not and cannot answer, is a claim that Dodd disallows from the first — not, however, by challenging Polkinghorne's views on theology but by challenging his views on science. Although, as Dodd puts it, he and Polkinghorne both purport to know something about the same things, they cannot even discuss physics, much less theology. Why not? Dodd considers that their disagreement is scientific, but that is so only if "scientific" is taken in the broad etymological sense of "pertaining to knowledge." For what these two physicists disagree on is not so much what they know about as it is their knowing. Theirs is not a disagreement within science, in other words, but a disagreement about the nature of science itself. And while Dodd declines to pursue the matter, saying that his purpose is not "to argue philosophical interpretations of physics," I would contend that the roots of his differences with Polkinghorne, theological differences included, lie just there — not in physics and not in theology but in philosophy.

My contention can be put more precisely. The basic question that divides Dodd's position from Polkinghorne's has two aspects. On the one hand, it is a question about what is going on in that exercise of the mind which is physics. Science, *scientia*, is a matter of knowing, *scire*. What, then, is the character of that activity? Correspondingly, there is the question of what physicists know as a result of exercising their *scientia*. Polkinghorne considers, for example, that they know the nature of light, what light truly is; Dodd, on the contrary, that properly speaking all they know is observations, which models and mathematical theory are no more than a convenient way to talk about. From a philosophical viewpoint, there is disagreement on an *epistemological* question and on a *metaphysical* question, a question about reason and a question about reality.

Dodd's remarks in response to Polkinghorne ought not to be made to carry more weight than they can support. They do, however, point toward the chief theme of the present essay, which, briefly stated, is that the dialogue between science and theology is difficult because it is never a dialogue. There is inevitably a third party to the discussion: philosophy. Questions of epistemology and metaphysics may get postponed or shunted off, but they cannot be dismissed. Any "interfacing" of science with theology will involve the same kind of philosophical questions about reason and about reality that Dodd begins to raise. Indeed, epistemology and metaphysics *are* the interface between natural science and theology.

In this regard it is pertinent to note in passing that the theological trends I mentioned earlier as precluding interaction with science also have in common a strong aversion to philosophy. To distinguish sharply between the "God of the philosophers" and either the God of revelation or the God of religious experience is to eliminate the philosophical ground on which, for a position like Polkinghorne's, science and theology have some hope of establishing mutual relations.

It is not to be expected that in a brief paper such as the one he presented at the Dunedin conference Polkinghorne should have done more than touch on his philosophical views. They can be found elsewhere, though, notably in the paper he contributed to a "study week" for philosophers, physicists, and theologians sponsored by the Vatican Observatory in 1987.[17] "Einstein," he remarks there, "was the last of the ancients."[18] To understand this somewhat startling statement is to understand the crux of Polkinghorne's position.

It is well known that Einstein resisted developments in quantum physics that took place in the 1920s; the question is why he did so. Polkinghorne suggests that while Einstein undoubtedly advanced what is understood about physical processes beyond even the greatest achievements of Newtonian physics, he nevertheless clung to Newton's view of those processes as clear, determinate, and capable of being visualized. Such a view is, to be sure, intuitively plausible. But the processes of what Polkinghorne calls the quantum world do not conform themselves to the expectations of common sense. Anything that can be visualized or imagined possesses, simultaneously, both position and momentum — as do the particles of Newtonian physics. Quantum realities do not. And while a great deal more would have to be said in order to state the difference in a scientifically rigorous way, the point that Polkinghorne wants to emphasize would remain. It is that if picturability is the criterion of objective reality, then the unimaginable, counterintuitive quantum world cannot be real. A choice therefore has to be made between denying that the quantum-mechanical account of (say) light is an account of what is really and objectively so, and denying that imagination, commonsense intuition, the ability to visualize, is the arbiter of scientific knowledge. That choice marks the watershed between "ancient" physics, Einstein included, and quantum physics as Polkinghorne construes it.

His own stand has been mentioned already. The quantum world, elusive though it is, has a rational structure. That structure is not imaginable. It is, however, intelligible; and "intelligibility is the ultimate guarantee of reality."[19] Taken individually, there is no straightforward way to understand quantum events: they are "random" in the technical sense of that word. Yet their overall pattern shows a statistical regularity that can be understood in terms of mathematical probabilities; and such an intelligibility, though it cannot be formulated in "classical" laws such as Newton's, is no less an intelligibility than they are.

It is impossible to overemphasize the importance of all this. If "intelligibility is the ultimate guarantee of reality," and if in quantum physics the relevant intelligibility is statistical, it follows that the quantum world is intrinsically indeterminate. Randomness is an objectively real feature of the universe at its most basic level of complexity. And this is just what Polkinghorne holds. The "uncertainty" of Heisenberg's "uncertainty principle" is not a lack of mental certitude on the part of physicists: it is a characteristic of what physicists know about. "The uncertainty principle arises from the nature of the entities with which we have to deal, not from our lack of dexterity in investigating them."[20]

Why is any of this important in relation to a conversation between science and theology? Because, as the objection raised by Dodd at the beginning of his response to Polkinghorne's Dunedin paper has already suggested, those who attempt such a conversation will do well to be clear about what sort of conversation is possible. And that means taking a stand, both on what sort of rational activity is going on when a scientist "does" science and a theologian "does" theology, and on what each of them knows as a result of doing it. The philosophical questions that belong to epistemology and metaphysics are implicit always, and ought to be made explicit. What is reason, and what is reality?

It is on that account that Polkinghorne's most extensive exploration of the interface between his physics and his faith is especially noteworthy. It has as its subtitle *The Relationship between Science and Theology* and as its main title, significantly enough, *Reason and Reality*. It is a remarkable book in several respects, not least among them the breadth of Polkinghorne's acquaintance with other positions, theological and philosophical, past and present. There is hardly a major figure in the debate whose work he is not acquainted with. At times his deference to predecessors and colleagues verges on eclecticism, but on the whole he draws on others for the sake of presenting what is, in the end, a coherent position of his own.

The theological program for which *Reason and Reality* considers conversation with science essential is, in effect, the program of *fides quaerens intellectum* mentioned above. As a Christian, Polkinghorne believes in a God who not only has created and not only sustains "all things visible and invisible," as the creed puts it, but also is actively involved in the world — the God, that is, of theism rather than deism. Is this religious and theological tenet "consonant" with what the same Polkinghorne, as a physicist, holds to be the character of the physical world? His (affirmative) answer is the same as the one mentioned already, in connection with his Dunedin paper. What makes its elaboration in *Reason and Reality* notable is the route by which it is arrived at. For the first step Polkinghorne takes is to ask about asking, to question questioning, to inquire about inquiry. Only then does he take up the much debated topic of the language or discourse in which rational inquiry finds expression; and not until "rational discourse" has been treated does he suggest the character of the reality that such a rational inquiry aims to understand and that such rational discourse aims to communicate.

Thus the first three chapters of *Reason and Reality*, although they necessarily bring in both scientific and theological issues, are at bottom philosophical. Together they articulate a position that Polkinghorne calls "critical realism," with equal emphasis on both words.[21] It is a *critical* realism in three ways. In the first place, despite his repeated references to "bottom up" investigation, he is certainly not an empiricist in any simplistic sense. What is known to physicists about the physical world did not come to be known by simple scrutiny — by what Lonergan dubs "taking a good look." Picturability, as has been noted already, cannot be made the criterion of what is real. Does this mean that the mind makes a contribution, over and above empirical observation? Yes; but Polkinghorne is not convinced that the contribution is simply the imposition a priori of mental categories, as Kant would have it. Nor does he accept the modified Kantianism of theologians like Lindbeck or philosophers of science like Thomas Kuhn.[22] Rational inquiry is a process rather than a punctilear event; the process is corrigible, subject to critique at every stage; and the criticism is made by continually referring back to the observed data that the inquirer is endeavoring to explain. That is a second way in which Polkinghorne's is a critical realism. He maintains neither that theory invariably precedes observation, nor the reverse. There is a developing, reciprocal relationship, which he sometimes refers to as "universe-assisted logic."[23] Yet the universe does not render its assistance to the mind by being ostensible. Gluons are no more the objects of direct inspection than God is, yet particle physics yields genuine knowledge, testable against observation, even if it is knowledge that stands always open to criticism and refinement.

Such is Polkinghorne's epistemology. On the metaphysical side, he is a realist in the sense of holding that the epistemic process he outlines yields results that correspond to what *is*, actually and objectively and independently of the process by which it is known. So much is clear, again, from his interpretation of Heisenberg's principle. But while Polkinghorne thinks that such a realism is deeply "instinctive," to physicists anyhow, it is not dogmatic or apodictically certain, not a philosophical "first." As the order of his chapters suggests, he accepts Kant's "Copernican revolution" to the extent of giving epistemological questions priority over metaphysics. And this is the third, most basic sense in which his position is critical.

Can the same critical realism be applied to religion? Polkinghorne thinks it can. In the first place, there is an empirical starting point. Joining the main current of modern theology — all of it, that is, except for Barth's influential, if reactionary, attempt to swim against the tide — he acknowledges religious experience as fundamental. There is plainly an enormous difference between "theophanic" moments and experimental observations made in laboratories, but Polkinghorne argues that it is a difference of degree, not kind. It is not, for example, that religious experience is private, while science concerns itself with publicly accessible fact. Rather, religion belongs, with art and ethics, to a realm of experience where personal engagement comes to the fore in a measure that is not ordinarily characteristic of science. And in either case, differences notwithstanding, a "bottom-up thinker" will endeavor to give a rational account of what he or she experiences. Intelligibility remains "the ultimate guarantee of reality," and to acknowledge the mystery, the ineffability, the uniqueness of "transcendent" or "disclosure" or "revelatory" experiences is not to foreclose on the effort to understand them.

The *mathematical* intelligibility that characterizes quantum-physical realities obviously cannot be equally characteristic of religious realities, although Polkinghorne does draw a remarkable comparison between the Christian creeds and Maxwell's electromagnetic equations: "they are strikingly compact" and "use a specialized vocabulary which requires as much unpacking as would the equations of physics"; yet "what has been boiled down in these concise credal statements is not unbridled metaphysical speculation but the distillation of Christian experience."[24] Still, the comparison is no more than suggestive, and to make it stick Polkinghorne has to consider nonmathematical modes of "rational discourse" as expressions of intelligibility. "Model," "metaphor," "symbol," and "myth" are terms that show up frequently in contemporary theology, and in considering them Polkinghorne engages directly or indirectly with theological thinkers like Ian Barbour and Sallie McFague as well as with physicists such as Bohr.

As will be clear by now, Polkinghorne is endeavoring to establish a kind of parallel between the scientist's and the theologian's efforts at articulating the intelligibility which is "the ultimate criterion of reality."

Summing up his argument in this regard, he writes that science and religion are both

> concerned with seeking to describe the nature of reality. The difference between them is not that between reasonableness and obscurantism. It lies, rather, in the nature of the aspects of reality that they are seeking to explore. One is concerned with the physical world, which we transcend and can manipulate. The other is concerned with One who transcends us in his love and mercy. Both incorporate appeal to experience. Science looks for the grounds of its understanding to experiments which are within its power to contrive. Religion depends upon those revelatory moments of divine disclosure which cannot be brought about by human will alone but which come as a gracious gift.[25]

But one further question remains. The summary I have just quoted is open to being construed as a kind of separate-but-equal policy. On such a reading, scientific and theological lines of inquiry do show certain similarities, but they run parallel to each other and never meet. While each is appropriate in its own sphere, the spheres do not overlap. This is not, of course, Polkinghorne's position. For religion's relationship with science he proposes instead an analogy with Edmund Dirac's development of quantum field theory.

It was the achievement of Dirac to resolve the notorious paradox, alluded to earlier, which had arisen from the fact that electromagnetic radiation has the observable properties both of waves and of particles. Polkinghorne insists that this *was* a paradox and that, as such, it was irrational and unintelligible. Equally, he emphasizes that Dirac's theory puts an end to the duality by bringing all the observable properties within a single, unified intelligibility. "It is *not* the case that we use a wave model at one time and a particle model at another and that is all we can say about it, as theologians sometimes allege. It *is* the case that we have a theory that combines wave and particle models without a taint of paradox and which is open to our rational inspection."[26] To draw the analogy, science and religion are both concerned with one reality — the universe, the real world. Theology aims at understanding that universe, as does science, though from a different viewpoint and in a different way. As the wave-model and the particle-model are complementary descriptions of light, so on a broader scale science and theology are complementary descriptions of one and the same universe. But if "complementarity" is to be more than a slogan, something analogous to quantum field theory is needed — some unifying "rational discourse" capable of embracing both scientific and theological explanations. The need is met by natural theology.

By natural theology, Polkinghorne means "an inquiry which one might define as the attempt to learn something of God through the exercise of reason and the general exploration of the world." While the attempt cannot help being metaphysical, as were the natural theologies of the past, it will also be

> more modest in its tone than its predecessors of earlier centuries. It speaks of insight rather than demonstration. Its aim is not the classic goal of proving the existence of God. Rather, it seeks to exhibit theism as providing a coherent and deeply intellectually satisfying understanding of the total way things are.[27]

And so we are back where we began, at the position Polkinghorne presents telegraphically in his Dunedin paper. It is not a position immune to criticism, even if one accepts his basic philosophical stance of critical realism and his (largely implicit) answers to questions of fundamental theology. I will mention two complaints that might be lodged.

It could be argued, for one thing, that God as Polkinghorne conceives him is not *God* enough — that when all is said we are not presented with a God who is truly transcendent. Polkinghorne aims for a conception of the Creator different from the absentee God of deism and from the marginal "God of the gaps," both of which he rightly considers anthropomorphic. But while he does not wholly miss his mark, neither does he seem able to articulate divine transcendence in such a way as to prevent God's being conditioned by the very space and time that, *ex hypothesi*, God has created.[28]

A second and related quarrel could be raised in respect of Polkinghorne's ambivalence, as it seems to be, about the point and purpose of natural theology in general and theistic demonstration in particular. Demonstration, we have seen, he abjures; despite the formal parallel between his natural theology and "rational theology" in the scholastic mode, the intelligibility of the existing world does not logically entail the existence of an intelligent Creator. It does cohere with, and to that extent support, belief in such a God; but the belief itself has its primary "anchorage" in experience, specifically the experience of hope, which Polkinghorne calls "the unconscious discernment that we live in a world which is a creation."[29] But surely it is a long way from hope as experienced to the doctrine of creation as Christianity has traditionally taught it, and to suggest that only after the doctrine has been articulated and accepted does the sort of reasoning which natural theology formalizes enter the scene is to carry modesty to extremes. If natural theology and religious experience are indeed consonant, it would seem there must be in the experience something that natural theology echoes, something like the inchoate conviction that Austin Farrer called crypto-theism. Conversely, there must be something akin to religious experience in the scientific act of grasping that the world is intelligible. Polkinghorne is no doubt right to locate the ground of religious faith elsewhere than in intellectual reasoning, but he comes close to making the distance between the two so great as to cast doubt on the theological relevance of his own project.

These objections are rather technical, however, and worth raising only because on the whole Polkinghorne provides what I take to be a very convincing answer to the question raised at the beginning of this section. Having prescinded from theological trends that halt conversation with natural science almost before it begins, I asked whether there is any evidence that something like the old definition of theology as faith's quest for understanding, and something like the old idea that what theology has to understand is all things in relation to God, would prove to be more hospitable. Polkinghorne's work is just such evidence. At the same time, it also suggests something of the complexity of the issues involved in the conversation. By way of conclusion I will attempt to sum up and sort out this complexity under five heads.

III

— 1 —

This essay has been, at best, an exercise in meta-conversation. Not only is it for the most part a report, but a report of a report — of a conversation as Polkinghorne reports it. My discussion here thus stands at not one but two removes from actual conversation between science and theology. Consequently, for example, I have made use of certain technical terms from physics, such as "quantum field theory," and have said that the proper expression for the meaning of such terms is mathematical in form. Yet there are no mathematical symbols in this essay, and with unimportant exceptions neither are there any in the works of Polkinghorne on which I have drawn. Readers must not only take it on trust that I have accurately mediated Polkinghorne's statements about the quantum world; they must also take it on trust that those statements convey in English prose what can be adequately stated only in equations. But if the intelligibility of Dirac's achievement in resolving the wave-particle duality with respect to light is, as Polkinghorne maintains, a mathematical intelligibility, then one has not grasped it, at least not fully, without grasping the unity that Dirac himself grasped *as* he grasped it, that is, in mathematical terms.

The point is important because of the significance Polkinghorne attaches to "the unreasonable effectiveness of mathematics." When he speaks of the beauty, economy, and elegance of physical theory, he is speaking of qualities which he, as a mathematical physicist, can experience at first hand. But while he rightly deprecates the often misleading statements of "gee-whiz popularizers," Polkinghorne himself is caught

in a comparable dilemma. On the one hand, he rejects the naive realism that takes picturability to be the criterion of what is real, insisting
instead that what is real is what is intelligible. On the other hand, however, his "revised natural theology" hinges on a kind of intelligibility
that can be conveyed to nonmathematicians only by simplifying it.

Polkinghorne's achievement in communicating his own insights to
nonspecialist readers is, in my judgment, of a very high order. Whether
they are correct insights, though, is a judgment of a different kind, which
could properly be arrived at only on the basis of technical competence
in physics — and in philosophy and theology — equal to Polkinghorne's.
Conversation that remains at the level of *haute vulgarisation* is likely to
be misleading, and can scarcely be other than inconclusive. Theologians
who want to talk seriously with scientists need to know science, and,
especially if the science is physics, their philosophy needs to be mathematically literate. Acquiring this literacy is difficult — one of the greatest
difficulties that impede conversation at the level on which it ought to
take place if it takes place at all.

— 2 —

Still, physics is not the only science. Polkinghorne naturally gives it pride
of place in exploring the interface between theology and science-in-
general, and there can be no doubt but that twentieth-century advances
in physics have done much to reshape that interface. Nevertheless conversation with theology cannot responsibly ignore the other sciences,
which raise questions different in kind from those that are of most interest to Polkinghorne. Debate continues, to take an unfortunate example,
over the compatibility of evolutionary biology with the Christian doctrine of creation. By insisting that creation in the proper sense of the
word does not refer to temporal origin, Polkinghorne does identify the
most basic issue. Still, it is one thing to argue that creation properly
means ontological dependence, and that this dependence is evinced in
the fact that the mathematical intelligibility of quantum-level realities is
not self-explanatory. It is something else to mount a parallel argument
for realities at the level of biological life, where mathematics plays a different and less central role in scientific explanation and where, for that
reason, a different notion of non-self-explanatory intelligibility would be
required as the centerpiece of a natural theology.

This is to say that a theology which would speak seriously about "*all
things in relation to God*" would have to generalize and extend Polkinghorne's argument, which draws mainly though not exclusively on
physics, so as to include all the other natural sciences.[30] But that exi-
gence can be met only by tackling yet another philosophical problem,
the relation of the natural sciences to one another. To refer to "*the* scientific worldview" is a commonplace, but is there any such thing? Or

are there only the partial views of discrete sciences, of physics, chemistry, biology, and so on? If the sciences do form an integral whole — and Polkinghorne, for one, is thoroughly committed to the idea that they do — then some account of their wholeness is needed. And with that arises one of the most disputed questions in the philosophy of science: reductionism. Can the intelligible regularities that chemists, say, investigate be explained by applying the laws of quantum mechanics? Is biology, in similar fashion, reducible to chemistry? And so on. Even to phrase the issue in this way is to distort it, for all the same epistemological and metaphysical debates are involved as were mentioned in connection with Dodd's objections to Polkinghorne.[31] That, however, is exactly the point. If conversation between theology and science is to get past the Genesis-or-geology stage, questions about the nature of science and how the sciences exemplify it must be on the table from the first. Those questions are made all the more difficult by specialization *within* science.

— 3 —

In the previous paragraph, as earlier in this essay, epistemology and metaphysics have been spoken of in connection with science in general and physics in particular. But philosophy has as much bearing on the theological as on the scientific side of the conversation — or it has, anyhow, if one takes such a position as Polkinghorne's, which acknowledges transcendence and mystery without being wholly apophatic or content to speak of God in negations only. The philosophical difficulties inherent in making "objective" statements about God are notorious, but natural theology stands or falls with the possibility of making them, even if they can only be made in language that is analogical, incomplete, and always corrigible. To put this the other way round, the question whether objective statements can be made only by natural science, or also by other kinds of "rational discourse," theology included, is a crucial question — and a philosophical one.

Divine *action* offers a classic, and fundamental, case in point. The problem is not hard to state: it belongs ineradicably to biblical faith that God not only creates but makes a difference in the created order; but if that is so, *how* can it be so, and more especially how can it be so in the light of contemporary science? If "intelligibility is the ultimate guarantee of reality," as Polkinghorne avers, can activity within the world be predicated intelligibly of God? Is it possible to conceive divine *agency* without at the same time conceiving God as *an agent*, that is, as one component, a finite one, within the world? And would such an agent qualify as *God*? I have deliberately omitted any discussion of Polkinghorne's own understanding of divine providence, which draws on what is rather inaptly named "chaos theory." It is an admirable effort at *fides quaerens intellectum*, though not, I think, entirely successful, for reasons alluded to above. At present, however, the point is simply that "action" and "agency," like "cause," are not unambiguous terms; their meaning needs to be clarified, as does the sense in which they do, or do not, apply to God. There is a long tradition of theistic philosophy that endeavors to do just that, and as Christian theologians have learned from this tradition in the past, so too it deserves to be heard from in the conversation with natural science today. Scientists need some comprehension of its grammar and vocabulary as much as theologians need to have some comprehension of mathematical thinking. Otherwise no real conversation is possible.

— 4 —

I have credited Polkinghorne with a definite position on basic philosophical issues regarding epistemology and metaphysics, but it is well to remember that his "critical realism" is by no means the only philosophy on offer. In English-speaking discussions of science and theology today the "third partner" is quite commonly Alfred North Whitehead, whose philosophy of process, explicitly influenced by the theory of General Relativity, has a theistic component that makes it congenial to many Christian theologians. Polkinghorne, although he acknowledges on some particular points an indebtedness to process thought, rejects it on the whole, judging it (correctly) to be incompatible with both his own understanding of quantum physics and his own understanding of God.[32] Less explicit, though not less important, is his rejection of the various philosophical idealisms begotten by Kant on Newtonian mechanics. Somewhat surprisingly, he makes very little mention of the analytic schools of philosophy, though they have certainly subjected both science and theology to scrutiny. The point, however, is that each of these alternatives to Polkinghorne's "critical realism" could provide the philosophical framework which, I have argued, is necessary to a conversation between science and theology — though the conversation would in each case take a very different direction. The fact that so many respectable philosophical options exist helps to explain why it is as difficult as it is to pose, let alone answer, the questions that define theology's interface with science.

Moreover, if philosophies are many, so are theologies. The present essay has not been theologically neutral; it began by taking up a position defined in part by its difference from trends I called the existential-pastoral-spirituality and the linguistic-biblical-narrative. Neither of these trends, I suggested, is amenable to cross-disciplinary interaction with natural science; but to reject them on that ground alone would be an obvious *petitio principii*. The very question whether and how far a conversation with the sciences can be carried on depends on, among other

things, the nature of religious faith, the authority of revelation, the extent of human depravity, the significance of religious experience, and
the purpose of theological discourse. All these questions belong, traditionally, to "fundamental theology," which is so named because such
questions need to be settled before going on to speak about God and —
perhaps — about all things in relation to God. It is possible to prescind
from such questions, as I have done for purposes of this essay, but not
to ignore them. Whether they are addressed all together as prolegom-
ena, or ad hoc in the way Polkinghorne addresses them, addressed they
must be. And depending on how they are answered, a conversation between theology and science will, again, work itself out in very different
directions.

— 5 —

I have been speaking of conversation between theology and science as
involving a metaphorical minimum of one scientist, one theologian, and
one philosopher. These concluding points have so far suggested that
even if each of the three interlocutors is conversant with both the others'
specialties, their interaction will depend on *which* philosophical movement, *which* school of theology, and to some extent even *which* natural
science they represent. If all of this were not enough to convince anyone that intelligent discussion of theology in relation to science is an
extremely convoluted undertaking, there is one thing more. In this essay
I have touched, and touched only lightly, on a single Christian doctrine,
that of creation, in the relations to a single science, quantum physics,
that it stands in according to a single author. Even the closely connected
doctrine of providence has had to be left out, although Polkinghorne
gives it as much attention as he gives creation, if not more. But while
creation is in some sense presupposed by other Christian doctrines, including providence, it does not follow that treating it in the light of
contemporary science resolves, even in principle, all the issues that arise
at the interface between science and theology. The very term "natural
theology" is defined partly by way of contrast with "revealed theology."
Above and beyond "the attempt to learn something of God through the
exercise of reason and the general exploration of the world," to repeat
Polkinghorne's characterization of natural theology, Christian tradition
asserts that something has been learned of God not from the world in
general but from particular divine disclosure.

    To be sure, the distinction between truths of natural and revealed the-
ology is itself a matter of theological debate, and Polkinghorne virtually
removes it by making religious experience the source of both. But while
he does recognize that the Trinity, the incarnation, "the resurrection of
the body, and the life everlasting" — all the articles of the Christian
creed, in fact, except the one about God as Creator — cannot be under-

stood in terms of natural theology alone, he nevertheless considers that natural science has a bearing on their intelligibility. Witness his recent Gifford Lectures, published as *The Faith of a Physicist*, which follows approximately the outline of the creed. It is a vast project, far beyond the scope of an essay even to sketch. And that is my final point. Not only does the rest of the creed raise a host of new questions, but each of those questions is complicated in all the ways suggested in my first four points. There is enough material for a great many scientists, theologians, and philosophers to have a great many conversations.

Notes

1. I have discussed Lindbeck's theological isolationism in some detail in "Turning Liberalism Inside-Out," *Method: Journal of Lonergan Studies* 3, no. 2 (1985): 51–69.

2. Stephen Hawking, *A Brief History of Time* (New York: Bantam Press, 1988), 175.

3. See Edward O. Wilson, *On Human Nature* (Cambridge: Harvard University Press, 1978), 191–209.

4. John Polkinghorne, "Theological Notions of Creation and Divine Causality," in Murray Rae, Hilary Regan, and John Stenhouse, eds., *Science and Theology: Questions at the Interface* (Edinburgh: T. & T. Clark, 1994; Grand Rapids: Eerdmans, 1994), 225–37.

5. John Polkinghorne, *One World: The Interaction of Science and Theology* (London: SPCK, 1986; Princeton University Press, 1986); *Science and Creation: The Search for Understanding* (London: SPCK, 1988; Boston: Shambhala Publications, 1988); *Science and Providence: God's Interaction with the World* (London: SPCK, 1989; Boston: Shambhala Publications, 1989); *Reason and Reality: The Relationship between Science and Theology* (London: SPCK, 1991; Philadelphia: Trinity Press International, 1991).

Shortly after the Dunedin symposium, Polkinghorne delivered the 1993–94 Gifford Lectures, published as *The Faith of a Physicist: Reflections of a Bottom-Up Thinker* (Princeton, N.J.: Princeton University Press, 1994). Somewhat more popular in tone are his two most recent books, *Quarks, Chaos, and Christianity: Questions to Science and Religion* (London: SPCK, 1994) and *Serious Talk: Science and Religion in Dialogue* (Valley Forge, Pa.: Trinity Press International, 1995), which embodies the William Belden Noble Lectures that Polkinghorne delivered at Harvard University.

6. Polkinghorne, "Theological Notions," 227.

7. Jürgen Moltmann, *God in Creation* (London: SCM Press, 1985), 36; see Polkinghorne, *Science and Creation*, 5. Moltmann is clearly alluding to Rudolf Bultmann's "demythologization" program.

8. Polkinghorne, *Science and Creation* 2, 99.

9. Polkinghorne, *Reason and Reality*, 80; more extensively, *Science and Creation*, 54ff.

10. Polkinghorne, "Theological Notions," 228.

11. On theology as a "meta-science" see especially *The Faith of a Physicist*, 46.

12. Polkinghorne, "Theological Notions," 229; *Reason and Reality*, 76. Polkinghorne's presentation of this argument in *Reason and Reality* is considerably clearer than the one in "Theological Notions," which even by his own standards is telegraphic. On the nondemonstrative character of his argument see also *The Faith of a Physicist*, 41.

13. Polkinghorne, "Theological Notions," 226.

14. "Response by Jack Dodd," in *Science and Theology*, 238–46; the quotation is at 244 and the italics are Dodd's.

15. Polkinghorne, "Theological Notions," 228; see also *Reason and Reality*, 25–27 and *Science and Creation*, 70.

16. Dodd, "Response," 238.

17. Polkinghorne, "The Quantum World," in Robert J. Russell, William R. Stoeger, and George V. Coyne, eds., *Physics, Philosophy, and Theology: A Common Quest for Understanding* (Vatican City State: Vatican Observatory; Notre Dame, Ind.: University of Notre Dame Press, 1988), 333–42.

18. Polkinghorne, "Quantum World," 333.

19. Ibid., 336; compare 341.

20. Ibid., 335.

21. See *Reason and Reality*, 5–8, 10–11, 14–15, 30–31, 41–44, 51–52, 68–69, and 96–98.

22. Polkinghorne, *Reason and Reality*, 14–15.

23. Perhaps Polkinghorne's best discussion of this aspect of his epistemology appears in *The Faith of a Physicist*, 32, where he uses the metaphor of an "epistemic circle."

24. Polkinghorne, *Reason and Reality*, 55.

25. Ibid., 59.

26. Polkinghorne, "Quantum World," 334.

27. Polkinghorne, *Reason and Reality*, 51.

28. See for example the unusually (for Polkinghorne) indecisive discussion in *Science and Creation*, chap. 4, esp. 58–64. At bottom, I think, the difficulty lies in the fact that Polkinghorne finds it necessary to think of the divine nature as complex and multiple, whereas for the theological tradition that is in other respects closest to his, two of the most fundamental attributes of God are *unity* and *simplicity*. Why one should think of simplicity as more appropriately ascribed to God than complexity is, of course, a large question — basically, a philosophical one. For Polkinghorne's own assessment of the matter see especially *The Faith of a Physicist*, 54, 59–61.

29. Polkinghorne, "Theological Notions," 226. There is a somewhat different account, complementary to this one, in *Faith of a Physicist*, 74.

30. I have reported on such a generalized argument in "Philosophy, Theology, and God," in Vernon Gregson, ed., *The Desires of the Human Spirit* (New York: Paulist Press, 1989), 120–43.

31. For Polkinghorne's views on the question of reductionism, see especially *The Faith of a Physicist*, 28–29.

32. See Polkinghorne, *Science and Creation*, 56–61, 73, 82–83; *Reason and Reality*, 46–47, 86; *Science and Providence*, 14, 21, 80.

8

Spirit and Matter

An Essay in Theology, Philosophy, and the Natural Sciences

– JOHN H. WRIGHT, S.J. –

Contemporary science requires us once again to raise the question of the relationship of spirit and matter. Answers to this question are frequent in the history of Western thought. But for us today these answers are either insufficient or simply mistaken. For example, the story of the creation of Adam in the book of Genesis describes God forming the first human being out of the dust of the earth, as a potter might form a statue, and then breathing into him the breath of life. (In Hebrew the same word [*ruach*] is frequently used for "spirit" and "breath.") While this picture has rich symbolic value, it is insufficient to give any real understanding today. On the other hand, René Descartes conceived the human body as a machine and the soul or human spirit as an immaterial substance in the brain, operating through the pineal gland, and so moving the body. He was actually reviving a position of Plato rejected by Aquinas, that a human being is a soul using a body.[1] This idea may have clarity, but we rightly regard the radical dualism it places in the human being as simply mistaken.

Karl Rahner takes over Aquinas's theory of prime matter and substantial form to explain the relation of spirit and matter, and he develops it brilliantly in the context of evolution. But he does not relate this to the scientific understanding of matter. The nature of matter, he maintains, is not a scientific but a philosophical question:

> What matter is in general and on the whole, is not a question for natural science as such but a question of ontology on the basis of an existential metaphysics; such an ontology can answer this question because it already knows what spirit is and thus on the basis of this metaphysical experience of the spirit can state what the material as such is, viz. that which is closed in its individuality to the experience of the transcendence of being as such.[2]

However, for Karl Rahner, spirit and matter are indissolubly linked in the universe:

In the realm of the one and yet pluralistic reality of the world, in so far as it is distinct from God its absolutely one ground, what we call spirit and what we call matter are at least in the actual order of reality irreversibly related to one another and...together, in spite of their differences, they constitute the one reality of the world, and they do not exist merely one beside the other as if enclosed merely by an empty space.[3]

Spirit, he tells us, is characterized by "being-conscious-of-itself, knowledge, freedom and transcendence towards God."[4] Spirit, then, means the inner principle of human life manifested in self-conscious intelligent, free activity.

Karl Rahner's view that science is unable to tell us the nature of matter may well be the case, but the issue that concerns us here is more than a question of relating spirit and matter philosophically. We wish to consider what science tells us about the structure of matter (if not its metaphysical nature), and to see how there is room here for the coming-to-be and the activity of spirit, as we experience this relationship in our own conscious awareness. How can we today conceive the relationship of spirit and matter in a way that makes sense to us, with our background of scientific understanding?

The Structure and Evolution of Matter

In looking at matter we have to go beyond both a commonsense view of matter and earlier scientific views as well:

In attempts to understand the mind-matter connection it is usually assumed that the idea of matter used in Newtonian mechanics can be applied to the internal workings of a brain. However, that venerable concept does not extrapolate from the domain of planets and falling apples to the realm of the subtle chemical processes occurring in the tissues of human brains. Indeed, the classical idea of matter is logically incompatible with the nature of various processes that are essential to the functioning of brains. To achieve logical coherence one must employ a framework that accommodates these crucial processes. A quantum framework must be used in principle.[5]

Matter, thus, may not simply be regarded as the stuff out of which chairs and apples, oceans and planets, etc. are made — what fills Newtonian space. Matter, rather, in the present view of science, must be seen as many-leveled structures of mass/energy particles. The search for the most fundamental particles has most recently ended with "quarks." There are said to be six of them. They are never found existing by themselves freely, but always as parts of the basic particles of atomic nuclei: protons and neutrons, or *hadrons*. There are, in addition, *leptons,* electrons which orbit the nuclei of atoms. These particles unite in certain conditions to form atoms of different kinds. The periodic table of the elements gives the number of atoms naturally occurring in the universe.[6] The history of their formation is the story of the evolution of the universe.[7] Atoms themselves unite to form molecules, a molecule being "a stable configuration of atomic nuclei and electrons bound together by electrostatic and electromagnetic forces. It is the simplest structural unit that displays the characteristic physical and chemical properties of a compound."[8]

We note, then, that successive constructions of particles yield more complex compounds. These resulting compounds function as units, with properties and characteristics that are not simply deducible from the constituent parts. The unified whole is somehow determining by a so-called "downward causation" how its parts are to function within the whole that has been formed.[9]

The complexification of matter proceeds, at least on planet earth, to the formation of living things. Viruses are on the border between living and nonliving things, because they have no cell wall and no nucleus in the ordinary sense. They are enormously complex molecules that multiply within true cells. Living things are first of all single cells, then colonies of single cells, and finally multicellular or organic beings, in which different cells have different functions for the benefit of the whole complex.

Plants are distinguished by their ability to capture the energy of sunlight directly into their own structures as they elaborate their cellular development from the surrounding earth and air and water. Animals are nourished from the molecules elaborated by plants or other animals.

The Emergence and Unity of the Conscious Subject

At the level of animals conscious sensation makes its appearance. As we human beings experience consciousness in ourselves, so we judge that animals likewise have consciousness; for they have eyes, ears, and other external senses that seem to function in the same way ours do. They see and hear, and are aware of doing so. This fact enables us to raise a question and propose an answer about the kind of unity found in these enormously complex things and then to extrapolate the answer downward to things lower on the evolutionary scale. Is a conscious animal fundamentally one being or an aggregate of many beings? This is not a scientific but a philosophical question, since "being" is not a category of scientific explanation.[10]

Things may combine in a purely external fashion, as when stones are heaped together. A heap of stones is at least as many beings as there are stones. The same is true of anything made of parts that are ordered together from without, as in the case of a machine. Each part simply does what it otherwise does outside the machine; but now in a particular context these activities are coordinated to achieve a special result. Gasoline, for example, explodes inside a cylinder and moves a piston, which moves wheels, which move an automobile. All this order is outside the parts, which as beings remain separate and distinct from one another.

This kind of unity is inadequate to account for the phenomenon of sense consciousness, for three factors are required for this consciousness, and when they are present consciousness is present:

1. The first requirement is that there be some kind of responsive activity to a stimulus of some kind. By "responsive activity" I mean that the conscious subject is not simply passively receiving some influence or other, but is actively responding to that influence. The responsive activity in question may be quite different from the kind of influence that stimulates it, but, generally at least, the response differs as the stimulus differs.

2. The second factor is that there be a further responsive activity to the initial responsive activity. It is necessary to sense one's sensing. For example, it is not enough that an eye respond to light; the brain must somehow further respond to the eye's response. (Sometimes infants are born without a cerebral cortex and die within days. They may have external senses that respond to stimuli, but there is no consciousness.) From this we see that there can be different kinds of consciousness as there can be different kinds of initial responsive activity. Thus the conscious experience of seeing is different from hearing or tasting or smelling, etc.

3. The third factor (and here the matter becomes unavoidably philosophical) is that both responses must belong to the same subject, to the same being, to the same ontological unit. If the eye and the brain were actually different "beings" rather than parts of one total being, then there would be no consciousness. The eye would respond to light, and the brain would respond to the eye's response, but there would be no consciously seeing subject. One and the same subject must both see light and perceive its own seeing.

What does it mean to say that the conscious knower is one being? This, as we observed, is not a scientific question, but a philosophical one. To call a thing a being is to designate what it is most fundamentally. As a being a thing is, and is actually one, i.e., undivided in itself as being, and divided from all other beings — though not unrelated to them. It is said to be per se one: in and through itself it is a single unity. If it were not one being, it would be many beings. This is the kind of unity required to have a conscious knowing subject: that one and the same subject both know and (at least implicitly) know its own knowing.

Furthermore, the unity of the subject is manifested by its capacity to compare the different conscious experiences. If one being sees and another being hears there would be no way to know that seeing is really different from hearing as a conscious phenomenon, though perhaps a kind of external test might be set up on the basis of different stimuli and different neural responses. But in our actual experience the comparison is made within the unity of the conscious subject.

Distinctively Human Conscious Activity

This then poses still another question: what is distinctive of human consciousness, i.e., of intellectual consciousness as distinct from sense consciousness? What is the responsive activity that constitutes "intelligence?" If the eye perceives color and the ear perceives sound (where "perceives" means "receives and actively responds to") what does intelligence perceive?

Most simply, intelligence perceives being, reality, actuality. It seems to me it does this in three ongoing acts: (1) The radical act of intelligence is to affirm the reality of what is given in consciousness: "Being is." I call this a synoptic judgment: a comprehensive affirmation of being or reality without yet analyzing *what* is given in consciousness. The affirmation is made spontaneously, without distinguishing either subject and object, or variety within the object. It constitutes the background and foundation for all intellectual activity. (2) The second act of intelligence is to distinguish differences within what is affirmed in the synoptic judgment: to recognize the difference between subject and object and that within the object this is not that. This activity is enormously complex and goes on constantly within the prior comprehensive activity. (3) A third kind of activity is synthetic, interrelating the aspects or things that the second, analytic activity has distinguished or discriminated. Here the endeavor is to achieve in synthesis all that synopsis has already affirmed. It involves comparison and reasoning of various sorts.

It seems to me that all intellectual activity is an elaboration and interplay of these three kinds of activity: the first is the primitive, foundational judgment of existence; the second is the analytical judgment of difference and diversity; the third is the elaboration and affirmation of the relations which bind together what has been discriminated. (Every sentence is an instance of this synthetic activity, wherein I affirm a number of diversities in relation to one another in some sort of unity.)

Finally, we may note that as intellectual consciousness is concerned directly with the awareness of being as such, of what it means to be actual or real, it includes all that the senses perceive under their special aspects (color, sound, etc.) but precisely now as being, as real. The same ontological subject knows both by way of intelligence and by way of the senses, and it is from the senses that the intelligence derives its content, i.e., what it knows, though not the way it knows it: "Nothing is in the intellect that was not previously in the senses (except the intellect itself)."

Intellectual consciousness also is concerned about modalities of being: about possibility, necessity, impossibility, and contingency. The knowledge of the senses does not itself extend to these modalities, though intellect can in some ways perceive them in the data of the senses.

Following upon the activity of conscious knowing, there is the activity of conscious willing, of desiring and choosing. We should distinguish here two kinds of choice. Choice is always a decisive preferring of one way of acting among a number of possible ways of acting, and in this sense is "free," not necessary. At the human level, we not only freely choose, but we freely choose to freely choose. This means that our choice not only concerns what we are to do, but ourselves as doing it. Just as human beings not only know, but explicitly know that they know, so they not only choose a certain way of acting, but choose to be choosing that way of acting. This kind of free choice makes us personally responsible for our free choices, for it reaches into our innermost subjectivity in choosing so that we choose ourselves as choosing. Other things may choose freely, with more or less spontaneity, what they are to do, but they do not choose themselves choosing it. Just as they know, but do not explicitly know that they know, so they choose, but do not choose to choose.

Levels of Being

These distinctions we have been making between animal and human ways of being conscious call attention to "levels of being." Some beings as such are higher than other beings. It is not just that beings are different from one another; some are better or superior or fuller beings. A being that knows not only by way of sensation, but also by way of intelligence is on a higher level than one that knows only by sensation. This is not just a question of an accumulation of several ways of knowing, or of other various activities, but it is also a question of the quality of the activity itself. Intellectual activity of itself is universal, comprehensive, and transcendental. Because it does not know under a particular aspect like sound or color, but under the aspect of being, anything that is or can be is a possible object of human knowing. Furthermore, the human mind is able to conceive and comprehend in some way all finite things as one universe. Finally, the human mind can go beyond whatever it now knows to seek through questions and exploration what may account for what it knows.

It seems reasonable to extend downward through other living and nonliving things the insight into the ontological unity of the subjects of action. Just as each human and animal is one being (as revealed through consciousness), we may suppose that each plant acting as a unity is also one being, and that each microbe is one being, and likewise each separately functioning molecule, each free atom, and even each free nucleus, proton, neutron, and electron. Wherever a distinct unity of distinctive action is found, there is found a distinct unity of being.

From the standpoint of empirical sciences it is enough to distinguish these levels of being simply by their differences in complexity. The kind and degree of complexification are sufficient to mark higher and lower levels of being. But structural complexity is not a philosophical or metaphysical way of indicating a level of being. We must be able to speak about what intrinsically makes a thing be what it is, and be on a certain level of ontological reality. The traditional language speaks here of "essence." Each being has its own essence. In the case of material essences it is customary to designate the determining, unifying principle of the level of ontological reality as "substantial form." What you name it is secondary to the need to recognize that there are different levels of being, and that there is some intrinsic reason in a thing why it is what is. A person unaccustomed to philosophical analysis, as distinct from scientific analysis may find this strange, but this philosophical analysis does not stand in contradiction to the scientific analysis and is required by philosophical reflection in terms of being.

It may well be that the scientific notion of "field" can be helpful here. Just as "space tells a body how to move and a body tells space how to curve," so a field tells objects how to arrange themselves and the objects configure the nature of the field. The field constituted by the forces associated with an atom or a molecule, including the DNA molecule, thus unifies the objects in space and manifests the substantial form of the object, if it is not itself this form. This is an instance of downward causation. We will explore below somewhat more in detail how this unification takes place.

Evolution of Matter and Spirit

For the present we need to ask how these successively higher levels of being come about through the evolutionary process. This is a particularly urgent question, since we will say that spiritual form at the human level itself is somehow emergent from this process. Karl Rahner observed:

> Since ... the spirit cannot be simply regarded as the immanent product of material development and evolution, it originates from a new creative initiative of God; this is an absolutely indisputable fact for a theist with regard to the world as a whole and hence does not present any special difficulties even as a new and absolutely original initiative.
>
> Yet, for a Christian, the question now posed [whether the development of matter contributes to the coming-to-be of spirit] need not be decided in

the negative as quickly as it appears to have been from what we have just said. First of all, it is not at all as straightforward even for the Christian understanding of the relationship between God and the world as already built up by Thomas Aquinas in his teaching that God as creator of the material world is the transcendental ground of everything but not the categorial and spatio-temporally localisable cause for a determined individual thing and indeed is seen to be working rather through "secondary causes" in this respect. There are difficulties even for this Christian understanding if the coming into existence of the individual spiritual souls at particular points in space and time were in no way the result of the world and of its natural development due to secondary causes and if, as it were, God's creative activity could be grasped *in vacuo* and in a "worldless" sense so that God's causality would be an activity in the world *beside* other activity of creatures, instead of it being the ground of all the activity of creatures.[11]

From an external point of view the evolution of matter involves three fundamental factors: random association of particles, the stable unity of some of these associations, and, underlying the process, the tendency of matter to ever greater complexity, to form these associations. It is this third element which an adapted Darwinism does not explicitly take into account, but where theology perceives the abiding causality of God as the transcendental ground of being, directing matter to its goal as the sustaining cause of its reality. It is of the nature of matter to form more complex unities, and insofar as these new unities represent higher levels of being, the causality adequate to the effect is not simply the material agents considered in themselves, but as instruments of the transcendent causality of God sustaining and moving all things. We are not describing a "God of the gaps," invoked to explain some mysterious effect that we cannot otherwise account for; rather we are speaking of the one who explains why there is something rather than nothing at all, and why this evolving world exists rather than some other conceivable reality.

The move toward greater external complexity of matter is accompanied by a more intense and centered within. This is the essential insight of Teilhard de Chardin in his account of evolution: "The degree of concentration of a consciousness varies in inverse ratio to the *simplicity* of the material compound lined by it."[12] Teilhard used "consciousness" here in an extended sense, to designate all interiority, all centeredness — from that within the smallest enduring particle of matter, up to the highest complex unity. The increasing concentration of this consciousness leads to the appearance of sense awareness in animals and finally to intellectual self-consciousness in human beings. In the human brain we encounter the most complex arrangement of matter in the universe.[13] Here the center within is "spirit."

In the process of this complexification we perceive not simply the agency of material particles, but, as Rahner observed, the causality of

one who is "the transcendental ground of everything but not the categorial and spatio-temporally localisable cause for a determined individual
thing." At a certain point in this complexifying process a condition is
reached where the unified complexity itself requires for its functioning
a centering unity that reflects perfectly upon itself, that knows explicitly
that it knows, and that wills itself willing; the human spirit comes to be,
in some way "the result of the world and of its natural development due
to secondary causes."

The Relation of Spirit and Matter

How does this field or substantial form affect the constituent energy/
mass particles? How does it make them into "one being"? Clearly,
external arrangement is an insufficient explanation. No doubt the arrangement of the particles in their spatial relations to one another is
significant; but that does not explain the new characteristics found at
the higher levels. Most of all, it does not explain the unity of consciousness at the animal and human levels. Most succinctly, then, form or field
makes the parts into one being by communicating an inner unified teleology, an interior orientation to a single immediate end of activity. All
the constituent particles have, from within the depths of their essential
reality, the same immediate and specifying goal.

Raising the question of teleology at this point may seem an unnecessary digression, but it lies at the heart of the matter. To a large extent
the primary difficulty in relating the physical sciences to philosophy and
theology arises from the question of teleology. Since the time of Francis Bacon and René Descartes the physical sciences have employed a
method that in principle excludes final causality or purpose as a source
of explanation or understanding. As a deliberate limitation of method,
this is altogether legitimate. To offer explanations of events and observations simply in terms of agents and the matter they act upon is a
justifiable procedure that yields a particular kind of understanding.

This kind of science has produced remarkable results, as we can see
around us; but in the minds of some persons the success of the method
seems to justify the elimination of all purpose or goal from the universe.
The method becomes in this way a metaphysics. This leap from method
to metaphysics is really a leap of nonteleological faith: without proof
one affirms the nonexistence of purpose. Jacques Monod clearly but unwittingly described this faith when he wrote about the development of
the modern scientific method in contrast to earlier efforts:

> To be sure, neither reason, nor logic, nor observation, nor even the idea of
> their systematic confrontation had been ignored by Descartes' predeces-
> sors. But science as we understand it today could not have been developed
> upon these foundations alone. It required the unbending stricture implicit

in the postulate of objectivity — ironclad, pure, *forever indemonstrable* [emphasis added]. For it is obviously impossible to imagine an experiment which could prove the *nonexistence* anywhere in nature of a purpose, of a pursued end.[14]

Various approaches to teleology are possible. We here continue the exploration of consciousness as a way to deal with it. We note that human beings consciously act for a goal or purpose. They intend to bring about certain results by the actions they perform. They do not simply observe what they do as another happening in the world; they know themselves as actively intending to effect something by what they do. Furthermore, at a prior level, they are conscious of choosing between finalities or purposes. They experience within themselves the possibility of acting in different ways to bring about different results. They choose among these ways of acting, and their choice is based upon purpose or goal.

The notion of purpose, thus, arises directly out of the conscious human experience of acting for an end and of choosing means to an end. We observe ourselves as intending some goal or purpose, like going on a trip, writing a book, or ordering a meal. In view of this purpose we choose some action that we perceive as conducive to the end. We act purposefully to achieve the goal we intend.

It is important to note two things about this: (1) we do not *create* the notion of purpose by an act of constructive imagination, rather we *discover* it embedded in conscious, human activity; and (2) we do this as part of the universe, brought forth by the evolutionary process.

1. We discover purpose embedded in human activity in two ways. First of all we perceive it in the different possible courses of action that we see lie open before us, in our power to perform them. At any given moment we experience an interior directedness to many different possible goals embodied in many different actions that we recognize to be in our power to perform. Secondly we experience ourselves as choosing among them: we decide which of the many possible goals now drawing us will be the actual goal to which we direct our activity. We experience ourselves as freely intending a particular good.

2. We do this as part of the universe, brought forth by the evolutionary process. We are beings who act deliberately and consciously for purposes, because when matter is organized in this very complex way with emergent self-consciousness and freedom to choose, it includes this awareness of a drive to a goal with the ability to choose among several possible alternative ways of reaching the goal. We are dealing with a way of acting that belongs to a portion of organized matter in the world, the human organism. *How* does this happen? If prior to the evolutionary emergence of human beings in the world finality or purpose

simply did not exist, the emergence of human beings would not itself produce directedness in action. For the human being knows but does not produce the directedness of its own possible actions. Likewise, it knows that it can make use of but not create the directedness of the activities of the world around it.

We may affirm then that a given acting cause (or combination of causes) does as a matter of fact *tend* to bring about a certain definite result. There is within activity as such a tendency to do one thing rather than another. It is not just happenstance that a particular activity yields a particular result. There is within a particular acting cause a *tendency* to act one way rather than another, and within the action there is the *tendency* or "intention" (in the radical and literal sense of word), to produce one particular concrete result rather than another. The present disposition of acting things anticipates the future. This is the radical meaning of acting for a purpose or goal.

This reflection upon teleology leads to the answer to two questions: how does the superior form or field influence matter, and how does the human choice affect the body's activity? The answer in both cases is the same: by determining from within the indeterminate finality of the constituent parts. Henry Stapp's account of the relation of brain activity to conscious human choice points to this answer in different words:

> If one now considers this system [of neuron patterns] (or actually a vastly more complex system based on the same principle of mutually exclusive self-sustaining patterns) to be embedded in the much larger structure provided by the whole brain, and recalls that the full representation of the brain provided by contemporary physical theory gives merely a representation of tendencies for responses, then the state of the brain, as represented by contemporary physics, will, prior to the excitation of one of these self-sustaining but mutually exclusive patterns, represent only the tendencies for the excitations of the various alternative patterns. The choice of which of these patterns is activated is, according to the contemporary laws of physics, a matter of pure chance.
>
> The basic idea of the present psychophysical theory is to identify the selection of one of these mutually exclusive self-sustaining patterns of neural excitations as the image in the physical world, as represented by quantum theory, of a creative act from the realm of human consciousness.[15]

When we call the inner principle of intelligent human life "spirit," we are differentiating it from matter, but simultaneously relating it to matter inextricably. Matter and spirit are more alike than they are different. As Rahner observed:

> What we call material has always been seen, at least in Thomistic philosophy, as a limited and in a sense "frozen" spirit, as limited being whose being as such, i.e., prescinding from the real negativity and limitation of this being (commonly called *materia prima,* which of itself does

not signify any positive reality), is exactly the same being which outside such a limitation means being-conscious-of-itself, knowledge, freedom and transcendence towards God.[16]

What matter and spirit share besides being itself is intentionality, the directedness of their activities to an end. The end intended by spiritual activity ultimately transcends all particular finite goods and aims radically at the good in whose reality the whole universe of being participates. The end intended by material activity is a particular concrete goal. But in both cases there is the intentionality of an end. The unifying power of spiritual intentionality can subsume into itself the intentionalities of the material components and thus draw them into the unity of the one being, which is then a compound of the spiritual and material. The spiritual activity of responsible, free choice is ultimately universal and comprehensive, able to communicate its own intentionalities to the material dimensions of the human being, and to grasp and intend the more particular goals that material activities intend. Thus it is able to direct from within some actions that are characteristically material; I can consciously and freely choose to move my hands, to walk, to speak aloud.

The spiritual activities of the human spirit are activities concerned with "being," without the limitations of particularity and concreteness characteristic of material activity. There is here a knowing that reflects perfectly upon the knower and reaches out to grasp the universe in one idea; a willing that not only chooses freely between possible courses of action but chooses the willer as choosing and opens out to affirm all that is valuable and good; an awareness that grasps one's own self-identity and can experience the absolute horizon of being communicating itself in loving and personal concern; a questioning that not only seeks the answers to particular problems but transcends the whole mystery of the existing universe to seek a ground and goal of all that is. All these activities point to a reality within the human person that is not reducible to the material with which it is intimately joined in the unity of one being. The inner principle of human identity that lies at the root of these spiritual activities has its center, its supporting basis of being and operations, not in the matter that it is unifying, but rather in its own subsistent reality by which it communicates unity and being to the matter with which it forms one substance. This is the relation of spirit and matter as we find them present in the human being and revealed in human consciousness.

Notes

1. *Summa Contra Gentiles,* Lib. 1, Cap. 57: "Positio Platonis de unione animae intellectualis ad corpus."

2. Karl Rahner, "Unity of Spirit and Matter in Christian Faith," *Theological Investigations* 4 (New York: Crossroad, 1982), 162.

3. Ibid., 166.

4. Ibid., 168.

5. Henry P. Stapp, *Mind, Matter, and Quantum Mechanics* (Berlin: Springer-Verlag, 1993), 3.

6. James Trefil reports on modern physical theory in its relation to the universe in "The New Physics and the Universe," reproduced in Timothy Ferris, ed., *The World Treasury of Physics, Astronomy, and Mathematics* (Boston: Little, Brown and Company, 1991), 365–71.

7. For a fine popular presentation of recent scientific views on matter, see George Ellis, *Before the Beginning: Cosmology Explained* (London, New York: Boyars/Bowerdean, 1993), esp. part 2, "The Scientific Understanding," 22–88.

8. *Reader's Digest Illustrated Encyclopedic Dictionary* (Pleasantville, N.Y.: Reader's Digest Association, 1987), 2:1093.

9. Holmes Rolston, III discusses several aspects of downward causation in *Science and Religion: A Critical Survey* (Philadelphia: Temple University Press, 1987), esp. 53, 89–90.

10. An excellent exploration of this question may be found in Richard J. Connell, *Substance and Modern Science* (Houston: Center for Thomistic Studies, 1988).

11. Ibid., 173.

12. Pierre Teilhard de Chardin, *The Phenomenon of Man,* 2d ed. (New York: Harper and Row, 1965), 60.

13. Joel L. Swerdlow, observes: "The human brain, with its many billions of cells, is the most complex object in the known universe" ("Quiet Miracles of the Brain," *National Geographic* 187 [June 1995]: 6).

14. Jacques Monod, *Chance and Necessity: An Essay on the Natural Philosophy of Modern Biology* (New York: Knopf, 1971), 21

15. Stapp, *Mind, Matter, and Quantum Mechanics,* 101–2.

16. Rahner as cited in ibid., 168.

9

Evolutionary Contingency
and Cosmic Purpose

– ERNAN McMULLIN –

Does the contingency of the evolutionary account of origins, particularly of human origins, make it more difficult to see the universe as the work of a Creator? Does it, effectively, rule out purpose at the cosmic level and leave us in a world from which religious meaning has departed? Some would answer yes to both questions. It has always been clear that chance played an important part in the Darwinian theory. But it seems easier, somehow, to construe evolution as God's mode of bringing about the divine ends when evolution itself is understood as a process whose general shape could be anticipated in advance, and could thus be relied on in the carrying out of the divine plan. The emphasis on the contingency of evolutionary outcomes on the part of writers like Monod and Gould could easily suggest that ours is a universe on whose processes purpose *could* not be imposed, not even by a Creator.

In this essay, I first want to outline two very different understandings of evolution. According to one, evolution is, in broad outline at least, predictable, given the right conditions; natural selection works in a more or less lawlike way to bring about increasing complexity. According to the other view, evolution is in no way predictable; contingency limits the operations of selection so heavily that outcomes simply cannot be anticipated, even in the most general way. One way in which the contingency of the evolutionary account of human origins might be countered from the theistic point of view would be to suppose that God "intervened," in one sense or another of that inadequate term, to bring about the appearance of humanity. But there is another alternative. In the final section of the essay, I sketch the traditional theological doctrine of God's eternity in order to decide whether, according to this account, the contingency of evolutionary processes need have the negative import often claimed for it in regard to cosmic purpose. If the Creator is understood to escape the limits imposed by temporality, would radical contingency still render evolutionary outcomes impervious to the Creator's purposes?

Predicting Evolution

You may not be familiar with the "extraterrestrial civilization equation" which was first formulated by radio-astronomer Frank Drake back in the 1960s. Drake and some of his colleagues were convinced that the powerful new technology of the radio telescope ought to be utilized in a systematic effort to discover whether radio messages were being beamed in our direction by extraterrestrial civilizations sufficiently advanced to generate such signals. To justify devoting precious time on these expensive instruments to such a quest it was crucial to estimate how likely it was that such civilizations existed, and if so, in what numbers. How likely would it be that one lay within, say, twenty light years of us? Even with one that close, the forty-year interval between message and response would make for slow dialogue!

At a conference on extraterrestrial intelligence sponsored by the National Academy of Sciences in 1961, Drake proposed the following equation:

$$N = R \, F_p \, N_e \, F_l \, F_i \, F_c \, L$$

N is the number of civilizations in our galaxy with both the capacity and the interest for interstellar communication. R is the mean rate per year of star formation averaged over the lifetime of the galaxy; F_p is the fraction of stars with planetary systems; N_e is the mean number of planets in such systems with environments favorable for the origin of life; F_l is the fraction of such planets on which life does develop; F_i is the fraction of these planets on which intelligent life with manipulative abilities arises during the lifetime of the local sun; F_c is the fraction of these latter planets that give rise to an advanced technical civilization; and L is the mean lifetime of such a civilization.[1]

It might seem as though this does not get us far toward calculating the value of N, given that there are seven unknown quantities on the other side of the equation. But Drake, and following him Carl Sagan, were not daunted by this challenge and proceeded to give a rough estimate for each of the seven. Sagan's figures for these are: 10, 1, 1, 1, 10^{-1}, 10^{-1}, for the first six. L gave him more trouble. Would a technical civilization quickly destroy itself so that its mean lifetime might be no more than one hundred years? Or would it control its impulses to violence and settle into a stable mode of existence that could last as long as the planet does ($>10^8$ years)? The first value of L would imply that N would be of the order of only 10, the second that N would be $>10^7$. As a compromise, Sagan settled on 10^6 as a reasonable estimate of the number of advanced technical civilizations in our galaxy. And this figure thereupon attained a certain status in the Extra-Terrestrial Intelligence (ETI) literature.[2]

There is obviously much that one could say about this rather carefree calculation.[3] But my interest here lies in Sagan's understanding of biological evolution as a process that, given the right environment, will necessarily occur and in the course of time necessarily give rise to intelligence. Without some such assumption, a value for N could not be estimated, not even in the roughest way. This way of understanding the operation of natural selection has, indeed, been a fairly common one. Textbook presentations of Darwinian theory often make it seem like a simple consequence of natural selection in operation: heritable variations that favor differential survival of descendants will tend to spread in the population. There may be additional complications involving geographical isolation, environmental change, and the like, but the impression is of a gradual but steady drift toward greater complexity. Organic structures become more complex as new organs develop and old ones find new uses. Intelligence itself, with the enormous advantage it confers in terms of survival and propagation, may then seem an almost inevitable development, if the time-scale be generous enough.

This "upward and onward" view of the action of evolution finds some support in the text of *The Origin of Species* itself:

> Natural selection acts, as we have seen, exclusively by the presentation and accumulation of variations which are beneficial under the organic and inorganic conditions of life to which each creature is at each successive period exposed. The ultimate result will be that each creature will tend to become more and more improved in relation to its conditions of life. This improvement will, I think, inevitably lead to the gradual advancement of the organization of the greater number of living beings throughout the world.[4]

But it was among philosophers, perhaps, that this view found warmest welcome, among those at least, who regarded evolution as the key to their cosmology and to their philosophy generally. Herbert Spencer formulated a "law" of evolution that would, he believed, hold not only for living things but for the physical world generally. Organic structure tends to become more and more differentiated over time, with new forms of integration constantly appearing. Following Lamarck, he maintained that the use or disuse of an organ could lead to hereditable changes of function. Later philosophers like Lloyd Morgan, Samuel Alexander, and Henri Bergson proposed theories of evolution that departed even more from the Darwinian norm than did Spencer's, while agreeing that evolution is a relatively steady and progressive process.

It is notable that those philosophers who have represented evolution in strongly progressivist terms have as a rule (Spencer would be an obvious exception) seen evolution as God's mode of action in the world. This conjunction finds its most striking expression, perhaps, in the work of Pierre Teilhard de Chardin. He sought an explanation for the steady "complexification" he found in the fossil record of life in a "psychic" or "radial" energy that operated directively, unlike the "tangential" energies treated in physics and chemistry. Though he allows for a degree of "groping" along the way, evolution is for him "a grand orthogenesis of everything living toward a higher degree of immanent spontaneity," "a spiral which springs upwards as it turns. From one zoological layer to another, *something is carried over: it grows, jerkily, but ceaselessly and in a constant direction.*"[5] So steady, indeed, in his view has the upward curve been that he felt entitled to extend it into the far future to an Omega Point where consciousness will finally be fully realized, a Final Cause in which an explanation will be found for the entire course of evolution that inexorably led in its direction.

Few other evolutionary philosophers were quite so confidently orthogenetic in their understanding of the evolutionary process. But philosophers, like the physicists and earth scientists who compute the likelihood of intelligent life elsewhere in the universe, have been on the whole more likely than biologists to see the operation of evolution in terms of *law*, of a force analogous to Newtonian gravity that relentlessly alters the composition of the gene-pool to create more and more complex organisms. In this understanding, evolutionary theory becomes a predictive resource and not just an explanation for the radiation of living forms in times past.

The Contingency of Evolution

Those who shaped the "new synthesis" in evolutionary biology over the past half century were never comfortable with the predictive uses of evolutionary theory by exobiologists and others, and were flatly opposed to orthogenesis in any shape or form. Ernst Mayr and Theodosius Dobzhansky were among those who expressed their skepticism about this way of understanding evolutionary modes of explanation. The most outspoken critic was, perhaps, George Gaylord Simpson, who in *This View of Life* developed an extended polemic against the assumptions underlying the predictivist account. He emphasized, in particular, the fundamental differences between such nonhistorical natural sciences as physics and chemistry and the historical sciences: geology, paleontology, and evolutionary biology. The latter deal with unique events for which the notions of law applicable in physics simply do not work. The complexity of the interactions between environment and gene-change is so great that any attempt to abstract "trends" or "tendencies" is bound to fail. "There is direction, but it wavers, and apparently random effects also occur."[6]

In *Chance and Necessity* (1971), Jacques Monod celebrated the decisive role of chance in evolution. Since mutations in DNA:

constitute the *only* possible source of modifications in the genetic text, itself, the *sole* repository of the organism's hereditary structures, it necessarily follows that chance *alone* is at the source of every innovation, of all creation in the biosphere. Pure chance, absolutely free but blind, at the very root of the stupendous edifice of evolution: this central concept of modern biology is no longer one among other possible or even conceivable hypotheses. It is today the *sole* conceivable hypothesis.[7]

Mutations are "chance" events for him in two different senses. First, they represent the convergence of previously unrelated causal chains: second, they are quantum events and hence essentially unpredictable. The course of evolution is thus itself unpredictable in detail. Yet despite the far-reaching consequences that Monod draws from this primacy of chance in the story of evolution (losing our "necessary place in nature's scheme" condemns us to "a frozen universe of solitude"[8]), he is still willing to allow that evolution follows a "generally progressive course," that its general direction is "upward," that an initial commitment in particular groups to a certain kind of behavior "commits the species irrevocably in the direction of a continuous perfecting of the structures and performances this behavior needs for its support."[9] So the operation of natural selection seems to restore a fair degree of directionality, and even of progress, to the course of evolution after all.

Stephen Jay Gould takes a much stronger line regarding the contingency of evolutionary change. He will have no truck with "upward courses" or "trends," or with predictability of even the most modest kind. And his emphasis is not on the randomness either of the mutations that afford the material for natural selection nor of the genetic drift in founder populations. Rather, it is on the lack, in general, of connection between the multiple lines of causality that affect singular historical events, such as changes in the gene composition of a population.

In his popular essays, he returns over and again to the flexibility of the evolutionary process that makes it something other than simple selectionist accounts would lead one to expect. In the title essay of *Eight Little Piggies*, he argues that the pentadactyl limb we share with so many other mammalian species "just happens to be." It ought not necessarily be taken to testify to some intrinsic adaptive advantage of five, as against some other number, of digits; the earliest tetrapods, in fact, had seven or eight digits. Rather, the number may derive from:

> the complex, unrepeatable, and unpredictable events of history. We are trained to think that the "hard science" models of quantification, experimentation, and replication are inherently superior and exclusively canonical, so that any other set of techniques can pale by comparison. But historical science proceeds by reconstructing a set of contingent events, explaining in retrospect what could not have been predicted beforehand. . . . Contingency is rich and fascinating; it embodies an exquisite tension be-

tween the power of individuals to modify history and the intelligible limits set by laws of nature. The details of individual and species's lives are not mere frills, without power to shape the large-scale course of events, but particulars that can alter entire futures, profoundly and forever.[10]

The nature of history and of historical science is the theme around which *Wonderful Life,* his lively account of the successive and conflicting interpretations of the Cambrian fauna found in the Burgess shale, is organized. He has long been a critic of the gradualism of the traditional Darwinian account of the operation of natural selection, urging instead a "punctuated equilibrium" in which long periods of stasis, when species remain more or less unchanged, are interspersed with moments of relatively sudden speciation.[11] In this ambitious work, he reconstructs the extraordinary original flowering of the major phyla of nearly all modern animal groups within a geologically (and biologically) brief interval of a few million years during the Cambrian period, beginning around 570 million years ago. What excites Gould most about the "Cambrian explosion," as it has been called, is not just the fact that the phyla appeared over such a relatively brief time nor that no new phyla have appeared since, but that the vast majority of the arthropod "ground-plans" found in the Burgess shale have no modern representatives. Put in another way, of the twenty-five or so diverse anatomical designs found in the shale, any one of which *could*, in Gould's view, have served as ancestor for a distinct phylum, only four survived the Cambrian period and gave rise to the modern animal phyla. It is this decimation of phylum-candidates, this "lottery" as he terms it, that Gould sees as testimony to the effects of historical contingency. The conventional response, of course, would be that the four surviving phyla were in some way better adapted for changing environmental conditions. Gould regards this as implausible. But even if this *were* to have been the case, under a different environmental scenario the list of survivors (he claims) would have been quite different. And everything that came later would then have taken a quite different direction.

Gould's emphasis on extinctions, particularly the great extinctions of life that marked the end of the Permian period, when up to 96 percent of marine species died off, and of the Cretaceous, when the dinosaurs vanished, is in some ways reminiscent of the catastrophism that enlivened geological debate two centuries ago. His claim is that in such episodes natural selection of the usual sort would cease to operate; it would in large measure be a matter of luck which among all the existing species would survive to propagate themselves in a depopulated world. Furthermore, the causes of such massive extinctions are a matter of chance, relative to the prior history of the affected populations. And so he concludes: "Since dinosaurs were not moving toward markedly

larger brains, and since such a prospect may lie outside the capabili-
ties of reptilian design, we must assume that consciousness would not
have evolved on our planet if a cosmic catastrophe had not claimed the
dinosaurs as victims."[12]

The strength of Gould's case lies in his insistence on the importance
of the web of necessary conditions in any explanation of a complex historical event, conditions, that is, in whose absence the outcome would
have been different, perhaps altogether different. One specific source of
contingency to which he often returns is the constraint set on possible
adaptive lines of development in a particular population by the avail-
ability in some corner of that population, for quite other reasons, of the
appropriate anatomical framework for that development. Thus, one obscure group (lungfish/coelocanth) belonging to the vast domain of fish
species in the Devonian period happened to have the sort of skeleton
that would permit the development of limbs, thus allowing locomotion
on land. Had those species not been present, as they might well not
have been, Gould remarks, amphibians could not have invaded the land,
which in that event might still be inhabited by insects only.[13]

Few have pushed the theme of contingency as far as Gould has done;
others have found his emphasis much overdone.[14] He is, of course,
right about the overall contingency of the evolutionary path actually
followed. But the question remains: how does one know what would
have happened if life *had* taken a different fork along the way? Or more
exactly: how can one tell that life on land would *not* have developed if
lungfish had not been around at the right time? Or that consciousness
would not have developed if an asteroid had not hit or if climate change
had covered Africa in forest three or four million years ago? Furthermore, the massive evidence for parallel evolution of such organs as the
eye or of physiologically very similar species ought to give him pause. It
seems as though contingency has in many instances been overridden by
strong selective advantage.

There appears, then, to be a considerable risk involved in adopting
either of the extremes above, the appeal to laws or tendencies that would
allow one to assert that life on land or the advent of consciousness
would assuredly have come about anyway, or the emphasis on radical contingency that allows Gould to conclude that *Homo sapiens* is
a "tiny twig on an improbable branch of a contingent limb on a fortunate tree." "Replay the tape a million times from a Burgess beginning,"
he remarks, "and I doubt that anything like *Homo sapiens* would ever
evolve again."[15] How *can* we be so sure either of the inevitability or the
improbability of the advent of consciousness?

Most evolutionary biologists and philosophers of biology seem to
adopt a middle course somewhere between these extremes, but this still
allows for a lot of latitude. Dobzhansky, for example, disagrees with

what he regards as an overemphasis on chance on the part of Monod. On the contrary, he remarks: "Viewing evolution of the living world as a whole, from the hypothetical primeval self-reproducing substance to higher plants, animals, and man, one cannot avoid the recognition that progress or advancement, or rise, or ennoblement, has occurred."[16] Though chance predominates in mutation and recombination, he goes on, natural selection serves to counterbalance this as an "anti-chance" factor. Thus, though the course of evolution cannot be predicted, "it does not follow that the human species arose by a lucky throw of some evolutionary or celestial dice."[17] In a recent assessment of the issue, Elliott Sober is more cautious. He is skeptical of the suggestion that the evolutionary process has in the past displayed progress or even direction. Though there may have been directional trends within specific lineages, all that the theory of natural selection allows one to conclude is that such trends are *possible*. It does not, however, allow one to anticipate them in advance; the multiple sources of contingency exclude this.

What may we conclude from this rapid survey? Macro-evolution is an irregular process, admitting of breaks, reversals, large-scale extinctions. Its course can, in principle at least, be explained *after* the fact, but it cannot be anticipated by us. The last billion years has seen an enormous growth in the variety and number of species. There has been a concomitant growth in the complexity of organisms that (according to some) can be construed as a form of progress; it has, however, proved difficult in practice to find an agreed definition of what "complexity" and "progress" should be taken to mean in this context.[18] Nevertheless, as the palaeontological and geological records come under closer scrutiny and genetic mechanisms come to be better understood, the fragile character of the causal skein leading up to the first appearance of humans becomes ever more evident.

What are the theological implications of this, if any? Belief in a Creator has usually gone hand in hand with a conviction that the human race has a special role to play in the story of the Creation: fashioned in the Creator's image, the only creatures so far known to us that are able freely to offer or to deny the Creator their love. Jews, Christians, and Moslems would be at one in supposing that insofar as we can speak of God's plans at all, we can assume that humans have a significant part in at least one corner of them. It would seem to follow, then, that the appearance of the human species would not, as it were, have been left to chance. If it was part of the Creator's purpose that humans should eventually make their entrance on planet Earth after a fifteen-billion-year preparation, can the story of that long prelude be as shot through with contingency as it seems to be? Conversely, if the contingency thesis be accepted, even if not in as radical a form as Gould proposes, does this not cast doubt on the belief that the Creator intended the cosmos to bring forth human beings? And if it does, would it not also call in question the whole notion of an omnipotent Creator whose purposes give meaning to a universe that would otherwise be pointless?

The frank anthropocentrism of the line of inquiry these questions open up runs counter, of course, to the instincts of scientists who sometimes call on a "Copernican principle" to justify their refusal to grant any form of privilege to humans. But Western theology is of its nature anthropocentric; it is concerned centrally with human destiny. When theologians hurdle the eons of evolutionary time that went to the making of human beings in order to concentrate on the relationship between those beings and God, the form their inquiry takes will necessarily appear alien to scientists who look on humans as one node, admittedly a particularly intricate node, in a vast network of living kinds. But if scientists ought to be careful not to rush too rapidly to judgment when their theological colleagues focus on human destiny, theologians have to take seriously what the sciences have to say about how human beings came to be here in the first place. All of this by way of apologia for an essay that clearly crosses the disciplinary divides!

Evolution and Teleology

Questions about whether human evolution can be viewed as the working out of divine purpose immediately recall a more conventional but no less spirited debate about the extent to which evolutionary explanation can be regarded as teleological. The common view is that Darwin banished teleological explanation from the field of evolution, a view, indeed, that Darwin himself and many of his opponents shared.[19] Yet we find some recent writers arguing, on the contrary, that evolutionary explanation is of its nature teleological in form.[20] The problem lies, as one might expect, with the ambiguity of the term "teleological." It is not necessary for my purposes here to explore that ambiguity in any detail.[21] Suffice it to say that right from its origins in the works of Plato and Aristotle, the notion of teleology could be carried in two very different directions.

On the one hand, a *telos,* or end, might directly involve mind. A teleological explanation would in this case involve an appeal to the agency of mind, to intentionality. One particular form played a significant part in the history of the natural sciences, where it came to be called the argument from design. In the *Timaeus,* Plato called on a cosmic Craftsman, the Demiurge, to explain the numerous traces of order found in the sense-world. Intelligible order testifies to the agency of *Nous* (Mind, Reason). The explanation of this order points not to a specific purpose but to the necessity of a Purposer. And again, the proponents of natural theology in the seventeenth century began from the clear evidences of adaptation of means to end in the anatomical structures and instinctive behaviors of the animal world. Since such adaptation would require a deep understanding of the needs of each kind of animal, a cosmic Designer of animal natures must be responsible. "Design" here refers to a form of order that testifies directly to the operation of a shaping intelligence in Nature. A teleological explanation in this first sense can serve, therefore, not just to explain a range of phenomena but, more significantly, to prove the existence of a being capable of carrying out the process of cosmic design.

This is the form of argument that Darwin undermined. His theory of natural selection aimed to explain exactly the sorts of adaptation that had earlier been used as evidence for an original Designer. When Darwin and his later followers claimed to have eliminated teleology from the science of living things, this was primarily what they had in mind. Not everyone was persuaded, of course, and among those who accepted the historical fact of evolution, some like Bergson proposed a different sort of teleological account of how it had taken place. Instead of transcendent Designer, they proposed a mind-like energy or impetus operating throughout the history of life, giving it its direction and meaning. They argued that natural selection alone, relying as it does on chance for the material it works on, could not possibly bring about the increasingly intricate and beautifully balanced structures that the history of the living world presents.

When defenders of the new synthesis, like Simpson and Mayr, reject teleology, it is this form of intentional explanation that they have in mind. One can see why they react so vehemently to it, since it calls into fundamental question the adequacy of Darwinian modes of explanation. Daniel Dennett is only the latest in a series of angry critics of the most prominent recent representative of this form of teleology, Teilhard de Chardin:

> The esteem in which Teilhard's book is still held by non-scientists, the respectful tone in which his ideas are alluded to, is testimony to the depth of loathing of Darwin's dangerous idea, a loathing so great that it will excuse any illogicality and tolerate any opacity in what purports to be an argument, if its bottom line promises relief from the oppressions of Darwinism.[22]

The feeling of loathing is obviously not confined to one side of the debate only!

It seems fair to say that teleological explanation of this basically idealist kind is almost universally disavowed among evolutionary scientists. The possibility that a "radial" energy or an *élan vital* of some sort is responsible for at least some of the goal-oriented aspects of macro-evolution cannot, of course, be definitively excluded. And the evident incompleteness of standard neo-Darwinian accounts can easily be taken to furnish grounds for this "heresy," as Dennett calls it. But as time goes on, the continuing extension of neo-Darwinian forms of explanation to the mountains of data that palaeontologists and biologists are accumulating makes the chances of the "heretical" view prevailing seem ever more remote. Nevertheless, its appeal, to nonscientists especially, is undeniable. It still, after all, seems counterintuitive that the intricacies of anatomical structure and function in the living world could be entirely due to natural selection operating on stray mutations, no matter how long the time-scale available. That evolutionary scientists do not find it so is doubtless in part due to their conviction that the teleological alternative is even less credible because of the challenge it offers to the standard methods of empirical science.

There is, however, a different sense (or set of senses) of teleology, traceable in this instance back to Aristotle rather that to Plato, that allows many to claim that evolutionary explanation is still basically "teleological" in form. The appeal here is not to mind or to conscious purpose but to function, to the role played by the part in the economy of the whole, for instance. Aristotle's *De Partibus Animalium* is full of examples of what he calls "that for the sake of which": the liver is for the sake of concoction; the fat surrounding the kidneys is for the sake of warmth, and so forth. This sort of finality is indeed taken by Aristotle to be a defining characteristic of living things. A functional-teleological explanation, as we may call it, has two parts. First the function of the part (e.g., digestion of food) is inferred, and then the significance of this function in serving the needs of the organism as a whole is implied. The liver is thus necessary to the well-being of the organism; Aristotle has much to say about the sort of hypothetical necessity that is involved in explanations of this sort.[23]

A related form of teleological explanation is directed to the processes that constitute the natural world. Aristotle explains such processes by specifying the terminus to which they regularly tend, this terminus being taken as in some sense a completion of the nature involved. Explanation here appeals to *telos* in the most literal sense. And for Aristotle it extends to *all* physical things, nonliving as well as living. The goal of the falling motion of heavy bodies, for example, is to return to the natural place of the body. Each nature's habitual way of acting maintains that nature's place in a larger cosmic order; it is a good both for the individual nature and for that larger order. Aristotle sees the paradigm of such goal-directed process in ontogeny, in the steady development from embryo to adult found in all living things. The maturity of the adult form is evidently the goal of the process from the beginning. This tendency of natural process to an end that is beneficial to the individual or the kind is not a conscious striving. It is found in elements like earth as well as in higher animals. There is no suggestion in Aristotle's account of the intentionality that Plato postulated as explanation of the traces of intelligible form in the sensible order. The sharp distinctions that Aristotle draws between the living and the nonliving, and between the rational and the nonrational, make it quite clear that the sort of immanent final cause he postulates as explanation of natural process is not to be interpreted as intentional, though critics from the seventeenth century onward have persistently misread him in this regard.[24]

Appeal to function and appeal to the *telos* of natural process are not the same but they are closely related and neither necessarily involves the causal action of mind or *élan vital* or the like. It is to these nonintentional sorts of teleology that those philosophers who see evolutionary theory as teleological in form are referring. Wimsatt, for example, argues that a trait is "selected," in the Darwinian sense, if it serves a function within the population in question. Likewise, it might be argued that the operation of natural selection is "for the benefit of the nature" and thus might be said to have a *telos* in Aristotle's sense.[25] The debate at this point gets quite complicated and all sorts of qualifications have to be considered.[26]

For my purposes here, these further discussions are not relevant. Even if one concedes that evolutionary explanation *is* teleological in this second sense, it does not imply that there is anything purposive about the processes involved. So it is of no help in our attempt to answer the theological questions posed by the contingency of the evolutionary process. Those questions, furthermore, are directed to macro-evolution; the teleology to which Wimsatt and others draw attention relates, so far as one can see, to micro-evolution only. We need to turn, then, in a different direction.

Purpose and Contingency

How *are* purpose and contingency to be related at the cosmic level? Popular writers on evolution, as we have seen, tend to see them as antithetical.[27] But not all evolutionary biologists are so quick to judgment. Simpson, for example, remarks:

> Adaptation is real, and it is achieved by a progressive and directed process. The process is wholly natural in its operation. This natural process achieves the aspect of purpose without the intervention of a purposer; and it has produced a vast plan without the concurrent action of a planner. It may be that the initiation of the process and the physical laws under which it functions had a purpose and that this mechanistic way of achieving a plan is the instrument of a Planner — of this still deeper problem the scientist, as scientist, cannot speak.[28]

He speaks of "long and continued trends" that are "kept going by natural selection," where "creative natural selection" is "the directive, pseudo-purposive factor back of adaptation"; he notes, however, that it is "not always the decisive factor in evolution and it never acts alone."[29] The trends can thus be interrupted, hence his insistence (as we have seen) that the course of evolution cannot be predicted in advance. Even though evolution is "a deterministic process to a high degree," the factors that have determined the appearance of human beings are so intricate and so special that though "human origins were indeed inevitable under the precise conditions of our actual history, that makes the more nearly impossible such an occurrence anywhere else."[30] Inevitable in one sense that it may have been, then, no finality could have been involved: "If evolution is God's plan of creation — a proposition that a scientist as such should neither affirm nor deny — then God is not a finalist."[31] A plan, somehow, but without "finality."

Gould would object to this talk of trends and plans and would place the emphasis on the fragility of the line leading to the human, a theme on which he and Simpson could agree. His own sympathies, he tells us, lie with the tentative solution Darwin once offered, in his correspondence with Asa Gray, of the dilemma of how God could permit the suffering that is everywhere to be found in nonhuman nature: perhaps one could hold that the *details* of the operation of nature are a matter not of law but of chance. The implication is that God is responsible for lawlikeness, with its overtone for purpose, but not for chance outcomes. The advent of *Homo sapiens* is "a wildly improbable evolutionary event," Gould remarks. It is a "contingent detail" of cosmic history, something that very well might not have happened, something that in consequence (Gould implies) cannot be attributed to purpose. Nevertheless, we "may yet hope for purpose, or at least neutrality, from the universe in general."[32]

The rather half-hearted suggestion on the part of both authors is, then, that there may be enough lawlikeness in the universe, despite the prevalence of contingency, to sustain some sort of claim for purpose at the cosmic level. But how? For one possible answer we might return to an objection posed by Simplicio, the Aristotelian, to Salviati, Galileo's spokesman, in the great *Dialogue Concerning Two Chief World Systems* (1632). If Copernicus were right about the earth's motion round the sun, a parallax shift ought to be noticeable in the relative positions of the stars. Yet none is seen. The alternative is that the stars are at an enormous distance from us. But then, to what purpose are these great spaces? Are they not "superfluous and vain"? To which Salviati replies that God may well have other plans in mind besides the care of the human race. And in any event: "it is brash for our feebleness to attempt to judge the reasons for God's actions."[33] Good advice still!

But suppose we put this objection again today. Our universe, we now know, is far, far greater in extent than Copernicus could ever have dreamed; space and time stretch out to the limits of human imagination. Does this not greatly enhance the difficulty for the theist? Perhaps not. Might it not be said that such great spaces populated by billions of galaxies that have developed over billions of years may have been needed in order that in a natural way the cosmos might give birth somewhere within it to human life one time or maybe a multiplicity of times? The contingency of the single evolutionary line might thus be overcome by the immensity of the cosmic scale. Evolutionary biologists are divided, as we have seen, as to whether, on general evolutionary grounds, life of a broadly human type would be *bound* to originate somewhere in all those myriad planetary systems. But assuming for the moment a positive answer to this question, the enormous space of evolutionary possibilities would then make it possible to maintain that there could be a cosmic purpose at work here on the part of a Creator, a purpose that the contingency of particular evolutionary lines would not defeat.

If God be conceived as a time-bound Creator whose knowledge of the future depends on a knowledge of the present, this way of swamping contingency in order to achieve a distant end would be appropriate. It does presuppose, of course, that human life would inevitably appear in a universe of this general sort, if it be large enough and long-lived enough. And this, some theists would object, we do not really know. There might very well be steps in the process that would require some sort of "special" action on God's part to enable them to occur. In a recent essay, Peter van Inwagen observes:

> Since the actual physical world seems in fact, to be indeterministic, it is plausible to suppose that there are a great many states of affairs that are not part of God's plan and which, moreover, cannot be traced to the free decisions of created beings. I very much doubt that when the universe was (say) 10^{-45} seconds old, it was then physically inevitable that the earth, or even the Milky Way Galaxy, should exist. Thus, these objects, so important from the human point of view, are no part of God's plan — or at least not unless their creation was due to God's miraculous intervention into the course of development of the physical world at a relatively late stage. I see no reason as a theist, or as a Christian, to believe that the existence of human beings is a part of God's plan.[34]

Realizing that this last suggestion is likely to shock the average Christian, van Inwagen adds a significant qualifier: "I am sure that the existence of animals made in God's image — that is, rational animals having free-will and capable of love — *is* a part of God's plan." Though he sees "no reason to believe," on theological grounds, that God planned this *particular* race of human beings, he is sure, on these same grounds, that *some* human-like race is part of God's plan.[35]

Like those evolutionary biologists who regard the contingency of the human line as an obstacle to describing the appearance of humanity as an outcome of purpose, van Inwagen takes contingency very seriously as a negative sign when attributing some feature of the universe to God's plan. (Note the "thus" in the middle of the passage quoted.) But he suggests a way in which such contingency can be, as it were, transcended, one that does not depend on cosmic scale. God may intervene miraculously in the causal process to ensure a particular outcome, in which case that outcome, despite the appearance of contingency from the scientific standpoint, would still be the result of plan, God's plan.[36] Here, then, is a second way in which the contingency of the evolutionary process leading to the human could be reconciled with the claim that the appearance of the human on earth is, nevertheless, is part of God's plan for the cosmos.

Van Inwagen does not develop this suggestion of a "special" action of some sort on the Creator's part at crucial steps in the development of life on earth. But a good many others have done so, and from a variety of widely different points of view. The most radical claim would be that of the defenders of so-called "creation science," who defend a more or less literal interpretation of the Genesis account of human origins.[37] A much more nuanced view would be that of Alvin Plantinga, who argues for the insufficiency of current evolutionary theory to account for various stages in the development of life, beginning with the appearance of the first living cell, and the consequent greater likelihood, from the Christian standpoint, of a "special creation" on God's part at crucial steps along the way.[38] And a very different approach again would be that of John Polkinghorne, who finds in chaos theory and quantum theory warrant for a causal "looseness" in physical process that would have been excluded in the Newtonian worldview. This leads him to suggest that God can operate in the ontological "gaps" thus opened up, communicating information without altering energy. God might in this way accomplish the ends of Providence without miracle, in the sense of an observable departure from the normal order of nature.[39]

These three accounts of divine action within cosmic process disagree fundamentally, particularly regarding the role to be played by natural science in illuminating the course of that process. But they implicitly agree in linking purpose at the cosmic level to a "special" action of some sort on the Creator's part within cosmic process. I am not going to discuss the merits and demerits of these views here. Instead, I propose to examine an alternative way of dealing with the challenge that contingency offers to our irremediably earthbound notions of a Creator as a Being whose action is guided by "purposes" and who "makes plans." Might not chance be one way for God to get things done? Does contingency hinder plan on the part of an agent who does not have to rely on a knowledge of the present in order to plan future outcomes?

Eternity and Teleology

In our discussions so far, we have made some simple, and on the face of it, plausible assumptions about the relationship between time and teleology. But what if these were to be challenged? What if the Creator be supposed to stand outside temporal process entirely? This, after all, has been the dominant view of the Creation within the Christian tradition from Augustine's day onward. It is true that it has been challenged in recent times, but it retains strong support among Christian theologians. Would such a view make any difference to our assessment of the significance of the evolutionary sequence? First, a quick outline of the view itself.[40]

Augustine saw God not as a Demiurge shaping an independently existing matter nor as a First Mover responsible for the motions of a world whose natures were not of the Mover's fashioning, but as a Creator in the fullest sense, a Being from whom the existence of all things derives. Such a Being cannot be operating under constraints, as the God of Greek philosophers did. Temporality is the first and most obvious constraint of the created world, a mark of its dependent status. A temporal being exists only in the present moment, without secure access either to its past or its future. Its past is no longer; its future is not yet. So even though both past and future are somehow constitutive of what "it" is, in a real sense, they do not exist. Such a being is evidently lacking, incomplete.

The Creator on whom the universe depends for its existence cannot be limited in this way. Time is a condition of the creature, a sign of dependence. It is created *with* the creature; by bringing a changing world to be, God brings time, the condition of change, to be. The act of creation is a single one, in which what is past, present, or future from the perspective of the creature issues as a single whole from the Creator.[41] God is not part of the temporal sequence that the act of creation brings to be; God is not one more temporal thing among other things. The Creator is "outside" time created, though the metaphor is an imperfect one. Calling God "eternal" is not a way of saying that God is without beginning or end, like Aristotle's universe.[42] "Eternal" does not mean unending duration; it means that temporal notions simply do not apply to the Creator as Creator. Nor does it mean "static," as nineteenth-century critics charged. In a famous formula, Boethius expressed it in lapidary terms: "Eternity is the whole, simultaneous, and perfect possession of boundless life."[43] God's life transcends the sort of dispersal that is the first characteristic of the creature; it is not subject to the kind of division that time-marking would require.

Creation and conservation blend together in this view, as do transcendence and immanence. Creation was not just a moment of cosmic origination a long time in the past, though we often speak of it that way since the first moment seems to call in a special way for a transcendent cause. Creation continues at every moment, and each moment has the same relation of dependency on the Creator. God transcends the world; the Divine Being in no way depends on the world for existence nor requires it as complement. Yet the Creator is also immanent in every existent at every moment, sustaining it in being. God knows the world in the act of creating it, and thus knows the cosmic past, present, and future in a single unmediated grasp.[44] God knows the past and the future of each creature, not by memory or by foretelling, then, as another creature might, but in the same direct way that God knows the creature's present. When we speak of God's "foreknowledge," the temporal "fore" has reference to our created reference-frame, within which the distinctions between past, present, and future are *real*. From God's side, however, there is only knowledge, the knowledge proper to a maker who is not bound by these distinctions.

This is familiar, of course. It is all very conceptual, as philosophers' talk of God inevitably is. It is no more than an exploration of an initial postulate concerning the act of creation, when that act is understood as a bringing into existence and a holding in existence, both entirely outside the range of our experience. How would such an account be supported? How does it meet the two major objections that Augustine already anticipated: Can this way of construing the work of creation be made compatible with the reality of human freedom? Does it not saddle the Creator with responsibility for all of the manifest evils of cosmic history? I am leaving these familiar and troubling questions aside in order to focus on a limited but perhaps more tractable issue: How does the apparent defeasibility of the evolutionary line leading to the emergence of *Homo sapiens* fit with the view that the act of creation is a single atemporal action on the part of God?

What I want to argue is that both Christian evolutionists who have assumed that the purposes of the Creator can be realized only through lawlike, and more or less predictable, processes as well as those who on the contrary infer from the contingency of the evolutionary process to the lack of purpose and meaning in the universe generally, are mistaken from the perspective of the traditional doctrine of God's eternality. Our notions of teleology, of purpose, of plan, are conditioned by the temporality of the world in which plans gradually unfold and processes regularly come to term. A Creator who brings everything to be in a single action from which the entirety of temporal process issues, does not rely on the regularity of process to know the future condition of the creature or to attain ends. God's knowledge of how a situation will develop at a later time is not discursive; God does not infer from a prior knowledge of how situations of the sort ordinarily develop. It makes no difference, therefore, whether the appearance of *Homo sapiens* is the inevitable result of a steady process of complexification stretching over billions of years, or whether on the contrary it comes about through a series of coincidences that would have made it entirely unpredictable from the (causal) human standpoint. Either way, the outcome is of God's making, and from the biblical standpoint could properly be said to be part of God's plan.

Terms like "plan" obviously shift meaning when the element of time is absent. For God to plan is for the outcome to occur. There is no interval between decision and completion. Thus the character of the process which, from *our* perspective, separates initiation and accomplishment is of no relevance to whether or not a plan or purpose on the part of the Creator is involved. Reference to "cosmic purpose" in this sense does not involve design in the traditional sense. That is, it does not point to features of the process or the outcome that specifically require the intervention of mind. There is nothing about the evolutionary process in itself that would lead one to recognize in it the deliberate action of a Planner. It does not *look* like the kind of process human designers would use to accomplish their ends. When critics of the Christian understanding of cosmic history conclude in consequence that we live in a universe lacking in purpose, it is this lack of independently *recognizable* design that they point to.

But the Creator is not a designer in this time-bound sense. And the contingency or otherwise of the evolutionary sequence does not bear on whether the created universe embodies purpose or not. Asserting the reality of cosmic purpose in this context takes for granted that the universe depends for its existence on an omniscient Creator. It does not mean that we are privy to that purpose, though the traditions of the Torah, the Bible, the Koran, would each imply a recognition of at least a part of it. Only to the extent that such a recognition were possible could one allow cosmic purpose to constitute a form of teleology (recalling that "teleology" refers to specific modes of explanation). When in the *Confessions,* Augustine looks back over his life and finally recognizes a Providence at work through all the contingency, it is to teleology of this sort that he is appealing.

Linking plan to Providence in this way gives rise to many other questions, of course. One would need, in particular, to distinguish between God's intending and permitting something to occur.[45] But the answers to those questions, important, indeed crucial, though they are, do not affect the contention of this essay: that if one maintains the age-old doctrine of God's eternality, the contingency of the evolutionary process leading to the appearance of *Homo sapiens* makes no difference to the Christian belief in a special destiny for humankind.

Notes

1. See I. S. Shklovskii and Carl Sagan, *Intelligent Life in the Universe* (San Francisco: Holden-Day, 1966), chap. 29.

2. In *Persons: A Study of Possible Moral Agents in the Universe* (New York: Herder and Herder, 1969), Roland Puccetti makes use of Sagan's analysis to conclude that "a correct analysis of the person-concept, combined with the not unreasonable belief in extraterrestrial natural persons, actually undermines the Christian belief in God" (143). His argument is that since the total number of communities of persons in *all* the galaxies could be as many as 1018, and since God could not be simultaneously incarnate in more than one person, there would be no way for God to become incarnate in all these communities within the life-span of the universe, as Christian belief would seem to require. The argument is fascinating but exceedingly porous. See Ernan McMullin, "Persons in the Universe," *Zygon* 15 (1980): 69–89.

3. See Ernan McMullin, "Estimating the Probabilities of Extraterrestrial Life," *Icarus* 14 (1971): 291–94.

4. Charles Darwin, *The Origin of Species* (Philadelphia: University of Pennsylvania Press, 1959), 221.

5. Pierre Teilhard de Chardin, *The Phenomenon of Man* (New York: Harper, 1965), 151, 149; emphasis in the original.

6. George Gaylord Simpson, *This View of Life* (New York: Harcourt, Brace and World, 1964), 189.

7. Jacques Monod, *Chance and Necessity* (New York: Knopf, 1971), 112–13; emphasis in the original.

8. Ibid., 169–70.

9. Ibid., 119, 124, 127.

10. Stephen Jay Gould, *Eight Little Piggies* (New York: Penguin, 1993) 77.

11. Ernst Mayr, a leading exponent of the synthetic theory, claims that an apparently discontinuous sequence of this sort can easily be incorporated into a broadly Darwinian account of evolutionary change; he recalls, indeed, that he had already indicated the need for such a modification in some of his own early work (*Toward a New Philosophy of Biology* [Cambridge, Mass.: Harvard University Press, 1988], chap. 26: "Speciational evolution through punctuated equilibrium").

12. Stephen Jay Gould, *Wonderful Life* (Cambridge, Mass.: Harvard University Press, 1989), 318.

13. Ibid.

14. See, for example, the extended polemic in Daniel Dennett, *Darwin's Dangerous Idea* (New York: Simon and Schuster, 1995), chap. 10.

15. Gould, *Wonderful Life*, 291, 289.

16. Theodosius Dobzhansky, "Chance and Creativity in Evolution," in F. J. Ayala and T. Dobzhansky, eds., *Studies in the Philosophy of Biology* (London: Macmillan, 1974), 309, 311.

17. Ibid., 318, 329.

18. Francisco Ayala, "The Concept of Biological Progress," in Ayala and Dobzhansky, *Studies in the Philosophy of Biology*, 339–56.

19. See Timothy Lenoir, *The Strategy of Life* (Dordrecht: Reidel, 1982).

20. See William Wimsatt, "Teleology and the Logical Structure of Function Statements," *Studies in the History and Philosophy of Science* 3 (1972): 1–80;

Larry Wright, *Teleological Explanation: An Etiological Analysis of Goals and Functions* (Berkeley: University of California Press, 1976). For a discussion of the pros and cons, see William Bechtel, "Teleological Functional Analysis and the Hierarchical Organization of Nature," in N. Rescher, ed., *Current Issues in Teleology* (Lanham, Md.: University Press of America, 1986), 26–48.

21. Contemporary discussions of teleology vary widely in the taxonomies they advance. See, for example, Wolfgang Kullman, "Different Concepts of Final Cause in Aristotle," in Allan Gotthelf, ed., *Aristotle on Nature and Living Things* (Pittsburgh: Mathesis, 1985), 169–76. See also Marjorie Grene, *The Knower and the Known* (Berkeley: University of California Press, 1974), chap. 9, "Time and Teleology"; Ernst Mayr, "The Multiple Meanings of Teleological," chap. 3 of Mayr, *Toward a New Philosophy of Biology*.

22. Dennett, *Darwin's Dangerous Idea*, 320–21.

23. See John M. Cooper, "Hypothetical Necessity and Natural Teleology," in Gotthelf, *Aristotle on Nature and Living Things*, 151–67.

24. Aristotle leaves unexplained why natures *should* act in this orderly way. Does the world just *happen* to be this way, or is there some prior reason why finality should govern nature in the way it does? Aquinas pushes the analysis a step further: "The fifth way is taken from the governance of the world. We see that things which lack knowledge, such as natural bodies, act for an end, and this is evident from their acting always, or nearly always, in the same way so as to obtain the best result. Hence it is plain that they achieve their end, not fortuitously but designedly. Now whatever lacks knowledge cannot move towards an end, unless it be directed by some being endowed with knowledge and intelligence" (St. Thomas Aquinas, *Summa Theologiae* I, q. 2, a. 3, in St. Thomas Aquinas, *Summa Theologica,* trans. Fathers of the English Dominican Province, 3 vols. [New York: Benziger Brothers, 1947], 1:14). This shifts the mode of explanation back to a teleological one in the first sense above.

25. This is reflected in the way in which evolutionary biologists themselves describe adaptation, using expressions like "in order to" (recall Aristotle's "for the sake of which"). Thus, for example, "Flowers may have evolved in order to lure bees from other plants," headline in a recent *New York Times* article.

26. Bechtel points out some difficulties in the analysis given by Wimsatt and Wright but argues that they can be overcome ("Functional Analyses"). The process of natural selection is, as we have seen, by no means the steady affair envisaged by Aristotle in his account of teleology. Furthermore, it is only part of the explanation, other factors (mutation, drift, environmental change) being in Aristotle's sense "chance" in nature and hence in conflict with teleological forms of explanation. It is interesting to note that when Aristotle defines chance (*tuchê*) in *Physics* II, he takes it to be an intersection of independent lines of causality, themselves separately determinate.

27. Critics like Dennett and Dawkins are not primarily thinking of the contingency issue when they reject any appeal to a Creator as a means of anchoring cosmic purpose. Their argument, rather, is that the Creator is an "idle wheel," that the neo-Darwinian argument, allied with standard astrophysical argument in cosmology, needs no further supplementation, no "skyhooks," in Dennett's metaphor. See Dennett, *Darwin's Dangerous Idea;* Richard Dawkins, *The Blind Watchmaker* (New York: Norton, 1987).

28. Simpson, *This View of Life,* 212.

29. Ibid., 210.

30. Ibid., 268.

31. Ibid., 265.

32. Gould, *Wonderful Life*, 291.

33. *Dialogue Concerning Two Chief World Systems*, trans. Stillman Drake (Berkeley: University of California Press, 1953), 367–68.

34. Peter van Inwagen, "The Place of Chance in a World Sustained by God," in T. V. Morris, ed., *Divine and Human Action* (Ithaca, N.Y.: Cornell University Press, 1988), 225.

35. At first sight, it might seem that the distinction van Inwagen draws here is the same as the one just discussed: the contingency of the particular evolutionary line leading to humanity is contrasted with the inevitability of finding human-like beings *somewhere* in a universe so vast. But, in fact, this is not the ground of the distinction he has in mind. Indeed, he rejects the suggestion that in a universe so large human-like beings would be bound to appear. Instead, he implies that it is sufficient for God to aim at the general end of bringing life to be somewhere in the universe, whereas the appearance of this particular race, not being "physically inevitable," need not be regarded as part of God's plan.

36. Van Inwagen is using the term "miraculous" in a broader sense than the usual one to cover, for example, physical sequences that could be imperceptible to us. And he warns against taking the term "intervene" to imply that God is in any sense external to the process; we simply do not have a word to convey a "special" action on God's part to bring about an outcome outside the ordinary run of nature. (I am grateful to Professor van Inwagen for our discussion of the ramifications of his essay.) If God were to "intervene" in a causal sequence, it would, of course, have to be in a *particular* sequence. So if (as van Inwagen supposes; see his "Doubts about Darwinism," in J. Buell and V. Hearne, eds., *Darwinism: Science or Philosophy* [Richardson, Tex.: Foundation for Thought and Ethics, 1996], 177–91) there is reason to believe that God intervened to supplement the evolutionary process leading to the appearance of the human race on earth, there would also be reason to believe that the existence of human beings on earth *is* a part of God's plan.

37. See, for example, Henry Morris, *Scientific Creationism* (San Diego: Creation-Life Publishers, 1974).

38. See Alvin Plantinga, "When Faith and Reason Clash: Evolution and the Bible," *Christian Scholar's Review* 21 (1991): 8–32. Two critical responses to his essay appear in the same journal issue: Howard J. Van Till, "When Faith and Reason Cooperate," 33–45; Ernan McMullin, "Plantinga's Defense of Special Creation," 55–79. Plantinga replies to them in turn: "Evolution, Neutrality, and Antecedent Probability," 80–109. A further comment: Ernan McMullin, "Evolution and Special Creation," *Zygon* 28 (1993): 299–335.

39. See John Polkinghorne, *Science and Providence: God's Interaction with the World* (Boston: Shambhala, 1989). For a critical evaluation of this proposal, see Steven Crain, "Divine Action and Indeterminism: On Models of Divine Agency That Exploit the New Physics," Ph.D. dissertation (Ann Arbor: Ann Arbor Microfilms, 1993).

40. See, for example, Alan G. Padgett, *God, Eternity, and the Nature of Time* (New York: St. Martin's Press, 1992), chap. 3: "The Doctrine of Divine Timelessness: A Historical Sketch." I am grateful to David Burrell and Fred Freddoso for our discussions of the issues arising in this section.

41. How to relate the temporality of the creature with the eternality of the Creator without either making temporality unreal (by assuming that the future already exists) or making God quasi-temporal, has vexed philosophers from Aquinas's day to our own. See Eleanor Stump and Norman Kretzman, "Eternity," *Journal of Philosophy* 78 (1981): 429–59.

42. See G. D. Yarnold, "Everlasting or Eternal?" chap. 9 in *The Moving Image* (London: Allen and Unwin, 1966), 139–52; Brian Davies, "A Timeless God?," *New Blackfriars* 64 (1983): 218–24; Julie Gowan, "God and Timelessness: Everlasting or Eternal?," *Sophia* 26 (1987): 15–29.

43. Boethius, *The Consolation of Philosophy*, 5.6.

44. Aquinas enters a formal defense of the thesis that God knows future contingent things (*Summa Theologiae* I, q. 14, a. 13). Such things are contingent relative to their antecedent physical causes, which is why temporal creatures like us, whose assessments of the future depend on a knowledge of such prior causes, can only conjecture about their contingent outcomes. But God knows these outcomes directly in their presentness as their Creator; the act of bringing them to be has no temporal divisions within it. Some of the analogies Aquinas draws on here need careful construal: "He who sees the whole road from a height sees at once all those travelling on it" (a. 13, ad 3); "His gaze is carried from eternity over all things as they are in their presentness" (a. 13, c.). Such analogies might suggest that our inability to predict a contingent outcome is simply due to our lack of proper vantage point: the various events taking place at this moment on the road just happen to be out of our sight. This in turn might be taken to imply that the future is already set, that it is only our powers of knowing that are unequal to the task of grasping it. But contingency is *real*, as Aquinas elsewhere makes clear. God knows contingent things that are future to us not as a viewer would features of a landscape already determinate but rather as a maker might, a unique sort of a maker who respects contingency in the cross-causal connections between the things made.

Debate about the manner of God's knowledge of future contingents intensified after Aquinas's day, particularly about how it was to be reconciled with the reality of human free choice. It came to a head between the Dominican supporters of Banez and the Jesuit followers of Molina at the end of the sixteenth century in the famous controversy *de auxiliis*. For an account of the subtleties to which this protracted discussion gave rise, see William L. Craig, *The Problem of Divine Foreknowledge and Future Contingents from Aristotle to Suarez* (Leiden: Brill, 1988).

45. For a wide-ranging treatment of this and connected issues, see, for example, the essays collected in Morris, *Divine and Human Action*, above.

10

Faith Reflects on the Evolving Universe

Divine Action, the Trinity, and Time

– WILLIAM R. STOEGER, S.J. –

Our knowledge of the natural world and of ourselves has exploded with the advance of the physical, biological, and human sciences. Though generated by specialists, it rapidly enters contemporary culture in many different forms, educational and journalistic, mythological and symbolic, and radically influences the perspectives we have of our world and ourselves, of our origin and our destiny, of the meaning and value of life and reality. The sciences give us a virtually complete and reliable set of models of how the material world functions and of its development from the Big Bang to the present. Though there are many lacunae in that account, there is every indication that they will be gradually filled by continuing the research paradigms which have governed investigations so far. Such success challenges theology and philosophy to articulate more carefully and more critically their own perspectives on reality, on origins and destinies, on God's relation with the world. Obviously, this must be done within the our cultural context, which is partially determined by science and technology themselves.

How to describe God's action in the world in a coherent and acceptable way — faithful to the sources of revelation and at the same time understandable in light of our scientific knowledge of creation — is the central question confronting theology and catechetics today. Identifying what counts as divine action within the context of faith and the believing community is fairly easy. Modeling how God acts, in a way compatible with our emerging understanding of physical and biological systems and with an "adequate" concept of God, provisional as that always will be, is much more difficult. A number of different theologians and interdisciplinary groups of scholars have recently begun treating this central topic more extensively.[1] A survey of literature on philosophical theology over the past forty years reveals that a significant percentage of it has direct bearing on this issue.

There is general agreement that divine action in the world falls into two broad categories: (1) God's creative and sustaining action of all that is not God; and (2) God's special action with respect to creation, e.g., God's revelation to God's people through the prophets and through God's "mighty acts," in answer to the prayers and the cries of God's people, particularly, for Christians, in the incarnation of Jesus the Christ, in his death and resurrection, and the sending of the Spirit. Each of these two categories presents its own problems. Part of the theological agenda is to give a unified account of divine action which embraces both. Some strands of theology in this century have held that there is no fundamental difference in God's special acts — there is no distinction to be made in the character and quality of the acts themselves from those which are according to the laws of nature, just in the interpretation given them by communities of faith. The language of special acts is therefore used symbolically.[2] In this essay I shall *not* follow this course. I shall assume that there have been and are special acts through which God expresses God's predilection and love for us, beyond God's creative and sustaining activity but consistent with it.

The problems facing any account of God's action in the world are in large part already apparent in a rather more focused and fundamental question: What is God's relationship to time and to temporal reality? Or, in what way does God embrace time and the realities in time, and in what way does God transcend time? Certainly, the account we give of how God acts in the world will depend in large measure on our answers to these questions. The issue of God and temporality cannot be treated prior to any consideration of God's action, as we shall see, but it provides a more direct avenue for attacking the key difficulties. Some of those which surface are God's knowledge of the future, the autonomy of creation and the freedom of human action, God's omniscience and perfection, God's immanence and vulnerability, the authenticity of God's response to us. Essentially — and paradoxically — if God does not embrace time, or participate in temporal reality in a concrete way, the ways God can act are severely limited.

There has been a spate of recent studies, long and short, on God and time. It has been a perennial issue in philosophy and fundamental theology since Aristotle. Here I shall deal with it again, not presuming to add anything particularly new, but rather attempting to present a brief, critical synthesis of where we find ourselves now. In light of scientific, philosophical, and theological work, here seems to have emerged promising approaches which can resolve this issue. In turn, an adequate treatment of God and temporality will provide a secure foundation for addressing the knotty problems connected with divine action. In fact, an adequate harmonization of God and temporal reality will contain in germ a solution to the problems of divine action.

The Starting Point

The first thing we must recognize is that in attempting to treat God and time, we are dealing with two very slippery and elusive realities. We have no adequate concept of either of them. We shall never have an adequate concept of God, and it is likely that we shall never have an adequate model for time. Neither physics nor philosophy have provided us with that, and probably are incapable of doing so. So our project seems doomed from the very beginning. Why continue?

The purchase on the God-time relation which gives us encouragement is that in creation itself and in our experience of revelation we are given innumerable concrete examples of God's link with time, and with temporal reality. We could not know anything of God except for that. We know something about time in its manifestations in material reality, but we are unsure of its origin and its basis. And we know even less about God. But we discover God and time irretrievably linked together in the world around us, in our experience of ourselves, in God's self-communication to us. This discovery is not the result of scientific investigation, but rather of philosophical and theological reflection on the full range of our experience, including our experience of scientific knowledge. God does act within our world on every level, while respecting the character and freedom of material reality. This link between God and temporal reality is most fully expressed in the mystery of the incarnation, and in all that flows from it — the life, death, and resurrection of Jesus, the sending of the Spirit, and the life and mission of the church. Our experience of these through faith reveals God's continuing active and intimate presence among us. Using that as a foundation, we can begin to tease out and elaborate the specifics about who this God really is, to the extent that is possible, what God's relationship to temporal reality must be, how God acts within the temporal-spatial manifold, and how God's involvement and action in time and the experience of time are to be understood.

An important conclusion will be that God's relationship to time is radically Trinitarian. A number of theologians, since Karl Rahner's groundbreaking retrieval of Trinitarian theology,[3] have emphasized this.[4] Our experience of God's self-revelation is radically Trinitarian. And thus the results of our probing into the relationship of God and time on the basis of the vast sweep of revelation will be Trinitarian. The Trinitarian character of God is revealed in God's self-communication to us and is thus essential to properly understanding both God's relationship to time and temporal reality and the levels and modes of God's activity in that context. At the same time, our experience of God's action helps us discern in part who God is and what God is not.

Thus, the more "traditional" approach to reconciling God's being with God's involvement in temporal reality is ruled out. In that approach, we assume a concept of God — as all-perfect, and therefore immutable, etc. — and a concept of time, and then on the basis of those concepts we specify the character of the relationship. We then interpret our experience of revelation in light of it. At that point we find that we must do considerable violence to divine revelation to maintain the character of the model of this relationship we have fashioned between God and temporal reality. That approach is flawed from the beginning, since we have no way of testing either how adequate our concept of time and temporal reality is, nor, more importantly, how adequate our concept of God is for this harmonization. While we can say that God must be all-perfect in some sense, what are the subtleties and distinctions such predication involves in light of who God is for us and in light of God as Trinity? Those cannot be known a priori, but only through accepting the divine relationships as they are revealed and given to us, appreciating them and reflecting upon their implications.

Furthermore, in appealing to our experience of God's action in the world, we must appeal to the full range of that experience, including what is given us in creation. And so our reflection on what the sciences, the humanities, the arts, day-to-day human experience reveal to us is just as important as what the traditional sources of revelation reveal to us. What is crucial is what our reflection with the "eyes of faith" on the full range of experience yields. Determining how physical and biological systems are constructed and how they function — with great autonomy — in space and in time, the origins and evolution of life and of consciousness within that manifold of rich possibility, sets constraints on how we can model God's interaction with reality and God's involvement in time — the way in which divine action is "apparent" as divine. How God's action is *not* experienced is just as important as how it is experienced!

This fundamental aspect of the research program leads to confirming what God's immanence in temporal reality means — that God is not present and acting just as another cause, to fill causal gaps. God is not just another person or thing in the universe which we can objectify and thus delimit. Rather, God is transcendently and immanently, and thus pervasively, present as that which gives existence and distinct character to all that is, the ultimate immanent ground (immanent precisely because God is fully transcendent) of the created, temporal universe.[5] God endows us and all things with existence and concreteness in such a radical way that God's presence and action is all but hidden from analysis. In fact, strictly speaking, God is *not* even found at "the edges" of time and space — for example, at "the beginning" of time or at "the end" of time — though, mistakenly, we often try to find God in a privileged and unambiguous way there.[6]

Resolving the Problem of God and Time

A notion of God we have inherited includes the fulness of existence and perfection, such that nothing can be added to God and nothing can be subtracted from God. God does not need anything or anyone else. Boethius based his concept of eternity on this divine plenitude.[7] Now absolute perfection, on the face of it, rules out any change. And, since time is conceived as the measure of change, absolute perfection seems to place God forever outside time and beyond time. This is the basic apparent incompatibility which, from the "traditional" point of view, is at the root of the God-time problem. It leads directly to the well-known paradoxes involving the "simultaneous" presence of all realities, temporal and transient though they be, to God;[8] God's omniscience and knowledge of the future and our freedom to act; God's eternal being and God's sensitive response and presence to us in time.

Clearly, this simplistic and non-Trinitarian notion of God and what God's absolute perfection implies has betrayed us. With it, it becomes impossible to do justice to our experience and knowledge of the dimension of divine revelation. Certainly we want to maintain that God is perfect in the fullest possible sense and possesses the fulness of being. But what that should or should not imply — what the implications of that predication are — cannot be determined a priori. Since we are making assertions at the very limits of language and understanding, it would be foolhardy to try to do so. What that perfect and absolute plenitude is consistent with, or not consistent with, can be measured or determined only by who God reveals God's self to be. Strictly speaking, in a rigorous application of this Boethian notion of eternity, the incarnation would be a contradiction. Any self-communication of God would be unthinkable and contrary to the divine essence so inflexibly conceived. And yet the fundamental character of God's revelation involves God's self-communication — in creation and in redemption!

In light of revelation and our appropriation of it, then, God's self-communication is full and complete — and, far from being contrary to the divine essence, is somehow its fullest expression. (The fullest expression in temporal terms of the usual concept of an all-perfect and immutable God could be total aloofness — absence of interaction and relationship.) And so we must broaden and deepen our notions of what divine perfection is and allows.

The type of modification to the "standard" notion of divine perfection which correctly reflects God's revelation to us and moves us in the right direction is to include in its essential character relationship and relatedness. The divine perfection is realized in the dynamism of Trinitarian relationships, which are described in terms of eternal generation and infinite love. The essence of God is to be in relationship. And that is fundamentally the motive for the creation of distinct beings and God's communication of God's self to them. God's perfection does not suffer in that network of relationships. God's infinite love and faithfulness, power and goodness, mercy and compassion are expressed in creating the vast but finite universe — sharing existence with it — and communicating and uniting God's self to it. God does not maintain God's absolute perfection by withholding relationship from all that is not God, not absolutely perfect, but precisely by creating and entering creation freely, being present to it and letting it be fully itself. God is so perfect that such relationships in which God enters fully and empathetically do not taint or derogate from God but rather enhance and express who God is.

And this priority of relationships in the divine being is coherent with and reflected in the underlying raison d'être of space and time. Space and time essentially embody the fundamental relationships among finite material beings. In creation there bursts forth a great variety of distinct but interrelated entities, which move in and out of material existence in their interactions and combinations with one another according to the regularities and influences which are inherent in them. Relationships among them are fundamental, reflecting the divine essence. But so is distinctness — separateness. Space and time, or space-time, is the internal consequence of many distinct finite entities in interactive relationship. Thus, from this viewpoint, it is not so puzzling that God should find entry into temporal reality compatible with God's being, absolutely perfect as it is.

God creates and interacts fully with God's creation, to the extent of communicating God's self to it in a continuous and pervasive fashion. God is permanently and totally involved in God's creation. And that creation involves time. Thus, God is permanently and fully present in time and in temporal reality. But that does not mean that God is limited by time. God is unlimited but fully supportive and available to temporal reality. At this point we see God's radical immanence in creation — enabled by God's radical transcendence of it.

As Thomas Torrance puts it, God can and does make a place for God-self within creation.[9] Creation reflects, imperfectly of course, who God is and is fashioned so that it is open and receptive, so that it can be completed and be intimately united with its Creator. From the Creator's side there is no limitation, no barrier. God's life and character are such that God can and does enter fully into the material world as Creator/ redeemer, sustaining it, completing it, transforming it — not in a way different from that for which it was destined, but precisely in a way which fully realizes that destiny and at the same time respects its autonomy, distinctness, and relative freedom. That full realization of creation's purpose and potentiality will only be achieved in "the end times," when at least for our segment of the universe, final and full reconciliation with God in Christ has been appropriated.

Time in the Natural Sciences

So far we have focused almost exclusively on God, as God manifesting God's self within temporal reality, in creation itself, and in God's self-communication to creation. But we need to summarize what the natural sciences, and philosophical reflection, reveal to us about time and about temporal reality, in order to appreciate more fully God's immanent and active presence within it. From this we shall be able to detect points of agreement, and a basic coherence, between what is revealed in God's self-communication about God's presence in and relationship with temporal reality and what is discovered within our investigations of material reality itself. This will serve to clarify how God is present and active within time and is affected in God's relationship with temporal reality, with us.

Developments in the physical sciences have clarified some key aspects concerning the status and role of time in material reality. We shall describe these. Furthermore, the natural sciences in general have revealed certain characteristics of reality and its history which underscore the importance of time and strongly impact the way in which we can describe God's presence and action in the universe. We shall see that these reinforce some of the key conclusions astute theological analysis has been emphasizing for centuries concerning God's action and presence within the universe.

Physics never defines time, but uses it as a fundamental concept. In doing so it abstracts from concrete physical reality the general notion of duration. Time is the measure of duration in physics. One needs to know how long it takes of a fluctuation to grow to a certain size, how much time (how long it will take) for a system to reach equilibrium, or how long it has been since the Big Bang. The evolution equations of a given theory are time-equations, and their solutions predict what a given system (e.g., the amplitude of certain of its parameters or its thermodynamic state) will be like at every point in the future, given certain initial conditions in the past, or what a system must have been like at every point in the past, given what it is like now. In order to measure duration (i.e., time) in the concrete, of course, we need a clock, or actually a set of clocks (one for each world line in the space-time manifold), whose regular motions enable durations of processes, or durations separating events in the same place and inertial frame, and in other places and inertial frames, to be compared.

Without going into the details, we can summarize what we know about time from the physical sciences in the following way.[10]

1. From special relativity, we discover that both space and time are not absolute, but are relative: they are given by the relationships between particles, or fundamental observers, in space-time. Thus neither space nor time can be considered as containers within which matter moves. In particular, the rate at which clocks tick relative to a given clock depends on the relative velocity (the inertial frame) of the clock, and simultaneity of events depends both on position in space and on inertial frame. Furthermore, as we have just seen, there is no privileged frame or clock which can provide an absolute temporal or spatial reference point. Thus, time is an internal characteristic of material reality, with its source in its inner relationalities. Matter (mass-energy) is ontologically prior to time and to space.[11]

2. The internal character of time is further emphasized in Einstein's general relativity, and in quantum gravity and quantum cosmology. So much so, in fact, that time can never be uniquely or cleanly separated from space, or from matter. In general, there are many times (infinitely many) which can be defined in general relativity — corresponding to the infinitely different ways we can slice the space-time into a stack of three-spaces. Internal variables play the role of time, e.g., the volume of a spatial slice, and time is completely derivative. Fortunately, for isotropic and spatially homogeneous cosmologies (Friedmann-Robertson-Walker models), there is a privileged cosmic time, defined by the surfaces of homogeneity. But this feature is special to such models and still derives from internal parameters characterizing them.

3. In quantum mechanics and quantum field theory itself, time is basically Newtonian and classical, that is, "container-like." But once we marry quantum field theory with general relativity to describe the physics of the universe immediately after the Big Bang before classical space and time are possible, time itself becomes very different from what it is in classical quantum field theory. It assumes the characteristics time possesses in general relativity. And, furthermore, it tends to disappear very close to the Big Bang — in the quantum-gravity-dominated Planck era. Time is probably not a primordial characteristic of matter at the very highest temperatures: duration may not make any sense in the way we normally conceive it. The wave function of the universe and the equation which specifies it (the Wheeler-DeWitt equation) do not depend on time. Time itself may originate only as the universe emerges from the Planck era itself.

4. The physics of nonlinear and nonequilibrium systems, which describe the phenomena of chaos and self-organization, also emphasizes the internal character of time, in a somewhat different and more concrete way.[12] So do the biological and the geological sciences.

5. In general relativity, causality is incorporated in its usual sense in physics in that effects cannot precede their causes. There can be no

closed time-like curves, or even close to closed time-like curves in an acceptable cosmological model. This causality is enforced rigorously, even though simultaneity and the measurement of time intervals are relative. In quantum field theory, causality is also very important and again strictly enforced. In quantum cosmology, some residual causality is maintained, but how it is to be interpreted is a matter of controversy.

6. Neither general relativity nor quantum theory can explain the arrow of time. What enforces the directionality of time? Some maintain that its origin is in the second law of thermodynamics, that is, in any closed system, the entropy, or measure of disorder, must always remain the same or increase — it cannot decrease. I doubt that this is the origin of the arrow of time. I believe with others that it is due to the directionality of efficient causality itself.[13] Some of Neville's philosophical insights also have important bearing on this issue.[14]

7. In contemporary physics, for both general relativity and quantum theory, the fundamental theoretical entities are the complete histories of a system in state space, rather than points of the state space. Thus physics really knows nothing of the "passing of time," as such. Furthermore, what is given in general relativity is really four-dimensional space-time, not individual three-dimensional spaces given at successive times.[15]

Among the other important conclusions of the natural sciences which strongly impact how we conceive of God's relationship to temporal reality and God's action in the universe are the following: (1) the radically evolutionary character of physical reality, from the Big Bang on; (2) the permanence and "reliability" of the laws of nature at every level — the regularities and detailed behavior of systems, depending on temperature, density, etc.; (3) the relative but strong autonomy of physical reality; (4) the possibility, which may never be confirmed by science, that there are very many other universes like ours, causally disconnected from ours; (5) the possibility, which may eventually be confirmed, that life and even intelligent life exists elsewhere in our observable universe. I shall concentrate on the first three of these.

The radically evolutionary character of creation as we have come to know it in cosmology and astronomy, in paleontology and biology, concretely expresses our origin in accessible physical, biological, and historical terms. We can point directly and in detail to how the earth originated and how we originated, as individuals and societies. These processes took time, and thousands of different intermediate stages were negotiated. From the point of view of God's creative act, God was and is working through these time-consuming, interconnected processes to bring about the world we see about us, and ourselves as part of it. God is very much at work in time — *creatio continua.*

Along with this, though the physical and biological reality is evolving, there are reliable and relatively permanent underlying regularities and patterns of behavior inherent in material reality which enable and effect that development without fully determining it. They are complemented by a certain amount of randomness and uncertainty at different levels, upon which the inherent regularities and processes can operate to produce variety and trigger diversification. There is no need for "intervention" in these evolutionary processes. They exhibit a strong and definite autonomy, a functional integrity,[16] apart from their radical contingency. It is that radical contingency, and the radical contingency of our world, which manifests their profound and ultimate dependence upon the divine. But the functional integrity and relative autonomy of physical reality strongly constrain how we can conceive of God acting in the world. It also serves to emphasize how profoundly immanent is God's activity in creation — in time. God's creative activity pervades creation at every level and is expressed in all that occurs. The dynamism of physical reality is an expression and the concrete realization of God's creative, life-giving power. I shall develop this more later in the context of a discussion of Trinitarian self-expression in creation.

The Metaphysics of Time and Temporal Action

Although physics reveals something about the character of time and prevents us from absolutizing it or separating it from material reality, it abstracts from some important aspects of time we really need to preserve in making the link between time and God. Recently Neville has brilliantly and strongly emphasized these.[17] Physics, as we have seen, really does not do justice to the passing or the flow of time, or to the way in which what is past affects and is carried over into what is present and what is future, and what is future gives meaning and direction to what is past and present. Though physics models histories of particles and the fundamental causal structure associated with congruences of histories and can describe how initial states evolve, it abstracts from the complex interrelationships among past, present, and future existing entities and situations and their identities. What is needed, as Larson points out,[18] is a metaphysics of time and temporal reality as part of an "ontology of determinateness," which takes these complex interrelationships into consideration. This what Neville has constructed.

An important aspect about temporal reality is "the togetherness" of these temporal modes and of the entities which realize them.[19] The different components of the past are all linked together and interrelated. Entities have their own identities and periods over which they endure. And some of those objects and persons exist now. What they are now, and what everything in the present is, depends upon and subsumes the past — in some way recapitulates the past and is strongly conditioned and influenced by the past. And what is future are those events and objects and persons which also take up the realities and accomplishments of the past and present and give them new and different expression. The significance of the past and present is partially revealed and achieved in the future.

A heightened form of this togetherness of temporal modes is found in personal identity. What a person is is revealed not only in what he or she is now, but in the whole history of his or her life. The past is not abrogated, but taken up in the person and moved forward to realize new possibilities and to be eventually completed. The spirit, accomplishments, and effects of Einstein's life, of Albert Schweitzer's, Beethoven's, the saints' lives — of each individual life — continue on as vital components of the present and the future. The present and the future would be different without them, without us.

Neville refers to this togetherness of the temporal modes — and remember time is a feature of finite material reality — as "eternity."[20] He stresses that time cannot be understood and is not the reality that it is without "eternity," nor would this eternity be what it is without time. They are inseparable aspects of the same thing. Eternity gives temporal reality its consistency and interrelatedness and gives time itself its flowing character. In this rather comprehensive view of temporal reality, what is past, what is present, and what is future all exist, but in different ways. We cannot privilege the present and treat past and future as completely nonexistent. The whole character, fabric, and significance of temporal reality derives from the past, present, and future.

Although Neville does not mention it, I believe part of this "eternity" — part of what effects this "togetherness" of temporal modes — is the laws of nature. These regularities and patterns of behavior endow temporal reality with its consistency and its functional integrity, which in turn enable the present and the future to build upon and take up the past, and past and present to envision and strive for the future — to realize their potentialities. Though temporal reality is marked by change and transience, that change and transience occurs relative to certain permanent and stable features, and even values, which are embodied in the laws of nature, not just as we have modeled them, but as they are realized in the regularities, interrelationships, structures, and processes which characterize material reality.[21]

If we are going to relate temporal reality to God, or rather God's presence and action to temporal reality, we must preserve something like this fundamental connection between time and "natural eternity," which, as Neville again stresses, provides an "ontological context of mutual relevance."[22] This in turn allows the temporal modes of past, present, and future, and indeed all things, to be understood in terms of their essential and their conditional features. All things possess their own distinctiveness but are at the same time fundamentally interrelated. What Neville provides in a sense is a way of understanding David Bohm's wholeness and implicate order becoming explicit in time and space.[23]

Eternity and God

The next step, roughly speaking, is to recognize time and particularly "the togetherness of temporal modes" which Neville calls "natural eternity" as expressions of God, of the "divine eternity." Since temporal reality and its delicate integration of the transient and the enduring are contingent — demand an ultimate explanation outside of themselves — they are properly the result of eternal creation *ex nihilo*. Neville says:

> Time's flow can be appreciated only sub specie eternitatis, for it is in fact a proper trait of the eternal creation ex nihilo, only partially grasped by finite beings in present consciousness, behind the veil of memory and anticipation. The eternal act of creation does not take time, for it encompasses all the dates of things as each is future, present, and past together in order for present time to move on. Yet the eternal act of creation, as regards the creation of temporal things, is characterized by an infinite internal dynamism. Although not taking time itself, the eternal creative act includes the singular pulse of present decisive creativity from moment to moment in infinite serial order.... Time's flow is fully real only as the internal character of the eternal act in which all times are together in an infinite singular series of continuous transformation.[24]

In elaborating this conclusion, it becomes necessary to critique continually and carefully our ideas of God, according to the best traditions of the negative way in theology and the very severe constraints the sciences and other disciplines, including philosophy, impose. In fact, one of the emerging realizations is the striking coherence these very different resources yield on this issue. As Neville summarizes the restrictions, divine eternity cannot be form, or *totum simul,* or pure goodness, or unmoved mover. Nor can it, or God, according to Neville, be modeled as an individual, as consciousness or "presence" or as the fullness of being, or as a determinate being.[25]

It is at this point that I begin to disagree with Neville. I agree very much with his general approach and direction, but I have some reservations with regard to his conclusions concerning divine eternity and God. I am in accord with him concerning the above restrictions, as long as the words are properly understood. I can see ways, though, in which God as fullness of being is a supportable predication. God, for Neville, as Creator is, apart from creation, indeterminate, indistinguishable from nothing. God's character arises from the act of creation itself.[26] This conclusion, I believe, contradicts many of Neville's other important conclusions. In particular, if this is all God is apart from creation, then it is hard to see how God can be the Creator and the ultimate explanation for all that is.

Certainly, we must avoid conceiving God as determinate within the world as other entities are determinate, or as a cause among other causes and functioning alongside them. And we must avoid, too, making God an abstraction. But we must at the same time preserve in our concept of God all that is needed for God to be the fulness of activity and the fulness of existence — "pure act." God in some sense is the infinite reservoir of being and activity who constitutes the context or background of potentiality which is partially realized in creation. As the infinite reservoir of activity God is transcendent. But God becomes fully immanent, accessible, and present in creation, precisely because of God's transcendence. God as infinite and pure act is, as such, inaccessible but becomes accessible in God's self-communication in creation.

I shall not enter further into a discussion of these issues here, but move on to consider how God as Trinity creates and interacts with creation. For it is only in that context that we can begin to integrate Neville's key insight regarding time, natural eternity, and divine eternity of creation *ex nihilo* with an acceptable account of who God is. God as Trinity will assume and subsume temporality without contradiction; time does find a place in God and the incompleteness of temporal reality is respected within God, as Peters,[27] O'Donnell,[28] Jensen,[29] Larson,[30] and others have correctly stressed.

God, Creation, and the New Creation

As we have already seen, God creates *ex nihilo* the complexus we call the material world with its laws of nature, and its internal operational characteristics at different levels. This includes space and time, not as primordial realities but rather as features concomitant to material reality's being finite and interrelated. They probably fully emerge only after the universe exits the Planck era, during which quantum gravity and quantum gravitational fluctuations dominate physical reality.

This entire complexus is a distinct and finite expression of God's being and continues to be animated and sustained by God's active presence. As such God continues to send forth his Spirit into creation to actualize the Word in finite expression of God in the world. This creative action continues through the evolutionary processes of this created complexus. God "calls forth"[31] different species and organisms from the complexus through its inherent dynamisms and processes, which are the realizations of the Word in the Spirit with which God has endowed it. The created complexus is completely dependent upon God for its character and existence, but enjoys its own autonomy and its own internally consistent potentialities for growth, development, the emergence of novelty, etc. This is the principal mode of God's action in the world, and it is realized in time, within a "natural eternity."

There are two aspects of this that are important to discuss: (1) the radical relationship to the created complexus to God and its openness to God's self-communication; and (2) the "hiddenness" of God in creation.

Creation as such is in a fundamental relationship with the Trinitarian God. In fact, that relationship constitutes it to be what it is. In a limited way creation reflects who God is and is the expression of God outside God's self, providing the avenue or medium for God's continuing and ever fuller expression of God's self *ad extra*. Thus, creation "makes room" for God and has been fashioned so that God can communicate God's self to it in the fullest possible way — compatible with each created being's capacities. Thus, creation's fulfillment is achieved in God's self-communication in incarnation, resurrection, and further sending of the Spirit. From a theological point of view creation is "designed" that way. It is centered in God and in God's loving self-communication. But notice that this involves God's radical entry into and acceptance of time and temporal reality. God's increasing self-communication to creation involves promise, preparation, and fulfillment, and those moments are intrinsically temporal. Redemption and the new creation are but further moments in the entire creative process, as is emphasized in Deutero-Isaiah and in the book of Revelation.

Notice, too, that the Trinitarian involvement is from the beginning. The Spirit hovers over the chaos and makes "nothingness" and the "chaos" itself receptive to the Word, from whom and through whom and for whom the Father creates and sustains all that is, endowing it with its own distinct and autonomous existence, its functional integrity, but also with an evolving capacity for both fuller expression of the divine Word and further heightened relationship with the Trinity. As the complexus evolves, certain entities within it become more organized and complex, eventually culminating in the capacity for self-consciousness, knowledge, and intelligent activity. As such, these, individually and together, are more expressive of the Word and more receptive to the power and presence of the Spirit. They are more "made in the image and likeness" of God, though still finite and time-bound. They participate more fully in eternity and in God's life, and thus are capable of a much fuller and more intimate — conscious and free — relationship with the Creator. That, as I have already mentioned, is fully realized in God's revelation, eventuating finally in the incarnation, in the death and resurrection of Jesus as the Word of God, and all that flows from it. Much more needs to be said here, of course. But I am only pointing in what I see as the general direction. This realizes and gives concrete substance to the "redemption" as the continuation and completion of the creation — the new creation, God perfectly united with God's creation, though distinct from it.

The second important aspect of this relationship of God with creation is paradoxically the apparent "hiddenness" of God in creation, and even in Jesus, as the culmination of the "new creation." Creation is spread out in space and time and possesses its own internal dynamisms and its own functional integrity, through which it evolves and develops. We do not find God in creation in the sense that God is lurking there as a causal complement to its own internal dynamisms, processes, and structures. Because of the functional integrity of the material world, that is unnecessary. It would also be contrary to who God really is and what creation in the richest theological sense really is. Creation *as such* is God's expression of God's self. That's why we do not find anything else but creation there! Creation is not a container where we find God; it is itself the expression and the revelation of God. Thus, God's presence, relative to our own misguided expectations, is hidden, precisely because the material world functions autonomously at its own level without "outside divine interference" or intervention. Creation can be probed and understood and modeled without reference to God. Our yearning is often to find God as something or someone determinate and special *within* creation. But that would not be God! Creation's necessary relationship to God is revealed only in its contingency. But that fundamental dependence is as crucial as it is pervasive. Because of it, God is radically immanent in the material world.

Thus, there is no need to have gaps in creation in order to "make room" for God, because God is already fully and profoundly present and active in every nook and cranny of it. Creation's autonomy and functional integrity do not marginalize God, but rather express God's active presence and God's respect for creation in the fullest way. Nor do they indicate God's absence or abandonment of creation, but rather God's full and abiding presence within it, though *not in a determinate way.* Like the air we breathe, God's presence and activity is so pervasive that we do not notice it. We cannot separate it out, because it is always there. We cannot distil it or prescind from it. And thus, creation — in its beauty, its intricacy, its interrelationships which constitute its autonomy and functional integrity — fully expresses God outside of God's self in finite form. It is the finite realization of God's Word, animated by God's Spirit.

Time and space are eminently suited — and necessary — to God's immanent presence within the material universe, and to creation's response to and affirmation of God's invitation to dwell among us at an ever deeper level. Since creation is a finite and imperfect expression of God, time and space allow that expression to continue and develop and improve, and for creation's response to develop and improve as well. In conscious organisms creation freely accepts God's invitation to share God's life and to live in harmony with God's presence, thus fulfilling its destiny. That process "takes time" and requires space. While God in God's self transcends time and space, God in God's Word and Spirit fully enters temporal and spatial reality, first constituting it and then uniting God's self with it. This completion is achieved as the finite realization of God's Word accepts union with the infinite in his destiny as Risen Lord in Jesus.

And yet, even in Jesus, there is a sense in which God remains hidden — relative to our unpurified expectations. For Jesus, though the infinite realization of God's Word, is still in finite and imperfect form. Jesus is still within the temporal and spatial confines of the material world and as such is subject to all its limitations and its internal operations. But Jesus works signs — and lives his life as a sign — pointing to the way in which we realize our destiny within material reality. Those signs and miracles do not become new patterns of activity within creation but rather reveal the profound potentialities already within creation and, more than that, attain in essence their realization. Death and all else continue as before. Jesus dies. But in Jesus' death, which induces his resurrection, everything else is given the possibility of achieving its ultimate completion and eternal significance as God's creation.

If this is to be possibility, however, and if that possibility is to be freely accepted out of love and not compulsion, if the autonomy of creation is to be respected, then the refusal of God's invitation must also be possible. And so, paradoxically, evil, sin and death remain painful realities within creation — but realities which themselves are challenged and overcome in Jesus' death and resurrection, challenged and overcome precisely by entering fully into those realities and struggling in love and commitment to overpower and transform them. Jesus does this as Yahweh's Servant, the suffering Servant portrayed in Deutero-Isaiah.

There is here a further and even fuller expression of God's radical immanence in creation, and in the new creation — an expression of how intimately and profoundly God has taken temporal reality with all its imperfections and limitations to God's self, and how thoroughly the Word and the Spirit of God are active in and vulnerable to space and time, redeeming space and time and material reality as a whole in that very vulnerability. This is not a conclusion we can reach by beginning with an a priori concept of God and relating that to time but, according to our starting point, only by accepting and critically appropriating what is given in creation and in revelation concerning God and God's active presence and involvement in the temporality and materiality of the universe.

Recent scholarship on the theology of creation in the Old Testament, particularly on Deutero-Isaiah and on the book of Job, has revealed an interesting and tantalizing coherence among all these themes: God's presence in creation from the point of view of science and theology, the link between creation and the new creation in the suffering Servant, the relative autonomy of creation, the imperfection and evil manifest in it, and completion of creation in death and resurrection.[32] The point that both Deutero-Isaiah and the book of Job make is that the justice (*mish-pat*) and power of God revealed in the suffering Servant is the same sort of justice and power of God in creation. It is characterized by radical immanence, vulnerability, loyal suffering, provisionality, struggle, not by coercion and overwhelming imposition of order and tight retribution. This is, in turn, of a piece with what is required to ensure the development and growth of the community: servanthood. That is, doing justice in society means preserving or restoring the correct balance by means of the servant-like power exercised by God in creation. A fundamental characteristic of the nature of the divine power in creation, and in the new creation which completes it, is that it takes into account and works through all other effective agencies by transforming and reconciling their turbulent energies,[33] not by resisting them or countermanding them. God is at home and accepts the seemingly unruly forces of nature, even the most violent and frightening — including the death and suffering they occasion — and channels them to God's own purposes. This is, in large part, the wisdom of God, which Job cannot understand. Nor can we. God dwells among us in a tent, not in an impregnable fortress. God intimately accepts the imperfections, seeming absurdities and reversals, the self-willed recalcitrance and wild girations, the struggles and prodigalities that constitute material creation. And God is radically and fully immanent in all those dynamisms; God does not stand apart from them. In fact God cannot be objectified apart from them.

Conclusion: God's Vulnerability to Time

God's continual struggle and work in creation and in the new creation through the Word and in the Spirit is driven by God's perfect love. This divine activity occurs within space and time; it is always active, never static or finished, as long as creation is incomplete or uncompleted, always moving and pushing forward. In its own imperfect way it reflects the infinitely and completely expressive and active love of God within the Trinity. This activity of creation in time and space does not add anything to God as God. But it does involve God changing in the sense that God struggles and works within the finite and imperfect — within space and time — to express God's self, without overwhelming or destroying the finite with the infinite.

The Trinitarian God does not change in the Trinity's essence or in perfection. But the Trinity's essence and perfection is to be active and to express God's self in infinite terms (*ad intra*) and in finite terms (*ad extra*). Therefore, God must take into God's self — include through the immanent action of the Spirit and the expression of the Word in creation and in the new creation — temporality and therefore materiality. This is simply because time and materiality are part of God's expression of God's self in finite terms, and God freely chooses through the Word and in the Spirit to act and respond within that temporal-spatial-material framework God has fashioned and sustained. God takes it to God's self in the fullest possible way in the incarnation, as we have already seen. This can be understood also in terms of correlative divine transcendence and immanence, as I have emphasized elsewhere.[34] God is fully and completely immanent in creation (and therefore not objectifiable or determinate within it), precisely because God is completely transcendent, and therefore completely available, not as something to be objectified and indicated there, but as the ultimate ground and existential context of whatever can be objectified and indicated in the space-time manifold.

This complete immanence through divine transcendence in creation, and in its completion in the achievements of the new creation, is only possible because God is a Trinity of essentially related "modes" of being God. If that were not so, God would be transcendent but isolated from involvement in creation — or even from being able to create and sustain in existence what is not God. Furthermore, since God is Originator, Word, and Spirit, God can be fully involved and intimately united with God's creation and yet unchanged in God's essential being. In fact, it is only because God can be in all circumstances unchanged in God's essential being that God can be so fully immanent in creation and communicate God's self fully to it in Word and Spirit. That would be impossible if God were not Word and Spirit, as well as Originator. Much more needs to be developed on this score. One of the pressing needs in theology is for an adequate Trinitarian account of creation which links this doctrine in an essential way with that of redemption and salvation in Christ as its precondition and first moment.[35]

Thus, from one important perspective, there is change in God, insofar as God expresses Godself in finite and material reality through the Word and in the Spirit, and thus in God's intimate and evolving relationships to all that which God has created. Torrance says:

> Space and time are affirmed as real for God in the actuality of His relations with us, which binds us to space and time, so that neither we nor God can contract out of them.[36]

However, there is no change in God, insofar as God is in God's self. God is no more faithful than God was, no more love than God was, no more pure Act and infinite Goodness and fullness of Being than God was. But those divine attributes have been expressed finitely in a fuller way than before. And God in God's Trinitarian being intimately unites God's self to those created realities. That does not change God as one term in that relationship. It changes what is not God — in the ever new life and action in space and in time.

Notes

1. The Vatican Observatory and the Center for Theology and Natural Sciences (CTNS) sponsor ongoing collaborative research in this area. See the published results of this initiative, Robert J. Russell, Nancey Murphy, and C. J. Isham, eds., *Quantum Cosmology and the Laws of Nature: Scientific Perspectives on Divine Action* [hereafter referred to as QCLN] (Vatican City State: Vatican Observatory Publications, 1993), and Robert J. Russell, Nancey Murphy, and Arthur R. Peacocke, eds., *Chaos and Complexity: Scientific Perspectives on Divine Action* [hereafter referred to as CC] (Vatican City State: Vatican Observatory Publications, in press), as well as an earlier preliminary volume, Robert J. Russell, William R. Stoeger, S.J., and George V. Coyne, S.J., eds., *Physics, Philosophy and Theology: A Common Quest for Understanding* [hereafter referred to as PPT] (Vatican City State: Vatican Observatory Publications, 1988; 2d ed., 1995). The Center of Theological Inquiry, in Princeton, New Jersey, is also pursuing annual consultations on the subject of divine action in the world, as part of a larger program. In both cases, researchers representing theology, philosophy, and the natural sciences are involved.

2. See Thomas F. Torrance, *Space, Time and Incarnation* (London: Oxford University Press, 1969), 54ff.

3. Karl Rahner, S.J., *The Trinity,* trans. Joseph Donceel (New York: Herder and Herder, 1970).

4. See John J. O'Donnell, S.J., *Trinity and Temporality* (Oxford: Oxford University Press, 1983); Robert W. Jenson, *The Triune Identity: God according to the Gospel* (Philadelphia: Fortress Press, 1982); Joseph A. Bracken, S.J., *Society and Spirit: A Trinitarian Cosmology* (Selinsgrove, Pa.: Susquehanna University Press, 1991); Ted Peters, *God as Trinity* (Louisville: Westminster/John Knox Press, 1993); Duane H. Larson, "The Temporality of the Trinity: A Christian Theological Concept of Time and Eternity in View of Contemporary Physical Theory," Ph.D dissertation, Ann Arbor, UMI, 1993; Duane H. Larson, "The Trinity and Time's Flow," *Dialog* 33, no. 1 (Winter 1994): 62–70, and references therein.

5. See William R. Stoeger, S.J., "Describing God's Action in the World in Light of Scientific Knowledge of Reality," CC.

6. At the end of his article, "Observation, Revelation, and Posterity of Noah," in PPT, Nicholas Lash points out in this regard that, "if...we keep in mind the *singleness* of the Word which God is and utters in his stillness — then we shall be brought to acknowledge...that we are as close to the heart of the sense of creation in considering and responding to an act of human kindness as in attending to the fundamental physical structures and initial conditions of the world" (213).

7. Boethius, *The Consolation of Philosophy,* 5, 6., and *De Trinitate,* 4.

8. Ted Peters, *God as Trinity,* 148–49. See also Robert Cummings Neville, *Eternity and Time's Flow* (Albany, N.Y.: State University of New York Press, 1993), 128–29.

9. Torrance, *Space, Time and Incarnation,* 75.

10. The issue of time in general relativity, quantum field theory, and quantum cosmology is well treated in an accessible fashion in two articles by C. J. Isham, "Creation of the Universe as a Quantum Process," in PPT, 375–408, and "Quantum Theories of the Creation of the Universe," in QCLN, 49–89. More advanced and scientifically specialized reviews of the problem are C. J. Isham, "Canonical Quantum Gravity and the Problem of Time," in L. A. Ibort and M. A. Rodriguez, eds., *Integrable Systems, Quantum Groups, and Quantum Field Theories* (Dordrecht and Boston: Kluwer Academic Publishers, 1993), 157–287, and Karel V. Kuchar, "Time and Interpretations of Quantum Gravity," in G. Kunstatter, D. E. Vincent, and J. G. Williams, eds., *Proceedings of the 4th Canadian Conference on General Relativity and Relativistic Astrophysics* (1992): 211–314.

11. See Isham, in PPT, 388–90.

12. See, for instance, Ilya Prigogine, *From Being to Becoming: Time and Complexity in the Physical Sciences* (San Francisco: W. H. Freeman, 1980), and Ilya Prigogine and Isabelle Stengers, *Order Out of Chaos: Man's New Dialogue with Nature* (New York: Bantam Books, 1984).

13. Lawrence Sklar, "Up and Down, Left and Right, Past and Future," *Nous* 15 (1981): 111–29, reprinted in Robin Le Poidevin and Murray MacBeath, eds., *The Philosophy of Time* (Oxford: Oxford University Press, 1993), 99–116.

14. Neville, *Eternity and Time's Flow.*

15. Isham, in PPT, 383.

16. This expressive term has been coined by Howard J. Van Till. As he himself points out, the essence of functional integrity, however, goes back to Basil of Caesarea (*Hexaemeron*) and Augustine (*De Genesi ad Litteram*). See Van Till, *The Fourth Day: What the Bible and the Heavens Are Telling Us about Creation* (Grand Rapids: Eerdmans, 1986), and his Templeton Lecture, "Evolutionary Science and the Forgotten Doctrine of Creation's Functional Integrity," Yale University, November 12, 1992, unpublished draft.

17. Neville, *Eternity and Time's Flow.*

18. Larson, "The Trinity and Time's Flow," 66.

19. Neville, *Eternity and Time's Flow.*

20. Ibid., 12 and passim.

21. William R. Stoeger, S.J., "Contemporary Physics and the Ontological Status of the Laws of Nature," in QCLN, 209–34.

22. Neville, *Eternity and Time's Flow,* 112.

23. See David Bohm, *Wholeness and the Implicate Order* (London and Boston: Routledge and Kegan Paul, 1980), and David Bohm and B. J. Hiley, *The Undivided Universe: An Ontological Interpretation of Quantum Theory* (London and New York: Routledge, 1993).

24. Neville, *Eternity and Time's Flow,* 172–73.

25. Ibid., 127–33.

26. Ibid., 153.

27. Peters, *God as Trinity.* See also Ted Peters, "The Trinity in and beyond Time," in QCNL, 263–91.

28. O'Donnell, *Trinity and Temporality.*

29. Jensen, *The Triune Identity.*

30. Larson, "The Temporality of the Trinity."

31. I am indebted to Michael Welker for stressing this aspect of the Priestly account of creation in an unpublished paper, "Creation in a Recent Perspec-

tive of the Natural Sciences and in the Biblical Perspective of the Priestly Writing," Center of Theological Inquiry Consultation, 1994; see also Michael Welker, "What Is 'Creation'?: Rereading Genesis 1 and 2," *Theology Today* 48(1991): 56ff.

32. Millard C. Lind, "Monotheism, Power, and Justice: A Study in Isaiah 40–55," *Catholic Biblical Quarterly* 46 (1984): 432; J. Gerald Janzen, "On the Moral Nature of God's Power: Yahweh and the Sea in Job and Deutero-Isaiah," *Catholic Biblical Quarterly* 56 (1994): 458. I am indebted to Dennis Hamm, S.J., for pointing this work out to me.

33. Janzen, "On the Moral Nature of God's Power," 465.

34. Stoeger, "Describing God's Action in the World in Light of Scientific Knowledge of Reality," in CC.

35. Two recent works in which some progress in doing this has been made are Nicholas Lash, *Believing Three Ways in One God* (Notre Dame, Ind.: University of Notre Dame Press, 1993); and Colin E. Gunton, *The One, the Three and the Many* (Cambridge: Cambridge University Press, 1993).

36. Torrance, *Space, Time and Incarnation,* 75.

11

Religion, Science, and Bioethics

– ALBERT R. JONSEN –

Religion and science have engaged in hostilities over the past four centuries. At times, the hostility was diplomatic, as one attempted to insinuate itself into the other or claim pieces of each other's territory. At other times, the hostility broke out into battle. The battle has often resembled the tumultuous naval engagements in the days of wooden ships and iron men. Fought amid the confusion of gunsmoke and noise, the great vessels lurch and lumber toward and away from each other. Gunshot tear gaping wooden wounds and tangle lines. Boarding parties hack flesh indiscriminately. Once exhausted, the battered ships separate and sail away to different quarters, losing sight of each other and seeking safe harbors. The controversies between religion and science have been similarly confusing, sporadic, and, above all, fought in great volleys of accusations. Often enough like the balls of the great guns, these accusations flew wide of the mark, which could not be clearly seen by either side. Broad theological affirmations were met by equally broad scientific retorts. Faith claims tried to refute empirical evidence; scientific theories were offered as indisputable proofs. Each disputant engaged in tactics for which it had not been trained.[1] Michael Buckley has chronicled some of these intellectual battles as perceptively as Patrick O'Brien describes the naval battles of the Napoleonic wars.[2]

The cosmology disputes of the sixteenth century and the evolutionary debates of the nineteenth were, from a distant view, battles of this sort. The cosmological dispute, after damaging the reputation of its greatest scientist among believers and enhancing it among his colleagues, soon became a historical oddity.[3] The smoke cleared, the noise faded, leaving the science untouched and religious integrity tarnished. Over the following century, religion and science sailed warily by each other, sometimes engaging in hostile action, sometimes entering ill-advised alliances to the disadvantage of both. Buckley writes of that momentous time in the history of ideas, "Over [those] centuries, 'physics, mathematics, medicine, every science' [he is quoting Marx] asserted their own autonomy.... Theology alienated its nature by generating a philosophy that functioned as apologetics. Philosophy eventually developed into natural philosophy which became mechanics. And mechanics established its own nature by denying that its evidence possessed any theological significance and by negating any theological interest."[4] In the nineteenth century, the war broke out again in full force. By the time of the evolution debate, peace talks were rendered impossible by mutual misunderstanding and the clamor and confusion of battle obscured truth on either side.[5] While the major Christian denominations retired early from the fray, that war is still fought in fundamentalist pulpits and school board rooms. The science depending on the evolutionary hypothesis sails serenely by, far enough away from the guns that it scarcely hears their retort or sees their smoke. One reads the history of these wars, wondering why they were fought and to what end all the turmoil and destruction.

In one place, and only quite recently, religion has met science not in enmity but in curious amity. One of the most stalwart fleets of religion, theological ethics, sailed into one of the most capacious harbors of science, modern medicine. Theological ethics met medical ethics; philosophical ethics soon joined the flotilla. All three quickly learned to sail together. Instead of a melee, a conversation ensued, which came to be called bioethics. That conversation began over troubled waters. It was by no means easy to communicate. The conversants spoke different languages, had different perspectives, and held different interests. Still, they found it possible to join in a common cause. I was an early participant in that conversation. By chance, I had been well educated in two distinct vernaculars of theological ethics, Protestant and Roman Catholic, and had more than a passing familiarity with philosophical ethics. Although not a physician, I became part of a medical faculty at the beginning of my teaching career. Thus, I have seen the forming of that fleet out of quite different intellectual allegiances. In this essay I offer my interpretation of the ways in which theological ethics, moral philosophy, and professional morality have, over the last thirty years, been able to sail together, criticizing and reinforcing each other.

The word "bioethics" was invented in the late 1960s. Like many inventions, it had dual, mutually unconnected, origins.[6] Both inventors were physician-scientists. One, Van Rensselaer Potter of the University of Wisconsin, thought it a suitable term to describe a study bringing together the evolutionary sciences devoted to human relationship to the natural environment and a broad range of humanistic values. The other, Andre Hellegers of Georgetown University, applied it to the study of the ethical implications of modern scientific medicine. Hellegers's interpretation prevailed. The 1976 *Encyclopedia of Bioethics* defined bioethics as: "the systematic study of human conduct in the area of the life sciences and health care, insofar as this conduct is examined in the light of moral principles and values."[7] As the field grew through the 1970s, scholars devoted their attention to the ethical questions arising in biomedicine: research using human subjects, genetic screening and genetic engineering, euthanasia, allocation of scarce medical resources. The broad ecological and environmental focus of Potter's conception was narrowed to the particular questions encountered in clinical medicine and health policy. A variety of scholars joined eagerly in this new study, which soon came, perhaps prematurely, to be called a discipline.[8] Still, a stream of scholarly articles began, many of them published in the medical rather than the theological and philosophical literature. Journals were founded; books published; conferences held. Faculty positions were established, mostly in schools of medicine. Government panels and commissions were set up with mandates to explore "the ethical, legal, and social implications" of various advances in medicine.

My entry into this new field came when, as a professor of moral philosophy and moral theology at the University of San Francisco, a Jesuit institution, I was invited to join an advisory committee to the Director of the National Heart and Lung Institute. The Committee was asked to study "the moral, ethical, social, economic and psychological implications of the totally implanted, nuclear powered artificial heart." My only qualification for joining such a committee was a sound education in moral philosophy and moral theology, gained during my Jesuit training and an excellent education in religious ethics at Yale University's Department of Religious Studies. I had no medical background and little knowledge of biology. However, during the year that the Artificial Heart Assessment Panel met, I was invited to come to the school of medicine, University of California, San Francisco, first as a visiting professor, then as the first professor of medical ethics. There I began to learn the language of medicine and the problems faced by its practitioners in an era of rapid technological advance. I began to make contact with the few others who were working in this field, particularly Dr. Hellegers at Georgetown and Daniel Callahan at his newly created Hastings Center, then called the Institute for Society, Ethics and the Life Sciences.

It is easy to ask the question, "what are the ethical implications of this or that?" It is extremely difficult to answer that question. First, it is not at all clear what "an ethical implication" is; it is even less clear when asked, as one often was in those days, about "the ethical and moral implications" since the two words are not readily defined or distinguished. It might be thought that the two classical disciplines, moral theology and moral philosophy, would help with the answer. However, both were, in the beginning, rather inarticulate: they had much to say about theories and principles of the moral life, but very little to contribute when it came to applying those theories and principles to so unfamiliar a realm as medical technology. Another tradition, professional medical ethics, was equally inarticulate, indeed, impotent. Its precepts, developed over centuries of experience with medical practice, were almost entirely limited to the etiquette of physicians dealing with each other. The emerging bioethics had a name, but little substance.

Through the 1970s, substance began to appear. It came from the inventiveness of the scholars who realized that their home disciplines had but partial answers to the problems they were encountering. They were forced to "invent" in the rhetorical sense of the term: "the art of discovering new arguments and uncovering new things by argument," in the words of Richard McKeon.[9] Theologians such as Paul Ramsey, James Gustafson, and Richard McCormick, philosophers like Daniel Callahan, Tristam Englehardt, and Stephen Toulmin went at the issues, not only with the concepts proper to their disciplines, but with an ingenuity that found in the materials of the matter at hand "new arguments." They created "new things" in the form of policy recommendations and practical resolutions for problems that, until they pondered them, had appeared to be dilemmas. Beside the traditional philosophers and theologians, students began to be trained in bioethics itself, a novel amalgam of the principles of moral philosophy, the techniques of moral theology, some jurisprudence, some sociology, and bits of medicine and science. During the 1980s, "bioethicists" became welcome participants on public commissions, professional committees, and even in the courtrooms, where legal disputes began to be colored by ethical questions. I served on the two initial federal commissions that Congress established to examine a range of ethical problems in medicine and biomedical science.

In the small territory of bioethics, the long war between religion and science had come to a truce. I have my own explanation for the cessation of hostilities: an explanation that comes from the peculiar education and the exceptional experiences I enjoyed. I cannot claim that this personal profile explains the evolution of bioethics; I merely suggest that the bioethics that has come into being owes something to the convergence of disciplines that I witnessed and participated in. Each bioethicist tells his or her own story about entry into this novel field and about the intellectual elements that constitute it. My story is but one view and I tell it, not as autobiography, but as a hypothesis about how bioethics "invented" itself.

My education in ethics fell into four parts. First, I was exposed to the "natural law" form of moral philosophy commonly taught in Catholic seminaries and colleges until recently. However, I did those studies at a time when the "scholastic revival" brought us the revitalized versions of natural law ethics shaped by Jacques Maritain and Yves Simon, as well as contact with the roots of that tradition in Aquinas and Aristotle. Second, I studied Roman Catholic moral theology on the edge of Vatican II, which provided both the ecclesiastical casuistry of the tradition and the

biblical and theological insights of the renewal prompted by such figures as Häring and Fuchs. Third, and most unusual for the Catholic
cleric that I then was, I had a rich exposure to Protestant theological
ethics, mentored by Yale's James Gustafson. We read authors not found
in Catholic reading lists: Luther, Calvin, Barth, Kierkegaard, and met
Paul Ramsey, Paul Lehmann, Paul Tillich, and Joseph Fletcher. Finally,
during my graduate years, I was introduced to the pragmatists and util-
itarians and to the metaethics that had swept postwar from the British
universities into American moral philosophy. This was an unusual education in ethics: most of my bioethical colleagues had absorbed parts,
but few had experienced the fourfold exposure that I had enjoyed. I believe that the fourfold exposure reveals the inner structure of modern
bioethics.

Clearly, the intellectual resources of each — natural law moral philosophy, Catholic moral theology, Protestant theological ethics, and
contemporary philosophical ethics — are deep and wide. I shall select
one feature of each that I found central, that has influenced my own
work and, in my opinion, has shaped bioethics. From Protestant theology, I select the theme of ambiguity, from Catholic moral philosophy
the concept of entelechy, from Catholic moral theology the method of
casuistry, and from contemporary moral theology the method of conceptual analysis. I shall try to show, in brief compass, how each of these
contributes to the practice of bioethics.

Ambiguity is not intended as a synonym for obscurity, uncertainty,
or doubt. Rather, it designates a profound view of reality: one in which
each facet of nature, history, and human experience reflects dual and antithetical interpretations. The Hebrew Bible presents Yahweh as terrible
in justice and gentle in love. The Pauline letters speak of flesh and spirit.
St. Augustine discovered two cities; Martin Luther divided theological
truth into law and gospel. Theologians struggled to understand the tensions and contrasts between sin and redemption, nature and grace, death
and resurrection. Among the moderns, Kierkegaard dwells on either/or,
and Reinhold Niebuhr on love and justice. As I entered the world of
Protestant theology, I was impressed by how often the great theologians invoked dualities of this sort. By no means universal or constant in
meaning, they appear again and again, with a frequency and force that is
absent in Catholic theology. In the earliest years of interest in bioethics, a
leading Protestant theologian, Helmut Thielicke, gave a major address in
which he exposed "the ambiguity of medical progress," in which saved
lives live wretchedly and genetically defective persons are preserved to
pass on their genetic defects to posterity. He then asked, "What is the
origin of this ambiguity?" and answered, "The Christian tradition has
always been aware of the mystery which here comes to light. It has seen
in this ambiguity a manifestation of the halflight between creation and

fall, between man as he was meant to be and as he presently is, standing in sinful contradiction to his intended destiny."[10] Catholic moral theology had never exploited the concept of ambiguity, preferring to dwell in the light of certainty shed by deductive natural law reasoning and ecclesiastical responsa. However, in the 1970s, certain Catholic theologians found ambiguity as an element of an old Catholic idea, the principle of double effect. Richard McCormick entitled a lecture "Ambiguity and Moral Choice,"[11] and several years later co-authored a volume with Paul Ramsey with the title, *Doing Evil to Achieve Good: Moral Choice in Conflict Situations.*[12] It is worth noting that both these theologians had been deeply involved in bioethics at the time they collaborated on that volume.

The concept of ambiguity is complex. One aspect of its complex meaning, however, fitted the emerging field of bioethics perfectly. The topics of that field were all problems created, as Thielicke had noted, by the progress of medical science. Inevitably, the problem arose because, in the words of McCormick and Ramsey's subtitle, a moral choice had to be made in conflict situations. The conflict consisted in the inevitable harms that were associated with the benefits of modern scientific medicine. Human experimentation subjected individuals to risks in hopes of conquering disease in the future. Threatened life is saved only to leave behind a damaged mind or body. Genetic diagnosis can predict disease but offer no cure. These "double effects" are inextricably linked and the moral choice is not "either/or" but "both/and." The moral question is how to proceed amid this ambiguity.

The nascent bioethics benefited from the centrality of a theme of ambiguity. It was made clear that such a practice as experimentation with human subjects is not an evil, treating humans as guinea pigs, but a practice that produces both benefits and harms, enhances human dignity and impinges on human rights. Policies about experimentation must attempt to maximize the benefits and protect dignity; minimize the harms and offenses. This theme, so congenial to Protestant theology, which maintains a doctrine of justification in which sin remains, and so compatible with the Catholic teaching about the "double effect" of many moral acts, provided a perspective on the new problems of biology and medicine.

It is not enough to have perspective. Ethics is not merely a view of things, but a view which affects and effects decision and action. Two features, drawn from Catholic moral philosophy and from Catholic moral theology, helped to provide this move from perspective to action. Catholic moral philosophy, built on deep foundations of Aristotelian and Aquinian ethics, had long given primacy to the concept of entelechy, or the end of action. Although much debased over history and battered by modern analytic philosophy, it also fitted into the work of the nascent bioethics. One of the constant features of the problems of bioethics is the presence of a beneficent intent. When the ethicists entered the halls of medicine, they found a tangle of technology, but behind it an ancient and still honored tradition, phrased in the maxim of Hippocrates, "benefit the sick and do them no harm or injustice." The technology had obscured the meaning of "benefit," since its could produce regular and inevitable effects that may not be appreciated by their recipients.

Among the many medical efforts to benefit, one in particular posed a paradigm problem, sustaining unconscious life. Saving life was seen by physicians as a primary duty; at the same time, physicians who appreciated the tradition of their profession heeded the appeal to a serious evaluation of what constitutes benefit to their patients. The aim and intent, then, of medical interventions became a constant topic of discussion: whether there was any intrinsic end to medicine itself, how the end of research differs from the end of medical practice, who should determine the aims and intents, and what should be done when there is little likelihood of success. Although much of this discussion was pursued with scant attention to the complexities and ambiguities inherent in the concept of end, aim, and intent, it was a productive source for the invention of argument. This encounter with a living tradition of professional ethics, built on the intent to benefit, added an important element to bioethics.

Such discussions are inevitably entangled in the circumstances of cases. Early in bioethics, the importance of the case as a unit of analysis was recognized. Cases, with actual patients suffering from real diseases, are the stuff of medical practice; medical practitioners find a case discussion more congenial, and more persuasive, than a theoretical reflection on principles. In the first major book of modern bioethics, Paul Ramsey noted, "medical ethics today must be 'casuistry'; it must deal as competently and exhaustively as possible with the concrete features of actual moral decisions of life and death and medical care."[13] Ramsey did dwell on cases with great ingenuity, but he never elucidated what a modern "casuistry" would look like. Stephen Toulmin and I attempted to do that in our *Abuse of Casuistry,* which was inspired by our mutual experience on the National Commission for Protection of Human Subjects, which Congress charged with the task of preparing recommendations to protect the rights and welfare of research subjects. We both noted how the commissioners could agree on particular cases while holding very different theoretical justifications for their positions.[14] From my own education in the classical casuistry of moral theology, enhanced by research into its history, I thought that analogical reasoning and the importance of circumstances in giving moral weight to principles were the keys to casuistic analysis. Toulmin provided an astute comparison between the role of moral theory and moral practice. While the discussion about the nature and utility of casuistry goes on, it has become clear that the view of moral theory, as articulated by philosophers such as Sidgwick and Broad, needed to be supplemented by a view of casuistry, not merely as the application of theory to cases, but as a mode of reasoning about analogous cases and circumstances. Modern bioethicists are, overtly or covertly, enthusiastically or unwillingly, all casuists.

The final contribution to bioethics came from contemporary philosophical ethics. The geniuses of modern ethical thought, such as Hume, Kant, and Mill, elaborated systems; the scholars of contemporary ethics began to deconstruct those systems, even before "deconstruction" was a term of art. The criticisms of the inner structure of utilitarian theory and, later, the criticism of the rational foundations of any ethical system, seemed to render philosophical ethics impotent and foolish. Yet it survived the period of sterile metaethics that reigned from the 1950s to the 1970s in American universities. Stephen Toulmin has argued that "medicine saved the life of ethics," by drawing the remote moral philosophers into the real, agonizing problems of medicine.[15] At the same time, many moral philosophers felt guilt at having so little to offer on the ethical problems posed by conscientious objection, the war in Vietnam, American racism, and poverty. The journal *Philosophy and Public Affairs,* founded in the mid 1960s, was dedicated to the conviction that moral philosophy should have a voice in these burning issues. However, the moral philosophy that survived metaethics was not unscathed by it. It brought with it, not the radical skepticism about rationality in ethics, but a heightened appreciation for rationality of argumentation. It had learned to make meticulous distinctions between concepts and to challenge the logic of moral argument. R. M. Hare, one of the principal advocates of the new moral philosophy, once told a bioethics conference, "The main — perhaps the only — contribution of the philosopher to the solution of these problems [in medical ethics] is clarification of the logical properties of tricky words like wrong, and the establishment of canons of valid argument."[16]

This may seem a modest claim, but it has momentous consequences. Ethics is rarely a cool, calm reflection; it is more often a contentious business. It opens up emotions, challenges commitments, confronts tragedy, and often leaves doubt and confusion where apparent certainty had prevailed. Articles can be written that disguise this turmoil, but let the ethicist enter a hospital conference room and the turmoil will be evident. The ability to clarify words, concepts, and arguments that comes naturally to a trained philosopher must be carried into the real debates and clashes of opinion and emotion that constitute bioethics. Prevailing ideas of the medical tradition, such as the concepts of "extraordinary" and "ordinary" care and the moral implications of each, required considerable clarification in the early days of bioethics. Skilled philosophers, such as Dan Brock, Dan Wikler, and Allen Buchanan, spent much effort in "clarifying the logical properties of tricky words," like "withholding" and "withdrawing," "omission" and "commission," for one of the most significant documents of bioethics, the Report of the President's Commission on the Study of Ethical Problems in Medicine, entitled *Deciding to Forego Life-Sustaining Treatment.*[17]

Thus, I find in my own education and experience the elements that, in my opinion, make up bioethics and contribute to its success: a theme of moral ambiguity, a concept of entelechy, a technique of casuistry, and a competence at conceptual analysis. Each of these elements derives from a distinct discipline (although they certainly overlap). It is for this reason that I prefer to call bioethics "an interdisciplinary practice" rather than a discipline. It draws on parent disciplines for different concepts and skills and brings them to bear on a changing subject matter. A younger bioethicist than I might note other features that have become more prominent, such as the influence of gender studies and ethnic studies. Other bioethicists of my own seniority might note that bioethics has imported notions of rights from jurisprudence and politics or cost-benefit analysis from economics. I do not deny that these elements are present, some with increasing visibility, in contemporary bioethics. I have done nothing more than reflect on my own experience within bioethics and ruminate on how my experience reflects some of the important features of the evolution of the practice.

Returning to my original thesis, namely, that bioethics represents an amicable relationship between science and religion, I close with an actual example. On June 20, Dr. Claire Randall, Rabbi Bernard Mandelbaum, and Bishop Thomas Kelly, the general secretaries of the National Council of Churches, the Synagogue Council of America, and the United States Catholic Conference, signed a letter to President Jimmy Carter. The letter began,

> We are rapidly moving into a new era of fundamental danger, triggered by the rapid growth of genetic engineering. Albeit, there may be opportunity for doing good; the very term suggests the danger. Who shall determine how human good is best served when new life forms are being engineered? Who shall control genetic experimentation and its results which could have untold implications for human survival? Who will benefit and who will bear any adverse consequences, directly or indirectly? These are not ordinary questions. These are moral, ethical, and religious questions. They deal with the fundamental nature of human life and the dignity and worth of the individual human being.[18]

The religious leaders exclaimed, "Those who would play God will be tempted as never before." These words could have been the clarion for another crusade like that against the evolutionists. President Carter, a religious man, must have pondered the letter, but, instead of responding, he forwarded the letter to the newly established President's Commission

for the Study of Ethical Problems in Medicine. I was privileged to be a
member of that commission. The commission had already embarked on
a study of the ethical issues attending genetic screening and counseling.
It recognized the complaint of the religious leaders that there was no
organized oversight of the rapidly expanding field of molecular biology
and its applications to medicine, commonly referred to as "genetic engineering." Thus, it undertook a study to respond to the religious leaders'
concerns. On November 16, 1982, it issued its report, *Splicing Life: The
Social and Ethical Issues of Genetic Engineering with Human Beings.*

The three religious leaders had spoken on behalf of their denominations. They had defined their questions as "moral, ethical, and
religious." The commission's first step was to ask those leaders "to
elaborate on any uniquely theological considerations underlying their
concern about gene splicing in humans." We wished to know whether
the popular language that they invoked, "playing God," had any sound
theological grounds: Was there a divine command against creating new
life forms or crossing species boundaries? Was this science infringing on
a divine prerogative? The three general secretaries appointed theological
committees to respond to our question. These theologians responded (in
the commission's summary words),

> Contemporary developments in molecular biology raise issues of respon-
> sibility rather than being matters to be prohibited because they usurp
> powers that human beings should not possess. The Biblical religions teach
> that human beings are, in some sense, co-creators with the Supreme
> Creator. Thus... these major religious faiths respect and encourage the en-
> hancement of knowledge about nature, as well as responsible use of that
> knowledge. Endorsement of genetic engineering, which is praised for its
> potential to improve the human estate, is linked with the recognition that
> the misuse of human freedom creates evil and that human knowledge and
> power can result in harm.[19]

The final words recall Helmut Thielicke's remarks about the theological basis of ambiguity. The commission realized that the theologians
and religious leaders, while speaking from their traditions, had essentially the "same concerns [that] have been raised — sometimes in slightly
different words — by many thoughtful secular observers of science and
technology." The concerns of religious and secular observers alike focused on the potential misuse of information and powers that could
do much good. The "moral, ethical, and religious questions" could be
framed in terms of the radical ambiguity of human choices, an ambiguity
that might be particularly telling to persons steeped in the biblical faiths,
but which could be perceived by any sensitive person. That ambiguity
could be spelled out in terms of the aims and purposes of the science
and technology, as well as of the persons who apply them. The commission brings to the three religious leaders another religious leader of

unquestionable authority, Pope John Paul II, who, in addressing a meeting of genetic scientists, stated his approval of genetic science "when its aim is to ameliorate the conditions of those who are afflicted with chromosomic diseases. . . . I have no reason to be apprehensive for those experiments in biology that are performed by scientists who, like you, have a profound respect for the human person, since I am sure that they will contribute to the integral well-being of man."[20]

In addition to aims, purposes, and intents, the ambiguity infects the consequences of genetic engineering. Thus, careful and continual inspection must review how scientific advances are translated into medical applications, with what effects on diseases and with what risks, with what evolutionary impact on the human species, with what influence on parental roles and responsibilities, social attitudes, and sense of personal identity. And, in all these considerations, evaluation of the desirable and undesirable, the more or less likely, the more or less serious, must be worked through. This is the casuistry of genetic medicine, continually looking to the similarities and differences between different cases. In doing this, great care must be taken to sharpen the understanding of concepts and strengthen the logic of arguments for or against certain applications. Responsibility for these tasks must be assigned, and the commission recommends to the president and the Congress how this might be done.

Splicing Life presents a paradigm of bioethics mediating between religion and science. It provides a safe harbor, where the threat of war or misunderstanding can be avoided by rational discourse that is to the point and in a common vernacular. Bioethics, like all human enterprises, is itself ambiguous and fallible. Some issues of contention it cannot seem to settle: abortion is the prime example. Other issues may arise between religion and science that will be intractable. Nevertheless, bioethics as it has emerged in the last several decades has created a unique forum for consultation and conciliation of disputes that might otherwise have broken into the confusion of hostility.

Notes

1. John Brooke, *Science and Religion: Some Historical Perspectives* (Cambridge: Cambridge University Press, 1991).

2. Michael Buckley, *At the Origins of Modern Atheism* (New Haven: Yale University Press, 1987); also Patrick O'Brien, *Master and Commander* (New York: Norton, 1990).

3. Pietro Redondi, *Galileo Heretic* (Princeton: Princeton University Press, 1987).

4. Buckley, *At the Origins of Modern Atheism,* 358.

5. Ronald Numbers, *The Creationists* (New York: Knopf, 1992).

6. Warren Reich, "The Word 'Bioethics': Its Birth and the Legacies of Those

Who Shaped Its Meaning," *The Kennedy Institute of Ethics Journal* 4, no. 4 (1995): 319–36.

7. Warren Reich, ed., *The Encyclopedia of Bioethics* (New York: Free Press, 1976), xix.

8. Daniel Callahan, "Bioethics as a Discipline," *Hastings Center Report* 1, no. 1 (1972).

9. Richard McKeon, *Rhetoric* (Woodbridge, Conn.: OxBridge Press, 1987), 59.

10. Helmut Thielicke, "The Doctor as Judge of Who Shall Live and Who Shall Die," in Kenneth Vaux, ed., *Who Shall Live?* (Philadelphia: Fortress Press, 1970), 154.

11. Richard McCormick, *Ambiguity in Moral Choice* (Milwaukee: Marquette University Press, 1973).

12. Richard McCormick and Paul Ramsey, *Doing Evil to Achieve Good: Moral Choice in Conflict Situations* (Chicago: Loyola University Press, 1978).

13. Paul Ramsey, *The Patient as Person* (New Haven: Yale University Press, 1970), xvii.

14. Albert R. Jonsen and Stephen E. Toulmin, *The Abuse of Casuistry: A History of Moral Reasoning* (Berkeley and Los Angeles: University of California Press, 1986).

15. Stephen Toulmin, "How Medicine Saved the Life of Philosophy," *Perspectives in Biology and Medicine* 24, no. 4 (1982): 736–52.

16. Richard Hare, "Can the Moral Philosopher Help?" in S. F. Spicker and H. T. Engelhardt, eds., *Philosophical Medical Ethics* (Dordrecht and Boston: D. Reidel, 1977), 52.

17. President's Commission for the Study of Ethical Problems in Medicine, *Deciding to Forego Life Sustaining Treatment* (Washington, D.C.: U.S. Government Printing Office, 1982).

18. President's Commission for the Study of Ethical Problems in Medicine, *Splicing Life: The Social and Ethical Issues of Genetic Engineering with Human Beings* (Washington, D.C.: U.S. Government Printing Office, 1982), Appendix B, 96.

19. Ibid., 53–54.

20. Ibid., 56; see also *Osservatore Romano* (October 24, 1982): 2.

Part III

THEOLOGY
– AND –
SPIRITUALITY

12

The Crisis of Transcendence and the Task of Theology

– PAUL CROWLEY, S.J. –

Ours is a perplexing time. It is marked, on the one hand, by the resurgence of religion and of religious power, especially in the political realm, and by a renewed interest in the practice of religion on the part of many. On the other, there seems to be a dearth of spirit, a nagging sense that underlying all the show of religion and religious clout is a spiritual emptiness that manifests itself in bloated materialism, cultural shallowness, social disintegration, and, ironically, in a blend of religious and political fanaticism — the return of apocalyptic imagination and the praxis of violence. There would seem to be an alienation so pervasive of human beings from their spiritual ground, nature, and destiny that it can only be attributed to a loss of transcendence, a massive cultural amnesia regarding the transcendent.[1] One could say that we have forgotten God and forgotten that we are not God.

If civilization is to survive, a sense of the transcendent must be rediscovered. By "the transcendent" here we mean the spiritual origin, context, and goal of knowing and loving, indeed of all acts of the human spirit, including those which eventuate in social and political projects. Rediscovery of the transcendent is not simply a matter of religious or cultural nostalgia; the cultural loss of a sense of the transcendent has been decried in a wide variety circles, religious and academic.[2] The presumption of this essay is that any rediscovery of the transcendent in our time will require the wisdom and insight of various intellectual and religious traditions, including the distinctive resources of Christian theology, where the transcendent is revealed in existential situations that are intrinsically personal, most especially in human suffering. Recalling the meaning of the cross, especially the path to transcendence revealed in suffering, Christian theology can help chart a path to a rediscovery of the transcendent appropriate to this dark moment in human history.

This essay will suggest that Michael Buckley has helped draw the lines of a vigorous theological response to the cultural loss of the transcendent. We begin with a presentation of the problem by one of the most creative intellectual voices of our day, that of Vaclav Havel, who calls for a rediscovery and renewal of our transcendental origins. Havel raises this as a question about the fate of God in our culture, but does not pursue the question theologically. In the second section we turn to Buckley's treatment of this problem in his various works on atheism, taking note of one of his central arguments, that theology must attend to its own sources in religious experience if it is to make serious a contribution to debates about God within intellectual culture. As Buckley has argued, when theology forgets its own "data" in religious experience, it presents itself to the world as cognitively empty,[3] and can hope to contribute little to any significant discussion about transcendence. In the third section we focus explicitly on Buckley's treatment of religious experience and find here two factors pertinent to a rediscovery of transcendence: the irreducibly personal nature of religious experience and the mediation of such experience within existential reality. The directionality of the experience of transcendence is toward the real, and this drives us into the reality of suffering. Finally, we turn to Karl Rahner, who, according to Buckley, offers a theological explicitation of a spirituality that speaks of the mediation of religious experience through the reality of the cross.

Situating the Problem: The Loss of Transcendence

In a recent address at Stanford University, Czech President Vaclav Havel leveled a challenge to Western intellectuals which, if delivered by a religious leader, might have been politely ignored. But the Stanford audience could not fail to listen to this quasi-prophetic voice echoing through the halls of one of America's most important shapers of intellectual culture, calling his listeners to a recovery of the transcendent. Starting with his reflections on his recent reading of the Czech-American psychotherapist Stanislav Grof, Havel noted that even scientific research opens up questions of transcendence which lead scientists directly into the realms of philosophical speculation.

> Nor do I believe that so many modern scientists who in their work have touched on matters difficult to understand, such as the mysteries of the origin and history of the cosmos, the secrets of matter, and of space-time, and the mystery of life, have taken leave of their senses when they speak of transcendence.[4]

The experience of the transcendent, he argued, is among the most basic of human experiences. Yet we have lost it. Havel describes a situation of spiritual impoverishment in the Euro-American cultural tradition that has been noted by many outside of it. This spiritual impoverishment has given rise to moral relativism, materialism, the denial of any kind of spirituality, a proud disdain for everything supra-personal, a profound crisis of authority and the resulting general decay, a frenzied consumerism, a lack of solidarity, the selfish cult of material success, the absence of faith in a higher order of things or simply in eternity, and [an] expansionist mentality that holds in contempt everything that in any way resists the dreary standardization and rationalism of technical civilization.[5]

The West is now facing the consequences of a loss of the transcendent, Havel argued, and must undertake a rediscovery and renewal of our own "transcendental origins," of the "experience of transcendence" which unites all of humanity, and of that transcendent dimension "without which [humanity] would not be and of which [humanity] is an integral part."[6]

Havel is characteristically nonprescriptive about what he means by the transcendent dimension of human existence. Nevertheless, his Stanford address limns the transcendent as the ground, general context, and directionality of human existence. Transcendence describes the ontological ground ("transcendental origins") of the human person as the mystery whence we come and to which all of our knowledge leads us in wonder; it describes the context ("that spiritual dimension that connects all cultures") within which this experience is realized as the realm of the human, where matter and spirit intersect; and it describes the basic experience of human existence as a knowing and loving that stretches beyond concrete historical moments into spirit ("man's relationship to that which transcends him").[7] It is the universal "spiritual" dimension that calls us to a responsibility to one another.[8]

But Havel concludes on a pessimistic note. The loss of the transcendent can be correlated dialectically with the horrors of this century, each contributing to the proliferation of the other. The prospects for a rapid recovery of our transcendental origins are not bright. "Given its fatal incorrigibility, humanity probably will have to go through many more Rwandas and Chernobyls before it understands how unbelievably shortsighted a human being can be who has forgotten that he is not God."[9] Though the rediscovery and renewal of transcendence is crucial, there is bound to be an expanding experience of darkness before that recovery is finally accomplished. On the basis of his own dark experience of human affairs, past and current, Havel is not so naive as to suggest that this can be accomplished within the scope of human history. While constructive human projects, religious and political, are absolutely necessary, they cannot accomplish within human history what utopian dreams might envision. Nor can these projects alone secure a rediscovery and renewal of a lost transcendence. Finally, a rediscovery of transcendence requires being claimed again by that which transcends us; it requires rediscovery of our givenness, of the ultimate conditions for the possibility of existence. As Martin Heidegger put it in one of his more rhetorical phrases spoken in the wake of World War II, "Only a god can save us now."[10]

The problem, then, is that humankind is in quest of a transcendence it badly needs to rediscover and renew, but seems fated from the start to fall short of that goal within history. Havel refrains from offering philosophical, much less, theological remedies for the problem he describes.[11] But no one seriously engaged in theology today can fail to see this as a critical problem for theology itself; failure to attend to it is to concede the terrain of faith to skeptics and to abandon that which most belongs to theology as its object: absolute transcendence as ground, context, and experience of a human existence. Put more positively, Christian theology should be engaged with this problem because it concerns the central claim of faith: that God, who is transcendent mystery, became flesh. In the incarnation, God has driven into the flesh and bones of human reality and has revealed that human reality as the embodiment of the transcendent within history, the place from which the luminosity of God shines forth.

Intellectual Culture and the Loss of God

Long before his magisterial work on atheism, Michael Buckley was tackling this problem.[12] What distinguishes his approach to this problem from many others is that he treats it not only as a problem for philosophical theology, but also as a problem of personal meaning, and finally of spirituality. We cover this vast topic by focusing on two aspects of Buckley's treatment of it: the loss of transcendence within intellectual culture as a challenge to theology, and theology's need to take into account the data of religious experience as it deals with this problem. Buckley points us toward a renewed spirituality along the lines of Karl Rahner's sober realism, which focuses on the transcendent meaning of the cross. Where Havel is entitled to stop short of theology, Buckley forges ahead, realizing that only a theological response is adequate to the mass and depth of the problem at hand. For finally it is a problem that concerns not simply the loss of the transcendent, but (as Havel implies) the loss of God.

In his magnum opus, *At the Origins of Modern Atheism*, Buckley describes the self-alienation of religion as one of the major factors contributing to the rise of atheism as a philosophic and quasi-religious stance. This was largely due to the eagerness of theologians during the time of the Enlightenment to mount arguments demonstrating the existence of God according to the methods and data of the empirical sciences, and to neglect the warrants for faith found in revelation and religious experience. Warrants for the existence of God were taken from natural philosophy, and later from physics, rather than the knowledge to be derived from the paschal mystery of the incarnation, death, and resurrection of Christ. Theologians themselves contributed to the rise of atheism by avoiding the data of religion and religious experience. But, as Buckley observes at the end of his book: "The god defined in religion cannot be affirmed or supported adequately over time without the unique reality that is religion."[13] Theology itself helped write the epitaph of God.

Ludwig Feuerbach's rejection of theism by collapsing the transcendent into the human person and reducing the experience of transcendence to an experience of the projected self reenforced the intellectual marginalization of religion begun in the Enlightenment and defined the terms of the modern crisis of the spirit that became manifest in various forms of atheism, philosophical and systematic. Buckley's telling insight into Friedrich Nietzsche is that he, along with John Henry Newman, saw that the "gradual but profound erosion of religious belief... constituted a massive cultural phenomenon." This cultural phenomenon is tied to the gradual irrelevance of the very notion of God among the intellectuals, and

> the emergence of a certain cast of mind in greater and greater predominance, one whose sensibilities and educational background, whose ambit of intellectual interests and engagements, defined human beings constitutionally unable to believe, to know, or to be convinced in any way of the existence of the Judeo-Christian god.[14]

For Buckley, the recovery of the transcendent is not simply a problem about understanding the theories of atheism; it is more profoundly a problem about the governing questions of an intellectual culture where God eventually became an irrelevancy, and of theology's role in bringing about that remarkable phenomenon. The irony is that this began to occur during the Enlightenment, a period in fact "obsessed" with religion.[15]

This approach to the problem is already explicit in Buckley's earlier works on atheism, where he views atheism not as an abstract speculative issue, but as a phenomenon related to the cultural and intellectual construal of religion and of God. In "Experience and Culture: A Point of Departure for American Atheism,"[16] Buckley explains how John Dewey separated religious experience from a transcendent religious "object" or God, and shifted the problem of transcendence from a problem about God to a characteristic of the experience of intellectual culture, which is largely one of indifference to the existence of God.[17] Freud added to the potency of Dewey's argument through "...methodological commitment to an understanding of experience as self-enclosed, pointing to no realities beyond itself. The origins and goal of inquiry were experiences, and its horizon was culture,"[18] a culture which had redefined religious experience and grown indifferent to any transcendent directionality of this experience.

The loss of a transcendent God is of course a spiritual problem of societies properly addressed by sociology, cultural anthropology, or social psychology.[19] But it is also an intellectual problem for philosophy and theology, which belong partly to the domain of intellectual culture. Here, too, one of Buckley's longstanding concerns becomes operative in the discussion: the alienation of the intellectual classes from questions of religion and the need for theology to address the crucial issues of our time on a basis which meets and engages the intellectual classes who are so influential in the shaping of our culture.[20] Buckley speaks eloquently to this matter:

> Ours is a unique situation. However pervasively religious alienation permeates all ranks of society in Western Europe, among people of the United States as a whole religious belief and commitment have persisted strongly. One will come upon a profound alienation here not among workers, the middle class, and the recent immigrants, etc. but among the intellectuals and professional elites in communication.

The consequences are pervasive:

> This climate of mind segregates religious thought from serious engagements in business or statecraft or higher education; it mistrusts discourse that introduces absolutes or transcendence or "truth"; it makes the authority of experience depend upon its codification in those experiential or quantitative methods that took their rise from the physical and biological sciences.[21]

And, returning to a theme he developed in *At the Origins of Modern Atheism,* he concludes:

> The academy and the media are among the most formative influences upon culture. While our generation and the next may continue allegiance to religious practice out of the training that has been ours, the influence of this alienation will eventually tell — as both Newman and Nietzsche said it would tell, in the formation of a culture in which "belief in the Christian God has itself become unbelievable."[22]

The substantive content of religion, the realm of the spirit, that which is named the transcendent, must show cause why it should be admitted into educated discourses, including the discourses of the universities.

Buckley's point is that theology cannot afford to ignore the questions and challenges which are raised by those outside its own academic domain,[23] for these questions and challenges are arising from the actual experience of human beings. Buckley argues that it is the "religious manifold" of experience, even the experience of the absence of God, which formal dogmatic theology has largely failed to include within its sources of data. And this *epoché* of the religious has itself been a contributing factor to the loss of belief in the transcendent God.[24] The kind of spiritual problem described by Havel can be adequately treated by theology only when it is seen as a problem about the intellectual construal of God and of religion, and not only a problem of cultural demise, and when theology looks to its own sources in engaging the problem.

Attending to Religious Experience

Buckley's understanding of transcendence bears directly on his concern for an inclusion of the "data" of religious experience in the tasks of theology. Yet it is no easy task to determine exactly what he means by the term "transcendence." His works range from philosophical theology, atheism, and the philosophy of science, to Ignatian spirituality, Jesuit humanism, and higher education. They cover vast stretches of intellectual history and are subtly undergirded by the principles of Richard McKeon's philosophic semantics, a method which stresses the polyvalence of words and their definitions.[25]

One of Buckley's earliest public forays into this territory was made in an unpublished talk entitled "Man and God as Spirit."[26] In this fascinating early work, Buckley carefully investigates the philosophical linkages between human immortality and the existence of God. "Is there any reality which exists or can exist independent of this three-dimensional thing which we call 'body,' or is substance (what is) simply to be equated with body."[27] He resolves the issue to one of spirit: the human person is essentially spirit, underlying the dichotomies and divergences between subject and object which we regularly experience in all acts of knowing; and that spiritual ego is sustained in existence by an "uncomposed and uncaused" spirit called God. The influence upon Buckley's work of Aquinas and Rahner is clearly evident here, although he refrains from developing the theological or religious implications of the ideas he proposes.

A later presentation of transcendence that delves into the religious implications of the question appears in "Transcendence, Truth and Faith: The Ascending Experience of God in All Human Inquiry."[28] In this essay Buckley describes transcendence as the "experiential basis of authentic faith" which occurs in the movement toward truth which is a common part of human experience, and which leads one, unthematically, to that horizon which calls for articulation through religious discourse. In this line of inquiry he is clearly influenced not only by Rahner's work on transcendental subjectivity, but also, as he says, by Dupré, Gilkey, Tracy, and others who

> argue to the justification and possible validity of religious discourse from
> human limit-situations in which ultimacy is experienced, at least as a

question, and for which only religious discourse is appropriate themati-
zation — such experiences as deep joy in existence or an anxiety before
the Void which contains an infinite threat to meaning and value.[29]

Transcendence is a "going beyond" or reaching beyond limit situations,
such as those posed by spiritual crises, in successive acts of knowing.
"We transcend anything when we know it; we transcend anything in
order to know it."[30] Transcendence is, then, the process by which we
move beyond present attainments in order to know more, and it also
denotes that final goal toward which we move when we know more:
that ultimacy to which we give the name "God."[31]

Yet transcendence is not a movement of self-abstraction, a movement
away from the categorical toward the suprasensible. If it is a "going
beyond," this can be grasped only by standing within the limits of categorical reality and finding there the conditions for the possibility of
transcendence.[32] We move toward the transcendent by moving toward
the real. "The drive towards reality and towards a final coherence to
reality are the same."[33] In the experience of knowing, for example,
human beings raise questions about the meaning of life, the fundamental questions of whether, how, and why things are as they are. Such
questioning, which is a driving into reality as it is, moves the questioner
beyond oneself in a regard toward the world, toward others, finally toward the infinite context within, and goal toward which, one's knowing
tends. At the same time, knowledge, whether religious or scientific, is in-
herently personal because it is gained only through a self-transcendence
that always entails the real historical person of the knower. The experience of transcendence cannot take place except through a human person
who actually exists.

If transcendence is understood in relation to the ultimate reality called
God, God is not an otherworldly goal, but rather the ground of the
movement of transcendence (the source), the context of the experience
(the "within which"), and the infinite horizon (the goal) toward which
all movement in self-transcendence tends. Thus, God is mystery — "that
which I cannot exhaust, which I cannot go beyond, which I cannot
transcend."[34] God is the nonthematic horizon which is the presupposition for an intellectually honest faith that finally becomes articulated
in the knowledge of that God who claims us in the truth of his self-
communication and who graces us with the capacity to entrust ourselves
in freedom toward the acceptance of this gift. "In the human choice
to live a life governed by fidelity to Truth, the self-surrender of the
human person intersects with the self-communication of God."[35] This
self-communication and free acceptance of truth are expressed in the
Christian commitment to a God who has communicated himself as the
embodied Logos in the particular person of Jesus Christ. For Christian

theology, that horizon toward which all transcendence tends is a horizon which has become immanent within human experience as a historical person.

From a theological standpoint, then, the path to a rediscovery of transcendence is rooted in a restoration of the personal dimension of faith.

> This restoration of the personal must also figure strongly in any assessment of the religious resources to be disclosed within contemporary culture. For Christianity also respects experience as a point of departure for religious consciousness and assent, but that experience is primarily and irreducibly personal.[36]

The recovery of the transcendent must entail a recovery of the personal, for "one will not long believe in a personal God with whom there is no personal communication, no interaction; and the most compelling witness to a personal God must itself be personal."[37] For Buckley this cannot be an a priori assertion; it is a claim made only as a consequence of the experience of the transcendent.

Transcendence is thus further specified as (1) the process of inquiry, where God is present as the context and directionality of the movement of transcendence; (2) the absolute claim that truth makes upon the knowing subject, as when one's conscience is illuminated for the freedom of decision; and (3) the assent to truth in such a way as to give definition to one's person, where God is present as "the realization of grace" and the meaning of one's life.[38] That the experience of the transcendent is personal experience also means that it is historical; it is experienced within the reality of human existence, not in escape from it. Therefore, theology must attend to the existential human condition as the locus of the experience of transcendence.

Buckley further develops this treatment of transcendence as an existential issue in a subsequent essay, "Atheism and Contemplation."[39] This essay anticipates Buckley's later work on atheism and highlights one of the abiding underlying preoccupations of *At the Origins of Modern Atheism*. Buckley argues here that atheism and contemplation, in theory and in practice, "raise the question of the focus of religious awareness and of its commitments."[40] The central problem the essay concerns is "religious projection" of the sort suggested by Feuerbach, and later by Sigmund Freud. There are significant differences between the two. In a brilliant analysis of Feuerbach, Buckley claims that what Feuerbach borrowed from Hegel was the reflexivity of the dialectical method, leading to the well-known conclusions that God exists for the human person only as an object of consciousness, and that this divine object known as God is simply the objectification of the essence of human nature, i.e., consciousness.[41] But Buckley also mines a gem from Feuerbach not commonly noted: "To enrich God, the human person must become poor; that God may become all, man must be nothing. What you attribute to God, you take and project — literally cast off — from the human person. The human is sinful, that God may be holy."[42] God is not only the projection of human consciousness, but a projection of perfection made by an imperfect, "sinful," self-alienated human consciousness: the antithesis of the ego. Human persons have a need for God because they have a need for the holy, that which is greater than they are and which will elevate them from the nothingness of sin to the assurance of being loved.

Freud picks up on this note of self-alienation and builds upon it in *The Future of an Illusion*, a further development of religion as projection, but now projection of one aspect of the self-alienated consciousness itself, the threatening father figure. Whereas in Feuerbach the person, even in self-alienation, projects a desired perfection of human nature, for Freud the projection reflects the condition of the human person in actuality: "actional, finite, and threatened," looking for a God "who will minister to a sense of worth and provide protection from the horrors of the future."[43] Freud thus molds the templates of academic discourse about religion for much of the twentieth century, evacuating religion of its substantive content in the spirit.

But, Buckley argues, the advances of atheism ironically intersect with another movement of our time, the quest for transcendence in what he describes here as "the development of contemplation and of an interest in the mystical life."[44] Buckley notes that ours is a time within which the search for transcendence has been accelerated. What Feuerbach and Freud cast as projection may in fact be an incomplete grasp of a dynamism of the spirit that is inherent to the human being, a dynamism toward transcendence. Feuerbach's insight is that this dynamism is inseparable from human consciousness; Freud's insight is that religious experience cannot be fully separated from the psyche and its processes, nor even totally from its neuroses. Their conclusion, however, that religious experience is the fruit of projection, fails to take into account the *terminus ad quem* of transcendence, that toward which the dynamism of the human spirit tends. They thus conclude to the denial of God.

It is at this point that Buckley proposes the mystical theology of John of the Cross as an alternative to theories of projection. John of the Cross describes "a process of entering into the mystery that is God, so that gradually one is transformed by grace and this grace moves through the intense experiences of darkness into the vision of the incomprehensible God."[45] John of the Cross shares with Feuerbach and Freud the fundamental insight that all religious experience is filtered through the structures of the psyche of the religious subject; it is irreducibly personal. For John of the Cross, however, this basic insight flows naturally from the Thomistic doctrine that whatever is received is received according to the mode of the one receiving it (*quidquid recipitur per modum recipientis recipitur*).[46] And for John of the Cross, central to this "mode of receiving" is the progressive experience of purification whereby persons are gradually transformed by grace and transcend themselves and enter into a graced union with God. This is a process, "an evolution in which the experience of the desert is the essential preparation for contemplation." But, further, it is an experience of suffering "in which the reality of the cross with its sense of abandonment figures critically as the final movement into union with God."[47]

This second dimension of suffering is described in what John calls the "night of the spirit" or the night of faith. In this experience, "the concepts, the systems of meaning, the symbolic structures by which reassurance is forthcoming" have fallen away. It is an experience of dark grace, of "emptiness, impurity, weakness, abandonment, and death."[48] It is expressed most eloquently in the cross of Christ, where utter darkness is also the locus of revelation. Buckley concludes, "Any serious following of Christ leads by way of reversals or disappointments or sacrifice or suffering into the awareness that God is beyond control and beyond form."[49] The quest for transcendence, then, is not only personal, but, more precisely, rooted in the suffering and darkness of human existence.

Buckley's work can lead to the conclusion that a theological response to the kind of challenge Havel issues — the contemporary need for a rediscovery and renewal of transcendence — must take two factors into account: (1) a retrieval of the personal, and (2) a theological framework that locates the immanence of the transcendent God within existential reality, especially the reality of human suffering. If humanity is to rediscover and renew the transcendent dimension, then these fundamental insights of John of the Cross which Buckley spotlights might well be pertinent. This retrieval may occur if we take seriously the fact that suffering is often enough the form of human experience in which the transcendent is encountered.[50]

The Transcendence of the Cross

A theological alternative must be found, then, to those views of the human person and of religious experience which, as in theories of projection, limit the reality of transcendence to human subjectivity, rather than viewing the structures and patterns of human experience, including suffering, as the filters through which transcendent reality is mediated. Buckley sees potential for such a theological alternative not only in John of the Cross, but also in the mystagogical theology of Karl Rahner. Here we turn to a brief consideration of Rahner's thought particularly apposite to a retrieval of the transcendent.

As we have noted above, Buckley presumes Rahner's well-known contribution to theology of a transcendental anthropology. That anthropology does not require further rehearsing here, beyond pointing out that for Rahner, every act of knowing and loving tends asymptotically, through successive acts of self-transcendence, toward the absolute. Rahner thus provides the theoretical framework for a purely philosophical retrieval of transcendence that leads into theological claims.[51]

Equally important, though, is another aspect of Rahner's treatment of transcendental experience: the fact that the transcendental is necessarily mediated through the categorical, through the historically contingent dimensions of human existence. This includes all that actually contextualizes human freedom, including various sources of suffering. This is the foundation for what Rahner calls "sober realism." It is this aspect of Rahner's mystagogy that pertains especially to a recovery of the transcendent.

In an essay on this topic entitled "Christian Pessimism," Rahner observes that the human predicament is one of "radical perplexity."[52] Inspired by 2 Corinthians 4:8–10 ("we are perplexed but not driven to despair" [aporoumenoi all'ouk exaporoumenoi]), Rahner argues that perplexity is a permanent existential of human life. Human existence is incomprehensible; no one theory about its meaning, no one philosophy, not even one religious or theological system, can encompass the entire mystery of human existence. The personal and social projects of human beings are oriented to the construction of structures of meaning, comprehensibility, and progress. People adopt beliefs and invest in dreams to realize social utopias, but such dreams are doomed to disappointment. As if anticipating a voice like Havel's, Rahner muses:

> There still echoes in our ears the triumphant cry of a humanity that once thought itself on the brink of self-fulfillment. Now, however, we feel that we do not really know any more, that all our ideals are rapidly wearing thin, that everything is dissonance, that all our ideals and programs are pitifully impotent in the face of an ever-increasing hopelessness.[53]

The inescapable fact is that much of human existence is dark, and this darkness cannot be totally overcome within history itself simply by the agency of human beings, despite all our good will and intelligence. A Christian is a person who is soberly realistic about life, its crosses, dyings, and surds.

But Christian realism does not lead to despair, for it is precisely within this experience of darkness, within the real, that God is revealed. This insight lies at the core of the meaning of the cross. The cross says that there is an intrinsic connection between the experience of decline, suffering, and death, both personal and social, and the movement of the human spirit toward transcendence. This movement begins in our facing reality as it is, not as hapless fatalists, but in an active surrender. This active surrender entails the acceptance of God's grace, a grace darkly given in the sufferings and surds of human existence. Not unlike John of the Cross, Rahner speaks of "falling into the abyss of God's incomprehensibility."[54]

The cross of Christ is therefore not accidental, but essential to a Christian approach to transcendence. "Christianity is the religion which recognizes a man who was nailed to a cross and on it died a violent death as a sign of victory and as a realistic expression of human life."[55] The cross not only reminds us of the harsh and dark realities of life, but also that we cannot evade them in the name of religion, or even in a quest for transcendence. The cross is a crucial part of the rediscovery of transcendence, for it reveals, like a prism, the full range of God's self-communication to human persons: the givenness of life (incarnation), the luminosity of death (crucifixion), and the reach of authentic hope (resurrection). The cross is agonizing partly because it signals the end of a life born in youthful hope. It declares that death is not simply a part of human life, but rather, as Simone Weil observed, it *is* the future, pressing upon us now as surely as the force of gravity that holds us fast to earth, even from the moment of our birth.[56] The finality of the incarnation, God's assumption of a human nature and deep union with a human person, is reached in the cross, where that personal human life comes to an end. Yet this particular death is not simply an incidental feature of Jesus' life, another variable; it is the specific way God has effected salvation in human history, where the entanglement of sin, suffering, and death are perfectly embodied in the scandal of the cross.

But the cross is also the locus of the revelation of transcendence. God does more than accept Jesus' self-surrender in the darkness of death. God sees this self-surrender as the permanent validity of Jesus' life, and raises it into divinity itself. The death and resurrection of Jesus are two dimensions of one revelatory reality held together in the unity of their meaning so that one dimension cannot be understood apart from the other. The death of Jesus is "subsumed into the resurrection"[57] and is the revelation of death itself as passage from birth through graced existence to personal finality in God.[58] The darkness of death thus becomes the revelation of transcendent hope, a revelation that could not have taken place apart from the stark brutality of the cross.

The cross is therefore the revelatory locus of transcendence. First, in the cross, the manifestation of God as a human being reaches its finality in the death imposed and in the suffering acceptance of it. Second, in the abandonment of the cross there is submission not simply to the sheer force of death, but also to the God of life. Third, the transcendence of God becomes transparent in the totality of the life of Jesus. In Christian faith, suffering and death, coalesced on the cross, become the "transhistorical" way of following Jesus by dying with him.[59] The path to transcendence is blazed through a sober realism about the place and meaning of suffering in human life.

Rahner's "Christian pessimism" describes a faith stance planted firmly in the dark reality of human existence. It is "pessimistic" because it boldly admits the fact that there are no short-range solutions to the perplexity of existence. It is "Christian" because it is precisely in the experience of darkness that the movement toward the transcendent takes place. This movement toward transcendence emboldens the Christian to find grounds for meaning, commitment, and hope, because ultimately the totality of human existence depends upon the transcendent God within whom we live and move and have our being (Acts 17:28).

The Quest for Transcendence

Havel's Stanford talk was delivered to an intellectually elite audience that was not largely concerned with mystical or systematic theologies. Many may well have shared the very intellectual predispositions about the irrelevance of the God-question that Buckley has described in various works on atheism. Havel's was essentially a discourse on political philosophy; his concern was the fate of democracy on the world stage. He was thus entitled to stop short of offering a specific philosophical, much less, theological response to the issues he raised. But this fact does not let theologians themselves off the hook. What Havel raises is a profoundly theological issue, for it concerns the human spirit in relation to that which transcends humanity. A theology which remains regional or preoccupied only with provincial questions of Christian faith cannot enter into dialogue with the Havels of this world or hope to be heard by the intellectual elites whom Havel addresses. On the other hand, a Christian theology which brackets its most fundamental insights in order to render itself admissible within the intellectual culture actually contributes to the problem.

Michael Buckley's lifelong work provides theologians a model for intellectual engagement with such questions and for participation in the contemporary quest for a rediscovery of transcendence. It is firmly planted in the real and seeks transcendence in the direction of the real; it takes most seriously the data of religious experience as proper to a theological response to existential questions; and it opens up dogmatic theology to those virtualities of spirituality inherent in it. Finally, Buckley's work demonstrates how theology, far from irrelevant to contemporary cultural crises, can make an indispensable contribution toward their solution if it is faithful to its own questions and sources.

Not least among these questions and sources is the cross, which cannot fail to remind us that, in fact, we are not God.

Notes

1. See Bernard Lonergan, *Method in Theology* (New York: Herder and Herder, 1972), 55: "The term, alienation, is used in many different senses. But on the present analysis the basic form of alienation is man's disregard of the transcendental precepts.... As self-transcendence promotes progress, so the refusal of self-transcendence turns progress into cumulative decline."

2. One of the most prominent of such calls to a renewal of transcendence was "An Appeal for Theological Affirmation," also called the "Hartford Appeal," which appeared in 1975 under the signatures of twenty-five religious leaders and intellectuals. Among the signatories were Peter Berger, William Sloane Coffin, Avery Dulles, Stanley Hauerwas, George Lindbeck, Ralph McInerny, Richard John Neuhaus, Carl Peter, Gerard Sloyan, and Ileana Marculescu. See *Worldview: Symposium on the Hartford Appeal* (New York: Council on Religion and International Affairs, 1975). Although critically reviewed, the Hartford Appeal was testimony to the fact that a concern for the renewal of transcendence is not confined to those of a "nostalgic" spiritual bent. Indeed, transcendence has also surfaced as a concern among some of the architects of the theology of liberation, most especially in the writings of Gustavo Gutiérrez and Jon Sobrino. Sobrino writes: "The historical reality of the poor is something that not only ought to be analyzed and responded to in accordance with its materiality, but ought to be the object of a spiritual experience, a reality that can 'implode' into our lives and so become a mediation of the experience of God." See Jon Sobrino, "Spirituality and Theology" in *Spirituality of Liberation: Toward Political Holiness* (Maryknoll, N.Y.: Orbis Books, 1989), 67. Also to be noted is the pronounced emphasis upon transcendence in some modern philosophers, notably Eric Voegelin, George Steiner, Emmanuel Lévinas, and Louis Dupré.

3. Michael J. Buckley, "Presidential Address: The Rise of Modern Atheism and the Religious *Epoché*," *Proceedings of the Catholic Theological Society of America* 47 (1992): 82.

4. "Havel Envisions Transcendent Democracy," *Stanford University Campus Report* 27 (October 5, 1994): 7.

5. Ibid., 8.

6. Ibid.

7. Ibid.

8. For Havel's views on universality and responsibility, see *Open Letters: Selected Writings 1965–1990*, ed. Paul Wilson (New York: Alfred A. Knopf, 1991), 194–96: "If Western young people so often discover that retreat to an Indian monastery fails them as an individual or group solution, then this is obviously because, and only because, it lacks that element of universality, since not everyone can retire to an ashram. Christianity is an example of an opposite way out: it is a point of departure for me here and how — but only because anyone, anywhere, at any time, may avail themselves of it."

9. Havel, "Havel Envisions Transcendent Democracy," 8. For a somewhat similar presentation of these themes, see Havel, "The New Measure of Man,"

New York Times, July 8, 1995, A17. Havel writes: "In today's multicultural world, the truly reliable path to peaceful co-existence and creative cooperation must start from what is at the root of all cultures and what lies infinitely deeper in human hearts and minds than political opinion, convictions, antipathies or sympathies: it must be rooted in self-transcendence. The Declaration of Independence...states that the Creator gave man the right to liberty. It seems man can realize that liberty only if he does not forget the One who endowed him with it."

10. See Martin Heidegger, "Nur noch ein Gott kann uns retten," *Der Spiegel* 31 (May 1976): 193–219. The interview, with commentary, appears in Günther Neske and Emil Kettering, eds., *Martin Heidegger and National Socialism: Questions and Answers,* trans. Lisa Harries and Joachim Neugroschel (New York: Paragon House, 1990). Havel holds that the fate of democracy itself depends upon a rediscovery and renewal of transcendence in its several meanings: as origin, context, and fundamental orientation of human experience. And, in other writings, this is tied to a rediscovery of God, in the loss of whom "man has lost a kind of absolute and universal system of coordinates, to which he could always relate anything, chiefly himself" (see *Open Letters,* 94–95).

11. "Unlike many ideological utopians, fanatics and dogmatists, and a thousand more or less suspect prophets and messiahs who wander about this world as a sad symptom of its helplessness, I do not possess any special recipe to awaken the mind of man to his responsibility to the world and for the world" (Havel, "Havel Envisions Transcendent Democracy," 7).

12. A concern about transcendence has been an abiding element of Michael Buckley's work from the very beginning. While Buckley's first book, *Motion and Motion's God,* a study on the theme of the demonstrations of the existence of God from motion, is strictly philosophical and does not explicitly state this concern, the transcendence of God is in fact central to the task, as Buckley traces the shifting contours of arguments to God from motion in Aristotle and Aquinas, Cicero, Newton, and Hegel. In many ways this work prefigures his later work on atheism, not only in its method, but also in its central preoccupation with the arguments for the existence of God. Buckley concludes this work by invoking Teilhard de Chardin: " 'I am not speaking metaphorically when I say that it is throughout the length and breadth and depth of the world in movement that a man can attain the experience and vision of his God.' " See *Motion and Motion's God* (Princeton: Princeton University Press, 1971), 275.

13. *At the Origins of Modern Atheism* (New Haven: Yale University Press, 1987), 362.

14. Ibid., 29.

15. Ibid., 37.

16. In Michael Buckley, "Experience and Culture: A Point of Departure for Modern Atheism," *Theological Studies* 50 (1989): 443–65.

17. Ibid., 451–53.

18. Ibid., 455.

19. See *At the Origins of Modern Atheism,* 34.

20. This is a major argument of *At the Origins of Modern Atheism,* which also claims that atheism, which began as the position of an intellectual elite became, by the end of the twentieth century, a worldwide phenomenon of "radical godlessness" (see 27–28).

21. "Eadem caritatis ratio...," unpublished commencement address to the Jesuit School of Theology at Berkeley, May 19, 1994, 5–6.

22. Ibid. For a similar discussion, see "Education Marked with the Sign of the Cross," *America* 163 (September 1, 1990): 100–103, esp. 102.

23. For further discussion of this point, see David Tracy, "Afterword: Theology, Public Discourse, and the American Tradition," in Michael J. Lacey, ed., *Religion and Twentieth Century American Intellectual Life* (Cambridge: Woodrow Wilson International Center for Scholars and Cambridge University Press, 1989), 194.

24. See "Presidential Address," *Proceedings of the Catholic Theological Society of America* 47 (1992): 69–83.

25. "Philosophic Semantics" is McKeon's method for mapping out patterns of thought across intellectual history and through diverse sources of thought, relying upon what McKeon calls the four coordinates of selection, interpretation, method, and principle. Buckley gives a very lucid presentation of these four coordinates in *At the Origins of Modern Atheism,* 21–25, and in *Motion and Motion's God,* 8–11. McKeon himself lays it out in "Philosophic Semantics and Philosophic Inquiry," in Zahava K. McKeon, ed., *Richard McKeon: Freedom and History and Other Essays: An Introduction to the Thought of Richard McKeon* (Chicago: University of Chicago Press, 1990).

26. "Man and God as Spirit," Starved Rock State Park Fall Weekend, 1966 (unpublished). Buckley describes these notes as "often personal in tone and provisional in outline, offered as a stimulus to subsequent discussion and to those meditations out of which issues wisdom" (1).

27. Ibid.

28. Michael J. Buckley, "Transcendence, Truth and Faith: The Ascending Experience of God in All Human Inquiry," *Theological Studies* 39 (1978): 633–55.

29. Ibid., 636.

30. Ibid., 641.

31. This, of course, is a common thread running through the transcendental Thomists. In addition to Rahner, see Lonergan, *Method in Theology,* chap. 4, "Religion" for a lucid presentation of these themes.

32. Buckley, "Transcendence, Truth and Faith," 645.

33. Michael J. Buckley, "Within the Holy Mystery," in Leo O'Donovan, ed., *A World of Grace: An Introduction to the Themes and Foundations of Karl Rahner's Theology* (New York: Seabury Press, 1980), 38.

34. Ibid., 39–40.

35. Buckley, "Transcendence, Truth, and Faith," 654.

36. Buckley, "Experience and Culture," 463.

37. Buckley, "Presidential Address," 83.

38. Buckley, "Transcendence, Truth, and Faith," 638.

39. Michael J. Buckley, "Atheism and Contemplation," *Theological Studies* 40 (1979): 680–99.

40. Ibid., 680.

41. Ibid., 685.

42. Ibid.

43. Ibid., 689.

44. Ibid.

45. Ibid., 690.

46. Ibid., 693.

47. Ibid.

48. Ibid., 696.

49. Ibid., 697–98.

50. Again, see Lonergan, *Method in Theology,* 55: "A religion that promotes self-transcendence to the point, not merely of justice, but of self-sacrificing love, will have a redemptive role in human society inasmuch as such love can undo the mischief of decline and restore the cumulative process of progress."

51. For Buckley's most thorough treatment of Rahner on these themes, see "Within the Holy Mystery."

52. Karl Rahner, "Christian Pessimism," *Theological Investigations* 22, trans. Joseph Donceel, S.J. (New York: Crossroad, 1991), 155. Some of what follows here is adapted from my article "Rahner's Christian Pessimism," to be published in *Philosophy and Theology.*

53. Karl Rahner, "Utopia and Reality," *Theology Digest* 32 (1985): 143.

54. Rahner, "Christian Pessimism," 160–61.

55. Karl Rahner, *Foundations of Christian Faith* (New York: Crossroad, 1978), 404.

56. See *The Iliad, or the Poem of Force* (Willingford, Pa.: Pendle Hill, 1956), 21–22.

57. Rahner, *Foundations of Christian Faith,* 266.

58. Karl Rahner, *On the Theology of Death* (New York: Herder and Herder, 1961), 72, 78–79.

59. Karl Rahner, "Following the Crucified," *Theological Investigations* 18, trans. Edward Quinn (New York: Crossroad, 1983), 160f.

13

"Bright Darkness"
and Christian Transformation

Gregory of Nyssa on the Dynamics of Mystical Union

– BRIAN E. DALEY, S.J. –

"Mysticism," like "hermeneutics" and perhaps "democracy," is a word that suffers from overuse. It can be wielded with negative connotations of obscurantism and logorrhea, as in Ko-Ko's specter of "sermons by mystical Germans who preach from ten to four" in *The Mikado;* or it can be used with a reassuring hint of compassion and hipness, as in Matthew Fox's invitation to be a "musical, mystical bear." As the Olympic skater said when asked if she was happy with a silver medal, it all depends on what you mean.

So when one asks in what sense, if at all, Gregory of Nyssa can be considered a mystical theologian, one is likely to receive a variety of answers. Understanding mysticism as an interior union with the God who is beyond all conceiving, a matter not simply of ideas but of intensely personal experience, Jean Daniélou saw in Gregory's work the first comprehensive attempt to describe such a contact with God in Christian terms; so Daniélou boldly bestowed on Gregory the epithet, "le fondateur de la théologie mystique."[1] Other scholars in the past century have agreed that Gregory's writings delineate a "mystical" knowledge of God, but are less convinced of the originality or experiential roots of his treatment, pointing out the continuities between his thought and the Platonic tradition,[2] or its similarity to mystical elements in the earlier Judaeo-Christian theology of Alexandria.[3] Still others — understanding mysticism essentially as noncognitive identification, in which the human mind's sense of selfhood is simply swallowed up, at least for a brief moment, in blissful union with the absolute Being who is beyond both knowledge and sensation — have been more sceptical about Gregory's qualification as a mystical theologian,[4] or have even flatly denied it.[5]

What Gregory's own experience of God may have been seems, from this distance, impossible to know; biographical details about him are almost completely lacking. What his philosophical and theological sources were, how much originality his work reveals, remains a fascinating but complex question. But if we simply accept, as a working definition of mystical theology, the Pseudo-Dionysius's assertion that "the most divine knowledge of God, received through ignorance, is obtained in virtue of an incomprehensible union,"[6] it is hard to deny that Gregory of Nyssa not only does describe such knowledge of God in his works, at length and with great subtlety, but that he presents it as the fulfillment of every intellectual creature's natural dynamism, the crown of our well-being. This is not to say that Gregory would go so far as either Plotinus or the Ps.-Dionysius in denying cognitive content to such union with the transcendent Mystery, or that he suggests the mind ever loses all consciousness of the difference between itself and its Creator — a consciousness that is the foundation of its relatedness to him. Nor does Gregory describe knowledge of God in the "bright darkness" of ecstasy simply in affective terms, or as characteristically a transitory, passive state, followed by a relapse into a more ordinary, conceptually focused kind of consciousness.[7] In Gregory's thought, our knowledge of God certainly has an ineradicably cognitive element, even if it is only the paradoxical realization, as we strain to conceive God, of the limitations of our positive concepts and the growing sense that God is always greater than our thoughts. Knowledge of God is also, for Gregory, developmental: part of a continuing process that begins in moral and intellectual conversion, includes the transformation of our behavior by virtue, and finds its perfection not in rest or static completion but precisely in continuous movement, in never coming to an end. Yet while these features may set his thought apart from some other ancient approaches to "mystical theology," philosophic and Christian, it is undeniable that for him, as for the classical Christian mystics who followed, the fullest possible knowledge of God is realized in a growing consciousness of one's own ignorance, as well as in a growing awareness of being one with God in and through Christ — of genuinely sharing, through Christ, in the living characteristics of the divine being.

To see what is characteristic of Gregory's mystical theology and what elements of it seem to be his personal contribution to the history of spirituality, it is important to glance briefly first at the mystical elements in the theology of the two authors in the tradition of biblical faith whose thought influenced his most strongly: Philo and Origen. In many passages of his writings, Philo expressed the conviction that knowledge of God, although beyond the natural powers of the mind itself, is the highest bliss the mind can enjoy. In *On Abraham,* for instance, he writes:

The one to whose lot it falls, not only by means of his or her knowledge to comprehend all the other things which exist in nature, but also to behold the Father and Creator of the universe, has advanced to the very summit of happiness. For there is nothing above God; and if anyone, directing towards God the eye of the soul, has reached up to him, let that person then pray for the ability to remain and to stand firm before him; for the roads which lead upwards to God are laborious and slow, but the descent down the declivity, being more like a rapid dragging down than a gradual descent, is swift and easy.[8]

Because God does not belong to the perceptible world, the mind cannot hope to comprehend anything more of him than the fact that he exists.[9] One reaches such an understanding of the existence of "the uncreated and divine being, the first good of all," in Philo's view, through a kind of inductive reasoning from the order and beauty of the world around us;[10] the human *logos* or reasoning faculty must detach itself from its own uttered *logoi,* the words or concepts that limit and define its comprehension of created things, so that it can be left alone to seek "that which alone is to be embraced with purity."[11] This vision of the mind is, first of all, a vision of the Logos, the image of God, as "the place...on which the unchangeable and unalterable God stands"; on the other hand, it is a vision of the ordered universe, "the world of the senses," which lies "under the feet" of the Logos who created it.[12] Yet there is ultimately a quality of self-transcendence in the created mind's highest knowledge of God, for Philo, that moves even beyond such contemplative thinking and that can be described only in images of ecstasy, loss of self-awareness, even drunkenness or frenzy. So in a famous passage of his treatise *On the Creation,* Philo first describes the uniqueness of the human mind among terrestrial creatures and its likeness to the universal mind that governs the world. By using its "wings," the mind can rise to contemplate the highest structures of the universe,

> ...and being led on by love, which is the guide of wisdom, it proceeds onwards till, having surmounted all essence intelligible by the external senses, it comes to aspire to such as is perceptible only by the intellect; and perceiving in that the original models and ideas of those things intelligible by the external senses which it saw here full of surpassing beauty, it becomes seized with a sort of sober intoxication like the zealots engaged in the Corybantian festivals, and yields to enthusiasm, becoming filled with another desire and a more excellent longing, by which it is conducted onwards to the very summit of such things as are perceptible only to the intellect, till it appears to be reaching the great King himself. And while it is eagerly longing to behold him pure and unmingled, rays of divine light are poured forth upon it like a torrent, so as to bewilder the eyes of its intelligence by their splendor.[13]

In this powerful text one can hear already, by anticipation, many of the central themes and images of later Jewish and Christian mysticism.

Origen, the most influential Christian source of Gregory of Nyssa's thought, also stresses the crucial importance of knowledge of divine realities as the ultimate fulfillment of our natural human longing. Much has been written about whether, or in what sense, Origen is a "mystical theologian."[14] It is certainly true that he gladly uses the language of "mystery," especially in his exegetical works, in speaking of the divine plan of salvation.[15] It is also true that he sometimes portrays the human quest for divine wisdom and knowledge as an unending journey toward a share in incomprehensible reality[16] and emphasizes, in fact, that the goal of that quest is not simply intellectual knowledge but a joyful and loving personal contact with the God who has been revealed in Christ; it is to "touch the hem of his garment," to "take him in our arms" as Simeon did, and find in him our "peace."[17] Nevertheless, the most striking aspect of Origen's treatment of our relationship with God, for all its affective warmth, is its fundamentally cognitive character: the luminous union with the Logos that puts an end to human longing is for Origen ultimately "the light of knowledge."[18]

So in his De principiis — a work apparently intended to sketch out a reasoned synthesis of the apostolic faith as the hermeneutical background for an authentically Christian spiritual exegesis of Scripture[19] — Origen emphasizes that the "vision" of the incorporeal God promised to the "pure of heart" is nothing else but "to understand and to know him with the mind."[20] And in his treatment, in the same work, of the eschatological fulfillment promised to rational creatures (De princ. II, 11.4–7), Origen presents union with God as the fulfillment of the mind's natural desire to know the causes of all things.[21] So he interprets our "being with Christ" after death, which Paul refers to in Philippians 1:23, as a chance finally to learn the secrets of the visible world and the meaning of Scripture that now tantalize us, in a heavenly "school for souls."[22] And since Jesus, the incarnate Logos, is for Origen always the chief revealer of God's mysteries, he will be the main object of contemplation for those in that school,

> but we will no longer understand him in that narrow form in which he has come to be for our sakes — that is, not in that circumscribed state which he had when placed on earth among men and women in our kind of body.[23]

The perfection of the rational creature, according to De principiis, is reached when "the mind, having grown in mental and sensible power to perfect knowledge, is now made perfect, no longer impeded by these fleshly senses, but when increasing in its intellectual measure it attains perfection, gazing on what is pure and, so to speak, at the causes of things 'face to face'. . . . "[24] So, later in the same work, Origen explains the Pauline phrase, "God will be all in all" (1 Cor. 15.28), precisely as the perfection of human knowledge of God:

> He will be "all" in every individual in this way: that whatever the reasonable mind, purged from all stain of vice and thoroughly cleansed from the cloud of evil, can feel or understand or think, all will be God, nor will he then feel anything else but God, but he will think God, see God, hold God, and God will be the shape and measure of all his movements.[25]

Just as God knows all things, so the perfected intellectual creature, made in God's image, will come to know all things in knowing him, and find in that knowledge its perfection and fulfillment.[26] If such knowledge can be called "mystical," it is certainly mysticism of a radiantly conscious kind.

When one turns to the passages in the works of Gregory of Nyssa that deal with human knowledge of God and human fulfillment, one finds both continuities with these two great Alexandrian theologians and new emphases. Like Philo and like his own Cappadocian contemporaries — but unlike Origen — Gregory emphasizes repeatedly that the created intellect can know nothing directly of the essence of God; all one can know of God is *that* God is, not *what* God is.[27] The reason, for Gregory, is that the nature of God is unlimited goodness, and "what is unlimited is also infinite (τὸ δὲ ἀόριστον τῷ ἀπείρῳ ταὐτόν ἐστιν)." So he writes in his fifth homily on the Song of Songs:

> The blessed, eternal nature surpassing all understanding contains all things in itself and is limited by nothing. For no name or concept, nothing associated with it in thought, can impose limits to it: not time, place, color, form, image, bulk, quantity, dimension, or anything else. Every good conceived as belonging to God's nature extends to the infinite and the unbounded. For evil has no place and the good is boundless.[28]

So Gregory boldly asserts the radical unknowability of the divine nature:

> This is the Being in which, to use the words of the Apostle, all things are formed.... It is above beginning, and presents no marks of its inmost nature: it is to be known of only in the impossibility of perceiving it. That indeed is its most special characteristic [ἰδιαίτατον γνώρισμα], that its nature is too high for any distinctive attribute [παντὸς χαρακτηπισιτικοῦ νοήματος ὑψηλότεραν]."[29]

The result is that the created mind, which knows through perceiving and identifying defined form, can only come to inadequate concepts of God's essence: concepts that are either negative in character, denying to God some qualities found only in finite creatures, or else formed simply from our experience of God's "operations" in the created world.[30] In contemplating the universe, one can gain at least some sense of the "skill" of the artist who created it: his wisdom, his goodness, his freedom — all qualities that "engrave on the soul the impress of a divine and transcendent Mind,"[31] even though they do not provide adequate concepts of what the divine, creative nature in itself is.

So God is, in God's own self, simply unnameable, Gregory argues at the end of his first book against Eunomius,

> ...incapable of being grasped by any term, or any idea, or any other device of our apprehension, remaining beyond the reach not only of the human but of the angelic and of all supramundane intelligence, unthinkable, unutterable, above all expression in words, having but one name that can represent his proper nature, the single name of being "above every name."[32]

The divine nature, he suggests somewhat earlier in the same work, can only be imagined fleetingly by a mind limited to categories of time and space, as something utterly beyond itself:

> Having traversed the ages and all that has been produced in them, our thought catches a glimpse of the divine nature, as of some immense ocean, but when the imagination stretches onward to grasp it, it gives no sign in its own case of any beginning.[33]

Alongside this stress on the radical unknowability of God, however, Gregory emphasizes with equal insistence the created intellect's paradoxically insatiable drive to penetrate the mysteries of the divine being. This dynamism, rooted in the natural desire of every created consciousness for what is good and beautiful,[34] is most fully exemplified for Gregory in the story of Moses, whose "ascent" to a direct experience of the mysterious reality of God becomes a model both for growth in moral virtue and for the achievement of human perfection.[35] So in the second, allegorically interpretative section of his Life of Moses, Gregory asserts that when Moses had progressed, by ascetical practice, to the higher levels of moral virtue, and had conquered his enemies both without and within, he was "led on to the ineffable knowledge of God (τῇ ἀπορρήτῳ ἐκείνῃ θεογνωσίᾳ)."[36] Such "contemplation of God" (θεοῦ θεωρία) involves no sense perception, Gregory assures us,[37] and continues to demand a steep and laborious "climb";[38] more important, it is ultimately realized only in the paradoxical act of voluntarily entering the "darkness" of complete ignorance, of moving beyond any ideas we may have of God, useful as they have been, into the deeper realization that God completely transcends our ideas. Gregory writes:

> Scripture teaches...that religious knowledge comes at first to those who receive it as light. Therefore what is perceived to be contrary to religion is darkness....But as the mind progresses and, through an ever greater and more perfect diligence, comes to apprehend reality, as it approaches more nearly to contemplation [θεωρίᾳ], it sees more clearly what of the divine nature is not to be contemplated. For leaving behind everything that is observed, not only what sense comprehends but also what the intelligence

thinks it sees, it keeps on penetrating deeper, until, by the intelligence's busy activity [πολυπραγμοσύνη], it gains access to the invisible and the incomprehensible, and there it sees God. This is the true knowledge of what is sought; this is the seeing that consists in not seeing, because that which is sought transcends all knowledge, being separated on all sides by incomprehensibility as by a kind of darkness. Wherefore John the sublime, who penetrated into the luminous darkness [ἐν τῷ λάμπρῳ γνόφῳ], says, "No one has ever seen God," thus asserting that knowledge of the divine essence is unattainable not only by human beings but also by every intelligent creature.[39]

This entry into the "bright darkness" of God's incomprehensibility, as the experience which both satisfies the highest desire of his nature and awakens in him a longing for a still greater conscious share in God's beauty and goodness, becomes for Moses — and for every human person, all of whom Moses represents — a process of eternal self-transcendence in knowledge and love: a process which Gregory, in an allusion to Philippians 3:13, elsewhere labels ἐπέκτασις, "moving beyond [oneself]."[40] So Gregory suggests, in a famous passage at the climax of his interpretation of Moses' "vision," that the perfection of our knowledge of God is precisely a process of restless, endless growth beyond the knowledge we already possess:

This truly is the vision of God: never to reach satiety in the desire to see him. Rather, by looking at what one can see, one must always allow one's desire to see more be kindled anew. Thus no limit could interrupt growth in the ascent to God, since no limit to the Good can be found, nor is our increase of desire for the Good brought to an end because it is satisfied.[41]

Gregory gives, in his other writings, various explanations for the basis in human nature on which this paradoxical relationship with God — this insatiable yet perfecting desire, this knowledge fulfilled in ignorance — is based. Being made in God's image, he argues in his *Great Catechetical Oration,* the human person has in his own nature "something akin to the divine": a kind of participation by likeness in the divine perfection, which allows him "to recognize the transcendent and have the desire for God's immortality,"[42] on the presupposition — common to many ancient theories of knowledge — that "like is known by like."[43] In several works, Gregory develops the related idea that by purifying ourselves from the sinful, self-generated passions that distort the image of God in us, we enable ourselves to reflect God's archetypal reality as in a mirror, so that by looking within ourselves we can come, indirectly, to a vision of God. So he writes, interpreting the sixth Beatitude:

The Lord does not say it is blessed to know something about God, but to have God present within oneself. "Blessed are the clean of heart, for they shall see God...." By this we should learn that if a person's heart has been purified from every creature and all unruly affections, he will see the Image of the Divine Nature in his own beauty....Hence, if someone who is pure of heart sees himself, he sees in himself what he desires; and thus he becomes blessed, because when he looks at his own purity, he sees the archetype in the image.[44]

The key to this ability of the soul to be for itself a reflection of the divine reality is clearly, in Gregory's view, moral purification: growth in virtue (ἀρετή), which reaches its summit in freedom from passion (ἀπάθεια). In the preface to the *Life of Moses,* Gregory makes the bold assertion that since the divine nature is goodness itself, "God himself is perfect virtue."[45] So the "garment" of virtues we so laboriously weave for ourselves, he suggests in the ninth homily on the Song of Songs, "imitates the divine blessedness and resembles the transcendent divine nature by [its] purity and freedom from passion."[46] And the *way* by which the believer accomplishes this purification, the pattern for this growth in virtue and freedom, is for Gregory the way of Christ; for Christ is the embodiment and revealer of virtue, the "founding source of passionlessness [ἀρχηγὸς τῆς ἀπαθείας]." For every disciple, the key to restoring the inner beauty that reflects the divine reality is to imitate him.

It is here, I would argue, in his understanding of the person and role of Christ, that Gregory of Nyssa's approach to human experience of and union with God — his "mystical theology," such as it is — takes on its most original and characteristic shape. It is not simply that Gregory, like Origen before him (if usually in somewhat cooler and more philosophical terms), stresses the central importance of personal love for Christ in the soul's growth to perfection. Certainly this is important for him; in the Song of Songs, for instance, as Gregory interprets it, the Bride cries out to Christ, the Bridegroom,

> How can I not love you who have loved me so much? Even though I am black, you laid down your life for the sheep that you shepherd. No greater love than this can be comprehended, that you exchanged your life for my salvation.[47]

But still more important, it seems, in Gregory's understanding, is the *person* of Christ, for it is there, in the transformation of a complete human individual by the Logos who has "taken him up" and made his humanity God's own, that Gregory seems to be offering both the model and the explanation of the "mystical" union of totally unequal realities that is the realization of human perfection.

Original, speculative, and somewhat puzzling by the standard of later Chalcedonian terminology, Gregory's christology could perhaps best be called a "christology of transformation."[48] The real news of the gospel, according to Gregory's letter to Theophilus of Alexandria against the Apollinarians, is that the transcendent and unchanging Logos of God has, in the man Jesus, taken on human nature and made it his own; as a result, "everything that was weak and perishable in our nature, mingled with the Godhead, has become that which the Godhead is."[49] From this perspective, Gregory defends his own picture of Christ against the Apollinarian charge that it implies two distinct Sons, the eternal Son and the man Jesus:

> He who is always in the Father, and who always has the Father in himself and is united with him, is and will be as he was for all ages....But the first-fruits of the human nature which he has taken up, absorbed—as one might say figuratively—by the omnipotent divinity like a drop of vinegar mingled in the boundless sea, exists *in* the Godhead, but *not* in its own proper characteristics [ἰδιώμασιν]. For a duality of Sons might consistently be presumed, if a nature of a different kind could be recognized by its own proper signs within the ineffable Godhead of the Son, so that the one element were weak or small or corruptible or transitory, while the other were powerful and great and incorruptible and eternal; but since all the traits we recognize in the mortal [Jesus] we see transformed by the characteristics of the Godhead, and no difference of any kind can be perceived—for whatever one sees in the Son is Godhead, wisdom, power, holiness, freedom from passivity—how could one divide what is one into double significance?[50]

Gregory's conception of salvation in Christ, in fact, as presented throughout his works, is nothing less than a transformation of our own human characteristics (ἰδιώματα), damaged and distorted by passion through our history of sin, into the characteristics of the God who is in himself virtue and transcendent beauty, through our union with Christ, in whom that transformation has first been fully realized. In Jesus, "the divine being, changeless and unvarying in essence, has come to be in a changeable and alterable nature, so that by his own unchangeability he might heal our tendency to change for the worse."[51] In the risen Christ, the believer can contemplate in faith, and can share both through natural kinship and through the sacraments,[52] a humanity now become divine by the substitution of divine for human characteristics. In him, the believer can recognize that although our human reality (τὸ ἀνθρώπινον) remains in some way unalterably itself, all its characteristics are now swallowed up in the infinite ocean of God's ineffable Mystery. In him, too, the believer can rejoice that God the Word, who is above all knowledge and naming in himself, and whose self-emptying in the incarnation is expressed by having taken on the human name of Jesus, has now bestowed on that one ἄνθρωπος "the name that is above every name," expressing the man Jesus' participation to a hitherto unguessed-at degree in the reality of God.[53]

For every Christian, Gregory argues in his treatise *On Perfection*, growth toward ἀρετή is made possible first of all through the reverent contemplation of the many names of Christ. Since the Savior has bestowed on believers "a partnership in his name" (i.e., "Christian") as "the one authoritative name" for them, it is only through learning the significance of his various titles in Scripture that they can come to realize what they themselves are called to be.[54] In doing this, Gregory argues, one gradually becomes an imitator and even an "image" of Christ, who is the "image of the invisible God," and so acquires the virtues that conform one to the divine beauty itself.[55] By taking up an individual instance of our common humanity and turning it, in his own transformation, into the "first fruits" of a renewed human nature, the risen Christ offers us both a model and an anchor within the divine Mystery:

> Just as the first fruit of the dough was assimilated through purity and innocence [through the transformation, in other words, of the ἰδιώματα of fallen humanity] to the true Father and God, so we, also, as [the rest of the] dough, will cleave in similar ways to the Father of incorruptibility by imitating, as far as we can, the innocence and stability of the Mediator.[56]

In becoming a disciple of Christ, one begins the process of transformation which, in Gregory's eyes, alone makes mystical union possible.

So it seems to be no accident that when Gregory takes up the Philonian metaphor of the "sober drunkenness" of mystical knowledge, he does so — on two occasions out of three — in the context of an allusion to the transformation of the Christian believer by participation in Christ's glorified humanity through the Eucharist.[57] So, too, in the course of his explanation of Moses' vision of "the back parts of God" from his hiding-place in a cleft of a rock on the top of Mount Sinai, Gregory does not fail to point out that according to Paul, "the rock was Christ" (1 Cor. 10:4):

> For, since Christ is understood by Paul as the rock, and since all hope for good things is believed to be in Christ, in whom, we have learned are "all the treasures of good things" (Col. 2:3), he who finds he shares any good must surely be in Christ, who contains all that is good.[58]

Christ in his very person, then, is for Gregory the key to understanding the possibility of a mystical knowledge of God, as well the necessary way to its realization. So he speaks of Christ as himself a part the infinite, inconceivable Mystery of God, whose incarnation in our world makes possible for us both a new understanding of God's goodness and a new participation in it. He writes in the treatise *On Perfection:*

> He who is beyond all knowledge and understanding, the ineffable and unutterable and inexplicable one, has himself become an "image of the invisible God" out of love for humanity, that he might make you once again into an image of God; his purpose was that he might be formed in you in his own form, which he has taken up, and that you might once

again be shaped through him to correspond to that form of the archetypal beauty, and so become what you were from the beginning.[59]

The place of Christ now, after his resurrection and glorification, is not only within the transcendent Mystery — his human characteristics now divinized, even as his divine characteristics were previously revealed in human terms; his place is also *within* the believer, who both carries Christ and is carried by him.[60] As a result, the believer himself gradually becomes divinized, too — not through total absorption into God but through a steady, endless process of "ascent" that involves a transformation of our fallen human ιδιώματα into the characteristics of God. So the Bride, in Gregory's reading of the Song of Songs, is not only "wounded" by Christ, who is God's "sweet arrow of love," penetrated by Christ's divine presence and touched by his revelation of the reality of God; she herself becomes, with Christ and in him, "an arrow in the bowman's hands," sharing in his incorruptibility and aimed by him, in turn, deep into the Mystery of God.[61]

How one interprets the "mystical theology" of Gregory of Nyssa depends largely, as I said at the beginning, on what one takes "mysticism" to mean. Despite the enthusiasm of some of his twentieth-century interpreters, those who make a clear distinction between Gregory's "mysticism" and that of Meister Eckhart or even of Ps.-Dionysius, let alone that of Eastern religions, seem to be closest to the truth. The "darkness" of which Gregory speaks in describing the human mind's ultimate place of encounter with the infinite God does not seem to imply a loss of consciousness, let alone a merging of identity between creature and Creator; the ἔκστασις of which Gregory occasionally speaks is less the love-wounded swoon of Bernini's St. Teresa than the recognition of the limits of language by a great rhetorician who is also a man of deeply perceptive faith. Like John of the Cross, Gregory is always concerned with the moral foundation of union with God, with virtue and "philosophical" praxis, and always takes pains to emphasize the cognitive implications of religious experience. Yet he does succeed, at the same time, in reviving and reshaping the Alexandrian insight that the human mind must ultimately move beyond its own cognitive categories in its quest for the fullness of truth and beauty and must rest simply in a sense of graced union with the God who is both utterly near and fundamentally unknown. In the process, Gregory succeeds in combining Philo's emphases on God's radical inconceivability with Origen's christocentrism. What is new in his approach to this unitive "knowledge" of the transcendent Mystery is the clarity with which he rests it on the paradox of Christ's own person as the place where the Mystery has come palpably near and where the absorption into God of all that is knowably human has already begun. As Gregory peers into the divine darkness, it is for him of paramount significance that his feet are firmly planted on the rock which is Christ.

Notes

1. *Platonisme et théologie mystique: Essai sur la doctrine spirituelle de saint Grégoire de Nysse* (Paris: Aubier, 1944), 6f. Daniélou is followed, if in somewhat less enthusiastic language, by Louis Bouyer, *The Spirituality of the New Testament and the Fathers,* History of Christian Spirituality 1 (New York: Seabury, 1963), esp. 362–68; *The Christian Mystery: From Pagan Myth to Christian Mysticism* (Petersham, Mass.: St. Bede's, 1989), 175–79, 210–16. This essay will also appear in *Studia Philonica Annual* 8 (1996).

2. So, for instance, Hugo Koch, "Das mystische Schauen bei Gregor von Nyssa," *Theologische Quartalschrift* 80 (1898): 397–420; Endres von Ivánka, "Vom Platonismus zur Theorie der Mystik," *Scholastik* 11 (1936): 163–95.

3. The principal exponent of Gregory's mysticism as a link in the tradition reaching from Philo and Origen to Ps.-Dionysius and Maximus Confessor is Walther Völker, *Gregor von Nyssa als Mystiker* (Wiesbaden: Steiner, 1955). Völker's approach was anticipated in the important articles of Aloisius Lieske, "Zur Theologie der Christusmystik Gregors von Nyssa," *Scholastik* 14 (1939): 485–514; "Die Theologie der Christusmystik Gregors von Nyssa," *Zeitschrift für katholische Theologie* 70 (1948): 49–93, 129–68, 315–40. For a perceptive discussion of the issues in the debate between Daniélou and Völker, especially on the question of Gregory's debt to Origen and on Origen's "intellectualism," see Henri Crouzel, "Grégoire de Nysse est-il le fondateur de la théologie mystique? Une controverse récente," *Revue d'ascétique et de mystique* 33 (1957): 189–202.

4. Franz Diekamp, *Die Gotteslehre des Hl. Gregor von Nyssa* (Münster, 1896) was willing at most to acknowledge that Gregory did not exclude the possibility of a direct human experience of the essence of God (111).

5. So Hermann Langerbeck, "Zur Interpretation Gregors von Nyssa," *Theologische Literaturzeitung* 82 (1975): 82–90 (reviewing Völker's book); Ekkehard Mühlenberg, *Die Unendlichkeit Gottes bei Gregor von Nyssa* (Göttingen, 1966); and Maria-Barbara von Stritzky, *Zum Problem der Erkenntnis bei Gregor von Nyssa* (Münster: Aschendorff, 1973), esp. 67–104. These scholars insist that even Gregory's stress on the unknowability of the divine reality, in which we are nevertheless called to participate, is essentially a philosophical argument rather than a reference to ecstatic personal experience.

6. *On the Divine Names* 7.3; see *Mystical Theology* 2; *Ep.* 1 (PG 3.1065A). For a helpful discussion of the characteristics of mysticism and (as it is more traditionally called) "mystical theology" in the Christian tradition, see Bernard McGinn, *The Foundations of Mysticism,* The Presence of God: A History of Western Christian Mysticism 1 (New York: Crossroad, 1991), xiii–xx.

7. For allusions to such occasional, ecstatic experiences of God, see, e.g., Plotinus, *Ennead* IV, 8, 1; Augustine, *Confessions* IX, x (24f.); X, xl (65).

8. *Abr.* 57f. (trans. C. D. Yonge; Peabody, Mass.: Hendrickson, 1993), 417. Cf. *Decal.* 81; *Det.* 86; *Legat.* 4; *OG* 44; *Praem.* 14; *Quod Deus* 143f. (In citing works of Philo here, I am using the abbreviations given in the *Studia Philonica Annual.*) For concise descriptions of Philo's mystical theology, see Henry Chad-

wick, "Philo and the Beginnings of Christian Thought," in A. H. Armstrong, ed., *The Cambridge History of Later Greek and Early Medieval Philosophy* (Cambridge: Cambridge University Press, 1970), 148–52; David Winston, "Was Philo a Mystic?" in Joseph Dan and Frank Talmage, eds., *Studies in Jewish Mysticism* (Cambridge, Mass.: Association for Jewish Studies, 1982), 15–39; *Logos and Mystical Theology in Philo of Alexandria* (Cincinnati: Hebrew Union College Press, 1985), 54f.

9. *Quod Deus* 62; see *Leg.* 6; *Mut.* 7; *Praem.* 40. In *Spec. Leg.* 1.20, Philo takes a somewhat different position, suggesting that God can be comprehended by the mind only as it transcends the world of sense and "visible essences."

10. *Leg.* 5; see *Post.* 167; *Leg. All.* 3.97–99; *Praem.* 40–46.

11. *Fug.* 92; see *Gig.* 52.

12. *Conf.* 95f. (trans. Yonge 242). In a recent paper, David Winston has argued persuasively that Philo's writings suggest all knowledge of God which we might call "mystical" — knowledge involving ecstasy, characterized by love and longing, and leading to a union with God beyond consciousness — is really knowledge of the Logos. The "vision" of God himself, described in *Praem.* 36–46, is, in Winston's view, simply a clear intellectual grasp of God's existence. See "Philo's Mysticism," *Studia Philonica Annual 1996*.

13. *Op.* 70f. (trans. Yonge 11); cf. a similar description in *Ebr.* 152; also *Somn* 2.232. For a classic treatment of the background and later tradition of Philo's image of "sober drunkenness," see Hans Lewy, *Sobria Ebrietas: Untersuchungen zur Geschichte der antiken Mystik*, Beihefte zur Zeitschrift für die neutestamentliche Wissenschaft 9 (Giessen: Töpelmann, 1929).

14. The genuinely mystical direction of Origen's thought, in continuity with that of Philo and Clement of Alexandria, has been emphasized especially by Walther Völker, *Das Vollkommenheitsideal des Origenes* (Tübingen: J. C. B. Mohr, 1931), esp. 91–144; see also Bouyer, *Spirituality,* 283–300. Henri Crouzel, in his magisterial study *Origène et la "connaissance mystique"* (Paris: Desclée de Brouwer, 1961), takes a more cautious approach, emphasizing the spiritual and contemplative character of the knowledge of God that Origen seeks to mediate to his readers, yet acknowledging Origen's reticence in describing the "ecstatic" or "enthusiastic" aspects of such knowledge (see esp. 527–31). See also Crouzel, "Grégoire de Nysse est-il le fondateur de la théologie mystique?" (above, n. 3), 200–202.

15. On this theme, see especially Hans Urs von Balthasar, *Parole et mystère chez Origène* (Paris: Cerf, 1936).

16. See, for example, the famous passage in *Hom. 17 in Num.* 4 (Griechische christliche Schriftsteller [hereafter GCS] 30.159–64).

17. *Hom. 15 in Lucam* 1 (GCS 49.93f.); for other allusions to "touching" Jesus' garments or Jesus himself in order to be saved, see also *Hom. 17 in Jer.* 6 (SC 238.172.11–23); *Hom. 1 in Lev.* 4 (GCS 29.286.1–9); *Hom. 4 in Lev.* 8 (ibid. 327.4–13). For a discussion of how Origen conceives and emphasizes a personal relationship to Jesus, see especially Frédéric Bertrand, *Mystique de Jésus chez Origène* (Paris: Aubier, 1951).

18. So *Comm. in Cant.* III (GCS 33.202.27–203.2), on the presence of the divine Spouse to the soul: "Sic et animae, cum quaerit aliquem sensum et agnoscere obscura et arcana desiderat, donec invenire non potest, absens ei sine dubio est Verbum Dei. Ubi vero occurrerat et apparuerit quod requiritur, quis

dubitat adesse Verbum Dei et illuminare mentem ac scientiae ei lumen prae-
bere?" For a further discussion of this point, see Crouzel (n. 14 above); McGinn,
Foundations 124–26.

19. See my forthcoming article, "Origen's *De principiis:* A Guide to the 'Principles' of Christian Scriptural Interpretation," in John Petruccione, ed., Καινὰ
καὶ Παλαιά (Festschrift for Thomas J. Halton).

20. *De princ.* I, 1.9.

21. *De princ.* II, 11.4.

22. Ibid., 6f.

23. Ibid., 6. Cf. *Hom. 27 in Num.* 12 (GCS 30.273.21–25; 275.11–13), where
Origen emphasizes that the main content of this eschatological knowledge will
be the meaning of the divine economy itself.

24. Ibid., 7.

25. Ibid., III, 6.3.

26. Ibid., IV, 4.10.

27. See, e.g., *Contra Eunomium* II, 67 (*Gregorii Nysseni Opera* [hereafter
GNO] I, 245.19–24); *On the Beatitudes* 6 (PG 44.1268B); *On the Inscriptions
of the Psalms* II, 14 (GNO V, 155.25–156.4): all that human wisdom can attain
to is the "shadows of God's wings," not the "wings" themselves. Cf. Gregory of
Nazianzus, Or. 28.5, 15. On Gregory's differences from Origen concerning the
intelligibility of God, see McGinn, *Foundations* 141.

28. *Ctr. Eun.* I.169 (GNO I, 77.17–20); see *Inscr. Psal.* I (GNO V, 46.8–
10: "the limit of what has no end is limitlessness (πέρας δὲ τοῦ ἀτελευτήτου
ἡ ἀπειρία)." Ekkehard Mühlenberg, in his celebrated study *Die Unendlichkeit
Gottes bei Gregor von Nyssa* (Göttingen: Vandenhoeck und Ruprecht, 1966),
has shown that Gregory is the first Christian theologian to conceive of the infinity and inconceivability of the divine nature as a positive characteristic of God,
rather than simply as proof of the limitations of the created mind.

29. GNO VI, 157.14–158.1; trans. Casimir McCambley, *Saint Gregory of
Nyssa, Commentary on the Song of Songs* (Brookline, Mass.: Hellenic College
Press, 1987), 118 [alt.].

30. *Ctr. Eun.* I, 373 (GNO I, 137.1–8; trans. Henry Wace, NPNF II, 5 [1892]
70); see *Life of Moses* II, 234 (SC 1.266): "The proper characteristic [γνώρισμα]
of the divine nature is to lie beyond every characteristic."

31. See especially the important discussion of this subject in *Ctr. Eun.* II, 142–
158 (GNO I, 266–71); see *Ad Ablabium* (GNO III/1, 42–48).

32. *On the Beatitudes* 6 (PG 44.1209A5f.; trans. Hilda Graef, ACW 18 [New
York: Paulist, 1954], 147).

33. *Ctr. Eun* I, 683 (GNO I, 222.19–25; trans. Wace, NPNF II, 5.99). For
this notion that the nature of God is "above every name," see also *Ctr. Eun.* II,
587 (GNO I, 397.27–31); *Hom. 6 in Cant.* (GNO VI, 182.1f.).

34. *Ctr. Eun.* I, 364(GNO I, 134.17–22; trans. Wace, NPNF II, 5.69).

35. See, e.g., *Beat.* 5 (PG 44.1249C7f.); *De Mortuis* (GNO IX/1, 29.9); *Moses*
II, 231–39.

36. It seems likely that Gregory borrowed the idea of constructing a life of
Moses out of the material in the Pentateuch and of interpreting it allegorically
as a model of human growth in virtue and knowledge of God from Philo's two
books *De vita Moysis.* However, the details of Gregory's work show surprisingly
few echoes of that of Philo; see David Runia, *Philo in Early Christian Literature*
(Minneapolis: Fortress, 1993), 256–60.

37. *Moses* II, 152 (SC 1bis, 202.5f.).

38. Ibid., 157 (206.1).

39. Ibid., 158.

40. *Moses* II, 162f. (210.7–212.13; trans. Abraham J. Malherbe and Everett Ferguson: *Gregory of Nyssa, The Life of Moses* (New York: Paulist, 1978, 95 [alt.])). Gregory is describing here what St. Bonaventure, inspired by Ps.-Dionysius, would later call the movement from the "illuminative" to the "unitive" or "perfective" stage in a creature's conscious relationship to the Creator: see Ps.-Dionysius, *De coelesti hierarchia* 3.2; Bonaventure, *De triplici via* 13.17 (Quaracchi ed. 8 [1898] 7). For a discussion of the traditional conception of the "triple way" of growth toward union with God, with bibliography, see the article of Aimé Solignac, *Dictionnaire de spiritualité* (Paris: Beauchesne, 1994), 16:1200–15.

41. *Hom. 6 in Cant.* (GNO VI, 173f.). Jean Daniélou popularized the idea that this process of ἐπέκτασις, or self-transcendence, is one of the most characteristic and central themes in Gregory's spiritual theology: see *Platonisme et théologie mystique,* 309–26. The word itself appears, however, only in this one passage; related verbal forms occur in several others (*Hom. 9 in Cant.* [GNO VI, 291.17]; *Vita sancti Gregorii Thaumaturgi* [PG 46.901C7]; *In Hexaemeron* [PG 44.121A3], directly alluding to Phil. 3.13; *Vita Moysis* II, 225 (SC 1bis, 262.5). For a description of the process in different words, also using Moses as its classical representative, see *Hom. 12 in Cant.* (GNO VI, 354.1–357.2).

42. *Moses* II, 239 (SC 1bis, 270; trans. Malherbe and Ferguson 116 [altered]).

43. *Catechetical Oration* (PG 45.21C8f.; D10–12); trans. Cyril C. Richardson, in Edward R. Hardy, ed., *Christology of the Later Fathers* [Philadelphia: Westminster Press, 1954], 276). For a discussion of Gregory's use of the Platonic concept of participation, see David L. Balás, Μετουσία Θεοῦ: *Man's Participation in God's Perfections according to St. Gregory of Nyssa* (Rome: Studia Anselmiana, 1966); see von Stritzky, 70–73. For his use of the notion of "likeness to God," see H. Merki, Ὁμοίωσις Θεῷ: *Von der platonischen Angleichung an Gott zur Gottebenbildlichkeit bei Gregor von Nyssa* (Fribourg: Presses universitaires, 1952).

44. For early expressions of this theory of knowledge, see Empedocles, Frag. 109 (Diels 31 A86); Democritus, Frag. 9 (Diels 68 A 135); Plato, *Timaeus* 45 CD. Gregory makes explicit use of the maxim in *De virginitate* 11.5 (SC 119.392–94); see Michel Aubineau's note *ad loc.,* with further references.

45. *Beat.* 6 (PG 1272 B; trans. Graef, 148f. [alt.]). Cf. *Hom. 3 in Cant.* (GNO VI, 89ff.); *De anima et re* (PG 46.89BC); *De virginitate* 11.5 (SC 119.392–96).

46. *Moses,* Praef. 7 (SC 1, 50.1–8). For a discussion of this important connection, in Gregory's work, between growth in virtue and contemplation, see Anthony Meredith, *The Cappadocians* (New York: St. Vladimir's, 1995), 59–62.

47. GNO VI, 272 (trans. McCambley 175f. [alt.]). Cf. *Hom. 11 in Cant.*: ibid., 334.

48. *Hom. 2 in Cant.* (GNO VI, 61.17–21; trans. McCambley 67 [alt.]).

49. For a fuller discussion of Gregory's christology, especially in response to that of the Apollinarian school, as well as further literature, see my article, "Divine Transcendence and Human Transformation: Gregory of Nyssa's Anti-Apollinarian Christology," *Studia Patristica* forthcoming (paper given at the Oxford Patristic Conference, 1995).

50. *To Theophilus* (GNO III/1, 126f.; trans. mine).

51. Ibid., 126f.

52. *Antirrhetikos adversus Apollinarem* 2 (GNO III/1, 133.6–9; trans. mine); see 53 (222.25–223.10).

53. For Gregory's development of the central role of baptism and the Eucharist in the involvement of the believer in the transformed life of Christ, see especially the *Catechetical Oration* 33–37; for his treatment of the role of faith, ibid., 38f.; for his sense of the "physical" solidarity of the whole human race, ibid., 32. For a full treatment of Gregory's understanding of the connection between the community of believers and Christ, see Reinhard M. Hübner, *Die Einheit des Leibes Christi bei Gregor von Nyssa: Untersuchungen zum Ursprung der "physischen" Erlösungslehre* (Leiden: Brill, 1974).

54. See *Antirrhetikos* 21 (GNO III/1, 161.13–26); *Hom. 2 in Cant.*(GNO VI, 61).

55. *Perf.* (GNO VIII/1, 173.15–174.20). Gregory's treatise seems clearly modeled on the first book of Origen's Commentary on John, which is also largely taken up spiritual exegesis of the various titles or ἔννοιαι associated with Christ in the New Testament.

56. Ibid., 194.4–196.15.

57. Ibid., 206.9–14 (trans. Virginia Woods Callahan, Fathers of the Church 58 [Washington: Catholic University of America Press, 1967]: 117 [alt.]).

58. *Hom. 10 in Cant.* (GNO VI, 308); *Hom. in Christi ascensionem* (PG 46.692). For a discussion of Gregory's use of this image, see Lewy (above, n. 13), 132–37.

59. *Moses* II, 248 (SC 1bis, 276; trans. Malherbe and Ferguson 118 [alt.]). See also another passage, just before this (*Moses* II, 244: 274; trans. mine): "Those who climb uphill in sand, even if they happen to take large steps with their feet, toil endlessly, since their steps always slip downwards in the sand, so that they undertake movement but no progress comes of the movement. But if someone, as the psalm says, has drawn up his feet from the miry pit and plants them on the rock — and 'the rock is Christ,' who is perfect virtue — then as much as he or she is, according to the advice of Paul, 'firm and unshakeable in the good' (1 Cor. 15:58), so much the more quickly will he complete the race, using the firm footing as a kind of wing and flying upwards on his way because of the firmness of good in his heart."

60. GNO VIII/1, 194.14–195.5 (trans. mine). For a similar emphasis on the eternity and transcendence of Christ, contrasted with his entry into human history to remake our humanity, see *Antirrhetikos* 53 (GNO III/1, 222.25–223.10).

61. So, e.g., *Hom. 7 in Cant.* (GNO VI, 207); Ep. 3.1f (GNO VIII/2, 20.3–23, suggesting that the "holy places" of Christ's life are within us). Cf. Meredith, 82f.

62. *Hom. 4 in Cant.* (GNO VI, 127ff.).

14

Cassian's Hero and Discernment

Some Reflections

– LAWRENCE S. CUNNINGHAM –

Among the many things to which Michael Buckley has turned his considerable intelligence is the subject of spiritual discernment. That is only befitting for a faithful member of the Society of Jesus, whose founder, Ignatius of Loyola, makes much of the subject in *The Spiritual Exercises*. I would not have the temerity to pronounce on Ignatian discernment but it may not be out of place in a volume which honors Father Buckley to offer some extended reflections on discernment, as it is described in the second of the *Conlationes* of Cassian. Ignatian discernment, after all, is hardly intelligible without taking into account the contributions of Cassian, whose writings were recommended by Benedict as he finished his *Rule* and, thus, through the Western monastic tradition, entered into the common patrimony of Christian spirituality (St. Thomas Aquinas was an assiduous reader of Cassian).

In this essay discernment (*discretio* or *diakrisis*) will be understood according to that biblical hope by which a person would know what is "the good and the acceptable and the perfect will of God" (Rom. 12:2); "proving what is well pleasing to God" (Eph. 5:10) so that "charity may more and more abound in knowledge" (Phil. 1:9). The classic definition of St. John Climacus will suffice for our purposes: "discernment is...a solid understanding of the will of God in all times, in all places, in all things...."[1] John goes on to say that for the beginner, discretion is a form of self-knowledge; for those on the Christian path it is the ability to distinguish the spiritual good from the evil, and for the more advanced it is that grace by which one can "light up what is dark in others."[2] John thus distinguished discernment as a personal interior act from the gift by which one person aids another to arrive at interior discernment. We shall see that both senses are pertinent for our discussion.

John Climacus, of course, reflected an understanding of discretion that goes back to the earlier desert tradition. John Cassian mediated that tradition to the West. Cassian's most pointed comments on discernment occur in the second of the conferences he gave (we presume) to the monastic community of Marseilles which he had founded. The literary form of the conferences is well known. Cassian takes on the persona of a narrator/reporter as he explains what he had learned of the monastic life and its essential doctrine as it had been taught to him by the desert *Abbas* he had met during his Egyptian sojourn with his companion Germanus. In that sense, the conferences are literally cast as tradition: Cassian and Germanus had left their Bethlehem monastery to go to the desert in order to seek, in the traditional form, a "good word." As the text makes clear, those who spoke with Cassian and Germanus, in turn, appeal to what they remember of their predecessors. Cassian and Germanus, in turn, had carried this "good word" to the monks in Gaul after, as we know, some longish detours in Constantinople and Rome.[3] The *Conlationes,* in short, reflect monastic ascetical doctrine that goes back in time for at least two generations and are cast as a remembered or recollected dialogue.

Early in the *Conlationes* we are introduced to Abba Moses. He is the main speaker in both conference one and in conference two. We know from the *Verba Seniorum* that Moses, a black African, was a renowned ascetic who had been a freed slave before taking up the monastic life. The sayings attributed to him in the *Verba Seniorum* do not deal directly with discernment, but there is appended to his name a series of short sayings which deal with spiritual direction collected by Abba Poemen.[4] The notorious tangles concerning the transmission and final canonical shape of the desert sayings need not detain us here.[5] What is evident from the sources is that Abba Moses was a highly regarded figure in the desert area of Scete. Cassian's invocation of him as the spokesperson for the teaching about discernment was, in effect, to introduce someone who had great charismatic authority in the desert because of his reputation for purity and the holiness of his life. In fact, in the first conference, Cassian says that none was more outstanding than Moses because of the "fragrance of the virtue he practiced and for the preeminence of his contemplation" (37).[6]

Cassian does not begin his discussion of discernment with its definition; he has Abba Moses satisfy himself with simply noting that discernment ("the ability to distinguish between spirits") is one of the gifts of the Holy Spirit mentioned in St. Paul (1 Cor. 12:10). The subject, then, is the *diakrisis pneumaton* of the Pauline tradition. What Cassian does do, however, is narrate, through the mouth of Abba Moses, a series of *exempla* taken from both Sacred Scripture and monastic lore to show what happens when people lacked real discernment. Of all the *Conferences* this second one uses the most number of edifying stories to make its teachings vivid.

There is one *exemplum* in particular that bears careful examination since it contains most of what Abba Moses wishes to teach Cassian. It is the story of the ascetic desert dweller, Hero, narrated in chapter 5 of conference 2. I will use that *exemplum* as an entry point for our discussion of discretion.

According to Abba Moses, Hero had lived in the desert for over fifty years following a regime of heroic fasting and solitude. He was so ascetic that when the monks came from their cells to participate in the Easter *synaxis,* he could not be persuaded to join them in the celebration of the resurrection liturgy or to enjoy the common hospitality of all the monks who ate at table when the liturgy was over. Deluded by an angel of light (i.e., Satan) he threw himself headlong down a well having been convinced by the angel that no harm could befall him. Hero was extricated by some fellow monks only to die two days later convinced that it was an angel and not a delusion that caused him to act so foolishly. Only the subsequent intervention of Abba Paphnutius kept him from being classified among the suicides and, thus, saving his name, which was then inscribed among those for whom the monks prayed in honor of the memory of his asceticism.

There are a number of emphases in this rather extraordinary cautionary tale worth singling out for consideration:

1. The fall from grace came about because Hero "preferred to be guided by his own ideas rather than to bow to the advice [*consiliis*] and conferences of his brothers and to the rules laid down by our predecessors [*maiorum*]" (64). In other words, Hero preferred to be his own spiritual director, and this preference, as the whole tradition insists, is a fatal one. His disdain, to repeat, was both for advice and the wisdom of the desert rules or traditions.

2. His stated reason for not coming to table (note: he excommunicated himself; exclusion from the common table was considered a stiff punishment in early monastic rules) was his fear that by the tiniest relaxation of his ascetical practices he might give the impression of laxity. His decision was not based on his own interior needs but framed outwardly toward others and what they might think of him. He desired to impress by his example but he was unwilling to learn or be guided himself. The sensitive reader will see the charge alluded to by Cassian: Hero is filled with pride masking as observance. There is, then, in this *exemplum* both the traditional "vainglory" and pride against which the monastic writers warned so insistently.

3. Though it sounds strange to contemporary ears, Hero was vulnerable to demonic temptation when, ironically, he had gone to the desert for the precise reason of wrestling with the demonic, overcoming it, and reaching toward that peace which derives from a fully cultivated purity of heart. In other words, he had lost the desert combat of struggling with the demonic. In fact, we might read the references to angels in the

story as a demonic subtext. Hero did not discern between those spiritual impulses which were of God and those which may well have come from sublunary forces frequently identified in ascetic literature with the fallen angels.

Each of these observations deserves some further consideration.

It was a commonplace among the early desert monks that one not only learned the way of asceticism from an elder who was tried in the life but one continued to seek out the advice of those who were fellow searchers for Christian perfection. Even the great St. Antony, as Athanasius tells us in his *vita* of the saint, sought out someone to teach him the way of asceticism as he embarked on his spiritual journey.

The going to the Elder or Spiritual Guide, however, was not only for the sake of apprenticeship. Authentic discernment derives from genuine humility (which can be described as knowing who one truly is), and humility can only come when everything one does or thinks is "submitted to the scrutiny of our elders" (67). Discernment, in other words, first means knowledge of the self before it means discerning the needs and problems of others. Humility, in the desert tradition, is linked with the willingness to manifest the heart to another, an elder.

What is the logic of this "manifestation of the heart"? The sorry story of Hero gives us an insight: Hero did not know who he was because he had set himself up as the one who alone scrutinized what was going on in his life. He did not have an outside source to serve as a check on the misread signals he was seeing in himself; what he took to be spiritual advancement was, in fact, a snare. It is also interesting to note that later in this conference Cassian will return to the issue of eating again (did he have Hero's example in mind?) to argue that excessive fasting like excessive eating is a sign of the lack of discretion; it is making a means into an end. In Hero's story, of course, there was something more than fasting going on; Hero not only refused food. He refused hospitality.

While it is true that the development of discernment through recourse to another is a hallmark of the monastic life in the Eastern Church institutionalized in the office of the Elder (*Geron*), the deeper insight that rests behind that praxis has a wider and more generally applicable meaning, namely, that the path toward spiritual maturity in the Christian tradition is not a solitary and individualistic matter. Fidelity to the Spirit of God is a dynamic process that implicates the one who hears God's call to grace from within the *community* who serves as the custodian of revelation. The nexus between one who goes to the elder for true discernment is, as it were, a micro-example of the larger truth, to wit, that there is no such thing as a do-it-yourself Christianity by which an individual qua individual remains unanswerable to the witness of the community. It is worthwhile remembering that Hero's great "No" was to the community at worship at the synaxis and the community as community at a common festive meal. Behind that, as we have noted, was his disdain for the "counsels" of the tradition and its "rules." That simple fact, in itself, belies the common stereotype that the desert ascetics were egocentrically individualistic or independent of liturgical praxis, a stereotype recently demolished in a careful study by Graham Gould.[7]

Lesson one, then, is that discernment is never reducible to the needs and inspirations of the "I"; it always implicates the community even when the community stands in the deep background as one wrestles with a profoundly personal problem. Put another way: when one listens to the Spirit in order to discern something, the presumption should be toward what the community has found to be useful/true/applicable, etc. That notion is embedded in the observation that Hero would not listen to the "rules [*institutis*] laid down by our predecessors" (64). Hero's fault was not that he was an ascetic traditionalist but that he had cut himself off from the common tradition of monastic Christianity with his schism made most clear by his refusal of table fellowship.

This emphasis on the need for community is not peculiar to Cassian. His contemporary, St. Basil of Caesarea, was not terribly sympathetic to the life of strict eremitism. There were a number of reasons for this but one of them, as he expressed it in his *Ascetikon* in the Long Rule was: "The doctrine of the love of Christ does not permit the individual to be concerned solely with his own private interests. . . . A person living in solitary retirement will not readily discern his own defects, since he has no one to admonish and correct him with mildness and compassion."[8]

Second, the fall of Hero comes from a not fully recognized act of pride on his part. He was so proud of his ascetic rigor that an act as innocent as participation in the liturgy might have compromised the view that he personally had about how other people saw him. Note that this is what he thought *about himself* and, in so thinking, became a prisoner of one of the evil thoughts (*logismoi* are more properly images/persistent scenarios that unfold in the mind) that keep one back from attaining that purity of heart which is demanded by grace.

There is a rich tradition of analysis going back to Origen and coming to Cassian through Evagrius of Pontus that analyzes the principal vices which haunt the minds and hearts of people. Cassian in the *Institutes* devotes a long section to an analysis of these evil *logismoi* of which the worst is pride. Whether it be pride or anger or accedia the effect is the same: an inability to be awake to virtue; clear about one's true relationship to God; trapped into states which lead to a kind of torpor and paralysis.[9]

It is beyond the scope of this brief reflection to outline the subtle psychology which the monastic tradition developed with respect to the *logismoi,* but one point needs to be made: the images/thoughts of which these writers spoke acted as a kind of wall that separated a person from directly confronting the action of God. Indeed (and here I follow the analysis of Evagrius), the *logismos* is not a pure idea but a kind of alluring picture, plausibly drawn, found in the sensibilities of a person which powerfully draws that person to it. The *logismoi* may be thought of as interior images that act as a barrier or a screen. Their exterior depiction has been the subject later of both artistic (e.g., Bosch) and literary (e.g., Flaubert) renderings, for example, of St. Anthony's temptations. However lurid such depictions are in the belletristic tradition, they do reflect an insight into the *logismoi*, i.e., that they are more like pictures or images and not abstract ideas. (Does it take us too far afield that given our media saturated culture we might well look back again at what Evagrius and others have said about the *logismoi* and their influence on our minds and hearts?)

What kept Hero from a sense of discretion, apart from his solipsism, was a picture of himself as perfectly observant, a picture, alas, that was false but persuasive enough to make him a bad judge of both whom he was and what he should be doing. It is the burden of discretion to be able to judge the quality of the picture/images generated in the human person. The picture/image was of particular interest to the monk since, as Evagrius says, "the demons strive against men in the world through affairs, but in the case of monks for the most part by means of thoughts since the desert deprives them of such affairs."[10] The final effect of the *logismoi* is, in effect, to erect, through the imagination, a false self and, as a contemporary spiritual master has written, "The 'I' that works in the world, thinks about itself, observes its own reactions and talks about itself is not the true 'I' that has been united to God in Christ."[11]

The precise character of the *logismos* of vainglory and pride is that the sufferer "fancies himself" superior by an image he might have of himself as a healer or the object of adulation or believes that people should be knocking at his door for advice or that others should be touching his clothing to experience the Sacred (all these examples are offered by Evagrius). Such vainglory leads inevitably to demonic pride; and that pride, Evagrius insists, is a form of insanity which induces the monk "to deny that God is his helper and to consider that he is in himself the cause of all virtuous action."[12]

This brings us to our third point: the *logismoi* that blind are, and this is the unanimous tradition of the desert, always inspired by the demonic. To be blunt: Hero was engaged in a psychomachia (as he had been for fifty years), and he lost. The reason he lost was simple: he was deluded by Satan who threw up an image that blinded him; the image was interior but it was compelling enough to make Hero judge wrongly.

It is interesting to read the story of Hero in the light of what Cassian has to say about pride in the twelfth book of his *Institutes*.[13] Cassian writes that while pride is the last vice to be fought against in the desert "combat," it is actually the first in time and origin since it comes from Satan and is thus the "beginning of all sins and vices" (xii.6). Pride cannot be overcome unless we recognize two very fundamental things: (1) we cannot overcome pride without the mercy and grace of God (xii.16), and (2) the mercy and inspiration of God is shown to us by others (xii.15), especially those "ancient fathers" who learned a simple and pure faith not derived from "dialectical syllogisms or the eloquence of a Cicero" (xii.19).

Since Cassian believes that pride is the *fons et origo* of all sin and vice, it should not surprise us that he puts the struggle against that primordial sin at the very heart of the desert struggle; to lose the battle with pride is, in effect, to lose the reason why one goes into the desert. In the case of Hero, to be specific, it gained him nothing to have been in the desert when he failed to resist the satanic urges of pride. Cassian puts the case in the precise language of the monastic struggle:

> Wherefore the Christian athlete who strives lawfully in the spiritual combat and desires to be crowned by the Lord, should endeavour by every means to destroy this most fierce beast [i.e., pride] which is destructive of all the virtues knowing that as long as this remains in his breast he not only will never be free from all kinds of evil but if he seems to have any good qualities, will lose them by its malign influence. (xii.32)

It is, of course, one thing to inquire into the many lessons of this ancient *exemplum* and quite another to ask whether its lessons have any staying power for those who do not go out to desert wildernesses to enter combat, who do not use the language of demonic powers, and who are not conversant with the vocabulary of the *logismoi*.

In other words: does the analysis of discernment/discretion embedded in this story of Hero translate into anything useful for us?

Before answering that query let us stipulate that people today do seek out the "Will of God" and people do desire, often on the cusp of crucial moments in their lives, to know the way they should proceed or not proceed. Let us further stipulate that such axial moments in a person's life often involve conscious decisions which are seen to be responses to what they see as the promptings of God's graceful interventions in their lives. Let us stipulate, not to put too fine a point on it, that people today do seek to discern how they are to live within the divine economy.

Once those stipulations are in place, then it seems that the homely *exemplum* of Cassian has some extremely fundamental things to say to every serious Christian.

First, and most fundamentally, religious discernment is an act of faith; it says, in effect, that what I decide and how I proceed (or do not proceed) is not a nakedly autonomous decision based solely on my own powers, my own perceptions, and the assessed values of this or that particular "award" or "end": to say, in effect, that my decisions and judgments are not done free of any reference outside myself. In that sense, at least, one submits to the authority of God which is, at its most basic, an act of authentic humility. That kind of humility, as Thomas Merton once wrote, is a kind of shorthand description of faith itself.[14] The very act of discernment is an act against absolute autonomy and, in the same act, a gesture toward relationality.

The faith of the Christian, however, is both personal and communal. We learn of the demands of faith and are nourished by it through stepping into the story and its performance (e.g., in the liturgy) which is to say, by participating in the handing down (*paradosis*) of the gospel in time and space. Cassian's pointed observation about Hero's reluctance to enter into the liturgical and fraternal life of the monastic fellowship was a shorthand way of saying that Hero lacked faith in the cumulative experience of those who had tried and tested the life of the desert. Hero's reluctance was both a demonstration of an unhealthy individualism but was also an act of faithlessness in the Spirit-guaranteed tradition of the tradition of piety (one could say that Hero denied the creedal affirmation that the church is "holy" as well as one, catholic, and apostolic).

Resistance to the accumulated wisdom of what the "cloud of witnesses" (Heb. 12:1) have learned over the centuries is a kind of denial of the Spirit's presence in the Christian; it is another form of individualism and, hence, an erasure of humility and an act of pride. That is not to say that every person who acts as a director or elder or "soul friend" is worthy of credence because of his or her "traditional" way of seeing things (everyone knows how dangerous such persons can be), but it is to say that any spiritual director or counselor who seems indifferent or antagonistic to the tradition of faith is, on the face of it, suspect. To trust such a person is, in effect, to have a Hero as a director, which is to say, someone who relies exclusively on his or her estimation of things detached from any sense of the community and its memory. All the more suspect, it is clear, would be any discernment which would take us apart from the common table of Eucharist and fellowship.

The above should not be read as an apologia for extreme traditionalism; it is to be read as a suggestion that discernment is best approached from within the parameters of an environment that admits of the hermeneutics of trust. We might add parenthetically that Cassian's conference ten may contain an example of the need for this sense of community discernment. After all, as Cassian points out, some of the more advanced and perfect of the Egyptian monks held to the "anthropomorphite" heresy until they were led, through persuasion and collective discernment, to abandon their simple-minded notion of God in favor of that which the Great Church held.

Indeed, the history of Christian spirituality offers many examples of how something new was discerned as needed for a time and place but the "newness" had to be judged against what had previously been received. St. Francis had to show that itinerancy was not antagonistic to monastic stability but only different just as Ignatius had to show that recitation of the choral office was not needed for all clerks regular. The struggles of a Mary Ward and Louise de Marillac to define new vocations for women struggled both with tradition and what was perceived to be a *Novum* in apostolic service. In all of these cases (and many others) it was a question of balance between tradition and genuine insight into the new, a "going back" as a prelude for "going forward."

As we live in a postmodern world of increasing familiarity with other spiritual impulses, the issue of how to be faithful to the community of the gospel and the new opportunities for spiritual experience become all the more acute. If, for example, William Johnston, Bede Griffiths, Thomas Merton, et al. are correct in saying that contemplative experience may be the first authentic ground from which interreligious sharing is to take place, then the issue of having faith in our own tradition before we seek for experience in another one becomes crucial. Otherwise, we run the risk of plunging into a well of facile syncretism which does no honor to our tradition or that of others.

When one reads the old desert ascetics closely it becomes clear that they were shrewd psychologists. Their lives brought them into close contact with the naked realization that the line between authentic spiritual experience and self-delusion was a thin one. That is why their warnings were so frequent about the abuses of the ascetic practices which led to a kind of false egotism and a sense of the self detached from the ground which made their live meaningful and whole.

In the final analysis, the tragic error of Hero was to confuse ascetic practice with the goal of the ascetic life, which was that purity of heart by which one came close to the Living God. Hero thought that his asceticism was the goal when, in fact, it was only the means to a goal. He did not "let go" or "forget" ascetic practice but became preoccupied with it to the point of obsession.

There is a curious paradox in the spiritual life (one which Ignatius of Loyola understood perfectly) and it is this: the practice or training (*askesis*) in the Christian life is described in terms of "rules" or "practices" or "discipline," but the function of those disciplines is to forget them once they are mastered so one may live in that freedom and liberty which is life with God. Spiritual writers as widely separated in time as Cassian and Meister Eckhart have used the example of learning to write or learning to play a musical instrument: at the earliest stages focus is on the correct skill in forming the letter or hitting the right note; it is only when those skills are assimilated that one "forgets" them in order to write or to play music. The same is true of the Christian path; the goal of rules/training/ascesis etc. is so to assimilate them that they are "forgotten" in order to get on with life: "A person must be penetrated with the divine presence, and be shaped through and through with the shape of the God he loves, and be present in him, so that God's presence might shine out to him....But at the beginning there must be attentiveness and a careful formation within himself, like a schoolboy setting himself to learn."[15]

That insight is not always fully appreciated even among contemporary Christian seekers. The Catholic tradition has accumulated a plethora of "disciplines" over the centuries which have become, as it were, the broad description of what people think being a Catholic Christian is. These disciplines often appear to be the criteria by which a person judges the self (or others) to be on the path to a more ample Christian life. There is no doubt that a disciplined life is part of being a Christian and the process of conversion necessarily involves an aversion. However, the process by which one shapes a Christian life is not the Christian life itself. Focus on the disciplinary process can be a form of obsessive behavior and not the "Christian Life" which so many imagine.

It is for that reason alone that discretion is so crucial both for those small matters which make up quotidian living as well as those axial moments when one may be in a position, with the help of God, to be prompted to make (to use Ignatian language) an election. When those times appear it may well be useful to recall Hero as we reflect on what we are to do or what the "Good Word" is for us as the wisdom of another, the witness of the Christian community, and the graces which God has given us converge into a privileged moment in which God speaks more insistently and more compellingly than any angel of light. After all, religious experience becomes (as it did for Hero) a temptation, as Michael Buckley once shrewdly noted, "only under the persuasion that the intensity of experience absolves one from discretion, critical reflection, and the doctrinal content of Christian faith, giving experience a priority over the unspeakable Mystery that approaches human beings through experience and transferring the religious guidance of a single person or of an entire community to an unchallengeable subjectivity, to sentimentality or superstition or excited enthusiasms."[16]

The full burden of discretion, of course, rests not only on the person who seeks to discern God's will but also on those who are companions on the Way. We are called upon to listen to the promptings of the Spirit as well as those agents with the Christian community who can aid us as we attempt to be listeners to what God says to us. Those who would presume to aid in the process of discernment should not only keep the story of Hero in mind but the stern warnings of St. John of the Cross in his *Living Flame of Love*,[17] who numbered the bad spiritual director along with Satan and the Self as part of the triad of blind men leading people on the path of destruction.

John of the Cross makes the very sensible, indeed, almost obvious, observation that people ought not to be spiritual guides (John never uses the word "director"; his preferred terms are *guia* [guide] or *maestro espiritual* [spiritual master]) if they have not had some experience in the life of faith. To speak without such experience is likened by John to those who attempt to create an art work but are reduced to hewing and chopping. John has subtle advice on the ways people should be led more deeply into the life of prayer but his more general point is germane to our topic. Just as a person should not be an autonomous agent in discretion so should soul-friends or guides remember what their function is: they "should reflect that they themselves are not the chief agent, guide, and mover of souls in this matter, but that the principal guide is the Holy Spirit... and that they are instruments for directing them to perfection through faith and the law of God, according to the spirit God gives each one" (#46).

It has been the particular genius of Ignatian spirituality in general and *The Spiritual Exercises* of Ignatius in particular to understand that the process by which a person confronts the call of Christ to conversion involves a series of contrapuntal activities. The exercitant stands before the Word of God and also his or her own self open to the process of conversion as well as aversion since, as Ignatius says, we are to erase our "disordered affections" not only to seek God's will but to order ourselves toward salvation. This "first explanation" in the *Exercises* is compactly stated but contains within it a large program. It demands ruthless self-examination, an openness to God's will and a direction toward a final end — salvation. This is all done within the context of the community from which the gospel comes and toward which the person is called. That community is typically represented by the director of the exercises who has already embarked on the path of conversion and election.

Cassian and Ignatius and John of the Cross all wrote at a particular time in history using a language peculiar to their time and place. They all had in common the experience both of solitude and community represented by the desert and the city. They all lived within the larger community which we call the *ekklesia*. Their descriptive psychology is not ours nor can we witlessly adopt their particular theological vocabulary without some effort of translation and modification.

For all those examples of cultural distantiation there are certain threads of continuity which reach down to our own time. The Christian life implicates not only the God of Jesus Christ and the person but the person who lives in community. In this restless period at millennium's end there are many who feel discomfort as members of the church.

There is a persistent temptation to go it alone with a self-made spirituality and a personal (i.e., individual) approach to the "care of the soul."
It does no positive good to lament this tendency if those who love the
church cannot, at the same time, take some responsibility for providing
an alternative vision. My suspicion is that no one has lived in a university setting for long (my own experience now reaches toward thirty
years) without encountering young people who feel a kind of animus for
the faith in which they have been raised. In meeting such persons we
have a correlative privilege to help them discern the deepest impulse in
their humanity.

To those students and others in similar situations it is bootless to roll
out apologetical ploys or persuasive tactics. The ancient spiritual masters
and mistresses offer more solid and less threatening advice. Ask who you
are *really* and to what (or better: whom?) can you respond in knowledge
and love? Be as open and as receptive as you can with a willingness
to recount failure and aspire for something more. Discernment, at its
deepest level, comes at the moment when we finally see that when we are
honest and open in the depths of our heart we will find, not nothingness,
but God. Karl Rahner once wrote that the most fundamental reason
against Christian belief is the very experience of life. He then goes on to
say that the opposite is also true:

> For what does Christianity really declare? Nothing else, after all, than that
> the great mystery remains eternally a mystery, but that this mystery wishes
> to communicate himself in absolute self-communication — as the infinite,
> incomprehensible and inexpressible being whose name is God.[18]

Discernment seems a small part of the Christian experience. In retro-
spect, however, its place in the Christian life is such that without it, we
might fall, like Hero, into the well of spiritual illusion:

> For though by this time you ought to be teachers, you need someone to
> teach you again the first principles of God's Word. You need not milk but
> solid food. . . . But solid food is for the mature, for those who have their
> faculties trained by practice to distinguish good from evil. (Heb. 5:12–14)

Notes

1. *John Climacus: The Ladder of Divine Ascent,* ed. Colm Luibhead (New
York: Paulist, 1982), 229.

2. Ibid.

3. On Cassian's life, see Owen Chadwick, *John Cassian,* rev. ed. (Cambridge:
Cambridge University Press, 1968).

4. They may be found in Benedicta Ward's *The Sayings of the Desert Fathers: The Alphabetical Collection* (Kalamazoo, Mich.: Cistercian Publications,
1975), 119–21. With respect to our subject, see F. Dingjan, "La discretion dans
les apophtegmes des pères," *Angelicum* 39 (1962): 403–15.

5. On such issues, Douglas Burton-Christie's *The Word in the Desert* (New York: Oxford University Press, 1992) is invaluable.

6. All citations in the text with the page number are from *John Cassian: Conferences,* trans. Colm Luibhead (New York: Paulist, 1985); the critical edition is *Jean Cassian: Conferences,* ed. and trans. Dom E. Pichery, Sources Chrétiennes 42 (Paris: Cerf, 1955).

7. Graham Gould, *The Desert Fathers on Monastic Community,* Oxford Early Christian Studies (Oxford: Clarendon, 1993).

8. *St. Basil: Ascetical Works,* trans. Sister M. Monica Wagner, C.S.C. (Washington, D.C.: Catholic University of America Press, 1950), 248.

9. For an excellent survey on the *logismoi,* see Tomas Spidlik, S.J., *The Spirituality of the Christian East* (Kalamazoo, Mich.: Cistercian Publications, 1986), 239–56.

10. *Evagrius Ponticus: The Praktikos and Chapters on Prayer,* trans. John Eudes Bamberger (Kalamazoo, Mich.: Cistercian Publications, 1972), 29.

11. Thomas Merton, *New Seeds of Contemplation* (New York: New Directions, 1961), 7.

12. *Praktikos* no. 14 in *Evagrius Ponticus,* trans. Bamberger, 20.

13. "The Institutes of John Cassian" in *A Select Library of Nicene/Post-Nicene Fathers of the Christian Church,* ed. Edgar C. S. Gibson, 2d series (Grand Rapids: Eerdmans, 1978). All citations in the text are to book and chapter from this edition.

14. In *New Seeds of Contemplation,* 181ff., Merton contrasts humility with despair, a juxtaposition pregnant with meaning.

15. Meister Eckhart, "Counsels on Discernment" in *Meister Eckhart: The Essential Sermons,* ed. Edmund Colledge and Bernard McGinn (New York: Paulist, 1981), 254.

16. "Discernment of Spirits," in *The New Dictionary of Catholic Spirituality,* ed. Michael Downey (Collegeville, Minn.: Liturgical Press, 1993), 274–75.

17. In *The Collected Works of Saint John of the Cross,* ed. Kieran Kavanaugh and Otilio Rodriguez (Washington, D.C.: ICS, 1979), 577–652. References in text by paragraph number.

18. Karl Rahner, *The Content of Faith* (New York: Crossroad, 1993), 68; the full essay "What Is a Christian?" originally appeared in *Theological Investigations* 5 (Baltimore: Helicon, 1966), 4–9.

15

Finding God in All Things

Jonathan Edwards and Ignatius Loyola

– WILLIAM C. SPOHN –

Christian discernment is the ability to attend to the presence and action of God in experience, the graced habit of "finding God in all things." It links religious experience to moral conduct because the presence of God invites the believer to live a life compatible with that presence and to collaborate with God's transforming intentions for the world.[1] As the habit of discernment deepens, it tends to integrate every moral disposition and choice into a life which responds to the glory of God, the One "in whom we live and move and have our being" (Acts 17:28). Ignatius Loyola and Jonathan Edwards are acknowledged as two of the masters of Christian discernment in Western Christian spirituality. However, the distance between sixteenth-century Rome and eighteenth-century Massachusetts has proven to be a formidable barrier to comparing their accounts of discernment. American Protestants shaped in the tradition of Edwards have not dispelled the myth of Ignatius as point man for the Counter Reformation assault on heretics any more than Catholics have moved beyond the dour Puritan rhetoric of "Sinners in the Hands of an Angry God."[2]

This essay will attempt to redress this unfortunate omission by arguing that the founder of the Jesuits and the Puritan divine offer convergent accounts of the experience of Christian discernment. Despite significant differences in theology and cultural location, their practical advice on judging religious experience indicates underlying agreement on how God transforms and guides Christians. These two phenomenologies of religious discernment converge on three main points:

1. Christian conversion produces transformed religious experience that is impossible for the unconverted.

2. Affections, the deep emotional dispositions of the heart, are the center of religious transformation and the principal sources of evidence for judgments of religious discernment.

3. Religious affections are the media of God's inspiration. This convergence may indicate the promise of critical spirituality: the experience of God is more similar than the diverse theologies which interpret it.

Edwards and Loyola developed their accounts of discernment from personal experience of trial and error in evaluating religious phenomena. Ignatius made enough blunders following his conversion from soldier into Christian pilgrim to force him to become critical about religious impulses and intentions. Excessive fasting, penance, and long hours of mystical contemplation nearly ruined his health and diverted his energies from practical ministry and the study of theology. *The Spiritual Exercises* gradually emerged as the result of almost twenty years of struggling to find God's will for his life.[3] Ideally, the Exercises should help those making them learn "discernment of spirits," that is, how to sort out genuine religious experiences from counterfeit ones. This series of meditations on religious themes and gospel stories is an experimental laboratory for learning how to respond to God. The retreat director helps the retreatant to notice which deep dispositions of the heart are "disordered affections" and which ones are ordered to God.[4]

Edwards learned the need for discernment in a different but equally challenging context, the American religious revival of the 1740s.[5] Certain doctrinal commitments underlay the pastoral crisis. Puritans believed with other Calvinists that the elect are predestined by God; they added the requirement of experience to predestination. Each Christian had to experience divine election in a life-transforming conversion and give an account of it in order to become a full member of the church. Until they had been "savingly wrought upon" by the Spirit of God, churchgoers were not considered to be saved, even if their conduct was upstanding. Consequently, Puritan pastors devoted a great deal of pastoral care to helping individuals discern whether they had in fact undergone genuine conversion. A century after their ancestors had arrived in the New World on their "errand into the wilderness," the Puritans of the Massachusetts Bay Colony were in religious decline. Fewer conversions occurred in each subsequent generation, more people were attracted to the vocation of prosperity than becoming "visible saints," and pastoral compromises were made to accommodate churchgoers who could not testify to the experience of godly election.

Although Edwards's youthful conversion had some false starts, it was not nearly as confusing as the tumult of the Great Awakening which swept the American colonies between 1740 and 1743. "Awakening" referred to sinners' waking up to the peril of divine judgment; usually it came prior to receiving the saving grace of Christ. Edwards mounted a theological defense of this "season of grace" but also criticized its excesses. Beneath the intense and often bizarre expressions of religious fervor provoked by the Awakening, he discerned a genuine revival of "true religion." The widespread response to the call for conversion indicated to him that God was vindicating traditional doctrine against latter-day unbelief and compromise.

When the floodtide of the Awakening ebbed, however, Edwards struggled to comprehend why so many promising converts had fallen away from true religion and returned to their old carnal ways. In Puritan theology these backslidings were deeply scandalous. Since God's sovereign election assured the "perseverance of the saints," the failure to persevere in grace meant that most of the conversions produced by the Awakening had been counterfeit. Edwards and his ministerial colleagues must have been deceived on a massive scale. How could they have authenticated so many conversions as genuine which turned out to be false? The genteel Boston divines who had objected to the dramatic preaching and high emotions of the Awakening now felt vindicated. The entire affair had been a delusion, certainly not the result of the Spirit of God, who would produce religion that was always calm, rational, and serene. Edwards responded with a series of sermons that became his famous *Treatise on Religious Affections,* which ranks with *The Spiritual Exercises* as a classic on Christian discernment.

Comparing Edwards and Ignatius poses a particular challenge to theological interpretation. Edwards was a man of prodigious intellectual gifts and enormous theological production.[6] His descriptions are often rich, and his conceptual explanations are relentlessly logical and systematically profound. Ignatius's gifts lay in other directions. He wrote like the man of action that he was: his two major productions, *The Spiritual Exercises* and *The Constitutions of the Society of Jesus,* are guidelines for decision and practice.[7] Their theological rationale is rarely expressed; it lies between the lines as the supposition for practical directives. While the breadth and force of Edwards's theological argument may overwhelm the interpreter, Ignatius's wisdom must be mined from laconic expressions of particular insights. My treatment of the *Exercises* will be more summary, on the presumption that most readers of this volume will be more familiar with Ignatius, particularly in the interpretation of Michael J. Buckley, S.J.[8]

Conversion: The Transformation of Experience

Christian discernment depends upon a qualitatively different form of experience which emerges from the event of religious conversion. Ignatius outlines two different sets of "rules for the discernment of spirits": one applies to those who are committed to Christ and the other to those who are not. Edwards offers an explanation for these different religious psychologies.

The Spiritual Exercises are a "school of the affections" which orders the dispositions of the one making them to follow the way of Christ. Those who direct retreatants in making the Exercises are not the prime instructors in finding God's will. That role is reserved to God, who works directly with the person.[9] However, some who begin this pedagogy turn out to be so poorly suited for discernment that they cannot make the full course of the Exercises. The director can infer that some retreatants are not ready for the challenge of the gospel from their resistance to the action of the good spirit and the ease with which the contrary spirit moves them. They resist the influences of God's spirit like a rock under a stream of water but soak up temptations like a sponge. The serious Christian acts just the opposite. The receptivity and resistance of the retreatant manifests the person's basic internal disposition.

Someone who is tempted "grossly and openly" and easily discouraged from serving God by the prospect of hardships, shame, and the loss of worldly honor is a person "not versed in spiritual things."[10] It would be a great disservice to tell people like this to "follow your heart" because their hearts are set on the wrong things. The retreat director should offer them some basic advice on Christian life and then send them home. They would be harmed by further instruction in discernment because it is "too subtle and advanced for such a one to understand."[11]

People who have a basic generosity toward God require an entirely different strategy. They are more likely to be tempted subtly "under the appearance of good" rather than by the pleasures of sinful behavior. They may run ahead of grace or have their good intentions sapped by discouragingly "realistic" thoughts and specious objections.[12] They receive a more subtle training in discernment while meditating on the life of Christ. A pivotal consideration of the Kingdom of God sets the basic experimental strategy for learning discernment. It evokes both the retreatant's affective attachment to Christ and the affections which could lead away from the Lord so that the retreatant can experience the contrast. The cost of discipleship — the prospect of labor, poverty, and rejection by others — is pitted against the attraction of discipleship, namely, companionship with Jesus in his struggle to establish God's reign by liberating the world from sin and oppression.[13] That affective contrast will form the litmus test of discernment which will guide the person long after the retreat is finished.

According to Edwards, conversion changes the fundamental affective orientation by expanding it beyond the contraction of self-centeredness. It alters the individual's psychological structure by imparting a capacity to appreciate God's beauty, a new sense of the loveliness of God. Edwards dealt with "carnal men" in a different way because their experience was unlike that of the elect. He preached rhetorical hell-fire only to those who seemed immune to any higher religious message, like the congregation at Enfield who were subjected to "Sinners in the Hands of an Angry God." Unredeemed experience is contracted because the heart is turned in on itself. Since it is dominated by self-interest, the only appeal a preacher can make is that of reward and punishment. In its original condition under the influence of divine love, the soul "was, as it were, enlarged to a kind of comprehension of all its fellow creatures" and extended to the Creator in love.

> Immediately upon the Fall the mind of man shrunk from its primitive greatness and extensiveness into an exceeding diminution and...as soon as he transgressed, those nobler principles were immediately lost and all this excellent enlargedness of his soul was gone and he thenceforward shrunk into a little point circumscribed and closely shut up within itself to the exclusion of all others.[14]

Detached from the expansive attraction of the divine beauty, the natural moral dynamics shrink to the narrowness of self-love. Religious experience does not necessarily cure this contraction of spirit. For years Edwards witnessed people obsessed with intense elations, visions, and inner promptings which they took to be God's direct commands. They presumed that the more intense their experience, the more assuredly it must be genuine. Edwards notes that these "hypocrites" actually took "more delight in their discoveries than in Christ discovered."[15] They thought of themselves as eminent saints and congratulated God for his good taste in choosing them. When rejoicing in God, they kept one eye on themselves. The fact that "they are great talkers about themselves" betrayed their self-preoccupation.[16] An affective transformation is necessary to draw the person out of self-obsession. God works through Christ "to bring the soul of man out of its confinement, and again to infuse those noble and divine principles by which it was governed at first. And so Christianity restores an excellent enlargement and extensiveness to the soul."[17]

The disclosure of the divine beauty enlarges the soul by inaugurating a new form of experience. The pattern of conversions in Edwards's Northampton congregation replicated his own transformation: converts were given a "sense of divine things" which permeated their experience of nature, other persons, ideas, and moral values. Even though the initial delights faded in time, the new capacity for appreciation remained. This gift resembled a power of sensation like taste or sight because it was direct and immediate, not the result of reasoning. Edwards consistently describes it as a "relish" or "sweetness" in language reminiscent of Ignatius's use of *sentir,* a direct savoring of spiritual realities. Transformed experience meant a new identity for Edwards. "Nature is an abiding thing" because it is the basis of operations and actions. If the person's operations are changed permanently, then the individual's nature has been transformed. Admittedly, the new convert would wrestle with old sinful habits, but "they will no longer have dominion over him; nor will they any more be properly his character."[18] These evil habits, extensions of a corrupt self-love, will no longer reign by default because a new source of motivation and action has been conferred in the new sensibility. When the heart begins to appreciate all things in relation to God rather than to self-interest, morality is transformed by this affective revolution.

Affections: Signs of Conversion and Principles of Discernment

Ignatius and Edwards look to the affections, the deep dispositions of the heart, for the primary evidence of their judgments of discernment. The presence of God is not detected by direct introspection but by an inference based on signs that are primarily affective. For Edwards the quality of the person's dispositions provides evidence that authentic religious conversion has occurred. For Ignatius the quality of the impulses that move the retreatant's heart are signs that indicate whether they are God's invitations or not.

Where are these signs found? In the affections, the basic desires and dynamic habits of the heart. Conversion to Christ changes the basic dynamics of the individual's character by redirecting it out of self-absorption to active engagement with God and the world. This new love for God expresses itself in various dispositions which are determined by their finality. Every desire is structured by its proper object, or in Edwards's succinct description, "a holy love has a holy object."[19] The holiness of God evokes a corresponding holiness in the one who appreciates it. We expect a holy love to be pure, reverent, zealous for integrity and to seek what is admirable and avoid what is base. By examining the finality of dispositions, one can judge their origins. Conversely, since Scripture makes clear the profile of the Spirit which originates these affections, one can confidently predict what the will will be oriented to. A holy love will be the result of the Spirit of holiness.

Ignatius states that the *Exercises* employs the will to elicit "acts of the affections."[20] These are the raw material for the experiments which will teach discernment. Many of the meditations of the *Exercises* are deliberate experiments designed to bring out the qualitative difference between the invitations of grace and the false appeal of temptations. They lead the retreatant to experience the tension between the attraction of God's glory (the public manifestation of divine beauty and goodness) and the lure of worldly honor, riches, and pride.

Ignatius divides the movements of the soul into two main classes of experiences: spiritual consolation and desolation. Subtlety is required because they do not neatly divide into feelings of pleasure and pain, attraction and repulsion. The affective quality of interior experiences must be examined to determine their origins and destinations. The primary type of genuine consolation "occurs when some interior motion is caused within the soul through which it comes to be inflamed with love of its Creator and Lord." This unique attraction orders all other attractions because of its distinctive depth: "As a result [the soul] can love no created thing on the face of the earth in itself, but only in the Creator of them all."[21] The moral priority of love for God is not deduced logically from the idea of a transcendent love. It is an affective corollary, an inference of the heart which is inherent in the aesthetic structure of the love itself. All other loves must be subordinate to this great love because they pale by comparison with it.

Secondly, Ignatius mentions tears "which move [the soul] to love for its Lord" as another typical form of consolation. Ignatius often experienced tears but knew that intensity of affect was not enough: it had to be ordered to love and service of God. Finally, all thoughts, impulses, desires, and intentions which lead toward God and salvation of the soul and neighbor are "consolations." The emotional quality of these movements displays their aim: they are increases "in hope, faith, and charity, and every interior joy which calls and attracts one toward heavenly things and the salvation of one's soul, by bringing it tranquility and peace in its Creator and Lord."[22] Consolation is the key because God leads the person through desires; this obedience is a response to an attraction, not bare duty heeding a divine command.

Spiritual desolation has a contrary destination. It is marked by diminishment of faith, discouragement of hope, and an absence of love. Temptations may have an initial appeal, but underneath they sadden the spirit, evoke "a gnawing anxiety" and "set up obstacles" to serving God and the neighbor.[23] These affective qualities have their own moral effect. Beset by "darkness of soul, turmoil within it, an impulsive motion toward low and earthly things...one is completely listless, tepid, and unhappy, and feels separated from our Creator and Lord."[24]

The origin of these interior movements must also be discerned, although it is easier to detect their destinations. The most radical form of spiritual consolation arises immediately and spontaneously, "without a preceding cause." It does not come in the ordinary train of thoughts, perceptions, or intentions but from a direct influence of God who "draws the person wholly into love of his Divine Majesty."[25] The total response is out of proportion to any finite thought or image; this type of consolation seems to exclude any doubt. Ordinary religious experiences, by comparison, arise from thoughts, perceptions, and intentions; they can lead one toward serving God or away from God. They are not self-authenticating and call for discernment.

Edwards gives a psychological rationale for the centrality of affections in religious discernment. He flatly states the main thesis of *Religious Affections:* "True religion, in great part, consists in holy affections."[26] To profess Christian faith involves experiencing the power and goodness of what one professes. Those who criticize religious emotion for being excessive and irrational do not understand human psychology which requires both "heat and light" in response to what is infinitely good, true, and beautiful. The skeptics of affective religion are themselves suspect: "they who condemn others for their religious affections, and have none themselves, have no religion."[27]

Edwards distinguishes affections from passions, which are sudden physiological reactions that do not arise from insight and can overpower the mind. Affections are always based on some apprehension and are "the more vigorous and sensible exercises of the inclination and will of the soul."[28] They are the whole person's integral response to what is agreeable or repugnant. Human appreciation is not only physiological; indeed, nothing is known that is not adequately appreciated. Affections break down the customary division between sensibility and rationality; they are "sensible exercises of the will...affections of the soul...sensation[s] of the mind."[29] Affections are deeper than inclinations or mere velleities. Although they are felt, they enter more deeply into the agent's character than transient emotions or feelings. Affections are the weight of one's deepest convictions and "habits of the heart" which dispose the person to regular patterns of conduct.[30]

The appreciation of the divine beauty, the capacity initially imparted in conversion, conveys a new understanding of religious truths and new inclination to moral values which is "entirely diverse from anything that is perceived in them, by natural men, as the sweet taste of honey is diverse from the ideas men get of honey by only looking on it and feeling it."[31] Edwards gropes for tangible metaphors to convey this new form of comprehension. He contrasts "mere notional understanding" with "the sense of the heart, wherein the mind don't only speculate and behold, but relishes and feels." It provides "a knowledge, by which a man has a sensible perception of amiableness and loathsomeness."[32] This felt, direct appreciation of qualities satisfies the person more profoundly than rational reflection. Similarly, Ignatius counseled the retreat director not to overload the retreatant with too much material for reflection. "For, what fills and satisfies the soul consists, not in knowing much, but in our understanding the realities profoundly and savoring them interiorly."[33]

Edwards, like Ignatius, analyzes affections according to their origin and goal, the two poles that determine their inner rationale. (Edwards also found it easier to detect their finality than their origins.) Even intense affections have an inner structure that can be rationally grasped. Affections are not merely spontaneous emotional releases; they are organized by the "proper objects" to which they are attuned. An affection "fits" specific qualities of its object.[34] For instance, love may be heartfelt and gratifying but unless it conforms to the actual qualities of the beloved, it will not be genuine love.[35] Each religious affection correlates with some specific quality of God and Christ, while all are rooted in the primary Christian disposition, love. The qualities of God and Christ should determine the responses to them. When God's personal beauty is disclosed in conversion, an entirely new proper object enters the person's experience; correlatively, it evokes new affections which are unlike any which the person has experienced before. Genuine love for God is based upon the personal "loveliness" or beauty of God. The unconverted may experience God as a force of nature and appreciate the divine "greatness," but they cannot appreciate his "holiness" or "loveliness." They do not experience the beauty of God's personal excellence. They might realize that God is omniscient, powerful and just but not that God is personally gracious, merciful, kind, faithful, and loving. The full goodness of God, the true proper object, has not yet been disclosed to them.

In summary, therefore, an affection and its object stand in reciprocal relationship since the object is the objective correlative for the affection, and the affection is the subjective correlative to the object. This correlation of qualities provides the basis for discerning the nature of religious affections and making the crucial judgment about whether genuine conversion has occurred. From the qualities of God made known in Scripture one can infer the appropriate or fitting affective responses in the true Christian.[36] From the other side, by examining our own affections we can judge whether they actually tend toward God.

This correlation between affections and the divine characteristics provides the epistemological justification for each of *Religious Affections* twelve signs for discerning true religion. The principal signs are:

1. Gracious affections do not come from any natural perception or cognition but from the indwelling Spirit of God. One does not come to appreciate these qualities "by a long chain of reasoning"; rather one perceives God's beauty immediately and intuitively in images, doctrines, values, and nature. Edwards's description parallels the deepest form of Ignatian spiritual consolation, the one "without preceding cause."

2. The disclosure of beauty, particularly the beauty of personal "loveliness," evokes a response that transcends self-interest. The person is absorbed in the "loveliness of divine things, as they are in themselves; and not [in] any conceived relation they bear to self, or self-interest."[37]

3. Genuine religious experience is also deeply engaging. The relish of God is simultaneously gratifying and moral. Grace does not abolish a legitimate self-love any more than benevolence banishes complacence and delight from love.

4. The divine beauty conveys a deeper understanding of the truths

of the gospel. Religious doctrines that were once opaque or unmoving become meaningful when the beauty of God shines through them. Traces of the beauty of God are visible in them, which conveys "the real evidence of their divinity, the most direct and strong evidence."[38]

5. The divine beauty elicits qualities in the convert which correspond to the character of God and Christ revealed in the history of salvation and definitively expressed in Scripture. While promoting every virtuous affection, grace will more especially bring forth "those virtues that were so wonderfully exercised by Jesus Christ towards us in that affair [of the work of redemption]...such as humility, meekness, love, forgiveness, and mercy."[39] Ignatius devotes most of the *Spiritual Exercises* to meditating on the life, death, and resurrection of Jesus so that the attractiveness of his values will take hold in the heart and imagination of the retreatant. Ignatius, however, emphasizes more active characteristics of Jesus which he expects to be echoed in the retreatant: generosity, zeal to save the world, and total dedication to doing God's will in bringing about the Kingdom. Edwards's spirituality has a more contemplative, aesthetic emphasis.

6. Appreciating the holiness of God should evoke a sense of personal finitude and sinfulness which grounds the affections of reverence and humility. Both Edwards and Ignatius had an abiding sense of sinfulness. Because their humility was more closely aligned to gratitude than to guilt, it was not self-absorbed but led them closer to God.

7. The beauty of the beloved should in time produce a beautiful character in the convert. The character of the Christian should manifest that order and proportion which were the classical marks of beauty. The various affections balance each other harmoniously: Christian joy can accommodate sorrow and religious sorrow has the potential for joy. Religious experience could be intense without being bizarre. Balanced Christian affectivity contrasts sharply with the excesses of pseudo-converts: self-obsession, fascination with visions and private revelations, spiritual arrogance, unbalanced zeal, erratic behavior, and moral complacency.

8. Christian practice, earnest, life long, and persevering through trials, is the most telling sign of all. It is also the one least likely to be found in counterfeit conversions.[40] Edwards had no illusion that conversion brought instant spiritual maturity; the new dispositions had to nurtured by consistent practice in the face of internal and external opposition. Ignatius had a comparably practical spirituality which soberly accepted the role of trials and humiliations in refining the motives of the companions of Jesus.[41]

Although no one can discern for certain whether another is converted, some of the signs will be public because affections are the "principles" or "springs" from which actions flow. A self-centered spirit will manifest itself eventually because it orders all things in relation to its own interest rather than to God. By contrast, whoever has the spirit of Christ will manifest the qualities of Christ and will live a godly life.

Affections: the Medium of God's Inspiration

Ordinary experience was extraordinarily transparent to God for Ignatius and Edwards. Each was able to find intimations of God's presence in their affective response to nature, history, human relations, political struggles, personal trials, and disappointments. Ignatius's favorite description of God was "the Director of Souls," since he was intensely aware of divine encouragement and guidance. The only prayer he judged indispensable for Jesuits was the examination of conscience because it would continue the basic fruit of the Exercises: an experimental attentiveness to God in daily experience. Edwards kept a series of notebooks entitled "Images or Shadows of Divine Things" since so many commonplace natural occurrences reminded him of God's characteristic qualities.[42] What was the medium of their inspiration? Not visions or peak experiences, though each had his mystical moments; not ideas or inner locutions; not lofty plans or utopian projects. The basic medium of inspiration for them was the affections, the deep desires of the heart, through which God's invitations resonated.

The text of the *Spiritual Exercises* is permeated with the language of the affections. Ignatius believed that it was possible to elicit "great desires" which would expand the heart to be open to God's action."[43] Retreatants should enter the exercises with "great spirit and generosity toward their Creator and Lord, and by offering all their desires and freedom to him."[44] One should expect conflict between immediate desires and the deepest aspirations during the retreat. In fact, a flat affect is probably a sign that the person was resisting emotional engagement and so the director should change strategies.[45] Ignatian "indifference" is not emotional neutrality but an inner freedom to finite goods which comes from being affectively anchored in the incomparable love for God and the companionship of Jesus; this should impart a readiness to accept whatever the Lord prefers for one's life.

The retreatant is instructed to begin almost every period of prayer by asking "God our Lord for what I want and desire."[46] Asking only for what one was "supposed to" desire would restrict prayer to formality rather than the self-disclosure necessary for intimacy. The weeks spent meditating on the life of Christ should move one beyond immediate desires and fears to the deepest level of desire, which would convey one to the fullness of life in God. "For Ignatius, the spiritual journey is essentially away from fragmentation and toward harmony, from the surface to the center, from spiritual imprisonment to inner freedom."[47]

The deepest affections are the decisive factors in making the "election," the life decision to which the meditations point. It can occur in three different ways. First, it can be a call which so radically draws the person to God that no doubts or competing values can register.[48] The second way of discernment is the usual one: "when sufficient clarity is received from the knowledge of consolations and desolations, and from experience in the discernment of various spirits."[49] Over a period of time the retreatant experimentally compares the various ways of life with the deepest desires which lead to God. Eventually, there will emerge a harmony between one path and the basic generosity and love for God. The third way of making the decision is more deliberately rational and calculating. It is employed only when there is insufficient affective experience to utilize the second approach. This more prudential way of choosing remains incomplete until it has been confirmed by an affective experience of divine consolation — in effect, until the richness of the second way can be experienced.[50] This confirmation comes when the way of serving God chosen in the election harmonizes with the basic paradigm of loving God which is found in the narrative of Jesus' passion and resurrection. It is further ratified by the fruits it produces in the person's life after the retreat.

Ignatius presumes that affectivity is the medium of inspiration. Through our desires God will lead us to the "ultimate concern" of loving God and in turn this great desire will be the sounding board against which all other desires can be evaluated. God does not often give direct "marching orders"; more usually, God invites by evoking desires in the person that echo God's desires for reconciling the world in the Kingdom.[51] Encountering the most authentic desires of one's heart becomes also an encounter with God since they echo God's intentions. Obviously, this does not happen on demand and these judgments are not infallible. Commitment flows naturally from these deeper desires since they resonate with what is central to the person's identity. Philip Sheldrake, S.J., writes that in this discerning contemplation, "our desires are transformed, intensified, concentrated to the point where choice, commitment and action inevitably follow."[52]

Edwards treats practical discernment in response to the serious pastoral problem of "enthusiasm" in the Awakening. In eighteenth-century vocabulary, "enthusiasts" were those who believed that God was directly and infallibly revealing his will to them to enact in specific circumstances. Edwards conceded that the tendency to enthusiasm which had undermined many religious movements in history had also discredited the Awakening. Some took a vivid mental image as God's personal revelation to them; others thought that God gave them assurance of salvation because certain scriptural texts suddenly came to mind;

others mistook certain impulses for God's command and ended up doing bizarre deeds.[53]

Edwards countered with a subtle psychology of inspiration. God does communicate with the saints, but not by new revelation or direct verbal command. The Spirit immediately engenders religious affections in the saint, and they become the medium of insight, intention, and motivation. For instance, the Christian does not recognize God's acceptance by an idea imparted directly by God, but rather "when the sinner feels such a submissive disposition towards [Christ that] this belief is as if he heard the voice of Christ calling him."[54] The witness of the Spirit that we are God's children comes in experiencing the "holy, sweet, humble dispositions and motions of heart, which are a participation of the divine nature."[55] On matters of faith the testimony of the Spirit provides a clarity beyond doubt, "an intuitive evidence, and an evidence that the nature of the soul will not allow it to reject."[56] Edwards does not connect this certainty with particular calls, as Ignatius does in the first way of making the election. Nevertheless, even that certainty is warranted by an affect of unmistakable character: radical love for God which draws the person wholly toward God's service.

Religious affections can prompt certain ways of acting by giving insight as well as motivation. As the person matures spiritually a discerning spiritual sense develops much like natural good taste. It makes judgments directly without discursive reasoning. One who "has a true relish of external beauty" can tell by the "glance of his eye" what is beautiful. "He who has a rectified musical ear, knows whether the sound he hears be true harmony" without reference to theories of musicology. An analogous good taste operates in religious and moral discernment.

Just as a well-trained palate will suggest to a chef what ingredients are missing from a sauce, a well-developed habit of virtue spontaneously indicates what is "suitable" behavior. The converted soul that has grown in sanctification operates in the same manner: "Yea its holy taste and appetite leads it to think of that which is truly lovely, and naturally suggests it; as a healthy taste and appetite naturally suggests the idea of its proper object." The mature Christian "knows at once what is a suitable amiable behavior towards God, and towards man," because the dispositions of love and reverence seek to express themselves in appropriate actions.[57] These "habits of the heart" suggest appropriate words and actions more astutely than would a gifted intellect that lacked these virtues.[58]

Sometimes the spiritual taste suggests specific ways of acting by operating through the affections. These suggestions are not immediate directives from the Spirit but flow naturally from the developed religious affections themselves. They offer guidance in the same manner that natural affections do. A benevolent person will have a sense of how to act toward a friend; while a self-centered individual is unlikely to notice or respond to the needs of others. The affection of benevolence has a built-in tendency, a scenario, for helpful and considerate behavior. Aristotle linked this guidance by virtuous inclination with practical wisdom, and Thomas Aquinas called it "knowledge by connaturality."[59] Edwards refers to it as "a kind of taste of the mind ... whereby persons are guided in their judgment of the natural beauty, gracefulness, propriety, nobleness and sublimity of speeches and actions."[60] Virtues and vices have a felt tendency toward certain behaviors because they are disposed to act consistently with ingrained preferences. These insights do not depend upon inference or conscious reference to standards. The homing instinct of virtue operates "more precisely, than the most accurate reasonings can find out in many hours."[61]

For both Edwards and Ignatius discernment based on sensibility is more important than conscious reference to rational norms of behavior. Nevertheless, discernment does not become a pure intuitionism oblivious to critical standards. Ignatius makes clear that spiritual discernment examines only options which fall within the moral bounds set by morality and the church.[62] For Edwards, the norms of Christian morality are internal to Christian habits of the heart just as the lessons gained from years of tasting sauces "rectify" the taste of a master *saucier*. Similarly, a developed spiritual taste clarifies the meaning of Scripture's moral rules, since "it causes the true meaning most naturally to come to mind, through the harmony there is between the disposition and relish of a sanctified soul, and the true meaning of God's Word."[63] The metaphor of harmony runs throughout Edwards's phenomenology of religious experience. There is a structural and valuational correspondence between a religious affection and its proper object which registers harmoniously.[64]

Transformed affectivity is the ordinary medium for recognizing the traces of God's presence in daily life for Ignatius and Edwards. "Finding God in all things" means that one expects not so much to have experiences *of* God as experiences *with* God. The daily fabric of existence becomes transparent to those whose focused intensity on God allows them to appreciate all things in God. This sensibility depends upon a fundamental moral orientation toward God and commitment to God's purposes in the world. The *Exercises* end with a meditation on discerning God's presence in everything. It is designed to evoke an appreciation of God's continuous self-giving to, sustaining of, and laboring in all creatures to bring them to the fullness of life.[65] Gratitude leads naturally to active, responsive love in offering oneself in return and commitment to carry out that offering through generous service.

Edwards's youthful conversion gave him a sense of God's presence in nature which seemed to last for the rest of his life. The universe is sacramental "for the beauty of the world is a communication of God's beauty."[66] The world was full of types which "lively represent" the beauty of the divine archetype.[67] Even though nature and human relations are often marred by sin, they still show forth the *glory of God,* the "shining forth" of God's perfections. Late in life, Edwards wrote that the saints experience a deeper meaning in the harmony and proportion of earthly values, including moral values. They appreciate these limited beauties as images of the deeper consent of hearts, of the soul to God. When they affirm the value of these images they also affirm the relation they have to God: each experience of appreciation and every choice of moral values is simultaneously an act of personal consent to God.

Mature Christians intend every finite value as part of their overall intention of loving God. They relate to all things in a manner appropriate to their relation to God. As God wills the flourishing of all of nature and the reconciliation of all things and persons in Christ, so does the Christian. This is the single-mindedness that Ignatius stipulated as the "first principle and foundation" for those making the Exercises.[68] This commitment does not denigrate these finite values but affirms them in the universal context which gives them their full value. Finite values and persons are not stepping-stones to get to God; their full richness and excellence stand out when God's glory, the divine goodness latent in them, shines out. The Puritan divine and the Basque mystic agree on a spirituality which is both radically affective and wisely discriminating. Moving along the disparate paths of their traditions, they came to the same conclusion: those who find all things in God will be able to find God in all things.

Notes

1. See John Mahoney, *Seeking Their Spirit: Essays in Moral and Pastoral Theology* (London and Denville, N.J.: Sheed & Ward, 1981), 63–134.

2. Jonathan Edwards, *Selected Writings of Jonathan Edwards,* ed. Harold P. Simonson (New York: Ungar, 1970), 96–113.

3. Ignatius of Loyola, *The Spiritual Exercises,* trans. George E. Ganss in *Ignatius of Loyola: The Spiritual Exercises and Selected Works,* ed. George E. Ganss, S.J. (New York: Paulist Press, 1991), 113–214. Ignatius's *Autobiography* is found in the volume edited by Ganss, 65–111.

4. Ignatius defines "spiritual exercises" as "any means of preparing and disposing our soul to rid itself of all its disordered affections and then, after their removal, of seeking and finding God's will in the ordering of our life for the salvation of our soul" (*Exercises,* 1).

5. See John E. Smith's Introduction to Jonathan Edwards, *Religious Affections,* ed. John E. Smith, in The Works of Jonathan Edwards (New Haven: Yale University Press, 1959), 2, 95; also Edwin Scott Gaustad, *The Great Awakening in New England* (New York: Harper, 1957). See Perry Miller, *Jonathan Edwards* (New York: Meridian, 1959) and *Errand into the Wilderness* (Cambridge:

Harvard University Press, 1956) for a vivid, if now disputed, interpretation of Edwards's thought and career.

6. Twelve volumes have been published in The Works of Jonathan Edwards by Yale University Press since 1957; at least an equal number are currently being prepared for publication.

7. St. Ignatius of Loyola, *Constitutions of the Society of Jesus,* trans. George E. Ganss, S.J. (St. Louis: Institute of Jesuit Sources, 1970).

8. See Michael J. Buckley, S.J., "The Structure of the Rules for Discernment of Spirits," *The Way,* Supplement 20, Apostolic Spirituality and Reform II (Autumn 1973): 19–37.

9. *Exercises,* no. 15 (this and subsequent references will be to the standard paragraph numbers).

10. *Exercises,* 9, trans. Joseph Rickaby, S.J. (London: Burns, Oates, 1915).

11. *Exercises,* 9.

12. See Ignatius, *Exercises,* 328–36.

13. Ignatius, *Exercises,* 97–98.

14. Jonathan Edwards, *Charity and Its Fruits* in *Ethical Writings,* ed. Paul Ramsey, Works of Jonathan Edwards (New Haven: Yale University Press, 1989) 253.

15. *Religious Affections,* 252.

16. Ibid.

17. Edwards, *Charity and Its Fruits,* 254.

18. Ibid., 341–42.

19. Edwards, *Religious Affections,* 260.

20. Ignatius, *Exercises,* 3.

21. Ibid., 316.

22. Ibid.

23. Ignatius, *Exercises,* 315.

24. Ibid., 317.

25. Ibid., 330.

26. Edwards, *Religious Affections,* 95. For a fine account of Edwards's psychology see Paul Lewis, "'The Springs of Motion': Jonathan Edwards on Emotions, Character, and Agency," *Journal of Religious Ethics* 22, no. 2 (1992): 275–97.

27. Ibid., 121.

28. Ibid., 96. Unlike the passions, the proper seat of the affections is the mind or soul. "As 'tis the soul only that has ideas, so 'tis the soul only that is pleased or displeased with its ideas. As 'tis the soul only that thinks, so 'tis the soul only that loves or hates, rejoices or grieves at what it thinks of" (ibid., 98).

29. Ibid., 100, 113.

30. "Habits of the heart" is borrowed from Alexis de Tocqueville, *Democracy in America,* trans. George Lawrence, ed. J. P. Meyer (New York: Doubleday, 1969), 287.

31. *Religious Affections,* 206.

32. Traces of the beauty of God are visible in them which conveys "the real evidence of their divinity, the most direct and strong evidence.... They therefore that see the stamp of this glory in divine things, they see divinity in them, they see God in them, and so see 'em to be divine; because they see that in them wherein the truest idea of divinity does consist" (ibid., 298).

33. Ignatius, *Exercises*, 2. Each evening of the retreat is devoted to an "application of the senses" to relish and deepen the results of the day's other times of prayer: see *Exercises* 121–26, 133, 134, etc.

34. Charles Taylor distinguishes spontaneous reactions from moral reactions that have some qualitative agreement with their object: "It seems to turn on this: in either case our response is to an object with a certain property. But in one case the property marks the object as *meriting* this reaction; in the other the connection between the two is just brute fact. Thus we argue over what and who is a fit object of moral respect, while this doesn't seem to be even possible for a reaction like nausea.... Our moral reactions have these two sides: that they are not only 'gut' feelings but also implicit acknowledgments of claims concerning their objects" (Taylor, *Sources of the Self: The Making of the Modern Identity* [Cambridge, Mass.: Harvard University Press, 1989], 6, 7).

35. *Religious Affections*, 255. See Roland Andre Delattre, *Beauty and Sensibility in the Thought of Jonathan Edwards: An Essay in Aesthetics and Theological Ethics* (New Haven: Yale University Press, 1968), chap. 6.

36. Reason and experience confirm in the saint what Scripture has revealed. Theologians today would pay more attention to the historical mediation of Scripture that depicts these qualities. Though no fundamentalist, Edwards's use of Scripture was analogical and typological rather than according to the historical critical methods that would emerge in the following century. For a contemporary treatment of the role of affections or "senses" shaped by biblical images of God, see James M. Gustafson, *Can Ethics Be Christian?* (Chicago: University of Chicago Press, 1975), chap. 4. Gustafson acknowledges his debt to Edwards and develops his position further in *Ethics from a Theocentric Perspective*, 2 vols. (Chicago: University of Chicago Press, 1981).

37. Edwards, *Religious Affections*, 240.

38. Ibid., 298.

39. Ibid., 346.

40. Ibid., 399. Edwards reviews all of the previous eleven signs to show that they all lead to and culminate in holy practice; see 392–97.

41. These themes are central in the key meditations of the *Exercises;* see 95–98, 146–47, and 167–68.

42. Jonathan Edwards, *Images or Shadows of Divine Things*, ed. Perry Miller (New Haven: Yale University Press, 1948).

43. See Edward A. Kinerk, S.J. "Eliciting Great Desires: Their Place in the Spirituality of the Society of Jesus," *Studies in Jesuit Spirituality* 16, no. 5 (1984).

44. Ignatius, *Exercises*, 5.

45. Ibid., 6.

46. Ibid., 48, 91.

47. Philip Sheldrake, S.J., *Befriending Our Desires* (Notre Dame, Ind.: Ave Maria Press, 1994), 97.

48. Ignatius, *Exercises*, 175.

49. Ibid., 176.

50. Ibid., 183.

51. "God's own Spirit dwelling in our hearts gently, and sometimes forcefully, impels us to desire what God desires, to intend what God intends" (William A. Barry, S.J., *Paying Attention to God: Discernment in Prayer* [Notre Dame, Ind.: Ave Maria Press, 1990], 59).

52. Philip Sheldrake, S.J., *Befriending Our Desires*, 102.

53. Even if private revelation were to occur — which is unnecessary since Scripture is sufficient — it would be no sign of genuine conversion. Such a revelation is only propositional; it does not disclose the divine loveliness: "it is not spiritual knowledge, for persons to be informed of their duty, by having it immediately suggested to their minds, that such and such outward actions or deeds are the will of God" (Edwards, *Religious Affections*, 279). For the sad story of the enthusiast James Davenport see C. C. Goen, Introduction to Edwards, *Awakening*, 51–62.

54. Jonathan Edwards, *The Miscellanies a-500*, Thomas A. Schafer, ed., Works of Jonathan Edwards 13 (New Haven: Yale University Press, 1994), no. 344.

55. Edwards, *Miscellanies*, no. 375.

56. No. 201.

57. Edwards, *Religious Affections*, 282.

58. "So an eminently humble, or meek, or charitable disposition, will direct a person of mean capacity to such a behavior, as is agreeable to Christian rules of humility, meekness, and charity, far more readily and precisely, than the most diligent study, and elaborate reasonings, of a man of the strongest faculties, who has not a Christian spirit within him" (Edwards, *Religious Affections*, 284).

59. Aristotle, *Nicomachean Ethics*, trans. Martin Ostwald, Library of Liberal Arts (New York: Bobbs-Merrill, 1962), 167, also 285, 291 on practical wisdom. For an account of practical wisdom, virtue and character in Aristotle, see Nancy Sherman, *The Fabric of Character: Aristotle's Theory of Virtue* (Oxford: Clarendon, 1989). See Thomas Aquinas, *Summa Theologiae* II–II, q. 60, a. 1, ad 2; also Mahoney, *Seeking the Spirit*, 65–67, 78–84.

60. Edwards, *Religious Affections*, 281. See Aristotle, *Nicomachean Ethics*, Book VI sec. 5 and 7; also Martha C. Nussbaum, *The Fragility of Goodness* (Cambridge. Mass.: Harvard University Press, 1986), chap. 10.

61. *Religious Affections*, 283–84.

62. Ignatius, *Exercises*, 170.

63. Edwards, *Religious Affections*, 285. Aquinas makes the same comparison between sound taste and practical wisdom: see Mahoney, *Seeking the Spirit*, 66.

64. "The soul distinguishes as a musical ear; and besides, holiness itself consists in spiritual harmony; and whatever don't agree with that, as a base to a treble, the soul rejects" (Edwards, *Miscellanies*, no. 141).

65. Ignatius, "The Contemplation to Attain Love," *Exercises*, 230–37.

66. Edwards, *Miscellanies*, no. 293.

67. Ibid., nos. 108, 119.

68. Ignatius, *Exercises*, 23.

16

Priest, Community, and Eucharist

– THOMAS P. RAUSCH, S.J. –

Among Michael Buckley's many interests is the church's priesthood. In 1969, having just finished his doctorate, he graciously put his own academic career on hold to accept a call from his provincial to become rector of the California Province theologate, then in the process of making its move from the hills and redwoods of the Santa Cruz Mountains to the streets and demonstrations of Berkeley. The assignment was primarily a pastoral one, to be religious superior and guide for Jesuit scholastics preparing for ordination, a role he filled for four years. The position involved him personally in the theology of the priesthood. After the 1976 Congregation for the Doctrine of the Faith statement on the ordination of women, *Inter insignores*,[1] the theologate faculty published a response, criticizing the Congregation's statement for the poor quality of its argument.[2] Michael Buckley was its chief redactor.

Buckley has also contributed toward the development of a more adequate theology of priesthood in apostolic religious communities, which for too long had been understood on the basis of the diocesan priesthood. In an article originally written for Jesuit scholastics preparing for ordination, he distinguished between a primarily cultic priesthood and one more prophetic in its orientation.[3] A cultic priesthood is characterized by an emphasis on sacramental ministry or by the liturgical prayer of the choral office; it describes the ministry of a parish priest or pastor who presides over the liturgical and sacramental life of a local congregation, the cathedral canon who serves the sacramental life of a major church, or the ordained monk whose life is devoted to the *opus Dei*.

Buckley described a prophetic priesthood as one devoted to the ministry of the word in its fullest sense:

A prophetic priesthood, one which was concerned to speak out the word of God in any way that it could be heard, assimilated, and incarnated within the social life of human beings, a priesthood which spoke with the religious experience of human beings and — as did the prophets of the Old Testament — coupled this care for authentic belief with a concern for those in social misery: the ministry of the word, the ministries of interiority, the ministry to social misery.[4]

Such a priesthood, though it does not exclude the liturgical, is primarily kerygmatic. It must be mobile, available for mission, not tied to a local parish or church. Buckley saw the Jesuits as embodying this kind of priesthood, one which represented a new form of the ancient *presbyterium*. Twelve years later historian John W. O'Malley published an article with a similar view of religious priesthood. Without explicitly using Buckley's distinction between a cultic and a prophetic priesthood, he makes basically the same argument, contrasting the "division of labor" between diocesan and regular clergy: "The former relates more easily to 'priest' — celebrant for the community and its public servant; the latter more easily to 'prophet' — spokesperson and agent for a special point of view."[5]

The apostolic religious priesthood sketched by Buckley and O'Malley is one exercised primarily "outside of the sanctuary." It represents a move away from an overly clerical understanding of ordained ministry, from the "sacral" model of priesthood which developed in the Middle Ages and dominated the Roman Catholic understanding of priesthood down to the Second Vatican Council. The sacral model, based on the medieval concept of sacred power (*sacra potestas*), defines priesthood exclusively in terms of the priest's relationship to the Eucharist, specifically, his power to consecrate. From this perspective, the priest too easily becomes not a minister but a sacred person, a mediator between God and God's people, marked by special powers, separated from the community by obligatory celibacy, special privileges, and clerical dress.[6]

Though the sacral understanding of the priesthood is rapidly disappearing today, the presumption that the essential relationship for the church's eucharistic life is between priest and Eucharist, rather than between church and Eucharist, is still very much present. Today, given the shortage of priests, an increasing number of local communities cannot celebrate the Eucharist, or can do so only occasionally with a priest who comes to the community from outside. In this essay I would like first, to investigate the relationships which link priest, community, and Eucharist by considering briefly the notions of presidency, priesthood, and the eucharistic assembly, and, second, to reflect on what a new understanding of these relationships might suggest for the church's eucharistic life as well as for the way that priesthood is lived out today.

Presidency, Priesthood, and the Assembly

Though we often speak of the priest as both presiding and celebrating, a more careful use of language speaks of the priest as the presider and the liturgical assembly as the actual subject or agent of the eucharistic celebration. We need to consider more thoroughly each of these realities.

Eucharistic Presidency

The New Testament does not specifically address the question of who should preside at the Eucharist. But scholars today generally argue that it was unlikely that any baptized member of the community could preside. As recent research has shown, eucharistic presidency went with the responsibility of presiding over the Christian community.[7]

The eucharistic presidency was never a "free-for-all," for ministerial leadership is evident in even the earliest writings.[8] Texts such as Acts 13:2 and 1 Corinthians 12:28 suggest that eucharistic presidency was a task of the prophets and teachers. In 1 Clement (c. 96) 44:4–6 it falls to the presbyter-bishops. The *Didache* (c. 100) recognizes that the wandering charismatic prophets can improvise when presiding (10:7), though here eucharistic presidency is in the process of being bound to office, as the author instructs the community to elect for themselves bishops and deacons with the encouragement that "they too conduct (*leitourgousi*) the liturgy of the prophets and teachers" (15:1). Note, however, that these bishops and deacons are not linear descendants of the apostles; they are local leaders elected by the community. Ignatius of Antioch (c. 115) asserts the bishop's authority over the Eucharist: "Let that Eucharist be held valid which is offered by the bishop or by one to whom the bishop has committed this charge" (Smyrneans 8:1).

The clearest description of an early Eucharist comes from the Apology of Justin Martyr, written around the year 150. In it, Justin distinguishes the "one who presides [*proestos*] over the brethren" (1 Apol. 65) from the assembly. Hervé-Marie Legrand notes that the term "presider" is not a "neuter" term, chosen for the pagans Justin was addressing, but one long used (from at least the time of Paul) to designate "those who preside over the life of the community, expending themselves, without, however, any special reference to the liturgy (see especially Rom. 12:6–8; 1 Thess. 5:12–13; 1 Tim. 5:17)."[9] In Justin we have clear evidence that presiding over the life of the community means presiding at its liturgy.

Priesthood

The task of presiding at the Eucharist is not seen in this early period as a sacerdotal role. A review of the liturgical tradition in the pre-Nicene church illustrates that ordination in the ancient tradition was to a pastoral office, not to an independent priestly office.[10] It is with Hippolytus of Rome (c. 215) that for the first time the bishop's ministry is described in sacerdotal terms (Apos. Trad. 3). Still, the perspective is the same as in Ignatius; the exercise of what Hippolytus calls the "high priesthood" follows upon the reception of a pastoral charge. In Legrand's words, the one to be ordained bishop is "elected by all, ordained,... receives an apostolic charism and a pastoral charge which includes the exercise of the high priesthood."[11] Similarly, in his study of the ordination prayers, Bernard Botte says: "In the early documents, episcopate, priesthood and diaconate appear not so much ritual functions as *charismata* designed to edify the Church."[12]

As the theology of the ordained ministry continued to develop, the language of priesthood became more common. Tertullian (d. 225) and Cyprian (d. 258) also spoke of the bishop as *sacerdos;* Cyprian extended the term to presbyters, but only in conjunction with the bishop. It is also with Cyprian that we find the first reference to presbyters presiding at the Eucharist without the bishop (Letter 5). Gordon Lathrop is correct in identifying the language of priesthood as metaphor, based on the bishop's liturgical ministry.[13] At the same time, by ordination into the episcopacy or the order of presbyters, the one ordained is incorporated into the church's pastoral office. A new relation now exists between the one ordained and the local eucharistic community, and consequently, a real (ontological) change has come about. Henceforth the bishop or priest in his sacramental ministry is able to act officially in the name of the church and thus in the name of Christ, or in the language of the tradition, *in persona Christi.*

The concept of the bishops and priests acting *in persona Christi* is an ancient one, based on the bishop's role as leader of the local church.[14] It appears for the first time in Cyprian, who says that the bishop presides at the Eucharist in the role or place of Christ (*vice Christi*) (Letter 63, 14).[15] As one who presides over the church and has been ordained, the priest acts *in persona Christi* in the church's sacraments and particularly in its Eucharist. At the same time, in the Middle Ages, some scholastic theologians spoke of the priest as one who acts *in persona ecclesiae* in virtue of his role as president of the liturgical assembly.[16] If the two representations are distinctive, they are also intrinsically related. As Edward Kilmartin argued, the priest cannot represent Christ outside the ecclesial context; therefore, the pastoral office "can only represent and act in the name of the Lord when it represents the life of faith of the Church."[17] The priest is able to act *in persona Christi* because he acts *in persona ecclesiae,* the body of Christ.

The Assembly

Finally, in spite of our often less than careful language, it is not the priest who celebrates the Eucharist, but the entire assembly with its president. This is the theology of the ancient church. Yves Congar shows this as the patristic view in the period between the second and the ninth centuries.[18] Legrand states that "an analysis of the liturgical vocabulary of the first millennium shows that all celebrate and that all offer the sacrifice."[19] To demonstrate this, he offers considerable historical and liturgical evidence. For example, a study of the verb "celebrate" in the Roman sacramentaries shows that the subject of the verb is always the "we" of the assembly, never the "I" of the priest.[20] From the East Syrian liturgy he gives the example of the bishop presiding without going to the altar, while a simple priest recites the anaphora, to illustrate that all celebrate as a body. It was only in the eleventh and twelfth centuries that a number of Western developments — a sacralization of the pastoral office, a shift in emphasis from bishop to priest, and the emergence of the concept of a self-possessed sacramental power — led to a sacral understanding of the priesthood which defined ordained ministry in terms of the priest's role in the celebration of the Eucharist.[21]

Recent liturgical theology has recovered the concept of the liturgical assembly. The language of the *General Instruction* which introduces the *Roman Missal Revised by Decree of the Second Vatican Council* (1970) regards the entire assembly as the primary agent of the liturgical action.[22] So does the new *Catechism of the Catholic Church* (no. 1140).

Some Practical Implications

From our review of presidency, priesthood, and the eucharistic assembly, it becomes more evident that the priesthood cannot be defined in terms of the priest's relationship to the Eucharist; the essential relationship for the church's eucharistic life is between church and Eucharist, rather than between priest and Eucharist. In this final section I would like to suggest some implications of this relationship. I do so somewhat tentatively, but also with the clear awareness that the question of the relation between community and Eucharist is becoming increasingly a critical one in the church.

Priestless Parishes

The problem of a community unable to celebrate the Eucharist is a modern one; as Legrand argues, it would not have arisen in the pre-Nicene church, for the bond between church and Eucharist was so strong in this period that the local community is not conceived without the Sunday Eucharist: "the essential is this: a local church always provides herself for her presidency, with the indispensable assistance of the heads of neighboring churches."[23] Pastoral leaders were never lacking; they emerged from the community which recognized their charism for leadership; but they would be presented for ordination. It was only later, in the medieval period, with the emergence of a sacral concept of priesthood, that the priest came to be defined in terms of his relation to the Eucharist, as we have seen.

For the contemporary situation, Legrand suggests that "once Christians are competent to preside over the upbuilding of their local church they are likewise competent to receive the ordination which entitles them to preside at the Eucharist."[24] Others have made similar suggestions. Twenty years ago Karl Rahner proposed recovering the concept of relative ordination, ordaining an individual for a sacramental ministry within the context of a particular community.[25] Others have made similar suggestions. Leonardo Boff calls for an extraordinary solution to meet the current shortage of priests in Latin America, the recognition of extraordinary ministers to celebrate the Lord's Supper as a true eucharistic sacrament, even though he suggests distinguishing it from the canonical Mass.[26] In Africa, where lay catechists so often function as unordained pastors, Raymond Hickey has suggested ordaining some of these catechists to serve as auxiliary priests who would work under the direction of a professional, seminary-trained priest.[27]

One contemporary development which would not be legitimated by the tradition is the practice of some groups or communities of choosing their own presiders without the approval of the larger church.[28]

Facing Issues

The institutional church needs to face the problem of the shortage of priests more straightforwardly. This is not the place to rehearse the statistics on the shortage of priests; the dimensions of the problem are well known. Even in the United States, where the ratio of priests to Catholic population is better than in most parts of the world, the number of parish communities unable to celebrate the Eucharist on Sundays continues to increase. In his study on the shortage of priests, Dean Hoge argues that the problem is not the result of a lack of spiritual vitality or a loss of faith in the Catholic Church; the research he examines suggests rather that it is "largely a matter of institutional policies."[29]

The institutional church has taken some steps to address the shortage of priests, but it could be argued that these steps not only fail to come to grips with the real issue, but that they are emergency measures which do not serve to enhance the relationship which ought to exist between a local community and the one who presides at its Eucharist.

Many dioceses have found themselves increasingly dependent on foreign priests, many of them students, or on retired religious, and while people are grateful for their service, the fact that there is a psychological distance of age or culture between the people of the parish and a significant percentage of their clergy can be a hindrance to the development of a vital local community. A priest should be able to represent the community in a genuine sense, as we have seen.

In some dioceses bishops are amalgamating parishes. Others have mandated that when new churches are built they should be able to ac-

268 THOMAS P. RAUSCH, S.J.

commodate larger numbers of people than present churches. Thus many Catholic parish assemblies will become even larger and more impersonal, in an age when Catholic people are seeking smaller, more intimate worshiping communities which can facilitate a deeper level of spiritual sharing.

In November 1989 the U.S. bishops approved the "Directory for Sunday Celebrations in the Absence of a Priest," a rite for a lay-led Communion service for Catholic congregations lacking a priest for Sunday worship.[30] But this effort is not without its own problems. Many priests are forced into become traveling sacramental ministers rather than resident pastors with a relationship to a local community. At the same time, there is a risk to a parish's Catholic identity. Some communities can become so comfortable with the communion services provided by local leaders that they are reluctant to welcome the occasional ordained celebrant, who is seen as coming to the community "from outside." They find their local services more meaningful, a better expression of their community life.

In the 1991 draft of a pastoral letter prepared for his archdiocese, Archbishop Rembert Weakland of Milwaukee specifically raised the question of having more parishes unable to celebrate a Sunday Mass by the end of the century than would be desirable. He also expressed concern that substituting a lay-led communion service for the Sunday liturgy could threaten Catholic identity and lead to a new kind of church different from the one received from the apostles.[31] Courageously going even further, the archbishop stated his willingness to present to Rome a married male candidate for the ordination to the priesthood when a Catholic community which met certain conditions of faith and vitality was not able to find a celibate priest.

His proposal was carefully circumscribed; as he said later, it was to be "only in extreme necessity and under very rigid conditions." But when the final draft of his pastoral letter was published on November 7, the archbishop disclosed that the Vatican Secretary of State had termed his proposal for priest-short areas and communities "out of place."[32]

A New Inculturation

The shortage of priests suggests that a new inculturation of the church's pastoral office is needed. In the period between the fourth and the tenth centuries the ordained ministry underwent a process of clericalization and sacralization. While a growing separation of clergy from laity was an unfortunate side of this development, the process was not entirely negative.

For example, one could argue that taking on titles, insignia, marks of distinction, and other signs of office borrowed in many cases from

Roman officialdom served to make the church and its ordained leaders more visibly at home within the hierarchical culture of the Roman Empire. The church was going through a process of inculturation. Today some of these titles and signs of distinction seem to us pompous, overly clerical, or out of date. But too often we have forgotten their original meanings. The word "pope" comes from the Latin *papa* and the Greek *pappas,* father, and was often applied to the bishop; the term "bishop," from the Greek *episkopos,* means overseer; "pastor" meant shepherd; "deacon" meant servant.

How well is the Catholic priesthood inculturated today? One could make the case that in many parts of the church the priesthood as it is presently expressed appears as something foreign. In many countries in Central and Latin American, local churches are still heavily dependent on foreign priests, mostly from religious orders. According to one commentator, in Guatemala, Nicaragua, Honduras, Venezuela, Panama, and Bolivia the Catholic clergy is around 80 percent foreign.[33] This suggests that after more than four centuries of Christianity, these churches have not yet been able to develop a truly indigenous ministry. In much of Africa celibacy remains something foreign to the culture.

It is also true that the clericalism which surrounds so many priests and bishops like an invisible shield keeps the priesthood from being adequately inculturated. Many Catholic clergy are separated from their co-religionists by dress, religious titles, clerical privileges (though these are vanishing rapidly), a single sex educational system, rectory living, and too often the lack of work experience in an ordinary job. I do not mean this to be an attack on clerical dress or religious titles. These can have their proper place within the context of today's well educated Catholic community which expects a certain professionalism of its priests.

But too often, a separatist and hieratic clerical culture builds walls between priests and people by insisting on status recognition; priests become "insiders" and the people "outsiders." Certainly clericalism is an obstacle to the kind of collaborative and personal leadership that Catholics desire from their clergy. Tim Unsworth, one of the more perceptive commentators on the contemporary priesthood, has observed: "Clericalism is on the wane but it still affects priests a great deal. The clerical culture is breaking down but it hasn't left us entirely. Many priests and most laity feel that it must break down completely before a new priesthood arises."[34]

As almost any university campus minister could testify, there are many young people today who would be willing to serve the church as priests, but they are not attracted by the clerical system they perceive as being included with the priesthood. Nor are they willing to give up the possibility of a married life. Whatever kinds of changes must ultimately be made, it is important today to exhibit more variability in the way priesthood is lived out. There should be other possibilities besides an exclusive parish ministry. There must be alternatives to rectory living and the clerical culture.

There are already signs of a greater flexibility in a new type of "worker priest" evident in the some dioceses in the United States, priests who have full-time professional jobs, live privately, and have a relationship with a parish community in which they function as priests on a regular basis. There are also signs of a new inculturation taking place in some parts of Latin America, India, and other countries where priests are more identified with those with whom they work; they dress simply, with only a small cross on the lapel marking them as priests.

Liturgical Implications

If the essential relationship for the church's eucharistic life is between church and Eucharist rather than between priest and Eucharist, there are some liturgical implications that need to be considered.

1. *Liturgical assemblies should reflect the fact that the entire community, not just the priest, celebrates the Eucharist.* In recent years liturgical scholars have sought to restore the liturgical assembly to its proper place. In an article entitled "Liturgy and Empowerment: The Restoration of the Liturgical Assembly," composer and liturgist Bob Hurd argues that the liturgical reforms of the Second Vatican Council have been less than completely successful because too often parish congregations fail to function as genuine liturgical assemblies: "we have been fitting the new particulars of the reforms into the political framework of the older liturgy. To put it succinctly, most parish liturgies continue to be *priest-centered liturgies with congregations* instead of *assembly-centered liturgies with presiders.*"[35] A priest-centered liturgy tends to reduce others to passive spectators. An assembly-centered liturgy seeks to share responsibility for the liturgical celebration with all present, under the leadership of the presider.

Hurd offers some practical suggestions, changing the entrance procession so that the priest is seen as a member of the assembly who presides rather than as the one around whom the procession centers, or letting the gift-bearers bring the gifts to the table rather than stopping at the foot of the altar.[36] Perhaps even more important is the way that presiders, liturgical planners, and ministers understand the nature of the worshiping community and their various roles within it.

2. *Concelebration should be an occasional, not a regular expression of presbyterial solidarity.* The practice of regular concelebration of the Eucharist by priests, made possible by the Second Vatican Council's Constitution on the Sacred Liturgy (nos. 57, 58), has recently come in for a reexamination.[37] In a very balanced article, John Baldovin situates

the question of concelebration within the context of the liturgical assembly and the baptismal dignity of all of its members: "Any theory of concelebration which begins with the ordained priesthood and ignores the central purpose of the eucharist as the unity of the gathered church will ultimately reach a dead end."[38] Because concelebration can symbolically underline an inequality of status in the assembly, frequent or regular concelebration can be a problem. The need to offer a stipend Mass is a questionable reason. Even more problematic is the idea that a priest should concelebrate because his status demands it.

Baldovin recognizes that concelebration is sometimes appropriate, for example, on occasions when the corporate ministry of the presbyterate is fittingly made evident. Concelebration can be warranted at major feasts or at a eucharistic celebration presided over by a bishop. An ordination liturgy would certainly be such an occasion. But there are other times when concelebration is not appropriate, for example, at liturgies where priests outnumber the lay people present or at daily Eucharists where there is no need to symbolize the unity of the priesthood. As Baldovin says, "[concelebration] is never merely a sign of honor or dignity, since the highest dignity one can have in the assembly is the status of being a baptized member."[39]

3. *A priest not needed for liturgical leadership can participate in the Eucharist as a member of the liturgical assembly.* Not all priests would agree with this. For many priests, formed in a sacerdotal spirituality which saw the primary meaning of the priesthood in "offering the holy sacrifice of the Mass" and stressed the importance of daily celebration, the idea of "merely" attending Mass appears as less than faithful to their vocation. They want to "exercise their priesthood."[40]

The church does not require that priests celebrate on a daily basis.[41] However some Vatican documents have taken the position that priests should participate at the Eucharist as priests, rather than by attending. The Sacred Congregation of Rites in 1967 stated that it is fitting that priests "participate in the Eucharist by exercising the order proper to them, by celebrating or concelebrating the Mass, and not by limiting themselves to communicating like the laity."[42] In 1972 the Sacred Congregation on Divine Worship in a Declaration on Concelebration said that priests should celebrate or concelebrate, and "should not communicate merely, as do the laity."[43]

Today many theologians and liturgists argue that regular concelebration emphasizes differences in status in the assembly rather than its unity, as we have seen, and many lay people are sensitive about liturgies that seem too clerically dominated. As Baldovin suggests, these new concerns and sensitivities were probably not envisioned at the time the postconciliar liturgical documents such as those cited above were written.[44] While we are still in a process of transition in terms of our personal appropriation of the liturgical renewal begun by the Council, we need to be open to the implications of that renewal and to the sensitivities of both laity and clergy. Certainly, the fact that an increasing number of priests choose to attend Eucharists when they are not needed as presiders should not be seen as a problem.

4. *The practice of solitary celebrations of the Eucharist should be allowed to disappear.* This practice, often referred to inaccurately as the "private Mass," probably concerns religious priests for whom the private Mass has too often become the norm more than it does diocesan priests.

The private Mass, understood as a Mass celebrated with just a server or some member of the faithful present, has a history that reaches back to at least the sixth century. But if this is a practice of long standing in the church, solitary celebrations of the Eucharist that is, Masses celebrated by a priest alone, without any other member of the faithful present, have been almost universally prohibited by church law.[45] This fact, rarely adverted to, suggests that somewhere deep within the subconsciousness of the church, the recognition that the Eucharist was the church's communal worship and not the private prayer of the priest still perdured.

However after the Second Vatican Council, the General Instruction of the 1969 Missal (no. 211) and the 1983 Code of Canon Law (c. 906) mitigated somewhat the prohibition against solitary celebrations. One result was that for religious priests, solitary celebrations of the Mass became more common. For many of them, it has become their most frequent experience of Eucharist. This is a personal matter, something they apparently find meaningful, and should be respected. But from the standpoint of the church's tradition, the solitary Mass represents a eucharistic practice which has almost no justification. The practice should be allowed to quietly disappear.

Conclusion

Our study of the relationships that link priest, Eucharist, and community has shown that for the church's eucharistic life, the essential relationship is between church and Eucharist, rather than between priest and Eucharist. The ancient church understood eucharistic presidency as a function of community leadership; it did not know the dilemma of a community unable to celebrate the Eucharist, for pastoral leaders who could be presented for ordination were never lacking.

Understanding the priest in terms of a relationship to a community, usually the local church, rather than in terms of a relationship to the Eucharist, has a number of implications for the issues facing the church of today, both practical and liturgical. Hopefully this study can help lead to a new understanding and perhaps reconsideration of some of these issues.

Notes

1. Congregation for the Doctrine of the Faith, *Declaration on the Question of the Admission of Women to the Ministerial Priesthood.*

2. Pontifical Faculty of the Jesuit School of Theology at Berkeley, "An Open Letter to the Apostolic Delegate," *Commonweal* 104 (April 1, 1977): 204–6.

3. Michael J. Buckley, "Jesuit Priesthood: Its Meaning and Commitments," *Studies in the Spirituality of Jesuits* 8 (1976).

4. Ibid., 150.

5. John W. O'Malley, "Priesthood, Ministry, and Religious Life: Some Historical and Historiographical Considerations," *Theological Studies* 49 (1988): 256.

6. See Thomas P. Rausch, *Priesthood Today: An Appraisal* (New York: Paulist Press, 1992), 15–22.

7. See Hervé-Marie Legrand, "The Presidency of the Eucharist According to the Ancient Tradition," *Worship* 53 (1979): 413–38; B. Botte, "Holy Orders in the Ordination Prayers," in *The Sacrament of Holy Orders* (Collegeville, Minn.: Liturgical Press, 1962), 5–23; Hans-Joachim Schulz, "Das liturgisch-sakramental übertragene Hirtenamt in seiner eucharistichen Selbstverwirkung nach dem Zeugnis der liturgischen Überlieferung," in Peter Bläser, *Amt und Eucharistie* (Paderborn: Bonifacius-Druckerei, 1973), 208–55.

8. Paul Bernier, *The Ministry in the Church* (Mystic, Conn.: Twenty-Third Publications, 1992), 47; Legrand, "Presidency," 414–15.

9. Legrand, "Presidency," 241.

10. See Schulz, "Das liturgisch-sakramental übertragene Hirtenamt," 243.

11. Ibid., 422.

12. Botte, "Holy Orders," 22.

13. Gordon W. Lathrop, *Holy Things: A Liturgical Theology* (Minneapolis: Fortress Press, 1993), 186–87.

14. See Edward J. Kilmartin, "Apostolic Office: Sacrament of Christ," *Theological Studies* 36 (1975): 244–46.

15. Legrand, "Presidency," 424–25.

16. For example, Peter Lombard argued that excommunicated priests were not able to confect the Eucharist because the celebrant offered the sacrament "quasi ex persona Ecclesiae," *Libri IV Sententiarum* D.XIII, c.i; see Bernard-Dominique Marliangeas, *Clés pour une Théologie du Ministère: In persona Christi, in persona Ecclesiae* (Paris: Beauchesne, 1978), 55–56.

17. Kilmartin, "Apostolic Office," 260; more recently Susan Wood has developed a similar argument, based on the priest's representational role, in "Priestly Identity: Sacrament of the Ecclesial Community," *Worship* 69 (1995): 109–27.

18. Yves Congar, " 'L'ecclesia' ou communauté chrétienne, sujet intégral de l'action liturgique," in J.-P. Jossua and Y. Congar, eds., *La Liturgie après Vatican II* (Paris: Cerf, 1967), 241–82.

19. Legrand, "Presidency," 432.

20. Benedicta Droste, *"Celebrare" in der römischen Liturgiesprache* (Munich: Max Hueber, 1963), 73–80; an exception is found in the rubrics of the

Gelasian sacramentary, but even here it is clear that the priest celebrates with the community, 80.

21. Rausch, *Priesthood Today,* 15–22.

22. Robert Cabié, *The Church at Prayer,* vol. 2, ed. Georges Martimort (Collegeville, Minn.: Liturgical Press, 1986), 191–92; see Burckhard Neunheuser, "The Relation of Priest and Faithful in the Liturgies of Pius V and Paul VI," in *Roles in the Liturgical Assembly,* trans. Matthew J. O'Connell (New York: Pueblo, 1981), 207–19.

23. Legrand, "Presidency," 437.

24. Ibid.

25. Karl Rahner, *The Shape of the Church to Come* (New York: Seabury, 1974), 110.

26. Leonardo Boff, *Ecclesiogenesis: The Base Communities Reinvent the Church* (Maryknoll, N.Y.: Orbis Books, 1983), 60–73; Susan Wood objects that divorcing jurisdictional authorization from sacramental empowerment results in a "functional" view of ministry and a congregationalist rather than sacramental model of church ("Priestly Identity," 123–25).

27. Raymond Hickey, *A Case for an Auxiliary Priesthood* (Maryknoll, N.Y.: Orbis Books, 1982), 78–79; see also Michel Bavarel, *New Communities, New Ministries* (Maryknoll, N.Y.: Orbis Books, 1983).

28. Legrand, "Presidency," 436.

29. Dean Hoge, *Future of Catholic Leadership: Responses to the Priest Shortage* (Kansas City: Sheed and Ward, 1987), 18.

30. *Origins* 18 (1988): 301–7.

31. Rembert G. Weakland, "Future Parishes and the Priesthood Shortage," *Origins* 20 (January 24, 1991): 539.

32. Weakland, "Facing the Future with Hope," *Catholic Herald* (November 7, 1991).

33. Phillip Berryman, *Liberation Theology* (New York: Pantheon Books, 1987), 1.

34. Cited in *Touchstone,* the newsletter of the National Federation of Priests' Councils, 3 (Spring 1992): 4.

35. Bob Hurd, "Liturgy and Empowerment: The Restoration of the Liturgical Assembly," in Michael Downey, ed., *That They Might Live: Power, Empowerment, and Leadership in the Church* (New York: Crossroad, 1991), 131–32.

36. Ibid., 143–44; see also Richard S. Vosko, "The Community Table: Assembly as Celebrant," *Modern Liturgy* 19 (May 1992): 17–20.

37. See for example, Eligius Dekkers, "Concelebration — Limitations of Current Practice," *Doctrine and Life* 22 (1972): 190–202; Robert Taft, "Ex Oriente Lux? Some Reflections on Eucharistic Concelebration," *Worship* 54 (1980): 308–25.

38. John F. Baldovin, "Concelebration: A Problem of Symbolic Roles in the Church," *Worship* 59 (1985): 33.

39. Ibid., 44. e

40. In this regard, see Robert Taft's comments on the reduction of the Eucharist *ut sacramentum* to the Eucharist *ut sacrificium* in traditional Catholic liturgical theology; "Ex Oriente Lux?: 321.

41. The 1917 Code of Canon Law obliged priests to celebrate several times a year; it also directed bishops and religious superiors to see that their priests cel-

ebrate at least on Sundays and holy days of obligation (CIC 805). In the revised 1983 Code daily celebration is "strongly recommended" (c. 904).

42. Sacred Congregation of Rites, *Eucharisticum mysterium*, May 25, 1967, no. 43, in *Vatican Council II: The Conciliar and Post Conciliar Documents*, ed. Austin Flannery (Northport, N.Y.: Costello, 1975), 126.

43. Sacred Congregation on Divine Worship, *In Celebratione Missae*, May 7, 1972, Introduction, in Flannery, *Documents*, 222.

44. Baldovin, "Concelebration," 44.

45. See Thomas P. Rausch, "Is the Private Mass Traditional?" *Worship* 64 (1990): 237–42.

Part IV

CATHOLICISM
– AND –
THE UNIVERSITY

17

The Catholic University under the Sign of the Cross

Christian Humanism in a Broken World

– DAVID HOLLENBACH, S.J. –

> The stone that the builders rejected
> has become the chief cornerstone.
> —Psalm 118:22

Today Catholic institutions of higher learning in the United States are surely at a kind of *kairos* — a fullness of time that is a moment of decision. How these institutions respond to the decisions that are upon them will set their courses over future generations in irrevocable ways. Michael Buckley's work on Catholicism and the university has repeatedly challenged the Catholic university to reflection on its identity that is both intellectually and religiously deeper than much that has been said on this matter. Buckley's writings, together with David O'Brien's historically informed reflections on the present conditions in Catholic universities, Pope John Paul II's apostolic constitution *Ex Corde Ecclesiae,* and George Marsden's study of the paths toward secularization followed by originally Protestant institutions, have raised recent discussion to a level of seriousness worthy of the issues that are at stake.[1]

This essay builds on and develops Buckley's insistence that the concern for justice is not only compatible with but required by the critical tasks of the university. He argues persuasively that the university as such should both possess and foster deep concern for the misery and suffering that mars the lives of so many persons in our world. Such care for those who suffer will in turn grow into a critical effort to understand how their misery might be alleviated. It will lead, in other words, to an effort to secure justice for all whose suffering is caused by human action or failure to act. This concern for justice is proper to the university because of the university's humanistic aims. In Buckley's words, this "care to develop a disciplined sensitivity to human misery and exploitation is not a single political doctrine or a system of economics. It is a humanism, a humane sensibility to be achieved anew within our own times and as a product of an education whose ideal continues to be that of the Western *humanitas.*"[2]

While presuming Buckley's affirmation that the concern for justice is demanded by the humanistic aims of the university, this essay will argue that more explicit emphasis on a distinctively Christian theme can contribute in indispensable ways to the appropriation of an enlarged sense of the requirements of humanism in contemporary Catholic higher education. It will advance the following multipart thesis: (1) the meaning of the cross is central to the identity of the Catholic university; (2) though the cross is the particularistic symbol of the distinctiveness of Christian faith, engagement with its meaning can open the university to a humanism that is more universal and inclusive than alternatives that overlook this meaning; (3) there is a special need to understand and appropriate the relation of the cross to human suffering and injustice, and the future identity of Catholic higher education will be heavily dependent on its efforts to respond to this need.

The argument for this thesis will be clearer once my reading of some of the issues faced by Catholic universities has been sketched.

The Pursuit of Christian Humanism

Many of the efforts to clarify the religious identity of Catholic universities over the past decade have appealed to the idea of Christian humanism as the link between their aims as universities and their relation to the Christian community of faith. These discussions seek to distinguish the Catholic university of today from the stance of defensiveness toward and isolation from the larger culture that characterized them in earlier generations. The founding of most Catholic universities in the United States occurred during the second half of the nineteenth century. This was a historical period in which the church was pursuing a strategy of resistance to many of the intellectual currents branded as "modernism" and "liberalism" by the Holy See. As Joseph Komonchak has put it, "Throughout the nineteenth century and the first half of the twentieth century, the church constructed itself as a countersociety legitimated by the counterculture of its basic faith. Central dogmas and devotions were articulated in such a way as to stress their anti-modern, anti-liberal meanings and implications. This counterideology was embodied in the structure of an alternate society."[3] American Catholic education in general and Catholic colleges in particular were major pieces in the edifice of this alternative. They became what have been called "custodial institutions" designed to protect Catholic youth from intellectual threats to their faith.[4] The teaching of religion featured strong emphasis on apologetics and ethics, while minimizing first-hand encounter with some of the most significant currents in modern philosophy, biblical criticism, and the critical social and historical study of the development of the Christian tradition.

This earlier pursuit of an alternative to many currents of modern thought was linked with resistance to an understanding of the political sphere that effectively restricted religious belief to the sacristy. Much of the sociology that emerged in the nineteenth century predicted that the growing "rationalization" of society, under the influence of technology and industrial economics, would result in the growing secularization of society and the privatization of religion. Indeed some forms of social analysis encouraged this outcome as normative and desirable. In the philosophical arena, reason was understood in a way that consigned religious belief to the domain of the irrational, sometimes understood benignly as harmless eccentricity, sometimes understood as dehumanizing illusion.

This latter charge that religion is irrational largely determined the place assigned to religious thought in the emerging secular university. Marsden has detailed the way this process occurred in the once-Protestant schools in the United States. In 1852, John Henry Newman's lectures entitled *The Idea of a University* stated the issue in terms that were relevant to universities throughout the nineteenth-century Western world. Newman identified the chief force pressing faith to the sidelines of intellectual life as the presupposition that belief is a matter of sentiment rather than knowledge. Religion might be useful to social cohesion or psychological satisfaction, but it lacks cognitive status. According to the prevailing view, even among those who view religion benignly, faith deals with personal preferences, not truth. In Newman's words:

> Religion was useful, venerable, beautiful, the sanction of order, the stay of government, the curb of self-will and self-indulgence, which laws cannot reach: but, after all, on what was it based? Why, that was a question delicate to ask, and imprudent to answer; but, if the truth must be spoken, however reluctantly, the long and the short of the matter was this, that Religion was based on custom, on prejudice, on law, on habit, on loyalty, on feudalism, on enlightened expedience, on many, many things, but not at all on reason; reason was neither its warrant, nor its instrument, and science has as little connexion with it as with the fashions of the season, or the state of the weather. . . . This day's philosophy sets up a system of universal knowledge, and teaches of plants, and earths, and creeping things, and beasts, and gases, about the crust of the earth and the changes of the atmosphere, about the sun, moon, and stars, about man and his doings, about the history of the world, about sensation, memory, and the passions, about duty, about cause and effect, about all things imaginable, except one — and that is about Him who made all these things, about God. I say the reason is plain because they consider knowledge, as regards

the creature, is illimitable, but impossible or hopeless as regards the being
and attributes and works of the Creator.[5]

The Second Vatican Council, echoing Vatican I, rejected this denial of
the cognitive status of religion.

At the same time, Vatican II affirmed the need to give full respect to
modes of intellectual inquiry other than those employed in theology. The
academic pursuit of knowledge possesses a legitimate autonomy that is
rooted in the intrinsic dynamism of the human mind. Inquiry should be
free from the dominating control by religion, theology, and ecclesiastical authority that had sometimes been restrictive of its proper scope in
the past. In the Catholic tradition one need only mention the "Galileo
affair" to indicate the damage done to both intellectual and religious
life by efforts to exercise religious veto-power over the results of intellectual investigation. The memory of such restrictions on inquiry was
surely a source of the Second Vatican Council's affirmation of the "just
liberty" and "legitimate autonomy of human culture and especially the
sciences."[6] In the words of the council, academic inquiry in all the disciplines — philosophy, history, mathematics, the natural sciences, and the
arts — "can do very much to elevate the human family to a more sublime understanding of truth, goodness, and beauty." Thus the inquiry
that is the lifeblood of the university can lead humankind "to be more
clearly enlightened by the marvelous Wisdom which was with God from
all eternity."[7]

In line with these emphases at the Council, Catholic universities in
the United States have been undergoing rapid changes that mirror the
shifting place of Catholics in American society and culture. The Catholic community has moved from being a sort of religious and cultural
enclave, largely insulated from the society around it, to a full and
free participation in the mainstream of its pluralistic environment. This
changed location of the church was brought about by the Council's renunciation of former claims by the church to a privileged role in political
society, by its acknowledgment of the reality of pluralism, and by the affirmation of religious freedom as the framework for the public role of
the church.[8] The American Catholic experience contributed much to the
council's thought on these matters. In a similar way, Catholic universities
have sought to demonstrate that the principles of academic freedom and
wholehearted respect for methods of rigorous academic inquiry mean
that they are true universities, not branch offices of the Holy See or
the local diocesan chancery office. Both American Catholics in general
and Catholic universities in particular have rejected that mode of pre-
Vatican II Catholic thought and practice known as "integralism" — a
view that in society and the academy all wisdom can be deduced from
religious or theological premises.

Such confidence that the pursuit of knowledge on its own terms can cohere with rather than contradict Christianity opens the possibility of a Christian humanism. Buckley's work embodies this kind of confidence. It does so in a way that is better informed by history, philosophy, and theology than many other examples. He argues that the drive to ultimacy inherent in every serious pursuit of knowledge leads to a convergence with the self-disclosure of God in Christian revelation. "The dynamism of the human mind inherent in all inquiry and knowledge — if not inhibited — is toward ultimacy, i.e., toward a completion in which an issue or its resolution finds its place in a universe that makes final sense, i.e., in the self-disclosure of God — the truth of the finite." Similarly, Christian belief seeks self-understanding in genuine knowledge. "The dynamism inherent in the experience of faith — if not inhibited — is toward its own understanding, toward its own self-possession in knowledge." Thus Buckley argues, "in their full development, the religious intrinsically involves the academic, and the academic intrinsically involves the religious."[9]

The Fragility of Christian Humanism

I agree with these statements. Nonetheless the provisos set off by dashes ("if not inhibited") are not minor matters. Buckley is of course aware of the possible impediments to the dynamism toward integration inherent in the religious and the academic. "This development is *de facto* always imperfectly realized at best or even seriously frustrated."[10]

These provisos, however, are an invitation to attend to the *de facto* impediments to the mutual completion of the academic and the religious by each other. Failure to attend to these impediments can lead to an analysis of the issues that misses the mark in practical deliberation about what can and should be done to encourage such mutual completion. On this practical level, I share John Haughey's concern that Buckley's description of the intrinsic relation between the religious and academic dimensions is "very optimistic"; it is stronger as a description of an ideal than as a strategy for action.[11] There is reason to be less sanguine about the practical working out of such integration than is suggested by the inviting description of the theoretical objective. A synthesis of this sort will be, at best, a fragile achievement today. Indeed, I think such fragility will always be a characteristic of any integration of the academic and the religious that is achieved in a Christian humanism in any historical epoch.

Concern about the practical versus the theoretical possibilities of a humanism that integrates the academic and the religious is not, I hope, based on a crude form of pragmatism. Concern for the pragmatic is, of course, a characteristically American trait, and it is subject to the anti-intellectual biases that have run deep in the culture of the United States, particularly among American Catholics.[12] An appeal to practicality that accepts such biases would be self-defeating for anyone interested in strengthening Catholic higher education. Rather, this concern is rooted in a reading of historical trends that are shaping the environment both around and within Catholic universities today. The historical record of American universities founded by Protestants suggests that is possible to have a correct theory of the intrinsic connection between the intellectual and the religious goals of a religiously inspired university, and yet on the basis of this theory to encourage developments that lead in practice to the alienation of these two aims from each other. This is suggested by George Marsden's observation that the secularization of American Protestant universities occurred despite, not because of, the intentions of those who led them. As Marsden puts it:

> One theme that emerges from the study of Protestant universities is that the loss of distinctly religious identity is not something that the Christians who led those universities directly chose. Rather, the long-term changes were largely the results of choices that in the short run promised to improve not only the university but also the quality of Christianity on its campus. So even from the perspective of attempting to sustain Christian identity, the choices were often the right ones for the immediate future.[13]

Marsden notes that the leaders of Protestant schools were responding to real cultural pressures and many legitimate demands to improve intellectual quality. The results of their decisions should encourage sober reflection among Catholics who face similar issues today.

On this point, the Dutch theologian Edward Schillebeeckx recently observed that there is a certain irony in the transition in Catholic intellectual life that occurred at Vatican II: "after two centuries of resistance to liberal modernity, at Vatican II Catholic Christianity embraced the humane ideal of modernity just at the time modernity began to distrust itself."[14] This recent intellectual self-distrust had its seeds in the earlier modern impulse to cast suspicion on all grand visions of the overarching meaning of human life and the cosmos, particularly those visions that are explicitly religious. For example, in 1918 Max Weber had characterized modern intellectual life in the West as marked by the "disenchantment" of "grandiose" reason.[15] In Weber's analysis, modern academic inquiry cannot provide answers to ultimate questions about the purpose of human life. Rationality had been recognized as instrumental; it deals with means, not ends. Thus the knowledge to be obtained in the university does not "partake of the contemplation of sages and philosophers about the meaning of the universe." This removes religion and metaphysics from the proper domain of the university.

Weber went further, anticipating more recent intellectual self-doubt in his admission that the ultimate significance of academic inquiry is itself touched by the forces of disenchantment. Whether the academic work of the lecture hall, library, or laboratory has any final significance is itself a value judgment "about which nothing can be said in the lecture room."[16] Indeed the value of the pursuit of academic inquiry is not finally a matter of intellectual judgment at all. It is an issue to be settled by a decision about which "demon" one will choose to grant functional divinity in one's way of life. But for Weber, the ultimacy one might grant to the academic muse in one's life is purely a matter of decision or preference, for the work of the professor provides no greater access to ultimate meaning than activities with less exalted self-understandings. The commitments of the academic world are no more ultimate than the gods of the ancient religions. A professor must face this fact "like a man."[17] This means bidding farewell to all academic claims to know the true and lasting meaning of even a part of what is real.

I think it is clear that Weber's description the historical situation of intellectual inquiry has become increasingly dominant in the academy since he first presented it. Today there are strong currents that challenge the capacity of reason to attain genuine knowledge of what actually is the case, not only in the domain of religion but in the humanities and even the sciences as well. Much postmodern thought has extended the critique of reason well beyond the domain where Newman saw it operative. The diversity of disciplinary methods and the deepening awareness of the cultural pluralism of our world discourage efforts to achieve an integration of the multiple forms of knowledge. Intellectual specialization can easily close academic disciplines, including theology, to insights that arise beyond the boundaries of their field of inquiry. This situation has led a number of contemporary thinkers to conclude that all we can aspire to in intellectual life are fragments of meaning that are not really the meaning *of* anything external to those who find them meaningful. These fragments of meaning are purely human constructs rather than vistas onto what is real or true. For example, Richard Rorty maintains that a culture that acknowledges this intellectual state of affairs would be one that "was enlightened through and through. It would be one in which no trace of divinity remained, either in the form of a divinized world or a divinized self.... It would drop, or drastically reinterpret, not only the idea of holiness but those of 'devotion to truth,' and of 'fulfillment of the deepest needs of the spirit.' "[18]

Thus our historical period is witnessing the return of an intellectual tendency that has appeared before with the Sophists in ancient Greece and with the nominalists of the late Middle Ages and early modern period — a tendency that denies the capacity of the human mind to grasp the truth of reality, whether this reality be mundane or divine.

As with the Sophists and nominalists in the past, this can lead to the reduction of intellectual undertakings to matters of power and will. In Weber's terms, words become weapons; politicized academic endeavors "are not plowshares to loosen the soil of contemplative thought; they are swords against enemies."[19] Suspicion of this sort is especially directed toward any claim to know the whole or the ultimate, even through a glass darkly. Thus it generates a bias against taking religious or theological matters seriously within the academic context that is even stronger than the belief that religion is a largely harmless illusion. Though the presence of these currents in the university is often exaggerated, it would be a mistake to underestimate their influence not only in the general academic environment but on Catholic campuses also. In my judgment they both threaten the academic project itself and undercut any attempt to uncover the connections between the religious and the academic.

The transformation of the socioeconomic realities shaping the contemporary Catholic university also needs to be taken into account in these discussions. Though the issue of the identity of the Catholic university is principally intellectual — how to conceive and actualize the relation of religious faith to the intellectual inquiry that is the defining activity of the university — a university is not a community of minds that floats free of social, economic, and political currents. A university is not only a community of intellectual inquiry; it is also a structured configuration of power in which influence, interests, and money shape the thinking of those involved.

It is inevitable, therefore, that the thinking that goes on in Catholic universities today is influenced by the social-economic location of those who support, staff, and study in them. Over the past few generations, the social-economic status of Roman Catholics has risen substantially. These institutions were almost all founded to respond to the needs of a poor, immigrant Catholic population that faced an economically and often religiously hostile environment. Immigrant Catholics needed protection from nativist prejudice and disciplined nurturance if they were to rise from the poverty in which most of them lived. Catholic colleges provided both. In fact, they succeeded beyond all the expectations of their founders. Today, for example, American Catholics of Irish, Italian, German, Polish, and Slavic ethnic backgrounds all rank higher in average income than do Protestants of British, German, and Scandinavian background. Irish-American Catholics outrank British-American Protestants in educational achievement.[20] In the wake of these transitions, the question of the distinctive identity of Catholics in general and of Catholic universities in particular has emerged with a pointed saliency (some say with an urgency that can fairly be counted as an identity crisis). The movement of many Catholics into the mainstream of American social and economic life is itself a positive achievement. At the same time, it means that the distinctive contributions of faith and tradition will not be automatically carried by ethnic and social identity. Economic success also raises the question of whether American Catholics will succumb to a kind of amnesia about their poor, immigrant roots. In my limited experience at one university, this historical amnesia is virtually total among most undergraduates today and is distressingly present among many Catholic university leaders. The fact that this is a side-effect of positive achievements rather than the outcome of deliberate choices makes it more subversive, not less so. The feeling of competence and achievement that accompanies this success leads many to a sense of entitlement that can obscure the vulnerability that is a part of the human condition.[21] This increases the difficulty of making practical connections between the academic task, the religious acknowledgment of the dependence of all human beings on God, and the call to have special concern for the poor.[22]

The problem can be roughly indicated by some numbers. In 1992 the median income for individuals fifteen years old and over in the United States was $15,190, the median income for all families was $35,353; the poverty line for a family of four was $14,228.[23] At the institution where I teach, Boston College, the cost of tuition, fees, and room for a resident student in the academic year 1991–92 was $16,847.[24] This means that the cost of attending Boston College for one year was significantly higher than the annual income of half of the individuals in the United States; it was only a bit below 50 percent of the total income of half the families in the country; it was higher than the cost for the total support of a family of four at the level defined by the government as marking the point of escape from poverty.[25] While Boston College is at the upper end of the price-scale for Catholic universities in the United States, its cost is representative of those Catholic institutions that aspire to be among the best in the country. As the pursuit of academic excellence continues, this cost is likely to increase, not decline. Financial aid, of course, is provided for some students who have lesser resources. But it is far from meeting the needs of many. These financial pressures mean that the best Catholic universities increasingly draw their students from families who would likely call themselves middle or upper-middle class but by any reasonable standard are more accurately described as rich.

This transition in the social-economic context is also evident in the fact that Catholic universities are now controlled by largely lay boards of directors, many of whose members are at the very top of the income ladder. One generation ago these institutions were staffed and administered largely by members of the religious orders that founded them. It is certainly true that the board members are aware of the dangers of private institutions pricing themselves out of the educational market, and a number of them are desirous of guiding their institutions in ways that respond to the needs of the poorer segments of American society. But it is also true that the link between the goals they set for the universities and a vision of economic success is a strong one. On the basis of my limited experience both on the faculty of my home institution and as a board member at two other Catholic colleges, I think there is at least some foundation for suspicion that the pursuit of institutional advancement at the best Catholic universities can be a tool serving the self-interest and privilege of the powerful.

I do not present these possible interpretations of what is going on in Catholic universities today to undercut the idea that religious and academic pursuits can be ultimately convergent. Again, I think that assertion is true. Rather, I offer them to guard against a too-ready confidence about the possibility of success in achieving such convergence today. If decisions of the leaders of formerly Protestant institutions made short-term sense but had negative long-term consequences for religious identity, the same could easily occur in Catholic universities today.

A few years ago, Martha Nussbaum wrote a much-noted study of classical Greek moral philosophy and tragedy entitled *The Fragility of Goodness*.[26] Nussbaum argued that the root of the Greeks' tragic vision was the experience that the multiple goods envisioned in their moral philosophies could come into genuine conflict through chance, fate, or luck. The Catholic university today is seeking to achieve multiple goods such as academic excellence, institutional reputation, financial support, service to the Christian community and broader society, and intellectually serious religious inquiry. It also seeks to avoid subordinating any of these goals to others in a way that denies that they are really part of the Catholic university's task. A sense of irony and even tragedy should warn us that working toward such inclusive goals is not likely to be a smooth and tidy process. While it would be a mistake to narrow the vision of what is aspired to, it would be equally wrong to expect its easy or total achievement. Therefore the effort to pursue the mutual completion of the academic and the religious through each other is likely to be characterized by a measure of conflict. Achieving the harmony of faith and reason is not something that can be simply presumed; we must also be prepared to struggle to attain it. This struggle may fail. We need the courage to admit this if we are to avoid making the conflicts worse than they need be. Some of the Greeks called blindness to such human limitation *hubris;* we might call it presumption or grandiosity. Christian faith, of course, is not the same as the Greek tragic vision. But the centrality of the cross of Jesus Christ suggests that we should be no less surprised than were the Greeks by conflict between the many goods sought in Catholic universities today.

The Cross and the Catholic University

The cross is a prominent feature in the very architecture of Catholic university campuses. One of the best of the Catholic institutions, one that has retained an exclusive commitment to liberal arts education, is even named the College of the Holy Cross. The pursuit of the humanistic ideal in higher education affirms that all truth discoverable by human beings has a proper place on such campuses, and I surely concur. At Harvard University, however, that great institution's former motto, *Veritas Christo et Ecclesiae,* is today to be found only on the old seal of the university still visible but rarely noticed above a side gate entering Harvard Yard. The old motto was long ago shortened to the apparently more universal and humanistic *Veritas.* This raises the question of whether all the crosses on the towers of Catholic campuses are fated to go the way of the *Christo et Ecclesiae* in Harvard's motto, becoming what Weber called "guaranteed genuine antiques"?[27]

Talk of the cross in relation to the university rightly raises two fears. The first is that reference to the cross will encourage a "sacrifice of the intellect." The cross can be invoked in a way that suggests one must choose between Christian belief and the full use of critical intelligence, sacrificing one or the other. For example, in light of his understanding of modern scientific rationality, Weber thought that an abandonment of the criteria of reason "is the decisive characteristic of the positively religious man." For Weber, the modern, well-educated believer inevitably "reaches the point where the Augustinian sentence holds: *credo non quod, sed quia absurdum est.*"[28] This danger is certainly present when the gospel's call to carry one's cross is invoked to legitimate moral teachings that cannot be supported by the reasoned reflection on human experience that is at the heart of the natural law morality so central in the Catholic tradition. But it makes its presence felt in many other areas as well. What follows should make clear that such uses of the symbol of the cross are rejected here.

The second fear is the more serious. Efforts to link the cross as the central symbol of one particular religious community with the university's aim to explore all systems of meaning found among the human race could seem self-contradictory. The university seeks to be universal in the scope of its inquiry. It cannot not grant the meaning-system of one segment of the human community the status of being the judge of all other such systems. No set of beliefs can be granted the status of trumps in the exchange of academic inquiry. All such beliefs deserve to be heard, and the invocation of none of them brings conversation and argument to a close.

In response to this concern, some recent commentators have appealed to distinctively postmodern self-doubts to argue that religion deserves a better hearing in this academic exchange than modern secular thought would have granted it. Weber admitted that his commitment to "value-free" science could not be justified on rational grounds but rested on a choice of his preferred "demon." This has been extended by many in our postmodern milieu to an admission that *all* intellectual orientations are shaped by the biases or cultural predispositions of their adherents. If this is the case, the subjectivity found in religion is not the exception in intellectual life but the rule. Thus there seems no more reason for excluding religious worldviews from the academy that there is for excluding, say, Freudianism, neoclassical capitalist theory, Marxism, evolutionary naturalism, or feminism. For example, Marsden has written that few academics believe "in neutral objective science any more and most would admit that everyone's intellectual inquiry takes place in a framework of communities that shape prior commitments. Such prior commitments might be arrived at on formal religious grounds or in some more informal way, but they [are] prior commitments nonetheless. Hence there is little reason to exclude a priori all religiously based claims on the grounds that they are unscientific."[29] The fact that religion shares the characteristic of subjectivity with other modes of thought becomes a reason for its inclusion. Marsden's point is valid, as far as it goes. Nevertheless, there is considerable irony in mounting a defense of the place of religion in the academic milieu through an appeal to something akin to relativism, even skepticism: religion is no more illusory than all the other illusions that are part of the intellectual game, so why single it out for exclusionary treatment? To be fair to Marsden, however, there is another way to interpret his appeal to postmodern self-doubt. It can be seen as an expression of humility before the truth rather than skepticism about the possibility of ever attaining it. And when it is seen this way, the meaning of the cross in the intellectual life begins to come into focus.

The postmodern intellectual epoch in which we live is characterized above all by a stance of suspicion toward all grand schemes of meaning, all ideologies, and all scientific and technological theories that claim total explanatory power. Who can escape the power of such suspicion in the face of the realities of the twentieth century? Science has been put at the service of genocidal slaughter at Auschwitz and the destruction of whole cities at Dresden and Hiroshima. Psychologies that aimed at the liberation of persons from hysteria have awakened a form of self-consciousness that threatens to become routinized narcissism. An economic-political ideology that promised to unshackle workers from their chains ordered tanks into the streets against them in Prague and Tienanmen Square, sent them to the gulag, slaughtered them in the killing fields of Cambodia, and finally expired without a whimper in the face of a velvet revolution led by poets, shipbuilders, and priests. Religions have fired conflict and terror against the innocent in the West

Bank and Gaza, in Belfast and the townships of South Africa, in Alge-
ria, the Sudan, and Kurdistan, in Ayodhya in Uttar Pradesh and Waco
in Texas, and in Bosnia today.

Such experiences have led late twentieth-century men and women to
a fork in the road. We can choose ironic detachment as a survival tac-
tic and "change the subject" when asked what it all means. Or we can
follow a path like the one that led the Buddha to affirm that the first,
though not last, Noble Truth is *Dukkha* — all is suffering, pain, sorrow, misery. Those who do not resort to irony as the opium of the
effete can readily say of our own century what St. Augustine said of the
achievements of the Roman empire: "you cannot show that men lived
in happiness, as they passed their lives amid the horrors of war, amid
the shedding of men's blood — whether the blood of enemies or fellow
citizens — under the shadow of fear and amid the terror of ruthless ambition. The only joy to be attained had the fragile brilliance of glass,
a joy outweighed by the fear that it may be shattered in a moment."[30]
When we look without flinching at the twentieth century, it is not unreasonable to draw the conclusion of both poets and mystics: the world
is on fire.

This encounter with suffering and misery has shattered the modern
West's hope in progress guided by enlightened rationality. It is the driving force behind the sensibility manifest in the wariness of professors
and students alike on contemporary campuses.[31] This wariness has obviously not brought the academic endeavor to a halt. But it has raised
the question of the meaning of all the effort that is expended by both
faculty and students today. At least a whiff of nihilism can be detected
in the atmosphere of the contemporary university. The question for the
university today, then, is whether it has any ground for its hope to uncover meaning that can sustain human life and guide the vast energies
of its scientific, political, economic, and cultural undertakings. Or is all
this activity simply a way of coping with life, filling the time between
young adulthood and death with activity that is perhaps interesting but
ultimately pointless?

To answer this question of meaning in the postmodern era, therefore,
demands squarely facing what has classically been called the "problem
of evil." This is the inexorable and unavoidable question at the end of
the twentieth century. This century has raised limit questions about the
significance of the academic endeavor as a whole. These questions touch
the work not only of theologians and philosophers but of every professor or student who asks, "Why am I doing this at all?" What is the
point of all this study and research in library and laboratory? Is it all a
veiled form of self-assertion that will likely add to the domination and
violence that has been so evident throughout this century? Is the one,
unifying meaning behind all the fragments of intellectual life finally that

the universe is hostile to human beings? Should we conclude on the basis of our experience that even God is malevolent toward us?

Resignation in the face of these questions leads to what H. Richard Niebuhr once called an "ethics of death": "We live and move and have our being in a realm that is not nothingness but that is ruled by destructive power, which brings us and all we love to nothing. The maker is the slayer; the affirmer is the denier; the creator is the destroyer; the life-giver is the death-dealer."[32] This description of the ultimate sounds very much like the goddess Kali, the Hindu deity who gives birth but who is portrayed with knife in hand, wearing a necklace made from the skulls of those she has slain. Is Kali the goddess whose icon should mark the towers and seals of post-Christian universities in the twenty-first century? If so, we are at the end not only of Christian humanism but of humanism *tout court*. And if this be the case, we also face the end of all the university has stood for throughout Western history.

It is in the face of such questions that the place of the cross in the effort to articulate a Christian humanism comes fully into view. The cross is the central symbol of the Christian religion, so if Christian humanism is not a dilution of Christianity but an expression of its inner logic, such humanism must have an integral connection to the meaning of the cross. In most theological discussions of the Catholic university today, the link between the intellectual aims of the university and Christian faith is articulated in terms of a theology of creation, with a strong stress on the human person created in the image and likeness of God. In such a humanism, human reason, understanding, and freedom are analogies or reflections of the reason, understanding, and freedom of God. Hence all the undertakings of reasonable persons in the university are seen as in continuity with the reality of God. But if the analysis of this essay is correct, this is like whistling in the dark to distract oneself from fear of what dimly lurks in the shadows. For today the reliability of human reason and the goodness of freedom are just what have been brought into question. In a world where human reason and freedom have produced the twentieth century, such a stress on the continuities of the human and the divine suggests not that God is on the side of the human but more like Kali — she creates only finally to destroy. Hence Christian humanism, if it is possible today, needs a different strategy from one that simply presumes the goodness of the human and then finds a way to say that God affirms this goodness.

This questioning of a humanism built on rosy readings of humanity's achievements has itself been one of the central strands in classical Christian theology, from Paul, to Augustine, to Luther, to Reinhold Niebuhr. Their questioning focuses on the cross of Jesus Christ as the result of human perversity. Because of the arrogance of pride and a lust for domination, human beings have a sinful propensity for evil that leads them to destroy the good and the innocent, including the One who showed them the meaning and reality of unconditional love. The *theologia crucis* of these thinkers has often been used in an anti-humanistic way. But there is also an interpretation of the cross that can lead to a profound humanism, a humanism that has the depth needed to withstand the disenchantment of what Weber called grandiose reason and the disillusionment produced by twentieth-century experience. It is a humanism that stakes its trust in all the undertakings of the contemporary university on a conviction that compassion, not malevolence, is the deepest attribute of the ultimate mystery behind the many shards of our fractured world.

For the cross is the sign through which Christians proclaim that the ultimate mystery that surrounds our lives embraces human suffering and shares human misery. The cross uncovers the central meaning of this mystery as compassion and divine mercy. Thomas Aquinas wrote that "mercy takes its name *misericordia* from denoting a person's compassionate heart (*miserum cor*) for another's unhappiness."[33] The motive of mercy is the misery or suffering of another. Through compassion one grieves for another's distress as though it were one's own. This, Thomas says, can happen in two ways. "First, through union of the affections, which is the effect of love." Relying on Aristotle, he sees friendship as the form of love that most leads to a compassionate heart. "For, since one who loves another looks upon his friend as another self, he counts his friend's hurt as his own, so that he grieves for his friend's hurt as though he were hurt himself." Thomas applies this description of mercy directly to God: "God takes pity on us through love alone, in as much as He loves us as belonging to Him," as friends. Second, one grieves with another through real union with the other in suffering, as when the cause of another's suffering actually touches not only the other but oneself as well.[34] Though Thomas does not say it explicitly, Christianity dares to affirm that the suffering and death of the cross really unite God to us in this second way.

For these reasons I think that any true humanism in a world bent by the afflictions and injustices we have witnessed in the twentieth century must be a humanism of compassion. A Christian humanism of this sort is humanism under the sign of the cross. For the cross tells us that wherever men, women, or children grieve, the ultimate mystery that surrounds our history grieves too. Wherever human beings suffer unjust torture and death, God is there, for God has *already* been there in Jesus as the one who endured the curse of crucifixion (Gal. 3:13). When such evils lead us to fear that the One beyond the many fragments of our experience is hostile, even our enemy, we need to hear the words of the Letter to the Hebrews, which describe Jesus as "the pioneer" of our faith and call us to "consider him who endured such hostility against himself from sinners, so that you may not grow weary or lose heart" (Heb. 12:2–3). If the Catholic university today is tempted to lose heart not only in its humanistic goals but also in its ability to integrate its religious tradition with its intellectual tasks, perhaps such a consideration can sustain and encourage it.

Such an appeal to the most distinctive and particularistic of all Christian doctrines may sound like a proposal to exclude non-Christians from a role in the Catholic university. It could also be heard as suggesting that intellectual work that apparently has little directly to do with social and psychological struggles with human suffering, such as that in the hard sciences, has no integral place in this vision. Both of these interpretations would be far from my intent. On the first point, taking the sign of the cross seriously in a Catholic university does not mean exclusion of other interpretations of the meaning of the ultimate mystery of existence. All interpretations of final meaning must be present in full and free discussion within any university worthy of the name. But taking the cross seriously does mean that the problem of human suffering must be directly confronted in the university. "Changing the subject" when the ultimate significance of our bloody history is raised will simply not do. Conversation and argument about all the answers offered to this question must be present. So followers of all religions and none must be engaged within the exchange.

Further, the cross speaks a message that can convey meaning not only to Christians but to all. For example, Gandhi remained fully a Hindu while also acknowledging that his encounter with the cross deeply affected the way he came to understand his own religion. Of Jesus, Gandhi believed that "the lives of all have, in some greater or lesser degree been changed by his presence, his actions, and the words spoken by his divine voice. . . . And because the life of Jesus has the significance and the transcendency to which I have alluded, I believe that he belongs not solely to Christianity, but to the entire world."[35] Thus Gandhi took a poem about war, the *Bhagavad Gita,* and reread it as a parable of nonviolence, both through the influence of reform movements indigenous to Hinduism and also because he learned to read the *Gita* in a new way through his interaction with the Christian story of the cross. Closer to home, Richard Rorty has observed that sorting out the role of Socrates and Christ in the making of Europe, and by extension the West, is a notoriously tricky business. For Rorty, the quest for purely rational philosophical arguments that give access to the foundations of ethics in Being is doomed to failure. For this reason Rorty has said a case can be made that the influence of the story of Jesus was more crucial than that of Athens in forming the ethic that finally brought about the revolutions of 1989 and overthrew Communist domination.[36] Both Gandhi and Rorty should be fully welcome in a Catholic university. Though neither is a Christian, both show that the cross can be a source of humanistic insight for believers and nonbelievers alike. And believers stand to learn much about the full meaning of the cross through engagement with the thinking of people like Gandhi and Rorty.

The question of whether this proposal lacks relevance to the hard sciences raises the longstanding modern issue of the relation of scientific and humanistic thought in a new form. But this new form is crucial. In its earlier, distinctively modern form, positivistic scientific thought made reductionist claims to be able to provide a complete account of all of reality. Today, that claim has been discredited not only in the eyes of religious believers but in most philosophy of science as well. The more pressing issue now is whether all science is simply what Plato called a "likely story" — perhaps true, but perhaps not. The justifications offered for scientific thought today are more likely to be pragmatic than positivistic for those who have pursued the issue of justification at all. But such pragmatic justifications need to take account of the full range of the social consequences of scientific discovery, not only those that are beneficial to humans and their environment. When such negative consequences are accounted for, the need for humility and perhaps a measure of compassion may be felt as essential to the continuation of the scientific endeavor at all. The cross calls the intellectual community to an acknowledgment that it is not made up of gods, that it deals with mystery at all times, and that not all that it achieves is free of the desire for domination and control. Such humility can be a source of the courage needed to continue the scientific undertaking, even though it has not abolished suffering and brought heaven to earth.

In light of the developments in the cultural self-understanding that sets the context of much university thinking today, therefore, it would seem that Christianity has much to contribute to enabling the university to achieve its humanistic objectives. This may be a moment not only of significant transition for Catholic universities but of openness to a fuller realization of the mutual completion of their academic and religious dimensions. The meaning of the sign of the cross may be one of the keys to such fuller realization. As Michael Buckley has argued, this will occur if we can broaden our understanding of humanism to include not only a celebration of the heights to which cultures can rise but a compassion for the depths of suffering into which they can fall. A humanism of compassion — a humanism of the cross — can guide the way.

Notes

1. Michael J. Buckley, S.J., *Redeeming the Promise: Some Jesuit Specifications in Higher Education*, forthcoming; George M. Marsden, *The Soul of the American University: From Protestant Establishment to Established Nonbelief*

(New York: Oxford University Press, 1994); David J. O'Brien, *From the Heart of the American Church: Catholic Higher Education and American Culture* (Maryknoll, N.Y.: Orbis Books, 1994); Pope John Paul II, *Ex Corde Ecclesiae* [*Apostolic Constitution on Catholic Universities*] (Boston: St. Paul Books and Media, 1990). Buckley's forthcoming volume develops and refines ideas that he initially developed in essays cited in the notes below and elsewhere.

2. Buckley, "The University and the Concern for Justice: The Search for a New Humanism, *Thought* 57 (June 1982): 223. See also his "Christian Humanism and Human Misery: A Challenge to the Jesuit University," in Francis M. Lazarus, ed., *Faith, Discovery, Service: Perspectives on Jesuit Education* (Milwaukee: Marquette University Press, 1992), 77–105.

3. Joseph A. Komonchak, "Vatican II and the Encounter between Catholicism and Liberalism," in R. Bruce Douglass and David Hollenbach, eds., *Catholicism and Liberalism: Contributions to American Public Philosophy* (Cambridge: Cambridge University Press, 1994), 77. See also Komonchak, "The Enlightenment and the Construction of Roman Catholicism," *Annual of the Catholic Commission on Intellectual and Cultural Affairs* (1985): 31–59.

4. Buckley, "The Catholic University and the Promise Inherent in Its Identity," in John Langan, ed., *Catholic Universities in Church and Society: A Dialogue on Ex Corde Ecclesiae* (Washington, D.C.: Georgetown University Press, 1993), 81.

5. John Henry Newman, *The Idea of a University*, ed. Martin J. Svaglic (Notre Dame, Ind.: University of Notre Dame Press, 1982), 21–22, 24–25.

6. Vatican Council II, *Gaudium et Spes* (*Pastoral Constitution on the Church in the Modern World*), no. 59. Citations from Vatican II documents are from Walter M. Abbott and Joseph Gallagher, eds., *The Documents of Vatican II* (New York: America Press, 1966).

7. Vatican Council II, *Gaudium et Spes*, no. 57.

8. Vatican Council II, *Dignitatis Humanae* (*Declaration on Religious Freedom*), passim, and *Gaudium et Spes*, nos. 53 and 59.

9. Buckley, "The Catholic University and the Promise Inherent in Its Identity," 82–83.

10. Ibid., 83.

11. John C. Haughey, S.J., "Theology and the Mission of the Jesuit College and University," *Conversations on Jesuit Higher Education* 5 (Spring 1994): 11.

12. See John Tracy Ellis, "American Catholics and the Intellectual Life," *Thought* 30 (Autumn 1955): 353–86, for the now classic discussion of the anti-intellectual bias of American Catholics. For a similarly well known account of this tendency in American culture at large, many of whose orientations the present essay does not share, see Richard Hofstadter, *Anti-Intellectualism in American Life* (New York: Knopf, 1970).

13. George M. Marsden, "What Can Catholic Universities Learn from Protestant Examples?" in Theodore M. Hesburgh, ed., *The Challenge and Promise of a Catholic University* (Notre Dame, Ind.: University of Notre Dame Press, 1994), 18.

14. See David Tracy, "Catholic Classics in American Liberal Culture," in Douglass and Hollenbach, *Catholicism and Liberalism*, 197–98. Tracy's allusion to Schillebeeckx is not a direct quote.

15. Max Weber, "Science as a Vocation," in *From Max Weber: Essays in So-*

ciology, trans. and ed. H. H. Gerth and C. Wright Mills (New York: Oxford University Press, 1958), esp. 148, 155.

16. Ibid., 152.

17. Ibid., 155–56.

18. Richard Rorty, *Contingency, Irony, and Solidarity* (New York: Cambridge University Press, 1989), 45.

19. Weber, "Science as a Vocation," 145.

20. Andrew Greeley, *The American Catholic: A Social Portrait* (New York: Basic Books, 1977), tables 3.6A and 3.4A, 62, 59.

21. See Robert Coles, *Privileged Ones: The Well-Off and the Rich in America,* vol. 5 of *Children of Crisis* (Boston: Little, Brown, 1977), esp. Part Six, for a discussion of some of the forms taken by the sense of "entitlement" among the well-off.

22. Both John Paul II and the U.S. bishops are clearly concerned about trends that point in this direction. See John Paul II, *Centesimus Annus,* no. 19, with its critique of "the affluent society or consumer society" in David J. O'Brien and Thomas A. Shannon, eds. *Catholic Social Thought: The Documentary Heritage* (Maryknoll, N.Y.: Orbis Books, 1992), 453–54; National Conference of Catholic Bishops, *Economic Justice for All: Pastoral Letter on Catholic Social Teaching and the U.S. Economy* (Washington, D.C.: United States Catholic Conference, 1986), nos. 327–38; Rembert G. Weakland, "Economic Justice and the American Tradition," in *Faith and the Human Enterprise: A Post-Vatican II Vision* (Maryknoll, N.Y.: Orbis Books, 1992), 108–28.

23. U.S. Bureau of the Census, Current Population Reports, Series P60–184, *Money Income of Households, Families, and Persons in the United States: 1992* (Washington, D.C.: U.S. Government Printing Office, 1993), Tables 13, 23, and xviii.

24. *Boston College Undergraduate Catalogue 1991–92.*

25. I am well aware that the official "poverty line" in no way marks a point where financial resources can be judged adequate for dignified human living.

26. Martha C. Nussbaum, *The Fragility of Goodness: Luck and Ethics in Greek Tragedy and Philosophy* (Cambridge: Cambridge University Press, 1986).

27. Weber, "Science as a Vocation," 154.

28. Ibid.

29. Marsden, *Soul of the American University,* 430. David O'Brien makes a similar move in *From the Heart of the American Church,* 9–11.

30. Augustine, *The City of God,* trans. Henry Bettenson (London, New York: Penguin Books, 1984), Book IV, 3, 138.

31. This self-doubt was prophetically anticipated in the late 1950s by one of the giants of American Catholic intellectual life, John Courtney Murray. Before the council and before the emergence of postmodernism as a self-conscious intellectual movement, Murray spoke of the end of the modern age in terms that are regularly heard on university campuses today. In his words: "Though the adjective 'modern' will continue to be used in advertising copy as synonymous with 'up to date,' it will from now on be increasingly used in scholarly circles as synonymous with 'out of date.' A new era has begun. Whatever its characteristics, they will not be those of modernity.... For instance, we no longer cherish the bright and brittle eighteenth-century concept of 'reason'; we do not believe in the principle of automatic harmony or the inevitability of progress. We have rejected the doctrine of modernity which asserted that government is the only

enemy of freedom. We see that the modern concept of freedom itself was danger-ously inadequate because it neglected the corporate dimension of freedom. We see too that modernity was wrong in isolating the problem of freedom from its polar terms — responsibility, justice, order, law. We have realized that the mod-ern experiment, originally conceived only as an experiment in freedom, had to become also an experiment in justice" (John Courtney Murray, *We Hold These Truths: Catholic Reflections on the American Proposition* [New York: Sheed and Ward, 1960], 197, 200); originally published as "Church, State and Political Freedom" in *Modern Age* 1 (Fall 1957). The influence of this sensibility on one sample of undergraduates at a Catholic university today is perceptively analyzed by Patrick H. Byrne, "Paradigms of Justice and Love," *Conversations on Jesuit Higher Education* 7 (Spring 1995): 5–17.

32. H. Richard Niebuhr, *The Responsible Self: An Essay in Christian Moral Philosophy* (New York: Harper and Row, 1963), 139–40.

33. *Summa Theologiae* II–II, q. 30, a. 1.

34. Ibid., II–II, q. 30, a. 2.

35. Gandhi, *The Law of Love*, ed. Anand T. Hingorani (Bharatiya Vidya Bhavan, 1962), 111. Cited in James W. Douglass, *The Non-Violent Cross: A Theology of Revolution and Peace* (New York: Macmillan, 1968), 56.

36. Richard Rorty, "The Seer of Prague," review of three works by the Czech philosopher Jan Patocka, *New Republic*, July 1, 1991, 40.

18

A Catholic/Jesuit University?

– WILLIAM B. NEENAN, S.J. –

The modern university traces its origins to medieval universities such as Paris and Oxford — which in turn found their immediate antecedents in the schools of monastic establishments. Why therefore should the possibility of the very existence of a university that is Catholic be a subject of serious discussion? Why is it a fairly common opinion among American intellectuals that the concept of a "Catholic university" is problematic, even oxymoronic?[1] Whatever the historical circumstances that have brought us to this point in the late twentieth century, many of the intellectual elite who define the discourse in such matters regard the issue of a "Catholic university" as something of an anachronism, posing perhaps a mild threat to the commonly accepted procedures of American universities, but one that is gradually receding. As Catholic universities emerge into the mainstream of American higher education, it is generally assumed that these institutions will no longer be "Catholic" in any confessional sense. They may indeed have notable Catholic alumni, be frequented by large numbers of Catholic students who attend popular liturgies sponsored by the chaplaincy, but as for their academic heart, these Catholic universities will be largely indistinguishable from secular universities. In this view Catholic universities, having appropriated the mores of mainstream American academia, are thus tamed, and so welcomed to the club.

If the metaphorical wall separating church and state runs through the heart of the cultural life of the nation, as Stephen Carter[2] and others have noted, should we be surprised that the ultimate questions — who am I? where do I come from? what is my destiny? — weighted as they are with theological implications, are largely disappearing from discourse in the university, the nation's principal cultural institution? The thesis of this essay is that these ultimate questions are among the proper concerns of a university and that in an increasingly secularized society the Catholic and Jesuit university has an important contribution to offer society; and that despite predictions to the contrary, prospects for this

299

particular species of university are encouraging though not completely assured.

To celebrate the life of Michael J. Buckley, S.J., I can think of no more appropriate endeavor than an exploration of the dynamics relating to Catholicism, the university, and contemporary cultural values. In his *At the Origins of Modern Atheism,* Buckley has argued that Christian apologists of the sixteenth and seventeenth centuries, by adopting the Cartesian and Newtonian conventions that God is known only by inference from the sensible universe, excluded the personal, experiential, and intersubjective relationships that are at the core of the Christian message.[3] Unwittingly therefore, these apologists effectively eliminated the only secure foundation for establishing the existence of the Christian God. Because they dismissed an appeal to all communal and personal religious experiences, including the call and demands of a personal God revealed in Jesus Christ, their writings logically and inexorably contributed to an alienation from the Christian religion. In other words, the purely philosophical natural theology adopted by Christian apologetics after the Renaissance can be said to stand paradoxically at the origins of modern atheism. Michael Buckley has thus identified one of the historical circumstances explaining how the Paris and Oxford of Aquinas and Duns Scotus have become the secular world of the modern university.

Even as many consider the issue of the "Catholic university" either closed or irrelevant, recently there has been in Catholic circles increased attention directed to the nature and viability of the Catholic university. Some of this attention has come from Catholic interests outside the academy, prompted by a feeling that the religious character of Catholic institutions has been dangerously attenuated. Concomitantly within Catholic universities — sometimes in response to these external concerns but also increasingly from a desire to promote something recognized as valuable — faculty, administrators, and trustees have been asking: what is a Catholic university? and how do we sustain it? Such questions should not be surprising. As Catholic colleges and universities have grown in size, financial stability, and academic stature, many of the traditional indicators of their Catholicity, such as the number of religious sisters, brothers, and priests of the sponsoring congregations active in the colleges, have dramatically declined.

These conversations within many Catholic universities are more insistent and self-confident than would have been possible twenty years ago. They are more insistent because secularization has grown apace in society in general, and in higher education in particular, and more self-confident because of the increased stature of many Catholic institutions. Their self-confidence may also be buoyed by the growing realization that they constitute a distinctive and important voice in American higher education.

Pope John Paul II and various episcopal bodies have indicated a strong and understandable concern that the "Catholic" nature of universities be carefully defined and measures adopted to maintain it. The Pope's 1990 apostolic constitution *Ex Corde Ecclesiae* has stimulated a series of conversations between the United States Conference of Bishops and representatives of the Association of Catholic Colleges and Universities. The central issue in these conversations has been how to reconcile the teaching responsibility of the hierarchy concerning doctrinal matters with the autonomy requisite for a Catholic college or university existing in the milieu of American higher education.

In *Ex Corde Ecclesiae* John Paul II, quoting from a document of a 1972 international conference of Catholic universities, asserts that

> every Catholic university, as Catholic, must have the following essential characteristics: First, a Christian inspiration not only of individuals but of the university community as such; second, a continuing reflection in the light of the Catholic faith upon the growing treasury of human knowledge, to which it seeks to contribute by its own research; third, fidelity to the Christian message as it comes to us through the church; and finally, an institutional commitment to the service of the people of God and of the human family in their pilgrimage to the transcendent goal which gives meaning to life.[4]

How these four characteristics of a Catholic university are to be grounded in institutions existing in various cultural situations worldwide is the object of ongoing deliberations. In the United States, efforts by the bishops to draft legislation implementing *Ex Corde Ecclesiae* engendered considerable apprehension among Catholic academic leaders fearful that good intentions aimed at maintaining Catholic orthodoxy might inadvertently damage what has been one of the great strengths of the Catholic Church in the United States, its system of higher education. Although full agreement has not yet been achieved on this important issue, recently both parties have arrived at an appreciative understanding of the issues involved.

The resolution of the juridical issues involving the hierarchical church and Catholic higher education is certainly desirable and continuing efforts should be pursued to that end. An important first step in this direction would be to address the basic question: What is the nature of the university as such? Is it not conceivable that the faculty of a department of theology could be impeccable in its orthodoxy but nested within a university structure that is either fully secular or deficient in some essential characteristic of a university? Would such an institution properly be called a "Catholic university?"

Only a relatively small fraction of the courses offered in Catholic universities relate to doctrinal issues. For example, during the 1994–95 academic year barely 5 percent of the courses taught at Boston College were offered by the Department of Theology and the Institute of Religious Education and Pastoral Ministry, even though Boston College offers major graduate programs in theology, Scripture, and religious education, requires theology courses for all of its undergraduates, and has a number of undergraduate majors in theology. At times, discussions concerning ecclesial and juridical issues seem to assume that the other 95 percent of the courses offered by a university are not relevant to its Catholic nature. Administrators and faculty at Catholic universities day in and day out devote the bulk of their time and energies to such issues as the relative priority to be given to doctoral programs in chemistry and nursing; whether the MBA program or the law school should be targeted for excellence; and to what extent resources should be used to reduce the student/faculty ratio in the freshman writing seminars. It is a contention of this essay that these questions are indeed intimately connected with the Catholicity of a university even though in ways that are not directly ecclesiastical. Administrators at Catholic universities sometimes feel that juridical conflicts involving one or two individuals in one department deflect attention from important problems facing all universities such as the maintenance of a strong faculty, promotion of the academic quality of undergraduate education, the provision of financial aid for needy students, and stress on racial and economic diversity among students — issues that also have a bearing on the Catholicity of a university.

It is therefore within a societal environment that is indifferent to Catholic higher education and an immediate context that is concerned for the prospects of Catholic higher education that the following points will be addressed in the remainder of this essay: definition of a "Catholic university," the Protestant experience, and characteristics of Jesuit education, with Boston College as a case study.

Definitional Issues

Many institutions are Catholic or a university but are not Catholic universities. A university is not rendered Catholic merely by existing in physical proximity to a cultural and liturgical center under Catholic auspices. The University of Michigan, for example, is not to be mistaken for a Catholic university merely because St. Mary's Chapel, a vibrant Newman Center which sponsors cultural and religious programs and provides liturgical worship for many members of the University of Michigan community, is contiguous to the campus in Ann Arbor. These two institutions are essentially autonomous, with distinct purposes even though serving overlapping constituencies.

A university is not a Catholic university merely because it possesses an endowed professorship in Catholic studies or supports a department of religious studies that may teach issues related to Roman Catholicism. Thus Harvard University with its Stillman Chair of Catholic Studies, the University of Iowa with its Religious Studies Department, or the University of Chicago with its School of Divinity are not for these reasons to be considered Catholic universities. These institutions are indeed "universities" but their identities are not directed intrinsically to goals that can properly be called "Catholic" simply because one or other program addresses issues of Catholic import.

An educational institution is not a Catholic university if its curriculum is primarily theological and its principal goal the professional preparation of priests and others for ministerial roles in the church. Thus Mundelein Seminary and the Weston Jesuit School of Theology, even though important Catholic educational institutions, are not Catholic universities. They serve purposes that are vital to the health of the Catholic community, but the scope of their academic offerings is too limited for them to be considered universities.

An issue outside the purview of this essay is posed by the existence of many institutions of higher education under Catholic sponsorship in such countries as Japan, Indonesia, and India. There are 143 members of the International Federation of Catholic Universities outside of North America. Are they to be considered "Catholic universities"? After all, only a few of the students and a small percentage of the faculty and administrators are Catholic and often the institutions cannot explicitly address issues central to Roman Catholic theology. Some might judge these institutions not to be Catholic universities. This would be met by a strong rejoinder from representatives of these colleges and universities. The issue of what is a Catholic university is a complex one, conditioned by varying cultural circumstances. These universities may offer lessons for Catholic universities in the United States whose faculty and administrators are increasingly non-Catholic.

The first step in defining a Catholic university is to emphasize that the noun is "university" and the adjective "Catholic." Thus institutions that meet the Carnegie Foundation's definition of "college" or "university" and that are members of the Association of Catholic Colleges and Universities are those that have *prima facie* claim to be both a university or college as well as "Catholic." In 1994, there were 1,402 institutions in the United States classified by the Carnegie Foundation as being either a Research University, a Doctoral University, a Comprehensive University or College, or a Liberal Arts College.[5] Of this number, 180 are currently members of the ACCU and presumably Catholic colleges or universi-

ties. These institutions are the largest concentration of Catholic colleges
and universities in any country in the world. Their aggregate enrollment
in 1994–95 of over 600,000 is greater than the total number of students enrolled in all Catholic institutions of higher education elsewhere
in the world. Are these 180 institutions "Catholic"? If so, what are their
prospects for maintaining their Catholic character into the next century?

Protestant Experience

The experience of Protestant higher education in the United States suggests that Catholic higher education is poised on the lip of a slippery
slope leading inexorably to secularization. George M. Marsden's *The
Soul of the American University* traces the evolution of many current
elite institutions from being enterprises defined and inspired by liberal
Protestantism to their present status as unabashedly and explicitly secular. Marsden's thesis is that the history of American higher education
can be described either as "the story of the disestablishment of religion"
or the "story of secularization."[6] Harvard, Yale, Williams, the University of Michigan, for example, have been transformed from institutions
more or less explicitly Christian in governance, selection of faculty, and
the regulation of student moral behavior into universities that stand at
a distance from any religious commitment. In 1924, the bylaws of Duke
University proclaimed that "the aims of Duke University are to assert
a faith in the eternal union of knowledge and religion set forth in the
teachings and character of Jesus Christ, the Son of God."[7] By 1988,
the goals of Duke University as found in its "mission statement" are
largely indistinguishable from other leading American universities: the
education of students for meaningful, productive and ethical lives; the
discovery of new knowledge; for the exchange of ideas; and the provision of medical, cultural, and recreational services. No longer does Duke
allude to Christianity in particular or to religion in general being integral
to the university.[8]

Marsden's thesis, however, is not clearly verified in all Protestant
institutions of higher education. Baylor University, the world's largest
Baptist university, is currently engaged in a self-scrutiny similar to
that occurring in Catholic institutions and is asking: what constitutes
the nature of a Baptist university and how can this Baptist character be maintained at Baylor? According to a statement approved by
the Regents of Baylor in 1994, "the mission of Baylor University is
to educate men and women for worldwide leadership and service by
integrating academic excellence and Christian commitment within a car-
ing community." The statement continues that "the University derives
its understanding of God, humanity, and nature from many sources:
the person and work of Jesus Christ, the biblical record, and Chris-

tian history and tradition, as well as scholarly and artistic endeavors. In its service to the church, Baylor's pursuit of knowledge is strengthened by the conviction that truth has its ultimate source in God and by a Baptist heritage that champions religious liberty and freedom of conscience."[9] The fact that such Protestant universities as Baylor still struggle with the meaning of religious identity indicates that the Protestant tradition in American higher education, although indeed diminished as Marsden has shown, is still extant in some universities. There are, of course, many small Christian colleges that maintain strong fundamentalist Protestant ties.

Marsden's analysis indicates there were three defining characteristics of the leading nineteenth- and twentieth-century Protestant colleges and universities: chapel service, parietal rules, and a capstone course in moral philosophy. These institutions sought the formation of a strong moral character nurtured by a biblically based religious practice and carefully monitored behavior. Graduates were expected to leave college with habits of personal virtue and a sense of public responsibility. The course of studies was not an essential constitutive element of the enterprise but simply the context within which the student's moral and social development occurred. There is a notable difference between this classical Protestant rationale for the sponsorship of colleges and the Catholic and Jesuit philosophy that has emerged in the United States. In this tradition a student's intellectual development is an absolutely essential component that occurs simultaneously with spiritual and religious maturation.

David O'Brien has suggested that Catholic colleges might not follow the secularization route of Protestant colleges because of the different historical moments when the colleges "moved away from their churches."[10] Due to the acceptance in the nineteenth century of the scientific method as the only path to truth, Protestant colleges often "sent theology off the campus and into the seminary, leaving the church with Sunday schools and sermons as its sole educational media for the laity."[11] Catholic colleges, on the other hand, adopted separate incorporation from their sponsoring religious congregations in the 1960s and 1970s when "academic freedom" and "autonomy" were the watchwords in higher education. Consequently as "Catholics...were creating independent boards and diversifying their faculties," they were also "expanding and strengthening their theology and religious studies programs ...and struggling to keep theology a vital element of the undergraduate curriculum."[12] Catholic colleges did not enter the mainstream of American higher education until after World War II, but serendipitously remained insulated from the forces that O'Brien associates with the secularization of Protestant colleges. They came of age only in the 1960s and 1970s with their identities still intact and were thus better prepared

to adapt to an emerging world of higher education which was more accepting of institutions that were both university and Catholic than might
have been true in the earlier decades of the century.[13]

Catholic Educational Tradition

Whatever weight may be attributed to the influence of these historical
circumstances on the evolution of Protestant and Catholic higher education in the United States, I contend that the two traditions are separated
by a fundamental difference in their basic philosophies. This difference
can be seen in both the manner and extent to which the two traditions
have been involved in educational efforts in the United States.

What has been the history of Catholic involvement in education in
the United States? And what lessons do we learn from this history that
might assist us in evaluating the prospects for Catholic higher education? Multiple reasons might explain the origins of the astounding
Catholic school system that has emerged in the United States — but
the basic fact is that over the past century millions of Americans have
been educated in Catholic schools, kindergarten through graduate and
professional education, by instructors, often vowed religious men and
women, who were as comfortable teaching secular disciplines as theological ones. Whether they studied arithmetic and geography in primary
school, Latin and social studies in high school, or organic chemistry
and macroeconomics in college, these students implicitly but powerfully
learned that secular disciplines were somehow part of their "Catholic"
education. Students educated in these Catholic schools were not faced
with an either/or but with a both/and: not either secular education or religious education but rather both secular and religious education under
the same roof.

There has been nothing quite like this in the Protestant tradition in
the United States. Protestant children have largely received their secular
education separate from their religious training: the former in the public school, the latter under church auspices in Sunday schools. In recent
years, the percentage of Catholic children receiving their education in
Catholic primary and secondary schools has declined as has the number of vowed religious men and women, but nonetheless the historical
record indicates a profound difference between American Protestant education and Catholic education. What is the reason for this difference?
Does this difference suggest a basis for believing that the secularization
experienced by Protestant colleges and universities need not presage a
similar destiny for Catholic colleges and universities? My answers to
these questions will emerge from an examination of the principles of
Jesuit education and how they are exemplified in one university, Boston
College.

Jesuit Education

I propose the following seven notes as characteristic of Jesuit education:

- an emphasis on excellence
- a concern for the individual
- knowledge put to useful purposes
- spiritual and religious development of students
- pursuit of knowledge as good in itself
- academic freedom extending to discussion of religious values
- a place for the church to do its thinking

Let me offer a brief explanation of each characteristic and indicate how I see it exemplified in the life of one Jesuit university, Boston College.

1. Striving for excellence should permeate everything a Jesuit college or university undertakes. Academic programs, extracurricular activities, architecture, liturgical worship, the maintenance of facilities — all should reflect the belief that the world in all its dimensions is a sacred trust and must be respected. For a university this responsibility is most acute in matters of the intellect and spirit. The precise expression of excellence, of course, must be conditioned by the overall goals of a particular university as well as the financial and other constraints that will necessarily vary from institution to institution. John Cogley once remarked that every cause had its own Jesuit sponsor. So too Jesuit universities in the United States have developed in different regions with diverse programs that serve different needs and clienteles.

The primary exemplar of excellence at any university must be in the way courses are taught, what faculty expect from students, and what students come to expect of themselves. An honors program, for example, should be rigorous and challenge the academically gifted students; a program designed for educationally disadvantaged students should be challenging but also responsive to their particular need — in both instances, therefore, students will graduate with enhanced qualities of mind and spirit fostered by programs that can be termed "excellent." Interscholastic athletics, played at whatever level an institution judges appropriate, should focus on success evaluated in terms of the athletes themselves and the contribution the sports program makes toward building a sense of community among students, parents, and alumni.

Research and scholarship, whether conducted in a large chemistry laboratory with a team of post doctoral and doctoral students, in a cluttered office of a graduate student puzzling over a text, or in a private study of a poet, should be characterized by integrity and the pursuit of excellence. The campus environment should evoke beauty and quality. Admittedly, not all universities can afford to build Gothic classroom buildings these days, but care in the construction and maintenance of even cinder block facilities should remind us that the Christian life embraces a love of things beautiful and a respect for the environment, with special care for one's home.

Liturgical worship at a Jesuit university, whether the annual Mass of the Holy Spirit or liturgies celebrated weekly in informal residence halls, should promote the reverence proper to sacred happenings. Participants in these celebrations should experience a sense of wonder and transcendence as well as a sense of community.

Excellence never occurs by chance but results from careful attention to detail combined with intelligence and creative imagination. Ignatius Loyola is a model in this regard. For sixteen years from his room in Rome he crafted with great care and diligence the *Constitutions* for the Society of Jesus. Only after long and protracted reflection on his and his companions' experience, after prayer that was open to the Spirit and to his own creative imagination that encompassed continents he had never seen and times he would never experience, was he satisfied with the governing document of the Jesuits that has been an inspiration for members of the Society of Jesus and others for 450 years.

Examples of excellence such as I have been discussing undoubtedly can be found in most Catholic universities and, apart from the question of religious services, at many universities in the United States. At Boston College they are found in the various undergraduate honors programs; in the Options through Education program whose educational, emotional, and financial support has resulted in a 90 percent graduation rate for students from educationally disadvantaged backgrounds; in research in the doctoral science departments that is recognized by peer review; in scholarship by instructors spurred both by a commendable professional pressure as well as a commitment to their students; in a Division I football program whose exploits on the field delight students and alumni and whose graduation rates are consistently among the highest in the country; and in a carefully planned building construction policy designed to enhance both the functionality and beauty of the campus.

2. The *Constitutions* of the Society of Jesus insist time and time again that a religious superior should give particular attention to the weaknesses, talents, and aspirations of each Jesuit in his charge in order to maximize his effectiveness. This *cura personalis* characteristic of internal Jesuit governance has traditionally been promoted in Jesuit colleges and is expected to permeate the culture of the institution. Even in large and complex universities such as Fordham, St. Louis, and Boston College, a student with extraordinary talents, particular handicaps, or simply the

bewilderment of a nineteen-year-old should be known by more than his or her ID number. Requests for a transcript from the registrar or for a room change from campus housing should be considered politely and with sensitivity, as should inquiries for an explanation of the grade given on a class writing assignment.

The ultimate theological basis for *cura personalis* at a Catholic university is the fact that "no one has ever seen God....Those who say, 'I love God,' and hate their brothers or sisters, are liars for those who do not love a brother or sister whom they have seen, cannot love God whom they have not seen" (1 John 4:12, 20). In addition to a concern for students, a Jesuit university should be a place where all — faculty, staff, and students — treat others and their values seriously and where one's bedrock convictions can be openly shared and received with respect. Whether Catholic, Protestant, Jew, or agnostic, a faculty member at a Jesuit university should be able and willing to discuss with a colleague one's most profound reflections on life. A Jesuit university has nothing to fear and much to gain from such exchanges.

Paul C. Reinert, S.J., long associated with Saint Louis University and a leading Jesuit educator of the twentieth century, recently wrote that a Jesuit university's most powerful attraction is the provision of mystery that can serve as a passage in either "specifically religious terms, or more generally in a personal spiritual awakening."[14] An atmosphere of openness and trust is a necessary condition for this exploration of mystery and of the transcendent — an atmosphere that is subverted by threat of coercion arising either within the university or, for example, from a confrontational relationship with the local bishop.

> Such an adversarial and judgmental atmosphere is not conducive to encounters with mystery, nor does it encourage faculty or students who fear that their beliefs are not acceptable to the church to enter into productive dialogue with teachers, colleagues or peers. Entering into the mystery cannot be forced through conformity and should not be compelled through threat or punishment.[15]

At Boston College there exists a fairly healthy climate of *cura personalis* for undergraduate students. The vast majority of their faculty strive to be accessible; there are small-enrollment courses in the college and departmental honors' programs; and the freshman writing and the senior capstone seminars provide frequent personal interaction with faculty. The offices of student development, housing, and the registrar are professionally staffed by personnel sensitive to student problems and foibles. The chaplaincy sponsors numerous weekly and daily liturgies, retreats are common, and personal counseling is readily available. Students guilty of rowdy behavior in the residence halls or charged with dishonesty in the classroom are held responsible for their actions but with allowance made for their age and immaturity. "Personal care" in a university should imply that juridical procedures are educational for the students and not simply judgmental and punitive. Unfortunately the graduate and professional students at Boston College, although constituting over 25 percent of the student body, do not enjoy the same support system that is in place for undergraduates. The spiritual and psychological needs of graduate students, although different from those of undergraduates, should not be ignored in favor of the often more visible needs of undergraduates.

The *cura personalis* regarding faculty at Boston College could be strengthened. Certainly there exist no constraints on the expression of one's values and viewpoints. There are, however, few structured opportunities for discourse among faculty concerning ultimate values. There have been some efforts to develop such exchanges that have been sponsored both by the Boston College Jesuit community and more recently by the Jesuit Institute, directed by Michael Buckley himself. Since the faculty, through the hiring process, their curricular decisions, and the research and scholarship options they choose, will ultimately determine whether Boston College remains recognizably Catholic and Jesuit into the next century, it is imperative to develop a faculty consensus concerning the values that are consistent with the Jesuit educational tradition.

3. In the Jesuit headquarters in Rome the base of a statue of St. Ignatius is adorned with the inscription *Ite inflammate omnes*. As if to qualify this inspiriting injunction, a fire extinguisher is affixed to a nearby wall! This little scene provides a metaphor for the purpose of Jesuit education — to inspire students to make a difference in the world and at the same time develop the intelligence and expertise so that one's efforts will be efficacious — good intentions combined with hard-headed realism.

The Jesuit tradition has always proposed the ideal of a contemplative in action. The graduate of a Jesuit institution should be involved in the world but always testing this involvement by recourse to prayer and reflection. In this way, one's enthusiasm is protected from degenerating into a self-righteous demagoguery and one's apathy is offset by continual spiritual renovation. It thus may be no accident of history that Jesuit institutions in the United States have been heavily involved in professional education.

At the dedication of Boston College's Thomas P. O'Neill Jr. Library, the president of Boston College, J. Donald Monan, S.J., pointed out that the thousands of students and faculty who in subsequent decades would enter the principal academic building on campus would be reminded by its name chiseled of the impact that this alumnus of Boston College was having on millions of citizens because of his long and illustrious political life. In other words Tip O'Neill was proposed as a model for Boston College graduates. Knowledge received at a Jesuit university should not lie fallow; it should be used to good effect for oneself and for others.

4. Jesuit educational efforts since their inception at Messina, Sicily, in 1548 have been directed toward the moral and religious development of students.[16] A student's formation of character can be promoted in various ways — the example of role models, words of advice, formal instruction in ethical reasoning, religious practices, and participating in others' life experiences. The virtuous life cannot be taught the way chemistry or calculus is taught. Virtue is not taught but "caught." One may see another's behavior and desire to emulate it or choose a profession that promotes it; one may witness another's suffering or battle with adversity and experience a conversion of heart. Such epiphanies cannot be planned; they happen in various and often surprising ways. Who cannot recall a word offered by a teacher at a pivotal moment in one's life either in encouragement or as a spur that crucially altered one's future life?

Principles of personal and social ethical reasoning should be taught in the curriculum. Clear thinking is essential for good and responsible behavior. Merely clarifying one's values, however, is not all that is needed for the virtuous life. One may clarify one's values and then decide to be a terrorist. To live the good life one must be responsive to three questions: what are the right values? how do I determine them in particular circumstances? and how do I carry them out in practice? At a Jesuit university, students should be taught the intellectual principles that govern a mature, moral life and be given the religious and ethical support that encourages their application.

At Boston College there are various courses in ethics tailored to the professional programs in education, law, management, nursing, and social work. In addition the combination of ethical reasoning and the concrete implementation of these principles, theory and praxis, is found in several notable programs. For a quarter century the Pulse Program has challenged undergraduates to question the prevailing paradigms of justice and love. It does this through interdisciplinary philosophy-theology courses combined with service placements that include tutoring disadvantaged students, assisting in programs for drug rehabilitation, and assisting homeless men and women. Professor Patrick Byrne, one of the founders of the Pulse Program, says the Pulse Program endeavors "to do what Christians down through the ages have always done — to draw upon all the intellectual and interpersonal resources we can to unveil narrowness and to broaden students' awarenesses about all that is truly entailed in both love and justice in the fullest sense."[17] The Pulse Program is thus not simply a volunteer service program. At its core is intellectual reflection on one's experience, an example of the Jesuit principle of contemplation in action. There are in addition at Boston College many volunteer opportunities in the Boston area, elsewhere in the United States, as well as in Belize, Jamaica, Ecuador, and Mexico, which bring students face to face with the harsh conditions of life common to millions of their brothers and sisters. Many of these programs also include formal elements of reflection on what a student has experienced. The chaplaincy sponsors over a dozen weekly campus liturgies as well as retreats with opportunities for prayer and reflection where students can sort out the problems that face all young people today.

5. The belief that the pursuit of knowledge is good derives in a Jesuit university from the Ignatian vision that God is to be found in all things; or as the Jesuit poet Gerard Manley Hopkins reminds us, "the world is charged with the grandeur of God." This insight flows from the religious conviction that the incarnation of God's Son has endowed all human activity with a sign-value, a sacramentality that points to God. The Jesuit theologian Karl Rahner has imagined St. Ignatius telling a young Jesuit biologist that once he has grasped the insight that God can be found in all things he should feel free to investigate any avenue of study, even the spiritual life of the cockroach.[18]

At a Jesuit university therefore the study of biochemistry, art history, and comparative political systems enjoys an intrinsic value with an ultimate religious basis. The Ignatian view assumes that a theologically intrinsic value for all academic pursuits is available to those who have first accepted, along with Hopkins, that "the world is charged with the grandeur of God." A glimpse of God's grandeur can also concomitantly emerge with a scientific insight or an artistic creation even if one is not searching for it.

The explicit articulation that the pursuit of knowledge has an ultimate theological basis is perhaps the hallmark of Jesuit education. It certainly is the mark that differentiates it from any educational philosophy, Protestant or Catholic, whose religious inspiration derives primarily from a desire to form the moral and religious life of its students through various parietal regulations and the devotional impact of chapel services.

The belief that all knowledge is good is the ultimate basis of the Christian humanism characteristic of Jesuit education from its origins. The phrase of the Latin poet Terence, "Humani nihil a me alienum puto" ("Nothing human is foreign to me"), was recast by the Ignatian insight and could be said to be the hallmark of Jesuit activities in the sciences, the arts, and architecture during the sixteenth, seventeenth, and eighteenth centuries. Obviously the Jesuits were on to something. As Ronald Modras has pointed out, they often found "themselves in the middle of any number of cross-fires. Their less accommodating Catholic critics viewed Jesuit affirmation of non-Christian cultures as toleration of idolatry and a betrayal of the Christian heritage. For anticlerical humanists like Diderot and Voltaire, the Jesuits were too spiritual. Because of their humanism, Blaise Pascal and the Jansenists found them too lax."[19]

The spirit of the Christian humanism of the Renaissance is reflected in the Boston College undergraduate core curriculum of fifteen courses in the liberal arts, the social sciences and the natural sciences. This curriculum is common for all undergraduate students whether in the professional schools or the College of Arts and Sciences. A humanistic emphasis is found in the various graduate programs in education, law, management, social work, and nursing that complements their properly professional training. And in recent years, Boston College has sought to recapture some of the traditional Jesuit concern for the fine and performing arts. These programs are mentioned not because they are uniquely Catholic or Jesuit, since they are found in many colleges and universities in the United States, but only to indicate that they can flow from and are significantly enriched by an incarnational view of the world.

6. Academic freedom is respected by American universities, including those that are Catholic and Jesuit. What distinguishes a Catholic and Jesuit university in this regard from most secular counterparts is an additional commitment to an understanding of the world that is not limited by space and time. Some contend that this openness to a belief in God must necessarily restrict academic freedom, that a Catholic university because of its confessional character necessarily circumscribes the free inquiry essential to a university. Although there have been historical examples of such restrictions — and some in the not too distant past — I do not believe they are endemic to the Catholic and Jesuit university. Any university — secular, private, or state-supported — is subject to intrusions that threaten its autonomy. The *Chronicle of Higher Education* periodically reports instances of benefactors and state legislatures seeking to limit who is admitted to graduate programs and what courses are offered to undergraduates. It is not surprising that society's cultural battles are waged within the precincts of society's principal social institution; the existence of such conflicts does not imply the absence of academic freedom.

Academic freedom in the university is not inconsistent with the responsibility of a Catholic and Jesuit university to offer a sympathetic yet critical attention to the specific tradition of the Catholic Church. The meaning of life, the place of death in this continuum, belief in God — issues that have been central concerns of most men and women through history — often find no place in the curriculum of the great private and public universities. In this respect they are deficient as universities. The mechanistic certainties that often characterized the spirit of the nineteenth-century research universities have recently come under fire by cultural critics in this postmodern age. Although postmodernism is sometimes characterized by an irrationalism that is antithetical to traditional Christianity, its challenge to the dominant paradigm of rationalism may result in a greater receptivity toward the Jesuit vision of life that views human concerns through a transcendent lens.

At Boston College there are numerous examples of how academic freedom thrives side by side with scholarship that addresses issues of ultimate values. The Law School has for years sponsored an annual conference on issues of good and evil raised by the Holocaust of World War II that are still, unfortunately, too much with us, as events in the Balkans and Africa remind us. The Jesuit Institute conducts ongoing seminars on topics such as technology and religion, the alienation of intellectuals from religion, and AIDS and the Catholic Church. The research interests of the faculty in the theology department and other disciplines often directly address issues of the theological implications of public and personal social morality.

7. Since the Middle Ages the university has been a place where the church does its thinking. The modern university has its origins in the schools of the medieval church, and the church's understanding of itself has often been enriched by its close ties with the university. While the modern Catholic university is not directly under the jurisdiction of the juridical church, it clearly exists as part of the broader Catholic community and seeks to serve the church by educating men and women to be mature members of the church, by reflecting on the religious tradition of Catholicism and the other great religious traditions, and by promoting dialogue between religion and modern culture.

In previous centuries the university has also been "a" place where the church did its thinking and trained its professional theologians. As we approach the twenty-first century we are entering an era in which theological reflection will be increasingly centered in universities simply because other theological institutions centers are shrinking in size, number, and importance. Until recently Catholic seminaries annually graduated large numbers of clergy with a certain theological sophistication that is essential for a vibrant church life. This is no longer the case. The number of diocesan and religious priests has declined dramatically even as the Catholic population has continued to increase. This diminution is seen in the Jesuit experience, which is typical also of the diocesan and other religious clergy. In 1964, there were 142 Jesuits ordained in the United States after receiving an extensive theological training in five theologates. In 1994, 33 Jesuits were ordained in the two schools of theology under Jesuit auspices, the Jesuit School of Theology at Berkeley and the Weston Jesuit School of Theology. Alongside this contraction in the number of those professionally trained in theology, the 1964 Catholic population of the United States of 44,874,371 had increased in 1994 by 33 percent to 59,858,042. Another notable development over the past thirty years has been the increase in the number of lay men and women studying professional theology. In 1964 there were no lay students in the five Jesuit theologates, while the enrollments of the two Jesuit schools of theology in 1994 included a large cadre of lay women and men.

Over these past thirty years as seminaries have declined as centers of theological training and scholarship in the United States, graduate programs have been established in various Catholic universities. In 1995 there are eight Catholic universities with doctoral studies in theology: Boston College, Catholic University, Duquesne University, Fordham University, Loyola University of Chicago, Marquette University, University of Notre Dame, and Saint Louis University. These programs enroll a preponderance of lay men and women. Even more dramatic has been the recent development of university-based programs in religious education. In the thirty years since the first such program was started at Loyola University of Chicago and twenty-five years since the second one was established at Boston College, there has been a veritable explosion of religious education programs associated with Catholic colleges and universities. In 1995 they number over fifty. The enrollment in these programs has also become increasingly lay, echoing the experience of the graduate theology programs at Catholic universities. There is no evidence that these trends toward university-based lay education in theology will be reversed; in fact they will most likely accelerate. If the Catholic Church of the twenty-first century in the United States is to possess a critical mass of professionally trained theologians aware of the rich Catholic tradition in theology and capable of passing it on to subsequent generations, it will primarily be the responsibility of the Catholic university to train them.

Boston College is attempting to meet its responsibility in this regard. It does so through its theology department, the Institute of Religious Education and Pastoral Ministry (IREPM), and the Lonergan Institute. The theology department offers both a master's program in theology and a Ph.D., the latter through a faculty that also draws upon the faculties of the Andover-Newton School of Theology and the Weston Jesuit School of Theology. The IREPM offers both masters and Ph.D. degrees to those preparing for work in professional church ministry. These graduate programs provided in a university setting serve the church directly by educating men and women in the Catholic tradition in contact with other Christian traditions. The Lonergan Institute at Boston College promotes the study of Bernard Lonergan, a noted Jesuit theologian, through the sponsoring of workshops and postdoctoral research in theology and the social sciences.

American/Gospel Pragmatism

A century and a half ago Alexis de Tocqueville noted that "the spirit of the Americans is averse to general ideas; and it does not seek theoretical discoveries."[20] In this essay there has been considerable speculation — a bit too much perhaps considering the topic addressed has been a pragmatic one: are there Catholic universities in America today? And if so, will there be any tomorrow? The answer given to the former question is yes, as seen from the example of Boston College. The central theme of this essay is that Jesuit education regards the intellectual development of students and the pursuit of knowledge to be core values for a university and that these values in themselves carry theological significance. It is this sacramental outlook which differentiates Jesuit education from other religious traditions that have sponsored universities. It is also the basis for my belief that prospects for the maintenance of a Catholic university tradition into the twenty-first century are hopeful.

Michael Buckley often sprinkles his conversation with the question, "What's the finality of this or that?" And Americans, ever pragmatic, ask, "What's the bottom line? How are we doing?" Michael, they are the same question! You might be more comfortable with the assurance that I consider both to be gospel-based: "By their fruits you shall know them" (Matt. 7:16). The finality, bottom line, and fruits of a university are multiple: the intellectual, moral and religious formation of students; the pursuit and acquiring of truth and knowledge; the intergenerational transmission of cultural and religious values; among others. Judged by these various criteria I consider Boston College and its sister Catholic universities to be succeeding fairly well. The task facing all universities, Catholic as well as others, is formidable; the responsibility of those privileged to serve in them is great; and the stakes for society are high. And hope is the virtue that calls us forward.[21]

Notes

1. A word on terminology. "College" and "university" are generally used interchangeably for the purposes of this essay unless otherwise specified. "Catholic" and "Jesuit" are not completely interchangeable. I assume that a "Jesuit" university is a "Catholic" university; obviously a "Catholic" university is not necessarily a "Jesuit" university. In current usage there is an anomaly involving the adjectives "Christian," "Catholic," and "Jesuit" as applied to "university." A "Christian" university implies fundamentalism; a "Catholic" university suggests greater openness; and a "Jesuit" university connotes for most a greater sense of inclusion. For this reason I favor the phrase "Jesuit university" in referring to Boston College, Fordham, and Saint Louis University, for example, since it implies both that the institution is Catholic and that it is in open dialogue with modern culture. The connotation of words experience a certain vogue that is subject to change. In certain circles "Jesuitical" is understood to mean "du-

plicitous" and "given to equivocation." These meanings are not employed in this essay.

2. Stephen L. Carter, *The Culture of Disbelief: How American Law and Politics Trivialize Religious Devotion* (New York: Basic Books, 1993).

3. Michael J. Buckley, S.J., *At the Origins of Modern Atheism* (New Haven: Yale University Press, 1987), 348.

4. John Paul II, Apostolic Constitution of the Supreme Pontiff, *Ex Corde Ecclesiae* (Association of Catholics College and Universities, 1991), 3.

5. The Carnegie Foundation for the Advancement of Teaching, *A Classification of Institutions of Higher Education* (Princeton, N.J.: The Carnegie Foundation, 1994), xiv.

6. George M. Marsden, *The Soul of the American University: From Protestant Establishment to Established Nonbelief* (New York: Oxford University Press, 1994), 61.

7. Ibid., *The Soul*, 422.

8. Ibid., 421.

9. Baylor University, *Mission Statement*, 1994.

10. David J. O'Brien, *From the Heart of the American Church: Catholic Higher Education and American Culture* (Maryknoll, N.Y.: Orbis Books, 1994), 104.

11. O'Brien, *From the Heart*, 104.

12. Ibid.

13. Ibid.

14. Paul C. Reinert and Paul Shore, "The Catholic University's Recognition of Mystery" *America* 172, no. 19 (May 27, 1995): 19.

15. Ibid., 20.

16. For a discussion of the origins of Jesuit education, see John W. O'Malley, S.J., *The First Jesuits* (Cambridge, Mass.: Harvard University Press, 1993), 200–242.

17. Patrick H. Byrne, "Paradigms of Justice and Love," *Conversations* (Spring 1995): 17.

18. Karl Rahner, S.J., *Ignatius of Loyola* (London: Collins, 1978), 16.

19. Ronald Modras, "The Spiritual Humanism of the Jesuits," *America* (February 4, 1995): 32.

20. Alexis de Toqueville, *Democracy in America* (New York: Colonial Press, 1899), 320.

21. The author is grateful to Mary Lou Connelly, Lynne M. McNamee, Robert R. Newton, and Margaret H. Preston for a number of useful comments.

19

Aiming High

Reflections on Buckley's Theorem on Higher Education

– FREDERICK G. LAWRENCE –

The U.S. Catholic University

In an article entitled "The Vatican and American Catholic Higher Education," Fr. Theodore Hesburgh, former president of the University of Notre Dame, said:

> What Europeans find hard to believe, because it is contrary to all their experience, is that most of our Catholic colleges were not founded by the hierarchy, but by religious orders of men and women; that they are not funded by the church or state, but privately by tuition, gifts, and grants; that religious and bishops do not govern most of our Catholic colleges and universities, but lay boards do, and that these lay boards will observe the university requirements whatever is said by others. The terrible basic dilemma is that the best Catholic universities are being asked to choose between being real universities and being really Catholic when, in fact, they are already both.[1]

Being a "real university" in the modern American context refers to the university form of organization as an internally differentiated complex that enables all the dimensions of science and scholarship and academic learning processes, including: (1) the training of future scientists and scholars; (2) preparation for academic professions; (3) participation in the processes of general education: (a) cultural transmission and cultural self-understanding; (b) social integration and the transmission of professional and specialized training and competencies; (c) formation of public opinion and consensus.[2]

The American university in its present state of cultural and social differentiation is an institution removed from the tutelage of religion and government. So-called private or church-affiliated universities are also independent of the state. Moreover, until the last twenty-five years, even publicly funded universities were free, at least to some extent, from societal imperatives to satisfy the desire of bourgeois society for saleable knowledge to "apply" productively in the manufacture of goods and services. The pressures of marketing and marketable skills in a globalized economy[3] are rapidly eroding this (in the classical sense) liberal[4] dimension of U.S. higher education.

The American university presupposes the institutional separation of state and church and the application to the U.S. context (via John Stuart Mill) of the continental university ethos of *Lernfreiheit und Lehrfreiheit* as first articulated in Germany by Wilhelm von Humboldt.[5] We call the theoretical and legal basis for the independence enjoyed by the "real university" in America (both from state control and to a great extent from official church authority) "academic freedom." The significance of this phrase was in part articulated in the 1982 *Recommended Institutional Regulations on Academic Freedom and Tenure* by the American Association of University Professors to the effect that a "college or university is a marketplace of ideas, and it cannot fulfill its purpose of transmitting, evaluating, and extending knowledge if it requires conformity with any orthodoxy of content and method."[6]

Hence if we allow Fr. Hesburgh's claim that American Catholic universities and colleges are "really universities," this means that Catholic universities are composed predominantly of lay professionals who employ the same methods and norms in their teaching and research as their counterparts in secular universities. For the most part, they are engaged in the pursuit of knowledge in autonomous spheres independent of any overall "Catholic position."[7] If Catholic colleges started out as places where Catholic youth could be cloistered for four years from the ways of the world and given a demonstration of the workability of Catholic doctrinal and ethical principles, in order to send them out ready to pay tribute to Caesar without losing their soul (to paraphrase a *Religious Bulletin* from Notre Dame in 1928),[8] that is no longer their ambition. Instead they are places of research and teaching which try with more or less success to join science and scholarship to general education. In an age of increasing differentiation (not to say fragmentation) of scientific and scholarly disciplines, what is meant by an "educated person" in these places is usually left up to faculty departments whose specialized approaches make up the content of the CORE curriculum of required courses. If cultural and social integration occur almost accidentally in the curriculum, rather than self-consciously or intentionally — and still less, paternalistically (as was the case until the early 1940s) — this does not differ appreciably from what generally happens in secular colleges and universities.

Fr. Hesburgh's statement above implies that American Catholic colleges and universities have not only been real universities but "really Catholic" as well. Some would argue that what is happening under the veil of freedom of research is the indoctrination of undergraduate stu-

dents against received Catholic teachings without the church's position
ever being being presented in its integrity; or, if it is presented, it is by
professors who no longer believe in the church and its doctrines.[9] While
it cannot be denied that this does occur, I would be hesitant to say that
Fr. Hesburgh's statement is patently false. Neither Fr. Hesburgh's complacency nor many of the standard alarms being raised do justice to the
complexity of the American academic situation.

In order to begin to comprehend this complexity, it is important to
recall that rather than a traditional society that has evolved toward liberalism, as was more the case for Europe's constitutional monarchies,
in the U.S. we have a republic self-consciously founded to incorporate
freedom. Still, however secularist or agnostic the liberal theories underlying it may have been, the American foundation was at least partly
couched in religious terms. For instance the key phrase from our Declaration of Independence, "created equal by nature and nature's God,"
appeals in neutral terms to the idea of creation, which is not demon-
strable by unaided reason, but only known to revealed faith. Again, the
U.S. disestablishment did not originally bring along with it that laicist
and anti-clerical animus associated with the advent of liberal states in
Europe. There is a space for the social and cultural effectiveness of religion, despite the juridical disestablishment of all churches and sects. In
the measure that Christian denominations manifest a social and cultural
vitality, even the restrictions ensuring academic freedom and protect-
ing against discrimination on purely religious grounds in universities
founded under denominational auspices historically have not kept university personnel (faculty and administrators) from actively espousing
Christian and Catholic meanings and values and promoting them by
policy, word, and, deed.

Let us use a document entitled "The Catholic University in the Modern World" by the International Federation of Catholic Universities to
spell out in an uncontroversial way the essential characteristics defining
what might be meant by Fr. Hesburgh's expression, "really Catholic":

> (1) a Christian inspiration not only of individuals but of the university
> community as such; (2) a continuing reflection in the light of the Catholic
> faith upon the growing treasury of human knowledge, to which it seeks
> to contribute by its own research; (3) fidelity to the Christian message
> as it comes to us through the church; and (4) an institutional commit-
> ment to the service of the people of God and of the human family in their
> pilgrimage to the transcendental goals which give meaning to life.[10]

As this makes altogether clear, a university can be "really Catholic" even
if it is not under official canonical jurisdiction.

If we understand "real university" and "really Catholic" in the ways
specified above, therefore, we may take Fr. Hesburgh to be claiming that

in at least some of the Catholic institutions of higher learning in the U.S. there are embodied both rigorous and honest unfolding of human inquiry without obscurantism or superstition, and the fulfillment of those four essentials of Catholic universities listed above. Whatever may be factually true, in principle there is no incompatibility between those four essential characteristics of a Catholic university and the root of academic freedom in the pure, detached, unrestricted desire to know. Indeed, if grace does heal and perfect nature, a genuinely Catholic university context should increase the chances for authentic academic freedom.

In fact, however, academic freedom often is not interpreted in light of such a sublime Christian intellectualism. The Roman Catholic Church has not finished making the transition from the heavily juridical and sovereignty-oriented ecclesiological emphases of the church in reaction to the Reformation and the Enlightenment in a smooth and frictionless manner.[11] As a result, the concrete truthfulness of Fr. Hesburgh's sanguine claim about American Catholic colleges and universities is a quite contingent matter, and fraught with exquisite tensions and difficulties.

Buckley's Theorem on Higher Education

I would like to consider these tensions and difficulties in the light of Michael J. Buckley's refreshing reflection on Catholic higher education in his Georgetown paper published in the wake of *Ex Corde Ecclesiae* in *America* magazine under the title "The Catholic University and Its Inherent Promise."[12] At the heart of this paper is a theorem that offers us a principle for a Catholic vision of the university:

> The fundamental proposition of the Catholic university is that the religious and the academic are intrinsically related. What does this mean?
>
> Any movement toward meaning and truth is inchoatively religious.... The dynamism inherent in all inquiry and knowledge, if not inhibited, is toward ultimacy, toward a completion in which an issue or its resolution finds place in a universe that makes final sense, i.e., in the self-disclosure of God — the truth of the finite. At the same time, the tendencies of faith are inescapably toward its own self-possession in knowledge. If allowed their true development, the religious intrinsically involves the academic, and the academic intrinsically involves the religious — granted that this development is de facto always imperfectly realized at best or even seriously frustrated.[13]

Buckley's breath of fresh air has to be set in the context of the tale told by George M. Marsden's book, *The Soul of the American University*.[14] It is a compelling history of the American academy whose drift is conveyed by its subtitle: *From Protestant Establishment to Established Nonbelief*. It tells us in breathtaking detail why it is that Buckley's theorem is not likely to get a serious hearing in the future policies and plans of American Catholic church-affiliated institutions of higher learning.

Marsden's tale is driven by modernity, which I understand to be the massive effective history brought about in Western culture by the Machiavellian twist given to the scientific revolution by the great early modern thinkers, Thomas Hobbes, René Descartes, Francis Bacon, Baruch Spinoza, and John Locke.[15] On this interpretation of the term, a first concern of modernity stems from Machiavelli's decision to pay attention only to "effectual truth."[16] Following the Florentine's teaching about *fortuna* and *virtu,* knowledge was to be reoriented toward power: in Bacon's formulation, science "in the relief of Man's estate"; and in the sixth part of Descartes's *Discourse on Method,* making man "the master and possessor of nature."

Modernity's famous "prejudice against prejudice" reoriented knowledge from the disinterested quest for the truth for its own sake to the acquisition of power in the sense of manipulative control. The Royal Academy of Science attempted to counter the verbalisms of scholasticism by ruling out any question or distinction that could not be settled by an *experimentum crucis* in the realm accessible to the senses. An empiricist version of what was taken to be the Newtonian method of science was installed as the only valid method of arriving at truth. Michael Buckley has masterfully depicted this cultural reorientation whose effects range from the deism of Descartes and Locke to the atheism of Holbach and LaMettrie.[17] He has also clarified how exclusive attention to instrumental reason went hand in hand with the denial of the cognitive value of religious experience.

This exclusive preoccupation with knowledge as power gravitates against the central argument of Michael Buckley's theorem that intelligent and critical inquiry is integral to the life of Christian faith, and that the supreme principle of intelligibility, truth, and goodness lies within the proper scope of the university's inquiry. Buckley would be the first to admit that his theorem belongs to "the ongoing tradition of questions and axioms"[18] specific to premodern philosophy and theology which grew out of the medieval equilibrium between Christian faith and Western culture. Catholic Christianity integrated the human spirit into the drama of creation, fall, and redemption within the real universal community of the church. It entered into a vital synthesis with the Greek noetic differentiation of theory — Aristotle's *episteme* — and with the genius of the Roman *imperium* for practical administration and law. As long as that equilibrium lasted, the church was "the superior civilizing force of Christian mankind,"[19] and so was the most impressive expression of supra-ethnic and transpolitical universality in the West. But this dynamic premodern synthesis of Jerusalem's *sacerdotium,* Athens's *studium,* and Rome's *imperium* has been dissolving for seven centuries with the breakdown of empire from 1300 to 1500, the prevalence of nominalism and the scientific revolution from 1500 to 1700, and the emergence and growing dominance of historical science and the critical retrieval of sacred texts, church history, and the history of dogma over against the church's authoritative interpretation of the truth of faith from the eighteenth century until the present.[20]

Consequently, for some time Christianity has ceased to play the role of the dominant civilizing force in Western culture. I take this to be the gravamen of Marsden's phrase "established nonbelief." Although Buckley's theorem is as normatively true now as it ever was, the facts of history have been rendering it an abstract velleity. I think that this is what David J. O'Brien was trying to get at in his response to Buckley;[21] and in his recent book, *From the Heart of the American Church: Catholic Higher Education and American Culture.*[22] But my analysis of what this means differs in many ways from O'Brien's.

In the measure that U.S. Catholic universities have followed or are following the pattern set by their Protestant counterparts,[23] Buckley's ideal flies in the face of the realities of Catholic higher education today. I think the critical mass of teachers and scholars in U.S. Catholic colleges and universities are already wedded to the empiricist interpretation of knowledge claims and committed to the cultural order sponsored by instrumental rationality — the managerial ethos with its rationalized or bureaucratic legitimacy. In the social sphere they cherish that combination of negative freedom ("freedom from . . .") and individuality which Alexis de Tocqueville euphemistically named "popular sovereignty." Those faculty members in the Catholic academy who would not somehow share in the Enlightenment sentiment that we have overcome the impediments of false or superstitious beliefs and the stultifying modes of life represented by the traditional doctrines, manners, and mores of especially Catholic Christianity are few and far between. So the problem is not that the dominant intellectuals in the Catholic academy today have any cogent argument against Buckley's theorem. It is rather that, through no fault of their own perhaps, they no longer share in that same tradition of questions and axioms from which it originated, and so they have no "feel" for it.

Most of the dominant academics in Catholic colleges and universities today have themselves been educated in a desacralized culture and society under the auspices of a secularist interpretation that begins to approach the "laicist" spirit of modernity. According to this spirit, as Hans Blumenberg has phrased its main thrust, modernity's humane self-affirmation entails surrendering illusory claims about God and about a sacred order of nature, society, and history.[24] To a like extent, this laicist spirit called forth a "clericalist" reaction (e.g., Joseph DeMaistre [1752–1821], Juan Donoso Cortes [1809–53], Joseph de Bonald [1754–

1840]) that favored resacralization and the restoration of the medieval synthesis of Jerusalem, Athens, and Rome.

As a prime example of the church's difficulties in relation to modernity, Robert Bellarmine, S.J., who formulated a theology of the church as a religious organization in the modern sense, tried to be the soul of enlightenment in his personal handling of the *cause célèbre* of Galileo Galilei and failed.[25] Within the dialectical tension between laicist progressives and clericalist reactionaries, neither he nor anybody else could save the church from "the stigma of obscurantism and the stigma of a force which opposes the freedom of scientific inquiry" still associated with it "even today, after the church has made its peace with science."[26]

In the wake of these stigmas, the intrinsic link between faith seeking understanding and understanding seeking the fullness of intelligibility and truth is almost always going to be misunderstood today. The stigma becomes socially and culturally effective in terms of a slur: "faith seeking understanding" and any university policy encouraging it are regularly misconstrued — even by Catholic interpreters — as an option for "sectarian fideism." Since the red thread running through Marsden's valuable book shows "faith" or "religion" always being understood in a *sectarian* sense, it supplies a historical demonstration of this tendency.[27]

Simply to aver that sectarian fideism has nothing whatsoever to do with what Buckley means by faith or religion within the tradition of questions and axioms to which he appeals does not help matters sufficiently. With the polarization of that tradition into the laicist and clericalist dialectic, the great law of dialectics holds sway, namely, that one holding a true position will always be construed as being in the counterposition opposed to that of the interlocutor. Thus, in the Platonic dialogues Socrates is always treated as a Sophist by the common man on the street, and as a common man on the street by the Sophist.

The main tendency is for academic freedom to be interpreted even by Catholic faculty and administration in terms of the anti-religious animus behind the idea of freedom as articulated in the context of the scandalous wars of religion. Hobbes and his liberal followers taught that no one is a more trustworthy judge in matters which concern oneself than that individual self, which runs contrary to the ancient advice, *nemo judex in causa sua*. But as Montesquieu, de Tocqueville, and the authors of the recently influential book *Habits of the Heart* have made plain, atomistic liberalism leads to the dissolution of civic liberty because it erodes all the many nonpolitical social and cultural conditions that make democratic liberty concretely possible. Be that as it may, on the anti-religious or laicist construal of academic freedom, free research and teaching would have to exclude the possibility that intellectual probity and taking the church's teaching office seriously can be compatible with each other: no one can be academically free and faithful to the teaching authority of the church. Of course, those who have been social-ized and acculturated into this "take" on academic freedom are more or less unaware of the Enlightenment epistemology at the basis of such an interpretation, and so assume, as David O'Brien himself seems to do,[28] that we have to choose between freedom and intellectual probity on the one hand, and fidelity to the church on the other.

The situation's opacity is enhanced by what we may call clericalist Catholics who also suppose that this is the only possible interpretation of academic freedom. They realize the threat to any kind of orthodoxy explicit in it. Their defensiveness is heightened when they see open hiring policies dominated by a majority prejudice against competent scholars who take their Christian commitment seriously. Then their way of dis-cussing and dealing with the threat furnishes further evidence motivating that majority prejudice. In an unfortunate way their behavior may begin to fulfill the criteria for what Ernst Troeltsch categorized as sectarian.[29]

It is important to emphasize that both the clericalizing sectarians and their laicizing opponents tend to be voluntarists[30] who couch the issues in terms of a power struggle in which academic freedom is deemed ir-reconcilable with commitment to the teachings of a faith community. In the conflict, the clericalist sectarians may present themselves as abusers of civility, and since by the time they start "making trouble," they have lost all significant power, their behavior tends to strengthen the laicist secularizers and to make it even less probable that a true understanding of academic freedom could prevail. Any attempt like Buckley's to show the intrinsic connection between the academic and the religious may be labeled as sectarian and so get marginalized.

In the context of the laicist/clericalist dialectic the construction of Buckley's theorem in sectarian terms will turn it into an authoritarian proposition regarding the whole of reality. Such a move runs counter to the modes of knowing characterized by Ernest Gellner as the commonly assumed modern and enlightened standpoint which has been institution-alized in the procedures of teaching, research, promotion, and tenure in today's university — "specialization, atomization, instrumental ra-tionality, independence of fact and value, growth and provisionality of knowledge."[31] We have to face the fact that in U.S. Catholic colleges and universities, the wrongly construed idea of academic freedom has also been institutionalized in terms of positivist conceptions of scientific and scholarly methods and norms. The codewords for this positivism, the so-called fact/value distinction, enforce a notion of "value-freedom" which not only pretends to neutralize values, but to relegate them to the realm of the irrational and the arbitrary.

We also have to face the fact that the postmodern or post-Enlightenment reaction to this pretense of "value-freedom" expands positivism into historicism and relativism: there are no facts, but only value-laden interpretations, or assertions backed by more or less power; the putative devotion to the truth is just a cover for racist, classist, or gender-based bias. When the business of the university becomes the "social construction of reality" in this sense, then what Buckley's theorem implies about truth is considered to be either a cover for another agenda or naively beside the point. Then the university becomes an arena for deliberate, organized bias. This is seen in the contemporary trend toward the politicization of academic discourse, as in the entire discussion of and implementation of so-called "political correctness."

It remains that these clericalist sectarian readings of "faith seeking understanding" and laicist anti-sectarian readings of academic freedom are actually subverted by Buckley's theorem. In principle, it articulates an ideal related to the open and conversational nature of the university as the institutionalized form of *studium*. It does not state or advocate a sectarian or dogmatic imposition upon the university, but rather implies a commitment to comprehensive openness entailed by both the university's noble birthright of academic freedom rightly understood, and the universalist ideal of Catholic Christianity.[32] Buckley would agree, this is the *Sitz im Leben* for authentic academic freedom.[33]

The American Political Context for University and Church

A second concern of modernity was to separate the public exercise of power and the law from all opinion about human nature, and in the first place this meant religious and especially Catholic opinion or belief. According to the political philosophies of Hobbes, Spinoza, and Locke, the exercise of power may be regarded as legitimate only if it is based on the voluntary and "rational" consent of those who will be governed by it.

Michael Buckley's application of an essentially medieval theorem to the modern Catholic university is reminiscent of the way John Courtney Murray, S.J., argued in the 1950s that modernity's separation of political power from religious authority is a valid application of Catholic Christianity's time-honored Gelasian conception of the relationship between the spiritual and temporal spheres: "Two there are." At the time of *We Hold These Truths* (1960),[34] Murray thought that the church's ancient prerogative of *libertas ecclesiae* was fully respected in the modern American system of religious disestablishment. The modern church is free to exercise its authority socially and publicly, but not politically, in accord with the distinction between the public order and the common good.[35]

According to Murray, the public order sets the conditions of civil liberty and equality before the law. The properly political sphere of the state or government has direct charge of this public order, and so legitimately wields public power in order to safeguard and promote it. Public order, then, is comprised of life, liberty, and the pursuit of property, which are social conditions for the individual and communal pursuit of the common good. The common good is a broader domain, of which public order is a subordinate part. It is comprised by the substantive ends, goods, or values of a society, which moderns like Hobbes, Spinoza, and Locke regarded as intrinsically controversial, and so causes of civil war; or, in the language of Madison's tenth *Federalist*, were the source of "factions." Nevertheless, Murray insists that the historical unfolding of the common good also occurs in the public sphere where the church and other subsidiary or voluntary associations function without the right to exercise direct political power; instead, they may wield the power of persuasion in order to influence public opinion directly; and they may thereby influence political power only indirectly.

Murray (and I suppose Buckley) would agree with Madison's idea that the chief intent of the Framers of the U.S. Constitution in separating church and state institutionally was not the privatization of religion, but only its disestablishment. Consequently, disestablishing any denomination or sect from the position of the official religion of the state is not the same as banishing religion altogether from the public sphere. Murray would insist that this is not possible if human beings are social and political by nature anyway. And indeed a case can be made that history has shown to some degree the concrete validity of James Madison's hunch that "religion and government will both exist in greater purity, the less they are mixed together."

I would argue that, like Buckley's theorem, Murray's theory has a normative validity. But as Murray came to see during and after the Second Vatican Council (roughly, from 1964 onward), that theory was based on a juridical or *de jure* view of social and cultural reality.[36] In the end, therefore, that theory is too abstract, and it has to be replaced by a more concrete, historically conscious perspective.[37]

Once we adopt a historically conscious perspective on the concrete reality of American pluralism, we see that the historical effect of disestablishment has also been what liberation theologians have called the privatization of religion and so of religious discourse and practice. The point of separating the publicly authorized use of power from religious opinion by the device of the institutional separation of church and state was to relegate the free exercise of religion to the private sphere of society in accord with the major liberal distinction between state and society as roughly coordinate with public and private spheres.

Hence, just as in U.S. higher education the socialization and acculturation of the vast majority of faculty members even in church-affiliated schools has yielded the virtual dominance of the anti-religious or laicist interpretation of academic freedom, so the American regime of disestablishment has had its own effect.[38] According to Johann Baptist Metz,

"In the Christianity of our time, the messianic religion of the bible has
largely become 'bourgeois' religion." As Metz explains:

> Under the cloak of "bourgeois" religion there is a wide split within the
> church between the messianic virtues of Christianity that are publicly pro-
> claimed and ecclesiastically prescribed and believed in (repentance and
> discipleship, love and acceptance of suffering) and the actual value struc-
> tures and aims of "bourgeois" practice (autonomy, property, stability,
> success). Among the priorities of the gospel, the priorities of "bourgeois"
> life are actually practiced. Under the appearance of the belief in repen-
> tance and the belief in discipleship, the "bourgeois" subject is set up —
> with an absence of contradiction that even it finds uncomfortable — with
> its interests and its own future.[39]

If Metz is right about our society, the ancient view of law as educa-
tive sheds more light on our concrete situation than the modern view
of law as a tool of power. Although in liberal democracy government's
role is to refrain from directly imposing any religious body's prescribed
ends on the public order, in the educational role that they necessarily
play, the laws of the state still espouse and to some degree sponsor
what since Rousseau have been called "bourgeois" meanings and values.[40] This influence is generalized and affects the life of the churches
under liberal democratic regimes: comfortable self-preservation is the
only public norm, and free choice is restricted only by the laws of the
market and of competition and the functional commands built into the
bureaucratic administration business requires. Deprived of public authority, religion is free to "market" its opinions to individuals who are
free to "buy" them or not. Apart from the most vulgar examples of
so-called TV evangelism, the language of "sensible" church fund-raising
or tithing campaigns shows just how true this is. It is not too different with the advertising used in college recruiting by church-affiliated
schools. In short, Metz's contrast of "bourgeois" religion and messianic
Christianity does not grow out of some nostalgia for the halcyon days
of medieval Christianity, but is a prophetic theological critique of what
has happened to Christianity in modern times.

These less than salutary effects of the privatization of religion accompanying disestablishment seem to fall beyond the purview of Courtney
Murray's analysis of church-state relations, in spite of its sensitivity to
the juridical opening left for churches to exercise direct public influence and indirect political influence. This has inspired a prize-winning
essay by Michael J. Baxter, "Writing History in a World Without
Ends" — a stunning critique of recent American Catholic historiogra-
phy.[41] Baxter claims that Murray's theory of the separation of church
and state supplies, "albeit in different ways," the underpinning for what
he calls "Americanist" historical constructions by such renowned American Catholic church historians as John Tracy Ellis, Jay Dolan, and

David O'Brien. In my opinion, Baxter relies too heavily on Donald Pelotte's interpretation of Murray's position,[42] which, on Baxter's rendition of it at least, does not grasp correctly the significance of Murray's distinction between public order and common good. Baxter also clarifies his own rendering of Murray's theoretical and historical defects by contrasting them with what he mistakenly takes to be the normative Christian position represented by John Milbank's Augustinianism in the influential *Theology and Social Theory*.[43] If I disagree with Baxter's failure to make the best of Murray on his own terms, I wonder if he is not correct about the role that a probably truncated version of Murray's theory played in the uncritical telling of American Catholic history by the Americanists. Similarly, if I disagree with much in what he conceives of as "Evangelical Catholic" underpinnings, I think there is something terribly right about his critical historical stance toward Americanist histories of Catholicism which "have constructed a world that mirrors the so-called 'real world' of U.S. politics; a world that separates religion and politics and relegates them to separate spheres"; and in doing so, these histories have helped to "establish a protocol in which substantive religious beliefs and practices are marginalized, if not altogether banished, as a way to make peace in a pluralistic setting."[44]

Baxter's critique, he tells us, is an application to the Catholic case of a heuristic thesis proposed by Hayden White in the article entitled, "The Politics of Interpretation: Discipline and Desublimation"[45] about academic history in general. What White says about the disciplining of historical imagination generally, and what Baxter says in terms of American Catholic historical imagination in particular are illustrations of the pervasive social and cultural effects of the liberal democratic regime that I believe will condition the reception of Michael Buckley's theorem about Catholic higher education.

In what follows, I would like to present my framework for analysis and a diagnosis of the situation of American Catholic higher education under the rubric of the politicization of university and church discourse. I will try to take seriously the concrete conditions for the reception of Michael Buckley's theorem on academy and religion.

A Conversational Framework for Analysis and Diagnosis

I believe that an adequate analysis will have to start from a notion of the already mentioned three foundations of order in Western civilization: *imperium, sacerdotium,* and *studium:*

Imperium refers to the domain of publicly authorized use of power, administration, law, military forces, armaments, etc. In the context of liberal democracy it is roughly coordinate with the state as distinct

FREDERICK G. LAWRENCE

from society; and it is concerned with public order in Murray's sense of the term.

Sacerdotium I take to mean the publicly lived answer to the questions, What do people look up to? What do they bow down to? precisely as it is formally or informally institutionalized in churches, denominations, or sects, but also in the form of civil religion, the manners and mores de Tocqueville called "habits of the heart."

By *studium* I understand chiefly the philosophical-theological justification for the given society's concrete solutions to *imperium* and *sacerdotium*. It is attained through the human investigation and interpretation of the cosmic Word in natural and human sciences, and of the revealed Word in theology. *Studium* is the organ for the transmission of civilization and culture in a society that is institutionalized in the form of schools, universities, etc.[46]

Since Machiavelli's revolution the theme of political theory has been not virtue in the premodern sense but power and the legitimation of power. The prevailing speech about these themes is usually couched in Weberian terms. Weber's is ultimately a voluntarist formulation that ends up reducing the legitimation of power once again to power. This formulation is absurd and gravitates against the noble American experiment of "government by reflection and choice instead of by accident and force." I would like to change the terms of the talk about legitimation to something at once more reasonable and more verifiable in reality by simply stating and not arguing that the real legitimation of power occurs not by power but by authentic human conversation,[47] a term that I will try to analyze more fully.

If we start to rethink taken-for-granted terms of political discourse in conversational terms, we can begin to conceive of both the church and the university as quintessentially organs of conversation, not of power. Both the church and the university are privileged organs of what in Germany has been called *Dauerreflektion*.[48] What does this mean? If we think of society as a set of meanings and values immanent in a people's way of life, then culture can be distinguished from society or civilization as reflection on the society's meanings and values: Do they hold water? Are they really worthwhile? In this sense then we may think of the church and the university as organs of culture, locales in which people are led to think critically about their ways of living, perhaps even in the light of eternity.

The state as the organ for the publicly authorized use of power may be rethought in conversational terms as well. Then we can restore its properly political aspect as the representative institution that through deliberation mediates between the social or civilizational dimensions of society and the cultural dimensions. Conceived in this way, political institutions integrate concrete possibilities in the economic order; in turn, the economic order integrates all the resources for capital formation and for the standard of living made available by current technology.[49]

Prior to being an exercise of publicly authorized power, however, the political order mediates policies and plans based on decisions. But when conceived in conversational terms, politics is not just "decisionist." Relevant decisions must be based on informed judgments; hence the need for deliberation. Informed judgments have to be based on verified insights; hence the need for reflection. But reaching verified insights depends on asking all the relevant questions; and this in turn depends upon people's basic openness or closedness. This is the crucial point, because a person's basic openness or closedness depends on the presence or absence in his or her life of religious, moral, and intellectual conversion.[50] Political scientists today generally fail to realize that the ambiguities of the political sphere, and so the ambiguities of power, ultimately reduce to the presence or absence of the conversions in personal and communal life. Both the ambiguity of power and politics, and the pejorative sense of "politicization" are rooted in presence or absence of basic conversions. But they are also correlated with the ambiguities of conversation and communication to which we now turn.[51]

A first type of communication may be *leisurely* and *recreational* if it is oriented toward the liberation both of our senses and of our minds and hearts; it may involve the experience of authentic ecstasy as in artistic or mystical experience; but the perversion of this kind may be termed *intoxicant* insofar as it involves the reduction of joy to fun, trivialization, or escape from reality. Intoxicant communication would include what Voegelin has described as the "magic of the extreme," as well as all forms of Pascal's *divertissement,* and addictive behavior.[52]

A second type of communication would be *pragmatic:* insofar as it involves effective acts of meaning geared toward getting things done efficiently by supplying information and issuing commands. The perversion of this type would be *strategic* or *manipulative* communication inasmuch as it is bent on destroying the conditions for the full exercise of personal responsibility on the part of one's interlocutors by keeping from them the requisite knowledge and power to decide for themselves. A lot of advertising and propaganda of any kind would be examples of this.

A third type of genuine communication is *substantive* or *constitutive.* It involves acts of meaning in which we make ourselves and the world we live in who and what they are to be. This is rooted in the primal theological meaning of Word, which implies that as humans we not merely have our world as worded, but we exist conversationally, as is brought out by Hölderlin's lovely poetic expression, *Das Gespräch wir sind,* The conversation that we are. The sphere of friendship, including what the classics call political friendship, epitomizes this type of communication. However, besides being well-formed, moral, and virtuous, persons as well as institutions can be deformed, immoral, evil, demonic. Unfortunately, such deformation, immorality, evil, etc. can enter into the fabric of the constitutive meaning of a culture and civilization, too, to render a society and culture pathological.[53]

The Politicization of University and Church

In the light of these analytic distinctions we can state more clearly what is meant by "politicization" in the pejorative sense. To speak of the politicization of university and church is to convey telegraphically that practices appropriate to the university and to the church are being subsumed into practices of power, so that *studium* and *sacerdotium* get reduced to *imperium,* even as the latter suffers from the increasing loss of the conversationally grounded distinction between legitimate power and sheer power. In our day this reduction is usually a function of letting the technological and the economic orders in the social sphere predominate — in accord with the so-called "bottom line" mindset — over the properly political order and the cultural spheres. When this happens, a society feels compelled to spend its entire social dividend on increased consumer production or capital formation, and the *noblesse oblige* of a cultural surplus spent on things that cannot be "used" in producing and consuming commodities tends to disappear.

Hand-in-hand with this reduction goes the overwhelming tendency in our society to reduce *constitutive* or *substantive* communication to *pragmatic* communication, which, because it is out of context, then becomes *strategic* or *manipulative.* Examples are endless: propaganda, brainwashing, public relations as deceit, advertising as temptation; insider loans and trading; the effort on the part of individuals or select groups to monopolize the public or social dividends of economic productivity, PACs, lobbyists, and so on.

This reduction of legitimate pragmatic communication to the strategic manipulation of power politics and what is euphemistically named "hardball" makes the people oppressed by it susceptible to the reduction of *recreational* or *leisurely* communication in religion, art, literature, dance, etc., to *intoxicant* communication. If "bread and circuses" are transformed into rock, drugs, and sports, the effects may be just the same. Such phenomena as schlock, kitsch, and the escapist drug culture — dope as "the opiate of the people" — introduce the major theme of the "aestheticization of politics"[54] as occurs in Nazi propaganda; or in certain techniques of Madison Avenue; or in shock tactics for the sake of shock as in the ACT UP demonstration at a recent Boston ordination ceremony.

These destructive transformations of communication are rooted in liberal democracy's penchant for turning over the normative hierarchy of human values[55] as religious, personal, cultural, and social values are reduced to the vital values of health and in general, "living by bread alone." This is what has brought about Weber's tandem of "experts without spirit or vision and voluptuaries without heart," Nietzsche's Last Man, and MacIntyre's regime of managers and therapists.[56]

In the case of the university politicization has college presidents telling incoming students that they will be taught to lead "full and productive lives," which means that they will be prepared to be good producers and consumers, period.[57] In recruiting programs universities are marketed as playgrounds for gaining the skills and rehearsing the strategies for success and winning. The goal of liberal education — which means education oriented to moral and intellectual conversion — is overshadowed by a veritable welfare state of student programs that are peripheral to actual study. The impression is given that the teaching faculty are individually contracted persons working for the administration. Deans and vice-presidents regularly refer to the president and the board of trustees as "the University," in such statements as, "The University hopes to have an athletic program of national stature"; or "The University is starting a five-year funding campaign," and so on. Again, the opportunity built into the university's very multidisciplinarity and cultural diversity for a hard-edged dialectic gives way to rhetorical moves in a power game of factions with mostly extra-academic agendas trying to gain control in a university regarded mainly as a business.

As far as the religious aims of the politicized university are concerned, the Jesus who suffered, died on a cross, and rose again to save us is rarely presented as a challenge to a radical revision of already-inculcated modern images of success. In "best-case scenarios," students may be exposed to a well-intentioned concern for social justice; but outside the context of the gracious Law of the Cross, such exposure can actually function as a new Pelagianism.[58]

As politicized in this sense the church too becomes another business for another market with another managerial bureaucracy with its "professionalized" service-purveyors.[59] To the extent that explicitly and authentically religious meanings and values do not transform our culture and civilization, they themselves are bound to be reinterpreted in terms of the prevailing meanings and values. But to mediate Christian or Catholic meanings and values into a cultural or civilizational context without being either accommodationist or triumphalist is something we have not yet learned to do regularly or well, and academic theology as presently functioning furnishes precious little help in the task.[60]

I close these reflections by pointing to the clue that may provide the key to the depoliticization of both university and church. We know from the outer Word made flesh in Christ Jesus and the inner word of the love poured out in our hearts by the Spirit who has been given to us by the Father and the Son that the mediation of religious and Christian conversion and values takes place conversationally[61] — something for which Michael J. Buckley has a unique genius.

Notes

1. See Theodore M. Hesburgh, C.S.C., "The Vatican and Catholic Higher Education," *America* (November 1, 1986): 250, 263. For a survey of the history of American Catholic higher education, see Philip Gleason, "American Catholic Higher Education: A Historical Perspective," in R. Hassenger, ed., *The Shape of Catholic Higher Education* (Chicago: University of Chicago Press, 1967), 15–53; see, too, his "American Catholic Higher Education, 1940–1980: The Ideological Context," in George Marsden, ed., *The Secularization of the Academy* (New York: Oxford University Press, 1992), 234–58.

2. For this description of the modern university, I depend on Jürgen Habermas, "The Idea of the University: Learning Processes," in Shierry Weber Nicholsen, ed. and trans., *The New Conservatism: Cultural Criticism and the Historians' Debate* (Cambridge, Mass.: MIT Press, 1989), 100–127.

3. For an acute description of the implications of economic globalization see Nicholas Boyle, "Hegel and 'The End of History,'" *New Blackfriars* 76 (March and April 1995): 109–19, 164–74. For instance: "For it is only on condition that you are accountable, that is auditable, that you are allowed to become part of the global market — and you cannot refrain from becoming a part of it without withdrawing from economic life altogether. If you are paid in money, or in any of the market's products, you will eventually — it is the logic of our age — be subjected to the rule of participation in the market: that your activities be quantified, that they be broken down into measurable units, comparable with the units into which the behaviour of others, anywhere in the world, has been broken down, and that you are allowed no standing in this new world order — for standing itself has to be a quantifiable good — that is not transparently related to your performance indicator, your input-output ratio" (115).

4. See Jacob Klein, "The Idea of Liberal Education," in *Lectures and Essays*, ed. R. B. Williamson, E. Zuckerman (Annapolis, Md.: St. John's College, 1985), 157–70. Compare David J. Levy, "Education as Recollection, Encounter, and Ascent," *Modern Age* 37 (Summer 1993): 323–31.

5. See Wilhelm von Humboldt, *Über die innere und äussere Organisation der höheren wissenschaftlichen Anstalten* (1810); and John Stuart Mill, *On Liberty* (1859). For an expose of Mill's ideas on education in their dependency on and differences from von Humboldt, see F. W. Garforth, *Educational Democracy: John Stuart Mill on Education in Society* (Oxford: Hull/Oxford University, 1980).

6. *Academe* 7 (1984):1.

7. See Philip Gleason, "American Catholic Higher Education: A Historical Perspective," in R. Hassenger, ed., *The Shape of Catholic Higher Education* (Chicago: University of Chicago, 1967), 53.

8. Cited by James Heft, S.M., "Academic Freedom and the Catholic University," in J. Apczynski, ed., *Theology and the University* (Lanham, Md.: University of America Press, 1987), 216.

9. See Mark Jordan, "On Defending Catholic Higher Education in America," *Communio* 13 (1986): 259.

10. Cited in G. A. Kelly, ed., *Why Should a Catholic University Survive?* (New York: St. John's University Press, 1973), 110–29 at par. 15.

11. See Hermann Josef Pottmeyer, "Kontinuität und Innovation in der Ekklesiologie des II. Vatikanums," G. Alberigo et al., eds., *Kirche im Wandel — eine kritische Zwischenbalanz nach dem Zweiten Vatikanum* (Düsseldorf: Patmos, 1982), 89–110.

12. Michael J. Buckley, "The Catholic University and Its Inherent Promise," *America* (May 29, 1993): 14–16.

13. Ibid., 15.

14. George M. Marsden, *The Soul of the American University: From Protestant Establishment to Established Nonbelief* (New York: Oxford University, 1994).

15. In this interpretation I am following Leo Strauss, "The Three Waves of Modernity," *Political Philosophy: Six Essays by Leo Strauss,* ed. Hillel Gilden (Indianapolis: Bobbs-Merrill, 1975), 81–98. See also my articles, "Political Theology and 'the Longer Cycle of Decline,' " in *Lonergan Workshop,* ed. F. Lawrence (Missoula, Mont.: Scholars Press, 1978), 223–55; "The Horizon of Political Theology," *Trinification of the World, Festschrift* for Frederick E. Crowe, ed. T. A. Dunne and J.-M. Laporte (Toronto: Regis College Press, 1978), 46–70.

16. Niccolo Machiavelli, *The Prince,* trans. H. C. Mansfield (Chicago: University of Chicago, 1985), 61–62.

17. See Michael J. Buckley, *At the Origins of Modern Atheism* (New Haven: Yale University, 1987).

18. See Alasdair MacIntyre, *Three Rival Versions of Moral Enquiry* (London: Duckworth, 1990); and *Whose Justice? Which Rationality?* (London: Duckworth, 1988).

19. Eric Voegelin, *From Enlightenment to Revolution,* ed. John Hallowell (Durham, N.C.: Duke University, 1975), 19.

20. Ibid., 19–20.

21. See "A Collegiate Conversation: Prof. O'Brien to Father Buckley," *America* (September 11, 1993): 18–19, and "Father Buckley to Prof. O'Brien," 19–23.

22. David J. O'Brien, *From the Heart of the American Church: Catholic Higher Education and American Culture* (Maryknoll, N.Y.: Orbis Books, 1995).

23. But see George M. Marsden, "What Can Catholic Universities Learn from Protestant Examples?" in Theodore M. Hesburgh, C.S.C., ed., *The Challenge and Promise of a Catholic University* (Notre Dame, Ind.: University of Notre Dame Press, 1994), 187–98.

24. See Hans Blumenberg, *Die Legitimität der Neuzeit* (Frankfurt: Suhrkamp, 1966).

25. On Bellarmine's ecclesiology, see Joseph A. Komonchak, *Foundations in Ecclesiology,* supplementary issue of *Lonergan Workshop* 11, ed. F. Lawrence (Chestnut Hill, Mass.: Boston College, 1995), 10. On his conduct in the Galileo case, see William A. Wallace, *Galileo and His Sources: The Heritage of the Collegio Romano in Galileo's Science* (Princeton, N.J.: Princeton University, 1984).

26. Voegelin, *From Enlightenment to Revolution,* 20.

27. Michael Buckley has given a succinct description of traits associated in "the popular mind" with the term "sectarian": "There are influences within the church that would make it narrow, with carefully monitored speech and inhibited public discussion, negative in so much of its focus, harshly critical of disagreement and of attempts at nuance, increasingly demanding public protestations of loyalty and right thinking, etc." ("Father Buckley to Prof. O'Brien," *America* [September 11, 1993]: 22). "Fideism" is a technical theological term denoting the polar opposite of "rationalism," which is the exclusion of the supernatural light of faith and of belief from thought and discourse. It is the exclusion of the natural light of reason and of nature *tout court* from thought and discourse.

28. See O'Brien, "A Collegiate Conversation: Prof. O'Brien to Father Buckley," *America* (September 11, 1993): 18–19.

29. On sectarianism, see Bryan R. Wilson, *The Social Dimensions of Sectarianism: Sects and New Religious Movements in Contemporary Society* (Oxford: Clarendon, 1992 [1990]). Wilson points out the limitations of Ernst Troeltsch on sects because of having been derived from medieval instances (3). See *The Social Teaching of the Christian Churches,* trans. O. Wyon (New York: Macmillan, 1931).

30. By "voluntarist" is meant anyone who, in a vulgarization of premodern faculty psychology, valorizes the faculty of will over the faculty of intellect. They turn out to be exponents of Nietzsche's "will to power," usually quite unintentionally.

31. See Ernest Gellner, *Plough, Sword and Book* (Chicago: University of Chicago, 1978), 122.

32. For a nuanced discussion of what I mean by Christian universalism, see Frederick E. Crowe, "Lonergan's Universalist View of Religion," *Method: Journal of Lonergan Studies,* ed. P. Byrne, C. Hefling, M. Morelli, 12, no. 2 (Fall 1994): 147–79, esp. 158–63.

33. For what I take to be a true interpretation of the relationship between ecclesiastical authority and institutions of higher learning, see Ladislas Orsy, "Bishops and Universities: Dominion or Communion," *America* (November 30, 1993): 11–16.

34. John Courtney Murray, S.J., *We Hold These Truths: Reflections on the American Proposition* (New York: Sheed and Ward, 1960).

35. For a clear treatment of this distinction, see Robert W. McElroy, *The Search for an American Public Theology: The Contribution of John Courtney Murray* (New York: Paulist, 1989), especially chap. 3, "Renewing the Political Order," 77–115.

36. For the development of Murray's thought, see J. Leon Hooper, S.J., *The Ethics of Discourse: The Social Philosophy of John Courtney Murray* (Georgetown: Georgetown University Press, 1986); and his "General Introduction" in John Courtney Murray, *Religious Liberty: Catholic Struggles with Pluralism,* ed. J. Leon Hooper (Louisville: Westminster/John Knox Press, 1993), 11–48.

37. See John Courtney Murray, S.J., "Old Things and New in *Pacem in Terris,*" *America* (April 27, 1963): 612–14, for a brief and trenchant contrast between the classicist mindset and the historically conscious one.

38. Sociologist John Donovan of Boston College reports that he has done an initial study which shows that the number of teachers at Catholic colleges and

universities who have been educated in the Catholic tradition is surprisingly low and decreasing swiftly.

39. Johann Baptist Metz, "Messianic or 'Bourgeois' Religion?" in Johann Baptist Metz and Jürgen Moltmann, *Faith and the Future: Essays on Theology, Solidarity, and Modernity,* ed. F. Schüssler Fiorenza (Maryknoll, N.Y.: Orbis Books, 1995), 17, 20; see also his "Theology in the Modern Age, and before its End," 30–39.

40. For trenchant reflections on this see Pierre Manent, "The Modern State," in Mark Lilla, ed., *New French Thought: Political Philosophy* (Princeton, N.J.: Princeton University, 1994), 123–33. A further meditation on this theme carried out in terms of Alexis de Tocqueville's analysis may be found in Ernest L. Fortin, "Pros and Cons of Disestablishment: Did the Separation of Church and State Benefit Religion?" *Crisis* 13 (April 1995): 23–27.

41. Michael J. Baxter, "Writing History in a World without Ends: A Critique of Three Histories of Catholicism in the United States," paper presented to the College Theology Society, Annual Convention, Holy Cross College, Worcester, Mass., June 3, 1995. The author, a graduate student at Duke University, was granted the award for the best paper by a graduate student. I refer to a typescript given me by Prof. Thomas Wangler of the Boston College Theology Department.

42. See Donald E. Pelotte, *John Courtney Murray: Theologian in Conflict* (New York: Paulist Press, 1976).

43. See John Milbank, *Theology and Social Theory: Beyond Secular Reason* (Cambridge, Mass.: Basil Blackwell, 1990). Milbank's book is brilliant in its dismantling of the secularist presuppositions of modern social sciences and in its presentation of postmodern positions. My sense is that he gives an anachronistically Augustinian reading of developments in modern Roman Catholic theology and adopts for himself an anachronistic Augustinian position propped on an almost postmodern and highly speculative retrieval of Augustine's reflections on music. I do not see how Baxter can characterize his position as "Augustinian/Thomist," for it turns out to be fideist in a quite Barthian manner.

44. See the final section of Baxter, "Writing History in a World without Ends."

45. This essay appears in Hayden White, *The Content of Form* (Baltimore: Johns Hopkins University Press, 1987).

46. Thinking about *studium* in a manner adequate to the contemporary issues of what may be termed education for the masses, the new learning, and specialization within the context of the concrete human good calls for a full-blown philosophy of education whose essential dimensions are limned in Bernard Lonergan, *Topics in Education,* Collected Works of Bernard Lonergan 10, ed. R. Doran and F. Crowe (Toronto: University of Toronto Press, 1993).

47. For suggestive remarks on distinguishing legitimacy this way, see Bernard Lonergan, "Dialectic of Authority," *A Third Collection: Papers by Bernard J. F. Lonergan, S.J.,* ed. F. E. Crowe (New York: Paulist Press, 1985), 5–12.

48. At an earlier stage of his political theology in the 1960s, J. B. Metz picked up this term from German sociologist Helmut Schelsky. However, the distinction between the "social" and the "cultural" used here is from Bernard Lonergan, "The Absence of God in Modern Culture," *A Second Collection,* ed. W. F. Ryan and B. Tyrrell (Philadelphia: Westminster Press, 1974), 102, 115.

49. On the political order as integrating the economic, and the economic as integrating the technological, see Bernard Lonergan, *Insight: A Study in Human*

Understanding, Collected Works of Bernard Lonergan 3, ed. F. E. Crowe and R. M. Doran (Toronto: University of Toronto, 1992), 132–34, 138–39.

50. On conversion and the distinctions among intellectual, moral, and religious conversion, see Bernard Lonergan, *Method in Theology* (New York: Herder and Herder, 1972), 241–43, and passim.

51. For a fuller treatment of the analytic framework that follows, see my "Lonergan's Foundations for Constitutive Communication," in *Lonergan Workshop* 10, *The Legacy of Lonergan,* ed. F. Lawrence (Chestnut Hill, Mass.: Boston College, 1994), 229–77.

52. See Eric Voegelin, "Wisdom and the Magic of the Extreme: A Meditation," in *Published Essays 1966–1985,* Collected Works of Eric Voegelin 12, ed. Ellis Sandoz (Baton Rouge: Louisiana State University, 1990), 315–75.

53. My distinctions among (1) recreational-leisurely/intoxicant, (2) pragmatic/strategic-manipulative, and (3) constitutive/self-destructive communication were inspired by a similar tripartite set of distinctions made by Eric Voegelin in "Necessary Bases for Communication," in R. C. Seitz et al., eds., *Problems of Communication in a Pluralistic Society* (Milwaukee: Marquette University Press, 1968), 53–66.

54. See Saul Friedlaender, *Reflections on Nazism: An Essay on Kitsch and Death,* trans. Thomas Weyr (New York: Harper and Row, 1984); Glenn Hughes and Sebastian Moore, "Affirmation of Order: Therapy for Modernity in Bernard Lonergan's Analysis of Judgment," in *Lonergan Workshop* 8, ed. F. Lawrence (Atlanta: Scholars Press, 1990), 109–33.

55. On the normative hierarchy of values see Lonergan, *Method in Theology,* 31–32.

56. See Alasdair MacIntyre, *After Virtue: A Study in Moral Theory* (Notre Dame, Ind.: University of Notre Dame Press, 1981).

57. See the analysis by Mark Schwehn, "The Academic Vocation: 'Specialists without Spirit, Sensualists without Heart,'" *Cross Currents* 42 (Summer 1992): 185–99; and his little book, *Exiles from Eden: Religion and the American Vocation* (New York: Oxford University Press, 1992). Schwehn is dean of Valparaiso University's Christ College; together with Dorothy C. Bass, director of that university's Project on Education and Formation of People in Faith, he has written a review of Marsden's *The Soul of the American University:* "Christianity and Academic Soul-searching," *Christian Century* 155 (March 15, 1995): 292–95. Its tack is similar to Buckley's in that it also stresses the reciprocal role of intellectual life in communities of faith.

58. That this need not be the case is manifest in an article reflecting on experiences in Boston College's Pulse Program on the part of its founder, Patrick H. Byrne, in "Paradigms of Justice and Love," *Conversations* (Spring 1995): 5–17.

59. For a helpful view of the church in modern Western societies, see Franz-Xaver Kaufmann, "I. Kirche für die Gesellschaft von Morgen," and "II. Christentum im Westen: Spannungsfeld der Verweltlichung," in Franz-Xaver Kaufmann and Johann Baptist Metz, *Zukunftsfähigeit: Suchbewegungen im Christentum* (Freiburg: Herder, 1987), 11–90.

60. For a wrestling with the problematic in all its complicatedness see Kenneth Surin, "*Contemptus Mundi* and the Disenchanted World: Bonhoeffer's 'Discipline of the Secret' and Adorno's 'Strategy of Hibernation,'" in *The Turnings of Darkness and Light: Theological Essays* (Cambridge: Cambridge University, 1989), 180–200.

61. See my "The Human Good and Christian Conversation," in T. J. Farrell and P. Soukup, eds., *Communication and Lonergan: Common Ground for Forging the New Age* (Kansas City, Mo.: Sheed and Ward, 1993), 248–68, as well as many other of the contributions to this volume heading in the same direction.

20

Catholic Universities

A View from Christian Ethics

− LISA SOWLE CAHILL −

This essay will address the special nature of a Catholic university from the perspective of a moral theologian and feminist, one who enjoys a longstanding and rewarding association with the Society of Jesus in higher education.[1] The essay pays tribute to Michael J. Buckley, S.J., a Jesuit, theologian, and man of the church. Michael Buckley has long engaged questions of the church and culture, of belief and the intellectual life, which are constitutive dimensions of Christian ethics.[2] In his writing and teaching about spirituality and mysticism, Buckley also lays foundations in faith for Christian discipleship and social responsibility.[3] As an officer and ultimately president of the Catholic Theological Society of America, he has been a crucial mediator between the theological community and the U.S. episcopacy.[4] Negotiations between these parties have been necessary in view of directives from Rome urging bishops to assert greater control over the academic freedom of theologians, particularly their views of sexual morality and gender.

In 1992, Michael Buckley came to Boston College as director of the Jesuit Institute. The Institute's mission is to enhance the Jesuit identity of the university by sponsoring interdisciplinary research, especially on religious and ethical questions "that emerge at the intersection of faith and culture." For instance, it has supported research on AIDS and the church, technology and religion, violence against Guatemalan Indian children, social ethics and cultural pluralism, Christianity and capitalism, Nazi medicine and the Holocaust. Recently, Michael Buckley has initiated a series of lectures by women theologians.

I take my lead from Michael Buckley's roles in maintaining a dynamic connection between the ecclesial and cultural contexts of the Catholic university and in supporting critical ethical investigation within the university. The participation of the Catholic institution of higher learning in the intellectual life of its culture, its social mission, and its place within the larger church, have, of course, been much discussed over the past decade. One factor has been the declining numbers of Roman Catholic faculty and students on our campuses; another has been overtures of the institutional church attempting to certify or guarantee the orthodoxy of the Catholic faculty who remain. Influenced, perhaps by the precedent of the great medieval universities, whose integration of faith and reason, broad use of cultural learning, and unparalleled contributions to the development of theology as a science have constituted something of a base point for understanding the nature of the Catholic university, much of the discussion has focused around distinctive qualities of Catholic theological inquiry such as sacramentality, incorporation of philosophy, universalistic thrust, analogical thinking, and positive approach to tradition itself. In terms of ethics, these values have warranted and supported ecclesial and theological — and hence educational — engagement with social and political structures, manifest most strongly by the modern papal encyclical tradition.

Much of the argument emerging from within Catholic universities has taken the tack of maintaining that these distinctive qualities and values in the theological and social traditions of Catholicism demand openness to culture, academic freedom, and the integrity of intellectual inquiry in the university as pursuing thoroughly and honestly all the difficult and perplexing questions of our day. This includes morality, which seems to be the area in which pluralism is of most concern to the episcopal hierarchy. In this essay, I want to try a different though complementary approach. I will consider the relevance of biblical resources to the interrelation of university, church, and culture, with special attention to the moral mission of the Catholic university.

Scripture has not been a prominent source in recent reflections on the nature of Catholic higher education. Associated with Protestantism, and even with the distinctiveness of Christianity "over against" culture, the Bible has not played much part in understanding the distinctively *Catholic* nature of the Catholic *university*. In reality, however, engagement with culture may also be warranted biblically, as for instance, by the strong indebtedness of the Gospels of Matthew and Luke to Jewish religion and Greek philosophical ideals, respectively; and in Paul's adaptation of the gospel to the milieux of the Hellenistic cities in which he founded churches. These interactions with first-century culture were not merely one-way "translations," but two-way transfers, in which the very meaning of Jesus as the Christ was refined and reappropriated. Since the interrelating of the whole of Scripture to the whole problematic of the Catholic university would be a vast undertaking, I will concentrate on two aspects: the relation of the university to the church as Christian community, and the moral identity of the university as Christian and Catholic.

My general thesis is that the church is formed and inspired by the gospel as preached by Jesus. In his life, death, and resurrection, Jesus makes the kingdom of God present; the kingdom reverses worldly hierarchies and has radical social effects. The churches of the first Christians were local and diverse, but they shared unity in their memories of Jesus and in a moral ethos centered on mercy, forgiveness, and inclusion.

The gospel and the moral ethos it entails have implications for universities which are explicitly Christian in the Roman Catholic mode. Like other universities, Catholic universities today are interdisciplinary communities of moral discourse. But Christian institutions are informed by a special commitment to pursue questions of transcendent meaning. Catholic institutions do so in relation to the theological and ecclesial traditions of Catholicism, but, as I shall attempt to demonstrate, the Bible provides us with a pluralistic rather than a unitary model for the nature of that "relation to." Given both the pluralism of New Testament models of church and the interdisciplinary and dialectical character of scholarly inquiry, tensions in that relationship should more often be resolved communally and dialogically than juridically.

I will structure my reflections in three parts: first, the nature of Christian community with its profound moral and social implications; second, the unity and diversity in the church that results from the expression of Christian commitment in diverse historical and cultural settings; third, the place of universities within the church, understood *as* Christian community, with strong moral dimensions and healthy internal pluralism. Finally, I will take up a statement on women, drafted by Gerry O'Hanlon, S.J., dean of the Milltown Institute, Dublin, and approved by the 1995 Jesuit General Congregation. While not directed exclusively to the university setting, the statement can serve as a model for Catholic engagement with social and intellectual issues of the modern world.

Church as Moral Community

Kingdom of God and Discipleship Community

By definition, the Christian church from its earliest existence has been a community of disciples centered on Jesus. Even in view of the long and varied history of the Christian churches, and of the diverse ecclesiologies supporting them, the "basic source for the Catholic Christian's understanding of the church remains the preaching of Jesus and the New Testament."[5] Christian communal identity takes its shape from the relationship to God and to other persons mediated by Jesus Christ, a relationship centered on the symbol "kingdom of God" (Mark 1:15; cf. Luke 8:1, 16:16; Matt. 4:23), i.e., on God's inbreaking reign or rule.[6]

During his lifetime, Jesus had a reputation for unconventional status-breaking behavior, which manifested the character of life in God's kingdom. Of special note were his approach to women as hearers of his words in their own right; his inclusive table fellowship; and his healing miracles, which restored ostracized persons to their place within the social fabric.[7] Jesus undermines conventional wisdom about fitting rewards and punishments, the social importance of hierarchies and terms of exclusion, and the role of God in upholding this order and exacting conformity to it.[8] The Sermon on the Mount (Matt. 5–7; Luke 6) portrays what life under God's rule is like (Matt. 5:3, 10, 19, 20; cf. Luke 6:20). According to the Beatitudes, God's reign reverses worldly expectations and rewards, redeems the poor and exalts the lowly, blesses the persecuted, and vindicates those who have had mercy on the sufferings of others. The parables evoke unexpected intuitions of the reality of God and of God's reign (Luke 8:9-10). The disciple of Jesus is to act like the Good Samaritan who forgot longstanding enmities when he saw a wayfarer abandoned by the road, dependent on a stranger's mercy (Luke 10:29–37). The Lord's Prayer is a prayer for the coming of God's kingdom, and it concludes by commending forgiveness of others to the disciple who would be forgiven by God.

Elisabeth Schüssler Fiorenza has argued that the Jesus movement "had experienced in the praxis of Jesus" a God who, as "all-inclusive love," had called not Israel's righteous, but its "social underdogs."[9] Marcus Borg sees Jesus as establishing "a community of compassion," so that "to take Jesus seriously means to become part of such a community."[10] In this community, servanthood reaches across social boundaries.[11] The experience of God in Jesus is active, practical, and social. In the parable of the Last Judgment, the one who will inherit the kingdom gives food and drink to "one of the least of these my brethren" (Matt. 25:31–46; see also Luke 16:19–21).

In sum, then, there is a unity in the moral ethos of the kingdom or reign of God communicated through the pluralism of New Testament memories of Jesus. However, the moral orientation of Jesus does not focus on the same issues that have been most controversial in establishing the Catholic identity of Catholic universities. As will be illustrated further in the next section, New Testament morality focuses on issues which belong more in the category of social justice than of sexual behavior; sexual behavior is important insofar as it exploits and dehumanizes others and disrupts community as "kingdom." Discipleship cannot be reduced to but does imply compassion for others, active solidarity in breaking down social stratifications which deprive some of the basic means of subsistence, and a special inclusive bias toward "the poor" or marginalized. Negative moral criticism is directed primarily at those who use positions of power to further exclusive hierarchies and rarely at the failings of those on the bottom rungs of the status structure.

LISA SOWLE CAHILL

Social Effects of Discipleship Community

Recent research on the social history of Palestine in Jesus' day and on the Greco-Roman culture in which early Christianity flourished suggests that communities of discipleship had radical cultural implications in at least three areas: economic relations, purity laws as defining social status, and the patriarchal family.[12] In the ancient world, economic relations were embedded in religious, political, and cultural ones, so that high or low status in one area was much more likely than today to be matched to a similar position in the others. For most people, access to material and social goods was dependent on establishing a patron-client relation to the power elites. The asymmetry of power resulted in high levels of insecurity and competition among persons of low status, and even put their survival in question. By idealizing sharing of goods across class boundaries, the early Christians challenged the economic system.

In ancient Judaism, purity laws were a way of sanctifying everyday life and of remembering and reinforcing the holiness of God's covenant people. However, purity laws could also reinforce distinctions between the elite and nonelite. Impurity could result from social occupation or physical conditions like disfigurement or disease, and sexual behavior, including menstruation and childbirth. Purity laws did not affect all Jews equally, since observance was tied primarily to Jerusalem and to the Temple cult. But they still generally helped to maintain the economic and social differences between the priestly and peasant classes.

In Greco-Roman culture, social, political, and material goods were channeled through the patriarchal family. Women were largely under the legal control of fathers and husbands and were often pawns in dynastic marriages (or divorces) engineered in order to enhance family position. The state under the Roman Empire mandated and controlled the procreation of citizens within marriage, cultivating the longevity and success of the ruling classes. By downplaying procreation, upholding fidelity and mutuality in marriage, loosening the religious control of heads of household over subordinate members, and offering virginity as an alternative to marriage, Christianity had a subversive effect on the patriarchal family as an institution of social control, especially control of women.

Some familiarity with the social history of the first Christian communities makes it possible to appreciate more clearly that the constructive engagement of Christianity with culture did not arise with Augustine, but is an important aspect of Christian origins. The social encyclical tradition, mediated through the pastoral letters of episcopal conferences around the world, advances a positive, critical, and transformative relation of the church to culture under the aegis of the common good, rights and duties, and the reasonableness of social cooperation and even a "preferential option for the poor." A New Testament perspective reveals that an activist relation of church to social structures is also implicit in the way the first Christians lived out the meaning of discipleship under the symbol "kingdom of God."

Unity and Diversity in the Church

Inculturation and Prophetic Critique

Early Christianity was not, then, on the whole sectarian. That is, it did not withdraw from the surrounding culture and religious traditions, as did the Essenes; nor did it repudiate all forms of cultural wisdom and moral value. Instead, discipleship communities, specifically as moral communities, accepted that basic cultural institutions (government, military service, household, and class-based employment) will provide the background for Christian formation and practice; saw some cultural values as compatible with Christian faith and appropriated them positively in Christian moral teaching; criticized other cultural values as inconsistent with Christian faith and with life in the kingdom; and always worked to embody a distinctively Christian way of life by "inculturating" it in a variety of geographical and social settings.

This led and still leads to unavoidable ambiguities in Christian moral identity and has created problematics which are still with us today in debates about the legitimate parameters of pluralism and the requisite degree of conformity to ideals. "The difficulty is in distinguishing relatively benign social and cultural patterns from those which endanger freedom and community in Christ."[13] The New Testament itself provides numerous examples. For instance, wealth was certainly not abandoned by all converts; Luke is concerned with the use of possessions precisely because members of his community had significant possessions of which to dispose. The phenomenon of house churches itself implies that some Christians were of sufficient means to own homes with large meetings rooms and ran households which included servants and even slaves. We have no reason to think that Jesus abandoned all purity observances himself, and Matthew's community still considered itself to be a viable and practicing extension of Judaism.[14] And even though the patriarchal household was reconstrued by Christians as having less ultimacy and more mutuality than its pagan counterparts, the *Haustafeln* (and the many feminist critiques of them) demonstrate that inculturation could bring accommodation.

Moreover, many of the critical ideals of Christianity were not absolutely unique in contrast to the culture. Purity laws were never developed in Judaism simply as a means of stratification, and the prophets had centuries ago cried out against oppression of the widow and orphan and

abominated the hypocrisy of elites for whom worship was mere ostenta-
tious status-seeking. Near the time of Jesus, women were receiving more
legal rights under Roman law, and faithful, companionate marriage had
always been admired, even if husbands were assumed to have the upper
hand. Unbridled lust was deplored and self-control praised by pagan
philosophers as well as by Christian authors. When Paul refers to nature and conscience, he is drawing on Greek philosophical traditions
extending back to Aristotle and beyond; even John's "high" christology draws on Greek philosophical conceptions of divinity, creation, and
logos. Engaging with the intellectual, religious, and cultural life of its
various neighbors brought dangers to the early Christian mission; but it
also provided elements out of which a new identity could be forged and
a language in which it could be communicated.[15]

Community as Church and Churches

The inculturation of first-century Christianity produced a number of
expressions in local churches. Diverse regional communities developed
gradually, as a result of growth, disagreements, and a mission outside
Jerusalem. They were also a response to the experiences and needs of
believers in different geographical, social, and cultural settings. It is
possible to speak of a fundamental unity among the New Testament
churches, but this unity is not juridically established. It is a unity of inspiration and experience, rooted in Jesus' proclamation of the kingdom
of God and in the confidence of post-Easter faith that God's kingdom
was and is made present in Jesus. What James D. G. Dunn calls the
"integrating center" of Christianity is the unity between the historical
Jesus and the risen and exalted Christ, along with the recognition that
the divine power which now sustained them was the Spirit of the Lord.[16]
Hence, a marked and obvious degree of pluralism exists among the local communities that embody the general meaning of church in the New
Testament period and shortly thereafter.[17] In Dunn's words, *"To recognize the canon of the NT is to affirm the diversity of Christianity."*[18]
Yet even these earliest local communities could rely on a sense of unity
which stemmed from the first Christian's self-understanding as a renewal
of Israel, the whole people of God in different times and places. Diversity and unity coexisted and were variously expressed and structured in
the "churches" as part of the "church."

In the New Testament, the term *ekklesia* appears most frequently in
the Pauline letters. It is frequently used for local Christian communities,
such as "the church of the Thessalonians" (1 Thess. 1:1), "the churches
of Galatia" (Gal. 1:1), "the church of God which is in Corinth' (1 Cor.
1:1, 2 Cor. 1:1). These local churches were constituted by even smaller
units, the house churches, which had memberships of anywhere from
ten to forty persons.[19] At the same time, *ekklesia* is used in a more gen-

eralized sense in the New Testament, as when Colossians 1:18 speaks of "the church" as the body of Christ, and Ephesians 5:25 avows that "Christ loved the Church and gave himself up for her." The word *ekklesia* appears in only one of the four gospels, Matthew. There it replicates the same ambiguity of local and general meanings found in Paul (Matt. 16:18: "Peter is the "rock upon which I will build my [entire] church"; and 18:17: the matter of a brother who refuses to be corrected is referred to "the [local] church"). Although Luke does not use the term "church," Acts does. Most references are to specific regional communities in Jerusalem (8:1), Antioch (13:1), Asia Minor (14:24), Syria and Antioch (15:41). Yet Acts 9:31 refers to "the church throughout all Judea, Galilee, and Samaria."[20]

"Thus, in tracing how Christians understood themselves as a church, one could argue for a logical progression from original unity to regional or ideological diversity and finally to universality."[21] The sense of belonging to a universal church certainly developed incrementally after the New Testament period, especially after Nicaea (325). Before that, the Roman church did not have the resources to exercise governance over other churches worldwide. The word "church" was able to refer structurally and administratively to the church universal only after Christianity became the only lawful religion of the Roman Empire in 385.[22]

New Testament Models of Church Unity and Authority

In the era immediately after the deaths of the first apostles, the era in which most of the New Testament was probably written, a diversity of church models characterized Christianity. Raymond E. Brown outlines several such models in *The Churches the Apostles Left Behind*,[23] analyzing each in terms of strengths and weaknesses. These churches vary in terms of importance of centralized structure versus dynamic flexibility, even, for instance, in traditions all deriving from Paul (the Pastoral Epistles, Colossians and Ephesians, Luke/Acts) which would have understood themselves to be in *koinonia* (communion) with each other.[24]

One community strongly emphasizing structure is that which produced the Pastoral Epistles, and its strength is "impressive stability and solid continuity designed to preserve the apostolic heritage."[25] The authors of the pastorals direct their warnings against teachers of deceptive new ideas, men who love controversies! The faithful are to be submissive to authorities, and the purveyors of innovations to be stopped from teaching (1 Tim. 1:3–4). "They must be silenced, for they are upsetting whole households by teaching for dishonest profit what they have no right to teach" (Tit. 1:11). "In the Pastorals, then, we have the ancestor of the theology of a deposit of doctrine, and such ecclesiastical developments as the approval of professors, imprimaturs, an index of forbidden books, and supervised church presses."[26] The danger here, as Brown sees it, is that measures assumed in moments of crisis become "a consistent way of life," taken out of context, and formed into "a universal and unconditioned policy."[27] As Brown concludes, "at certain times the greatest peril facing a well-ordered institutional church is not the peril of new ideas but the peril of no ideas. The community described in the Pastorals would be perfectly safe if no one thought any other ideas than those handed down."[28]

A different model appears in the letters indisputably attributable to Paul, such as Corinthians and Galatians. Here "church" refers most often to local communities ("the church of God which is in Corinth," "the churches of Galatia," "in every church"), lending credence to the idea that, in the New Testament at least, Christian identity as church did indeed spring historically from conversion experiences within local communities and households, united around faith in the one Jesus Christ, which then communicated with one another. Colossians and Ephesians, later letters in the Pauline "school," take Paul's emphasis on body and transform it into an ideal image of church as a corporate entity. However, the stress is not on the institutional identity of church, but on the body of Christ as a growing community united by love (see Col. 1:17–18; Christ himself, not an ideal church type, is "before all things," the head of the church, and the source of its unity). Brown, noting that any church must become institutionalized if it lasts long enough and attracts a large membership, still comments that people do not love institutions as such and rarely give themselves for them; rather, institutions exist to serve the people. "But if the church is loved in a personalized relationship, it becomes a cause that attracts generosity from generation to generation."[29]

As Brown himself concludes in the book, a study of New Testament ecclesiologies demonstrates a pluralism that is instructive for the church. No one model is fully adequate, but always stands to be complemented by another. The New Testament is not a monolithic blueprint for theology, ethics, or church order, and certainly not for the positions to be explored within Catholic universities. Its very diversity has enabled the church to adapt historically to various challenges and contexts, drawing on themes or images which are useful at the time in encouraging faithfulness to the gospel. The New Testament itself provides four "gospels," and several other expressions of Christian witness besides. The historical church may also go back to these to renew its own identity and to take its lead not only from their content, but from the very fact of their diversity.

Catholic universities should not be understood as advocates for or bastions of pluralism over against ecclesial structures or positions whose uniformity has been constant from biblical times and guaranteed by biblical precedent. Rather, the dialectical ferment often experienced as one of the chief assets of intellectual inquiry in a university setting reflects the multidirectional and occasionally fractious energy of New Testament theologies, practices, and ecclesiologies themselves.

The Catholic University: Religion, Morality and Culture

A Community of Moral Discourse

A university is by definition an interdisciplinary venture in scholarship and learning. Although contemporary academic specialization often deters deep and frequent collaboration across fields, the university still provides an unparalleled opportunity for intellectual inquiry enriched by disciplined research in multiple intersecting areas, all informed by and conversing with the special problems and insights of the times.

One theological ethicist, James M. Gustafson, sees the university as a potential community of moral discourse in which conventional moral standards and values can be reexamined and new social issues addressed. Universities have at their disposal great resources of information and thought which can be brought to bear on value questions as they arise in research and in policy. The universities will never become "centers of moral infallibility," nor does clear moral thinking lead ineluctably to praiseworthy moral action. But sophisticated moral discourse about values would "constitute a significant contribution to the liberal education of students, and to American society."[30] Unfortunately, however, Gustafson does not find the ethical conversation in most universities to be of consistently high quality. The situation has not changed much since Gustafson formed that opinion in 1972.

What are the liabilities that beset university faculty as moral analysts and moral leaders? For one thing, intellectuals often assume their moral impulses enjoy a certitude proportionate to that earned by assiduous investigation in their research specialties. For another, too many intellectuals, like others in our culture, accept too quickly that moral pluralism must mean moral relativism. An important compounding factor is the prevalent cultural assumption — an assumption certainly shared by most of the research elites — that "real" knowledge is gained only on the model of scientific investigation. Absent the empirical demonstrability of a moral claim, it becomes relative to individual choice. Autonomy and the technical pursuit of good consequences — as unquestioned moral guides — become the sole criteria of judgment.[31]

The contribution of the theologian to the moral discourse of universities, according to Gustafson, should be to raise the level of discussion by bringing to bear the more profound insights of religious traditions.

(Here he has in mind a secular or at least pluralistic institution.) The theologian can introduce "both information and ways of thinking about moral issues that have developed out of the experiences of [those] who have sought to do what is right and good in response to the moral purposes of the ultimate power."[32] Both philosophical and practical problems raise for many people the kinds of questions which can be articulated in terms of "ultimacy" or the "transcendent dimensions" of life. The theologian can make these questions explicit, and pose them in terms of the final significance of political and professional life; of the grounds on which we value certain aspects of human life over others; of the grounds on which we can sustain those values against evil forces; and of the reasons we sacrifice a good, such as life, for another good, such as justice. Such questions can also be posed in religious terms: "What or who is worthy of our faith and our loyalty?...In and for what can the human community hope?"[33]

A Catholic university defines itself in principle and on the whole in terms of a religious identity. What does this mean? Fundamentally, it means that Gustafson's questions of ultimacy, and their relevance to moral analysis and excellence, are given a high profile institutionally, not just at the initiative of the individual theologian or theology faculty. In New Testament perspective, moral questions are questions about justice, which includes justice for "the poor." These questions shape the institutional ethos and assume priority among the institution's purposes. Since the Middle Ages, Catholic universities have been absorbing and reformulating the intellectual life of their culture in response to just such questions.

Catholic universities today — drawing on their traditions of natural law and natural theology, the social encyclicals, and great thinkers such as Cardinal John Henry Newman and John Courtney Murray — have a distinctive commitment to engage with, learn from, and contribute to intellectual inquiry in the arts and sciences, civil society and public life, and interreligious and intercultural dialogue and cooperation. The distinctive contribution to moral discourse of the Catholic university will be equally deeply rooted in faith-inspired New Testament moral and social values. These are compassion, active solidarity, and preferential option for the poor, which are coherent with Jesus' kingdom preaching, his life, death on the cross, and resurrection. These are not sectarian values, but values which faith illumines and which reasonable, humanistic discourse can recognize.

Catholic universities should therefore subject to constant critical scrutiny the individualism, relativism, technologically mediated utilitarianism, political self-interestedness, and economic opportunism that so pervade the U.S. cultural mindset and our knee-jerk value system. Here the pope's recent critique of the value trajectories which can turn modern liberal cultures into "cultures of death" hits home.[34] A Catholic university can heighten the potential of learning in the arts, sciences, and professions to contribute to a more humane and more just society in which immediate goals and interests are subsumed under more global values and meanings, such as the solidarity of the human community and the equality of each member within it.

The Catholic University, Moral Discourse, and the Church

In *Ex Corde Ecclesiae,* John Paul II alludes to his personal enrichment by the university's "ardent search for truth" and its commitment to "think rigorously" as well as to "act rightly."[35] He continues, "a Catholic university is distinguished by its free search for the whole truth about nature, man and God," and commends the "universal humanism" of Catholic education, which permits "impartial" research of truth "without fear, but rather with enthusiasm."[36]

Traditionally, the possibility of attaining theological and moral truths through intellectual and scientific work has been very important to Roman Catholicism. This note is sounded in the pope's affirmation of the unity of all truth, and of faith and reason.[37] "Theology has its legitimate place in the university alongside other disciplines. It has proper principles and methods which define it as a branch of knowledge."[38] In the contemporary university, theology is a discipline carried out among colleagues motivated by the "ultimate questions" about God, humanity, life, and death. In the Catholic university, these questions are pursued on the basis of a shared dedication to the Roman Catholic tradition of Christianity as a secure bearer of insight into these realities. Non-Catholic members of the community can and do appreciate, support, and participate in the quest for values and for just social practices which are distinctive of the Catholic orientation to higher learning. Theology develops the intellectual implications of this process's specifically religious dimension and interacts with the tradition as well as the culture by means of scholarly inquiry, critical argument, and reliance upon the intersecting disciplines available in the university context.

What is not always so clear is the practical form the moral discourse of the Catholic university should take, particularly in its dynamic relation to traditions, teachings, and prophecy promulgated via the pastoral and administrative functions of the "universal" church. Both of these functions are exercised through episcopal offices which reach within a defined hierarchical structure from the church's "command central" to its most divergent regional expressions. To what degree should structured, hierarchical church authority intervene in the moral community of the university to guide or monitor its culture-engaging inquiry into religious and moral values?

Ambiguity about the appropriate role of the Catholic university in participating freely, honestly, and rigorously in the intellectual and scientific investigations required by its academic identity; about the nature and extent of its critique of society; about its appropriation of cultural insights in revitalizing its religious, theological, and moral heritage; and about its fidelity to the universal church in undertaking these tasks, has been much in evidence in recent years. Rome, local bishops, universities, and theologians have had great difficulty in reaching a mutual understanding about the manner and degree of influence local ordinaries (acting at Rome's behest) should exercise on universities, especially regarding the research of theologians on their faculties. Rome's overriding concern is with orthodoxy on moral issues, particularly those involving sex and gender, much less so of economics and politics. A recent survey on Catholic identity, conducted by Fordham University, yields the not surprising finding that while a bare majority of bishops (51 percent) see control of the hiring of theology faculty in Catholic universities and colleges as outside their role, 92 percent of higher education respondents would agree with this assessment.[39]

The relation between local ordinary, as representative of ecclesiastical authority, and the Catholic university, particularly as home of a theological faculty, is treated ambiguously in *Ex Corde Ecclesiae*. A community of cooperative roles is affirmed, but theology is still perceived as transmitter of orthodox doctrine, presumably guaranteed by administrative sanctions within the university. Moreover, the theological faculty within the Catholic university is one expression, but not the sole expression, of its Catholic Christian identity. That identity consists in a dynamic relation with culture which is both receptive and prophetic. But *Ex Corde Ecclesiae* tends to focus on individual faculty and to see the university and its administration as conduits of official, ecclesiastical criteria for the approval or censure of individual faculty members, especially theological faculty. This does not address the real issue, which is the fostering of genuine community between universities and local ordinaries (and the bishops' conference), between theologians and bishops, and within a moderate plurality of perspectives within the church on Catholic identity and morality. Without it, no amount of canon law loopholing or noose-tying will resolve the proper function of theological inquiry in the Catholic university or the North American church or mediate successfully the dialogue of church, university, theology, and culture.

A recent letter from the Congregation for the Doctrine of the Faith provides perspective on Vatican overtures to Catholic universities in the way it defines *communio* as "the key to ecclesiology."[40] The Vatican letter emphasizes that, although the universal church may validly be seen as a communion of churches, the unity of the church in the institutional sense must not be threatened. The document cites the formula of *Lu-*

men Gentium: "The church in and formed out of the churches (*ecclesia in et ex ecclesiis*)."[41] It immediately qualifies this formula with the insistence of John Paul II that it is "inseparable" from its opposite: "the churches in and formed out of the church (*ecclesiae in et ex ecclesia*)."[42] The letter quite clearly magnifies the latter, even attributing to the universal church the character of a Platonic, preexisting model which is both "ontologically and temporally prior to every individual particular church."[43] This document also reinforces a unified and hierarchical episcopacy, reflecting the priority of the universal church, and the derivative nature of local churches. "As the very idea of the body of the churches calls for the existence of a church that is head of the churches, which is precisely the church of Rome ... so too the unity of the episcopate involves the existence of a bishop who is head of the body or college of bishops, namely the Roman pontiff."[44]

A one-sided emphasis on structure and authority will result in a dead church, unless enlivened by the spirit of love and community witnessed by Paul himself and by some of his later followers. Unless a community of trust exists first, not only does the institutional arm of the church lack true Christian "authority," as essentially an ability to command respect on the basis of a recognizable representation of Christ. Even worse, there could be no genuine mandate for theologians in light of the common good, no possibility of their being called by and affirmed in the university community to carry out their special vocation of reflection and teaching. If the moral heart of the gospel is respectful and supportive solidarity in community, then the church should embody such relations internally. More importantly, forgiveness, mercy, compassion, and inclusion should be the moral virtues and prophetic teachings for which the teaching church as "authoritative" should have the most care and concern.

Although pluralism of theory and liveliness of scholarly interaction are the best way of pruning out dead or deformed theological branches, there will undoubtedly come times when a bishop feels the obligation to distance a theological position from the collection of those that are helpful for the refinement of doctrine and the encouragement of common life. This is part of the identity formation of and by the church as community. However, juridical sanctions either against Catholic universities or against individual faculty members would do little to attract "the faithful" or a skeptical culture to the church's moral positions. Theological and ethical investigation and occasional correction in the Catholic university both need to illustrate a communal experience of Christ for which we can credibly claim that 1 Corinthians 13 serves as the norm. "Academic freedom" appears favorably in no. 29 of *Ex Corde Ecclesiae* (and footnote 15), as compatible with the search for "the truth and the common good."[45] The Roman Catholic presupposition of faith and reason's compatibility should make the Catholic university especially hospitable to the integrity of the theological enterprise.

The Jesuits, Catholic Identity, and Social Critique

I will conclude with one recent example of Catholic social critique which represents the specific commitments of the Society of Jesus. In the earliest documentation of the Society, including Ignatius's autobiography, the phrase recurrently defining Jesuit mission is "to help souls." By this was meant the whole person, and it was a task fulfilled by providing sustenance for spirit, mind, and body.[46] The Jesuits preached, directed retreats, taught catechism, heard confessions, and encouraged frequent reception of the Holy Eucharist. Yet they also "helped souls" by establishing orphanages and homes for prostitutes, by freeing debtors from prison, and eventually by establishing schools for rich and poor around the world. Howard Gray, S.J., reinterprets this mission for today:

> The Society of Jesus exists within the Church in order to help people (a phrase especially dear to Ignatius Loyola), and specifically to help people live in ways which embody the values of the Kingdom preached by Jesus. By origin and repeated confirmations of that origin, Jesuits must work with people in the world as it is in order to try to form a world as it could be, a world of peace, of justice, of love.[47]

At their thirty-second General Congregation in 1974–75, the Jesuits adopted "Decree 4," which contained a statement which has since been programmatic for Jesuit universities: "The mission of the Society of Jesus today is the service of faith, of which the promotion of justice is an absolute requirement."[48] Research institutes and programs of learning which emphasize Christian identity as "man or woman for others" are plentiful on Jesuit campuses. Examples at Boston College include not only the Jesuit Institute, but the Faith, Peace and Justice minor; the Pulse Program, which combines social service with theological study and reflection; the Jesuit Volunteer Corps for graduates; and a new doctoral program in theological ethics. The special identity of Jesuit educational institutions has been described as a conviction that moral excellence is the ultimate goal of education, and that scholarly excellence plays a vital role in achieving it.[49] In defining moral excellence and justice in our century, Catholic social teaching has appropriated the Enlightenment insight into essential human equality. Catholic social ethics demands that all classes and all peoples be included in the common good; defends human rights and "the dignity of the person"; and has given rise to liberation theology. Around the globe, Jesuits have been especially visible proponents of the "preferential option for the poor."

At its 1995 thirty-fourth General Congregation, the Society addressed the "unjust treatment and exploitation of women" (an issue already identified by the thirty-third Congregation) on the basis of the conviction that it is "a central concern of any contemporary mission which seeks to integrate truth and justice."[50] Recognizing that they cannot speak on behalf of women, the Jesuits express their support for women who speak out courageously on their own behalf; they note that discrimination and violence against women continues in many forms worldwide; they recognize that as a men's religious order, they "have been part of a civil and ecclesial tradition that has offended against women."[51] They invite their brother Jesuits to listen carefully to the experience of women in preparation for solidarity and action together. Among the specific examples are several which pertain to universities: "explicit teaching of the essential equality of women and men in Jesuit ministries, especially in schools and universities, support for liberation movements for women which oppose their exploitation and encourage their entry into political and social life,... genuine involvement of women in consultation and decision-making in our Jesuit ministries,... promotion of the education of women and, in particular, the elimination of all forms of illegitimate discrimination between boys and girls in the educational process."[52]

The statement also provides a model for theological appropriation of church teaching. It refers to Catholic social teaching as seminal, and notes developing magisterial recognition of women's dignity. Yet it acknowledges that certain questions about women's role that have already been advanced culturally still need time to "mature" in the church. Jesuits will be able to participate in that process through "committed and persevering research, through exposure to different cultures and through reflection on experience," all of which advance "the underlying issues of justice."[53]

The concluding line of this mission renewal refers to the "God of love and justice" who is transforming our world, so that "there is neither Jew nor Greek, there is neither slave nor free, there is neither male nor female, for you are all one in Christ Jesus (Gal. 3:28)."[54] The statement has taken the New Testament vision of solidarity and reappropriated it in intellectual and practical cooperation with the cross-cultural revolution toward women's emancipation. Continuity with biblical, theological, and ecclesial resources is affirmed. Yet the prophetic commitment of the Society on this issue is directed toward the church as well as cultures worldwide. Jesuits themselves, all those who collaborate with them, and all who read their declaration, are invited to embody gospel values by dramatically reconstituting justice in dialogue with the cultures of our day.

Notes

1. Having majored in theology at the University of Santa Clara, I shared the weal and woes of graduate student life with Jesuit classmates at the University of Chicago Divinity School in the early 1970s. I have taught for two decades at Boston College, where I serve on the Advisory Board of the Jesuit Institute, now directed by Michael Buckley.

2. Michael J. Buckley, *At the Origins of Modern Atheism* (New Haven: Yale University Press, 1987).

3. Michael J. Buckley, "The Rise of Modern Atheism and the Religious *Epoché*," Presidential Address, *Catholic Theological Society of America Proceedings* 47 (1992): 75–83.

4. For instance, in 1989–90, Michael Buckley chaired a committee of the board of the CTSA to address the issues implied by the newly published Profession of Faith and Oath of Fidelity. After intensive work and consultation, the final draft of this committee's report was completed in April 1990, unanimously received by the officers and directors of the Society, distributed to CTSA members, and made available to bishops as a basis for further discussion. In his capacity as executive director of the NCCB Committee on Doctrine, Buckley also worked closely with the Joint CTSA/CLSA [Canon Law Society of America] Committee on Cooperation Between Theologians and the Ecclesiastical Magisterium. This committee produced the document *Doctrinal Responsibilities* (*Origins* 19, no. 7 [1989]: 97–110), which is a model of dialogue between theologians and bishops, in cases requiring that doctrinal ambiguities or disagreements be resolved.

5. Michael A. Fahey, "Church," in Francis Schüssler Fiorenza and John P. Galvin, eds., *Systematic Theology: Roman Catholic Perspectives,* 2 vols. (Minneapolis: Fortress Press, 1991), 2:30.

6. The precise role of this imagery in the teaching of the historical Jesus can be debated, particularly in view of controversies about Jesus' own eschatological or even apocalyptic expectations. See John P. Meier, *A Marginal Jew: Rethinking the Historical Jesus,* vol. 2: *Mentor, Message, and Miracle* (New York: Doubleday, 1994), 350, 452.

7. See John Dominic Crossan, *Jesus: A Revolutionary Biography* (San Francisco: Harper, 1994).

8. See Elisabeth Schüssler Fiorenza, *Jesus: Miriam's Child, Sophia's Prophet* (New York: Continuum, 1994); Marcus J. Borg, *Jesus in Contemporary Scholarship* (Valley Forge, Pa.: Trinity Press International, 1994), 149–50.

9. *In Memory of Her: A Feminist Theological Reconstruction of Christian Origins* (New York: Crossroad, 1983), 130.

10. Borg, *Jesus,* 154. On compassion as essential to a New Testament ethics, see also John Donahue, *The Gospel in Parable* (Philadelphia: Fortress, 1988).

11. *Jesus' Call to Discipleship* (Cambridge, England and Oakleigh, Victoria, Australia: Cambridge University Press, 1992), 3.

12. For a more complete discussion of Christianity's effects on economics, purity, and family, along with citation of scholarly resources, see Lisa Sowle Cahill, "Sex and Gender Ethics as NT Social Ethics," in John W. Rogerson, Margaret Davies, and M. Daniel Carroll, eds., *The Bible in Ethics* (Sheffield, England: Sheffield Academic Press, 1995); and "Sexual Ethics: A Feminist Biblical Perspective," *Interpretation* 49 (January 1995): 5–16. Representative scholars upon

whom I have relied are Halvor Moxnes, *The Economy of the Kingdom: Social Conflict and Economic Relations in Luke's Gospel* (Philadelphia: Fortress Press, 1988); Jacob Neusner, *Purity in Rabbinic Judaism: A Systematic Account, the Sources, Media, Effects, and Removal of Uncleanness* (Atlanta: Scholars Press, 1994); Peter Brown, *The Body and Society: Men, Women and Sexual Renunciation in Early Christianity* (New York: Columbia University Press, 1988).

13. Thomas W. Ogletree, *Hospitality to the Stranger: Dimensions of Moral Understanding* (Philadelphia: Fortress Press, 1985), 141.

14. See Anthony J. Saldarini, *Matthew's Christian-Jewish Community* (Chicago and London: University of Chicago Press, 1994).

15. See Wim Beuken and Seán Freyne, eds., *The Bible as Cultural Heritage,* Concilium (London: SCM Press; Maryknoll N.Y.: Orbis Books, 1995).

16. James D. G. Dunn, *Unity and Diversity in the New Testament* (London: SCM Press; Philadelphia: Westminster Press, 1977), 371.

17. Fahey, "Church," 23.

18. *Unity and Diversity,* 376. We must recognize "how *few* the essentials are and how *wide* must be the range of acceptable liberty." See also, "Unity and Diversity in the Church: A New Testament Perspective," *Gregorianum* 71, no. 4 (1990): 629–56.

19. These churches were responsible to local figures of authority, such as bishops, presbyters and deacons (Phil. 1:1, Tit. 1:5), but the hosting householders also had some authority over the community, particularly the right and responsibility to refuse admittance to false teachers (2 John 10).

20. Raymond E. Brown, S.S., "New Testament Background for the Concept of Local Church," in *Catholic Theological Society of America Proceedings* 36 (1981): 1–2.

21. Ibid., 4. In the NT, a word which is often used to express the oneness, communion, or fellowship of Christians is *koinonia* (Acts 2:42).

22. Edmund Hill, O.P., "Church," in Joseph A. Komonchak, et al., *The New Dictionary of Theology* (Wilmington, Del.: Michael Glazier, Inc., 1987), 192–93.

23. Raymond E. Brown, *The Churches the Apostles Left Behind* (New York: Paulist Press, 1984).

24. Ibid., 22.

25. Ibid., 37.

26. Ibid., 38.

27. Ibid., 39.

28. Ibid., 40.

29. Ibid., 54.

30. James M. Gustafson, "The University as a Community of Moral Discourse," *Journal of Religion* 53, no. 4 (October 1973): 399. This was his inaugural lecture as University Professor of Theological Ethics in the University of Chicago Divinity School.

31. See Charles Taylor, *The Ethics of Authenticity* (Cambridge, Mass. and London, England: Harvard University Press, 1991).

32. Gustafson, "The University," 407.

33. Ibid., 409.

34. John Paul II, *The Gospel of Life* (*Evangelium vitae,* March 30, 1995).

35. The *Apostolic Constitution on Catholic Universities, Origins* 20, no. 17 (October 4, 1990): 267.

36. Ibid.

37. Ibid., 269.

38. Ibid., 271.

39. Joseph A. O'Hare, S.J., "Catholic Institutional Identity in Higher Education," in Msgr. Charles J. Fahey and Mary Ann Lewis, eds., The *Future of Catholic Institutional Ministries: A Continuing Conversation* (New York: Third Age Center, Fordham University, 1992), 93.

40. Congregation for the Doctrine of the Faith, "Some Aspects of the Church Understood as Communion," *Origins* (June 25, 1992): 108–12.

41. Ibid., 109, citing *Lumen Gentium,* no. 23.

42. Ibid.

43. Ibid.

44. Ibid., 110.

45. *Ex Corde Ecclesiae,* 271.

46. John W. O'Malley, S.J., *The First Jesuits* (Cambridge, Mass., and London: Harvard University Press, 1993), 18.

47. Howard J. Gray, S.J., "The Mission," *Boston College Magazine* 5 (Spring 1991): 33.

48. *Document of the Thirty-Second General Congregation of the Society of Jesus* (Washington, D.C.: The Jesuit Conference, 1975).

49. Frank H. T. Rhodes, "The Mission and Ministry of Jesuits in Higher Education," address on the 200th anniversary of Georgetown University, *America* 161, no. 3 (1989): 56.

50. As cited in Arthur Jones, "From Marble Halls to Cinder-Block Walls: The Jesuits, Worldwide, in Transition," *National Catholic Reporter* (June 15, 1990): 21.

51. The text of this statement was published in full by the *National Catholic Reporter* (April 7, 1995), 14.

52. Ibid.

53. Ibid.

54. Ibid.

Epilogue

Eucharisticon Fraternitatis

– LEO J. O'DONOVAN. S.J. –

Dear Mike,

As we close this volume of tribute on the occasion of your sixty-fifth birthday, I have the honor to thank you personally for the life and work that prompted our congratulations. We have written to celebrate a philosophical theologian of amazing erudition and energy, a committed man of the church and the university, a Jesuit priest of searching spirituality. But through all the scholarship presented here in tribute, we have also remembered a friend whose company on the journey to God has been a grace and a joy for us.

It was a good fortune for all that your father, Colonel Michael Buckley, having graduated from West Point in 1923, was on leave in his hometown of Coalinga, California, in the fall of 1925 and there met young Eleanor Fletcher, a native of Pullman, Washington, who had graduated from the University of California at Berkeley in 1924 and was teaching at Coalinga High School. Within two months, the new teacher was engaged to the young officer, whom she has described as "a decisive, witty, mobile military man of great good health."

As to the decisiveness, there has never been any doubt. When your father was sent to the Philippines, your mother followed later in June on a transport ship, which docked in Manila Harbor on July 1, 1926, at ten o'clock in the morning, after which the young couple were married at 11:00 a.m. in the Jesuit Church with a luncheon that followed at noon. Before returning home for Christmas, 1927, and a new assignment at Ft. Benning, your parents welcomed a daughter, Barbara. Another sister, Patricia, was born three years later; the next year, you arrived at Letterman Hospital in San Francisco; and then your brothers, Fletcher and Tom, followed some years later by young Ted, who died at only five years of age.

It was a typically devout Catholic family that thus grew in number and experience, praying the rosary together and centering its religious life on the Mass. Your father, regularly calling you Mickey, tells of your speaking about becoming a priest when you were five years old and then later celebrating Mass in your bedroom. (In later years, I understand, you even formed your own church and excommunicated a Prefect of Discipline for miscreancy against the community). Verbal from the very beginning, you caused Sr. Mary Charles, at the grammar school in Ft. Bragg, North Carolina, to shake her head "at how talkative such a little boy could be."

Your high school years required adaptability, again because of your father's army career. At Bellarmine Prep in San Jose, you never came home before five, I am told, because you were sent to jug for talking in class (which nevertheless had the beneficial effect of contributing to a cleaner campus). Staying at Bellarmine for freshman and sophomore years, when the family moved to Japan, you completed your junior year at Yokohama American High School and then your senior year at Red Bank Catholic High School from 1948 to 1949, where, not surprisingly, you won prizes for both debate and extemporary speaking.

Four years earlier, you had spoken with your family about entering the minor seminary, suggesting that "a rare flower should be cultivated well" — but meeting with the firm parental decision that you were going to the Jesuits at Bellarmine. On August 14, 1949, you left again for the Jesuits, but now to enter the Sacred Heart Novitiate in Los Gatos, California. (A difficult time for the family, since Teddy had just died, and your two sisters were also leaving for Trinity College in Washington.)

Your early years in the Society, leading up to your ordination in 1962 by Archbishop Joseph McGucken, represented a typical course of studies for a Jesuit at the time. Two years of noviceship, followed by the classical and humanistic studies of the Juniorate, led to your philosophical studies at Mt. St. Mary's in Spokane, Washington, where you completed a bachelor's degree in 1955 and two philosophical master's degrees the next year. Fr. Clifford Kossell, S.J., dean at that time, could be especially proud of the "golden dozen" scholastics among whom you numbered and with whom you encountered Aristotle and St. Thomas for the first time. Your regency, which the Society so wisely interposed between foundational and theological studies, brought you back to Bellarmine Prep for three years, to teach Greek, Latin, and English.

At Alma College for your theological studies between 1959 and 1963, you were fortunate to study with Fr. Joe Wall, a brilliant theologian and also a specialist in Jesuit spirituality and the Spiritual Exercises, a man who died far too young but whose interests you have in so many ways taken up to fulfill. After your year of Tertianship at St. Andrä in Austria, an essentially pastoral and spiritual conclusion to Jesuit studies, you followed the advice of Cliff Kossell and others and enrolled at the University of Chicago under the mentorship of Richard P. McKeon. Your doctoral dissertation, subsequently published as *Motion and Motion's*

God by Princeton University Press in 1971, set out to clarify how differently the theme of demonstrating God's existence from motion appears in each of the philosophical systems of Aristotle, Cicero, Newton, and Hegel.

In contrast to an *inquiry* into the solution of the problem of God's existence you pursued *semantics,* the "effort to understand, to trace a literal series of meanings for each system;...to so situate a theme in terms of its philosophical coordinates that its one or several meanings comes through, that it becomes an unambiguous proposition." The four authors you so skillfully chose for study each represent distinctive methods: a problematic method in Aristotle, an operational method in Cicero, the logistic method of Newton, and the dialectical method of Hegel. From the four, recognizing the singular ambiguity of the statement that the existence of God can be proved from movement, you learned a fundamental and enduring appreciation for philosophical pluralism. In contrast to both dogmatism and relativism, "the ambiguities of the theme and the infinitude of possible statements sustain the continuity of philosophy, and the dialogues of philosophers become the exploration and extension of the thematic concerns of men." The question of God is thus inevitable, always and everywhere posed by human thought embedded in the transience of time. It is also unavoidable with respect to the ultimate commitment of human lives. At once discriminating and irenic, this project also saw the beginning of your sustained interest in the dialogue of science, philosophy, and theology.

Later you would be elected by your Province to represent it at the thirty-second, thirty-third, and thirty-fourth General Congregations of the Society of Jesus (1974–75, 1983, and 1995). But it was at the opening of the thirty-first General Congregation on May 7, 1965, that Pope Paul VI gave his memorable charge to the Society to address "the fearful danger of atheism threatening human society." Two years earlier, you had already published a first article on Sartre and the antinomies of atheistic humanism. Now the theme was to take on increasing importance and urgency.

But first a major turning point in your academic life occurred when, after a year of teaching philosophy at Gonzaga University in Spokane, the California Provincial asked you to become the Rector of the Province's theologate, Alma College. Moving there in the summer of 1969, you oversaw the successful move to Berkeley, where Alma became the Jesuit School of Theology in Berkeley and joined the newly established Graduate Theological Union.

The circumstances of your new position deeply affected your teaching and scholarship, as well as your priestly and personal life. Your "Letter to the Ordinands" of spring 1972 is still quoted and admired for its sensitive discussion of God's entry into human life above all in our weakness. During these years, you became a leader in the renewal of Ignatian spiritual direction and the individually directed Spiritual Exercises of Ignatius. Some years later, this emphasis led to your gathering bishops in California for retreats, at the first of which Cardinal Manning of Los Angeles and Archbishop Jean Jadot, at the time Apostolic Delegate, participated.

The suffering of which you had written so movingly had also become your own personal experience, as a severe case of lupus, first appearing in 1970, emerged as one of the two great trials in your life. Family and friends across the country were apprehensive about the outcome of your cortisone treatment, which in the event proved happily to set the disease in remission. How easy it is to see now, looking back, what strength for others you would draw from this trial!

We have all benefitted as well from your Roman stories, the accompaniment of your service as a visiting professor at the Pontifical Gregorian University from 1973 to 1975. But Berkeley had become too obviously the "natural locus" for the work of your maturity as a scholar, and so you returned there for another eleven years of service, which included two fruitful years as Scholar in Residence at the University of Santa Clara (1981–83).

From the many articles you wrote during this period, I recall several that are especially typical. Writing on "Transcendence, Truth, and Faith" in *Theological Studies* in 1978, you argued that an ascending, cumulative search for truth is intrinsic to good faith in human experience. It "must underlie any confessional faith-commitment, if it is to be authentic, if faith is not to be based on bad faith." You had discovered Karl Rahner and agreed with him that philosophy is an inner moment of theology. You found in Einstein a witness to the purifying contribution of science in its relation to religion and in Ricoeur a deep sense of the "geological fault" within human beings, at once infinite in our striving for knowledge and finite in our perspective.

Unwilling to bracket the figure of Jesus, you established the thesis that in Christ "the self-surrender of the human person intersects with the self-communication of God." Combining a sense of process and priority, you saw the acceptance of Christ "not...as a single moment of decision, but as a lengthy process of freedom, complicated in its history and taxing in its moral demands, wherein one moves gradually into the light through a prior, lived commitment to the truth that is available in life and in its choice."

A similarly central paper appeared the next year, again in *Theological Studies,* on "Atheism and Contemplation." Here you contrasted the contention of Feuerbach and Freud that religion is projection, on the one hand, and, on the other, the renewed interest in contemplation and mysticism, with the great Spanish Carmelite John of the Cross as your preferred witness. For some years John had spoken to you quite personally. Now you counseled that "the focus of theology should be less to refute Feuerbachian and Freudian analysis than to provide an alternative to the processes they elaborate of anthropological assimilation and psychotherapy." Great energy has been expended in interpreting the masters of suspicion. Is it not time, and urgently so, you asked, to interpret John and contemporary spiritual masters such as Karl Rahner with comparable intensity?

How shall I describe the next, difficult transition in your life, as you moved to Washington to serve as the executive director of the Committees on Doctrine and Pastoral Research and Practices at the National Conference of Catholic Bishops from 1986 to 1989?

You had, of course, worked on Archbishop Quinn's Commission on Religious Life and had written articles on documentation from the Holy See and on the 1985 Extraordinary Synod on religious life. Once in Washington, you served with utter dedication and great élan. It was a happy time for me, certainly, as I lived in the same Jesuit community with you in the last year of that service. Together with Archbishop Oscar Lipscomb, as chairman for the Committee on Doctrine, we traveled to Rome for discussions about the document "Doctrinal Responsibilities," before it was finally presented for approval at the Bishops' Conference in June 1989. (During this year I learned how early your sense of order required you to arrive at an airport. Indeed, more recently, I hear, you were planning to fly to Cleveland and arrived early enough at the Boston airport to board a plane to Denver instead, later, when half way there, inquiring why the pilot reported the weather conditions in Denver instead of in Cleveland. Or, as Michael Himes has quoted you saying yourself: "My grasp of the contingent is not strong.")

During this period, *At the Origins of Modern Atheism* was published by Yale University Press in 1987, an occasion for much praise — as well as your own sighs of relief. Your major work to date, the book is learned, dramatic, searching, urgent — and marvelously written.

It may trail "clouds of the kindness of others," as you so generously acknowledge, but it is also entirely typical of your own penetrating intelligence, breadth of culture, and sensitive faith. None of us can imagine its being authored by anyone else. Indeed, it stands for so many as a worthy, and in fact more analytically probing successor, late in our century, to Henri de Lubac's magisterial *The Drama of Atheist Humanism* (1943).

You have shown us, Mike, how ambiguous and pluriform the notion of atheism is, "a confused history whose assertions can be identical in expression and positively contradictory in sense." Drawing again on the work of Richard McKeon for the armature of your investigation, your inquiry pushes back to the theologians Leonard Lessius and Marin Mersenne in the early seventeenth century, proposes Descartes and Newton as the most influential figures at the dawn of modernity, and interprets Baron Paul d'Holbach and the encyclopedist Dennis Diderot as the climatic representatives of Enlightenment atheism.

More important, you asked *how* this was possible. Your effort, as you subtly and persuasively wrote, was "to understand what has taken place as it emerged, rather than mount an effort of advocacy or of attack." A twofold question, then: "In the generation of ideas, how did so powerful an idea as atheism arrive? In the reflections of theology, what can be learned from such 'a tremendous event'?"

The great merit of your study, now widely recognized, is that you account both for the philosophical dialectic involved in the transition from theism to atheism and for the theological miscalculations that made another outcome unlikely. Friedrich Nietzsche and Cardinal Newman alike saw a great shadow descending on Europe at the end of the nineteenth century. But they were not in a historical position to discern how impoverished a God had been defended against the criticism of naturalistic philosophers who were intent, for good reason, on understanding the *working* of a purportedly self-sufficient universe. When the theological doctrines of Christ and his community in the Spirit were left aside in the effort to explain what Christianity really means in its life and practice, all the breadth of Christian culture and experience fell out of the argument between the critics of theism and a church that defended itself on almost purely philosophical grounds.

Implicit throughout this book as well as your entire scholarly life is the conviction that theology must be a concrete and historical discipline. From your undergraduate and graduate studies through to your reading of Gadamer, Rahner, and Ricoeur, I think you have become increasingly convinced, and convincing, that the history of ideas is not only indispensable to their understanding but also to their critique and development. Historical consciousness as you advocate it entails neither pure historicism nor historical relativism. Rather, it draws one deeper at once into the sacred, inviolable realm of the human conscience, asked to choose how it will enact the truth, and likewise toward the one way of truth proposed in the figure of Jesus of Nazareth, proclaimed as its Lord by a Spirit-filled community through the centuries.

But that, I am now astonished to realize, was fully nine years ago. Since then, you have served as professor of philosophical theology and of history and the philosophy of science at the University of Notre Dame, from 1989 to 1992, and then moved to become professor of systematic theology at Boston College and the director of the Jesuit Institute there. At Notre Dame, you further pursued your interest in the dialogue of science and religion. A visiting fellowship at Clare Hall, Cambridge

University, deepened your friendship with Nicholas Lash, whose sense for the interpenetration of paschal mystery and ordinary experience so complements your own.

I pause to recall a probing essay of 1989, "Experience and Culture: A Point of Departure for American Atheism." Taking Dewey and Freud as paradigmatic figures for our current situation, you argue there that "the eclipse of God" is represented in the United States especially among highly cultivated, educated, or elite groups. In this context, "the immediate task of theology is not to attempt answers." Rather, "theology must first clarify the religious problem lying hidden or unarticulated within the intellectual culture and raise to the level of understanding and expression what is still indeterminately contradictory to belief." An honest search for the genuine questions of our society, in other words, is essential for an honest theology.

American culture offers significant resources for such inquiry, just as religious faith can offer to our culture a restoration of the primordial primacy of the personal dimension in human life and community. Here, as you rightly noted, the quality of the church's own life will be decisive, whether, namely, it is perceived as a scandal or as a sacrament, a community of compassion and justice, reverent and forgiving, reenacting in its own life of suffering love what the Lord it worships did in his own. With the straightforward intensity we all admire in you, you closed by asking whether one may not assert theologically "that the contemporary state of unbelief...in the U.S. is something of a judgment upon the presence of the church itself within the culture."

In response to this challenge, you have of course served the official church on many occasions and the theological community in a formal way as well, not least as president of the Catholic Theological Society of America from 1991 to 1992 and through its *Report of the Committee on the Profession of Faith and the Oath of Fidelity* in 1990. But in a still broader vein, you have also challenged your academic colleagues throughout the country to consider the inherent promise of Catholic universities today and how they must develop a new humanism that includes commitment to justice. You have argued forcefully for the intrinsic relationship between religious faith, inescapably seeking understanding, its own self-possession and knowledge, and academic inquiry, tending "toward ultimacy, toward a completion in which an issue or its resolution finds place in a universe that makes final sense, i.e., in the self-disclosure of God."

In the early 1980s, you had recalled Pope Paul VI's appeal, in his great encyclical "On the Development of Peoples" (1967), for "a renewed consciousness of the demands of the Gospel...at this turning point in human history." You had also recalled the General Congregation of the Society of Jesus in 1974–75, committing itself to evaluate and judge all its apostolic endeavors by two interrelated criteria: its service to the faith and its promotion of social justice. More recently, acknowledging the warning against politicization or instrumentalization of university life, you have drawn on the long tradition of Jesuit humanistic education and argued that today an integral, holistic education requires an expansion and innovation of the humanities "into a sense of human solidarity," enabling students to hear the human pain and social injustice which calls out for understanding and redress.

More recently, you have refined this argument by recalling how Ignatius of Loyola came only late in his life to recognize the ministerial importance of higher education and the role of humanistic studies in it. Humanism today, retrieving and fulfilling the humanistic ideal of the Renaissance, must *understand* and *be willing* "to pay the price of a more just and a more humane society" (again quoting the Jesuit General Congregation). Indeed, as you continue to reflect on the experience and documents of the thirty-fourth General Congregation, which was held last year and emphasized the necessity for intercultural and interreligious dialogue, I look for your argument about the full dimensions of a humanistic and scientific education to become still more persuasive.

But then, Mike, we look for the fulfillment of so many other projects from your pen. With pride, we learned of Cardinal Ratzinger's invitation that you present a paper on the systematic theology of the papacy next fall in Rome. With the students and faculty at Oxford, we look forward to the D'Arcy Lectures, to be delivered there in a year or two. Above all, we anticipate your advancing your study of modern atheism further into the nineteenth and twentieth centuries. Having often taught Darwin myself, I am anxious to see you locate him in relation to the other great influences on our late twentieth-century mindset.

Yes, Mike, we look forward all the more to your future work because it has been such a pleasure to celebrate the past of it. You are, my dear friend, a remarkable example of someone whose person and work so very closely cohere. At once classical and very contemporary, reverent before tradition but always ready to review it, you have also been always a faithful friend and a very honest one. For so many of us whom you have attracted "like flypaper," in your brother Tom's words, this effort in your honor has evoked endless memories of time spent together.

For myself, whether editing a text or consulting with the bishops' conference, on vacation in Maine or at dinner in Rome, at the theater in New York or galleries in Washington, at prayer by the sea or in the air, the flux of our time as friends has always been borne by the intelligence and even more the generosity of your conversation in the course of the journey. You have, I think, greater confidence in human reason than I do. But we share, I am sure, two interlocking convictions: that the human mind and the human heart are instinct with longing for a goal that faith assures us is real, the homecoming to God of all the human family through Christ and in the Holy Spirit.

And so it is, as this volume closes, that all who have written and all who will read it look to join you in finding, or perhaps still better, seeking God, God in all things — and all things in God.

Contributors

DAVID B. BURRELL, C.S.C.
Theodore M. Hesburgh Professor of Theology and Philosophy
University of Notre Dame

LISA SOWLE CAHILL
J. Donald Monan Professor of Christian Ethics
Boston College

PAUL CROWLEY, S.J.
Associate Professor of Theology
University of Santa Clara

LAWRENCE S. CUNNINGHAM
Professor and Chair of Theology
University of Notre Dame

BRIAN E. DALEY, S.J.
Catherine S. Huisking Professor of Theology
University of Notre Dame

LOUIS DUPRÉ
T. Lawrason Riggs Professor in the Philosophy of Religion
Yale University

ROGER HAIGHT, S.J.
Professor of Theology
Weston Jesuit School of Theology

CHARLES HEFLING
Associate Professor of Theology
Boston College

MICHAEL J. HIMES
Associate Professor of Theology
Boston College

DAVID HOLLENBACH, S.J.
Margaret O'Brien Flatley Professor of Catholic Theology
Boston College

PETER HÜNERMANN
Professor of Fundamental Theology
Katholisch-Theologisches Seminar of Eberhard-Karls-Universität,
Tübingen

ELIZABETH A. JOHNSON, C.S.J.
Professor of Theology
Fordham University

ALBERT R. JONSEN
Professor and Chair of Medical History and Ethics
University of Washington

NICHOLAS LASH
Norris Hulse Professor of Divinity
University of Cambridge

FREDERICK G. LAWRENCE
Associate Professor of Theology
Boston College

ERNAN MCMULLIN
Cardinal John O'Hara Professor of Philosophy
University of Notre Dame

WILLIAM B. NEENAN, S.J.
Academic Vice President and Dean of Faculties
Boston College

LEO J. O'DONOVAN, S.J.
President
Georgetown University

STEPHEN J. POPE
Associate Professor of Theology
Boston College

THOMAS P. RAUSCH, S.J.
Professor of Theology
Loyola Marymount University

WILLIAM C. SPOHN
John Nobili, S.J. University Professor
University of Santa Clara

WILLIAM R. STOEGER, S.J.
The Vatican Observatory
Tucson, Arizona

JOHN H. WRIGHT, S.J.
Emeritus Professor of Theology
Jesuit School of Theology at Berkeley